BISHOP FABIAN BRUSKEWITZ

A Shepherd Speaks

Bishop Fabian Bruskewitz

A Shepherd Speaks

IGNATIUS PRESS   SAN FRANCISCO

Cover photo by Adrian Bartek
Cover design by Riz Boncan Marsella

© 1997 Ignatius Press, San Francisco
All rights reserved
ISBN 0–89870–626–2
Library of Congress catalogue number 96–78017
Printed in the United States of America ∞

CONTENTS

Part One: Our Trinitarian Faith

Part Two: The Church

Part Three: The Liturgical Year

Part Four: The Sacraments

Part Five: Living the Christian Mystery

Part One

OUR TRINITARIAN FAITH

Father, Son, and Holy Spirit

The Central Mystery

A famous author once wrote: "The way by which God comes to us and we go to God is not left to our choice but is pointed out to us by God Himself. What is that way? Revelation teaches us that the God to Whom we must go is God in Three Persons, Father, Son, and Holy Spirit, and it discloses to us the wonderful play of relations between God in Three Persons and each one of us." One of the most ancient creedal statements in the Church's history (the Athanasian Creed) begins, "Whoever wants to be saved must profess the Catholic Faith, and this is the Catholic Faith, that we worship Trinity in Unity and Unity in Trinity. . . ."

THE HOLY TRINITY

The *Catechism of the Catholic Church* states: "The mystery of the Most Holy Trinity is the central mystery of Christian faith and life. It is the mystery of God in himself. It is therefore the source of all the other mysteries of faith, the light that enlightens them. It is the most fundamental and essential teaching" (CCC 234). The *Catechism* goes on, "The ultimate end of the whole divine economy is the entry of God's creatures into the perfect unity of the Blessed Trinity" (CCC 260).

From the time of Pope John XXII in the year 1334, the first Sunday after Pentecost has been the Solemnity of the Most Holy Trinity, celebrating a dogma of our faith that, had God not revealed it, we could never even suspect, namely, that in the absolute and total unity of God, without compromising simple and complete oneness, there are three Divine Persons. There is one eternal Lord and God, and yet there are the Father, Son, and Holy Spirit, separate and distinct in Personhood as they are one and indivisibly incomprehensible in essence.

Liturgists tell us that the feast of the Holy Trinity should be looked upon as a solemn *Te Deum* of gratitude over the Church's blessings received during the Christmas and Easter seasons, as a synthesis of Christmas, Epiphany, Easter, Ascension, and Pentecost.

All the sacraments and blessings of the Church are done and given in the name of the Holy Trinity. For us Catholics each day of our lives should begin and end with the sign of the cross on ourselves, done in the name of the Father, and of the Son, and of the Holy Spirit. All the psalms in the Liturgy of the Hours are concluded with a trinitarian doxology (the Glory Be).

We must often pray that when it comes time for us to die, to close our eyes on earth for the last time and open them to look at God, we will have a priest at our side who will commend our soul in the name of the Trinity. As the ritual indicates: "Go forth, O Christian soul, in the name of God the Father almighty Who created you, of Jesus Christ, the Son of God, Who suffered for you, of the Holy Spirit Who has been poured out upon you." Our Catholic life should begin and end in the name of the Blessed Trinity.

TRINITARIAN PRAYER

The official prayer of the Church, the sacred liturgy, uses almost always a type of trinitarian prayer that dates to the earliest days of the Church. There are very old indications of prayer and adoration given to each Divine Person of the Blessed Trinity, but the kind of prayer that is most common is directed to God the Father, through Christ, the Son, and in the Holy Spirit.

In the current usage of the Roman Rite, the great consecratory prayer (sometimes call the Canon of the Mass, or the Eucharistic Prayer) always concludes with the well-known, magnificent trinitarian doxology (through Him, with Him . . .). Already our third pope, Saint Clement, in the year 96, prayed in his writings "to the Father, through Christ, the Son, and in the assurance of the Holy Spirit".

When he was at the stake, about to be martyred for the faith, Saint Polycarp, the Bishop of Smyrna in the year 167, prayed: "I praise You, Father, because You have found me worthy of this day and this hour. For this and Your other benefits, I render You praise and glory, through the eternal and heavenly High Priest, Jesus Christ, through Whom and with Whom, together with the Holy Spirit, be glory now and in ages to come." Experts tell us that these words of Saint Polycarp were most likely extracted from the text of the Mass as he used to celebrate it.

This way of praying is rooted in the New Testament, and indications of it can be found in the Epistles to the Ephesians (1:3–14; 2:4–5; 18–22), to the Romans (8:3–17), to the Galatians (4:4–6), and in the First Epistle to the Corinthians (6:19–20).

Why did God choose to reveal the mystery of the Holy Trinity to us?

It is beyond our understanding, although not contrary to human reason. Even after its revelation, this mystery remains totally "other", as is God Himself, Whose interior life it is.

God decided to tell us about His innermost life because it is that very life we share in sanctifying grace. His present, utter, and absolute happiness is our destiny and the goal of our existence. Saint Francis of Assisi, after reciting the Glory Be, exclaimed one time: "My God, how small You would have to be if I were to be able to understand You!" Saint Bernard of Clairvaux wrote: "To wish to fathom the mystery of the Trinity is boldness; to believe it is happiness; and to realize it is everlasting life."

MAY 27, 1994

The Personality of Jesus

I

What Jesus claimed about Himself He also proved to be true, because God confirmed by extraordinary signs that Jesus truly is His legate, His envoy, the Messiah, and God Himself. Among these extraordinary signs, preeminent among which are miracles, is the sign of Christ's personality. While this is not a miracle in the strict sense of the term, His human personality is so exceptional that anyone taking the time and effort to view it fully and with an open mind will be immediately struck by its outstanding beauty and splendor.

The Gospels are mainly catechetical books and not, strictly speaking, biographies of Jesus. Their main concern is not to give accurate chronologies and physical details or tell about mental states. Their prime interest is to give the sayings of Christ, His prayers, specimens of His miracles, and His parables and to narrate the Passion and Resurrection that are the beginning of the Christian proclamation (the *kerygma*). However, by careful study of the Gospels, one can come to some view of Jesus' personality. He did not teach as a philosopher but as One Whose teaching was involved with His very Person. Hence, in a certain sense His teaching and His personality are identical.

The Person and personality of Jesus are distinct. The Person of Jesus is the same as the Person of the eternal Word of God. Jesus is not two persons, human and divine, but rather one Person, unique and singular. Christ is one Divine Person, with both a human and a divine nature. In His human nature He is, teaches the Council of Chalcedon, like us in all things but sin (Heb 4:15). Since Jesus is true Man as well as true God, He has a human body and a human soul. By His personality, then, is meant the disposition in His human soul by which He related to other realities and values.

In reflecting on the Self-revelation by God in Jesus Christ, we must consider the totality of what God speaks in His Word made flesh. Christ's doctrine, personality, miracles, sayings, and the like are part of a whole, a unity in multiplicity and complexity.

Picking up the Gospels, let us look briefly at various aspects of our Lord's human personality, never forgetting, of course, that He is also divine. Jesus was above all a man of *simplicity*. From the entirety of the Gospel text, we see that our Savior's speaking and preaching involved something totally new in the history of religion, yet the way He spoke and preached was utterly simple and free from harshness.

Jesus taught us to love our enemies and pray for those who persecute us (Mt 5:44; Lk 6:27). He said there was rejoicing over one repentant sinner (Lk 15:7). The justice of the disciples must shine before the Father rather than before men (Mt 6:1). The parables, although they contain sublime insights, are very simple in their format: a farmer going to sow seeds (Mk 4:3), a wedding dinner (Lk 14:16), a lost sheep (Mt 18:12).

Our Redeemer announced the kingdom of God clearly and simply with astonishing ease, although He was a very young rabbi of about thirty years of age (Lk 3:23) and did not frequent the rabbinic schools (Jn 7:15). The deepest mysteries are expressed by Jesus in the simplest language with astoundingly natural ease. Profound thoughts that transcend even the work of great philosophers seem to be owned by Christ with a discursive and almost notional possession. His ease in speaking about spiritual and moral topics does not appear to be something He labored to acquire.

Jesus taught from simplicity of heart. He said our speech is to be simple and generally without oaths (Mt 5:34). Our religion is to be always genuine and free from hypocrisy. Alms, prayers, and fasting are to be done discreetly (Mt 6:2–6). Our morality is not to be merely external but internal as well (Mt 5:21–22). Formal casuistry is to yield to love of neighbor and interior dispositions of our hearts (Lk 11:39–52). However, mere religious sentiment or emotion is not enough (Lk 6:46). Moral goodness consists in sanctity and internal clarity and serving God with an undivided heart (Lk 11:34; Mt 6:24).

Christ's personality enabled Him to see the divine shining in the world. His "other-worldliness" was not impoverishment of spirit or doctrinaire hatred of the world. On the contrary, He loved the world as His Father did (Jn 3:16) and was aware of the world as He pursued the things of heaven. He spoke beautifully about sowing, harvesting, reaping, winnowing, the lilies of the field, the birds of the air, the signs of rain and storms and seasons, grain and wheat, seed, wine, bread, oil, fish. In His preaching He could talk about women kneading dough, about a hen gathering her young beneath her wings, about the loss of a coin, or about children who form make-believe processions, now like a funeral—now like a wedding, about cattle that fall into a pit, about sparrows that fall from a branch, about the hair on our heads, and about mothers giving birth. His speech was full of life and never pessimistic.

Although He vigorously practiced fasting and enjoyed solitude, His earthly life was evidently less rigid and less frightening to His contemporaries than that of Saint John the Baptist. He even visited the houses of His enemies, the Pharisees (Lk 7:36). He talked with the despised tax collectors (Mk 2:13), and He was capable of warm and extended human friendships. He felt keenly the betrayal of Judas and the denial of Peter (Lk 22:39–62).

In sharing our human condition to the full, our Lord knew sorrow and wept (Jn 11:32–36; Lk 19:41–44). He knew hunger, thirst, and fatigue (Lk 4:2; Jn 4:6). He was fond of children (Mk 10:13–16) and enjoyed visiting the homes of His friends (Lk 19:1–10). Though He spoke as one having authority and not like the scribes (Mk 1:27), He was obviously capable of charming not only individuals but vast throngs of people, whom He filled with admiration and enthusiasm.

Yet Christ was not a radical political or religious revolutionary. His simplicity of personality was a sign of His prudence and moderation. He came, He told us, not to destroy but to fulfill (Mt 5:17). Although He told us not to put new wine into old wineskins (Mk 2:22) and never to patch old clothing with new cloth (Lk 5:36), He was careful and slow in communicating the startlingly novel "good news" and in revealing His full and true identity (Mk 4:11). He kept in His own life and insisted that His disciples keep in theirs the positive precepts of the law of Moses, the Torah. Even when He preached against the scribes and Pharisees, He required His disciples to obey them "because they sit on the chair of Moses".

In studying the human personality of Jesus, we can learn, under His grace, a marvelous lesson from His simplicity. He told us: "Learn from me" (Mt 11:29), and one of the great instructions He gave us was that we were to be "as wise as serpents and innocent as doves" (Mt 10:16).

JANUARY 29, 1993

The Personality of Jesus

II

Jesus, the Son of God and Son of Man, is, as our Catholic faith proclaims, true God and true Man. In His human nature, like ours in all things but sin, Jesus' human soul gave evidence of a human personality that was (and is) magnificent and glorious.

There are many aspects of our Lord's human personality that are striking and beautiful. Anyone casually picking up the Sacred Scriptures and reading the Gospels with an unprejudiced eye cannot but be amazed and overwhelmed by the splendor of Jesus as He is depicted by the evangelists. The historical veracity of the Gospel accounts shows many signs by which God approves and authenticates the message and acts of Christ, by which Jesus Himself in His human and divine nature is vindicated in His claims and titles. Among these signs, which include prophecies and miracles, is the sign of His exceptional and unique personality.

Everyone who looks at the personality of Jesus is almost immediately struck by His inexpressible *humility*, which shows itself in so many ways. In His earthly life, our Lord's humility was displayed in His accessibility. He said: "Come to me, all . . ." (Mt 11:28). He was always available and near to His apostles, who were the special object of His care and teaching (Mk 4:13; Mt 13:36). He seemed to live with them in intimate and familiar daily life. He was accessible to the crowds who gave Him no time for relaxation (Mk 1:36; Lk 5:15). He was accessible to the sick (Mk 2:3) and to sinners and was even called their friend (Mt 11:19), and He was accessible to children (Mk 10:13). Thus His humility made Him totally "open" to all of humanity.

Our Savior shows His wonderful humility also in His patience. He did not work miracles merely to satisfy His enemies' demands (Mk 8:11), and when He worked miracles, He often admonished the recipients of His healing love to be silent lest they excite violent, unnecessary, and unwise nationalistic commotion (Mt 16:20). He wanted all to understand His life as one of humble service, for He came "not to be served but to serve" (Mk 10:45). He often scolded the disciples when they did not understand the lowly dimension of the kingdom of God and disputed about honors, present and future, even on the last night, when He washed their feet to help them better understand (Jn 13:12). Jesus also taught humility by His example. Saint Peter wrote: "When he was reviled, he did not revile in return; when he suffered, he did not threaten" (1 Pet 2:23).

The humility of our Redeemer is clear also from His attitude toward His heavenly Father. He said only God can be called good (Mk 10:18) and that those who hear and keep God's word are more blessed than the womb that bore Him and the breasts that suckled Him (Lk 11:28). His food is doing God's will (Jn 4:34). Only those who are as humble as little children can enter God's kingdom (Mt 18:4). Only the humble accept the "good news", while the proud resist the gospel (Mt 11:25). Jesus is God, but even in the mystery of the Blessed Trinity, He is, while on earth, a recipient of God's totality (Mt 11:27). In His divine nature He is one with the Father (Jn 14:9–10), but in His human nature the Father is greater (Jn 14:28).

Consideration of Christ's humility is even more striking when we see that He never displayed any consciousness of sin on His part, although He was very much aware of its reality in the world of men. He warned Saint Peter to watch and pray because of the weakness of the flesh (Mt 26:41). Jesus never acknowledged any sinfulness, although He instructed His disciples to acknowledge their sins (Mk 6:12). He used severe prophetic language to reprove sinners (Mt 12:34). Of all men, He alone could ask: "Which of you convicts me of sin?" (Jn 8:46). He always acted as One Who saves, coming to rescue what is lost (Lk 19:10), to give His life (Mk 10:45), to announce grace and forgiveness to the repentant (Mk 2:17), to be a doctor for the sinful (Mt 9:12), and to pour out His blood for the remission of sin (Mt 26:28).

It is clear that Jesus was conscious, even in His human nature, of His messianic dignity and divine Personhood. Yet He bore this knowledge and consciousness humbly. He received the crowds' acclaim while meekly riding on an ass (Mk 11:7), and He declared it was not for Him to distribute the first places in the kingdom (Mt 20:23). In His human nature He did not know the day of His Second Coming (Mk 13:32). Although He sometimes acknowledged His kingly and messianic function, as expected by the Jews, He always included in this another lowly messianic function in Jewish tradition, that of the Suffering Servant of Yahweh (Is 53; Lk 9:22). He refused the kingship offered by the people when He multiplied the loaves and fishes (Jn 6:14–15). In humble obedience, even though Peter and the apostles tried to dissuade Him, He continued His journey, which led to the cross (Mk 8:32–33).

Christ demanded that His followers carry a cross (Mk 8:34). He struggled against the hyper-legalism of the Pharisees (Mt 9:11). He courageously went to Jerusalem in the face of danger (Lk 13:31–33), and He bravely faced His arrest and execution.

Our Savior taught with power (Mt 7:28). He walked unharmed through His hometown folks who tried to throw Him over a cliff (Lk

4:30). He drove the money-changers from the temple with uncommon valor (Mk 11:15), and He stopped those sent to arrest Him with only a word (Jn 18:6). He understood the fickle nature of the multitudes and the passing character of their adulation. He cried over their refusal to accept Him fully and follow Him properly (Mt 11:21), yet He was willing to go it alone (Jn 6:66), to take the long view and forfeit temporary success for long-term gain. He cast fire on the earth (Lk 12:49) and, although He is the Prince of peace, brought into the world not peace but a sword (Mt 10:34).

As members of His Church, as His followers, we must be prepared, as He warned us, to endure the hatred of all because of His name (Mk 13:13). With the help of His grace, we must strive to be endowed with His humility and strength, making over our own personality into His. His humanity simultaneously conceals and reveals His divinity. By carefully studying His humanity, we get a glimpse of God, and we are touched by all of heaven. "Learn from me", He told us, "for I am gentle and lowly in heart" (Mt 11:29).

FEBRUARY 5, 1993

The Personality of Jesus

III

When God intervened decisively in human history by becoming incarnate in order to redeem us, He assumed our human nature without diminishing or foregoing His eternal divine nature (which, of course, would be impossible). The Divine Person of Christ also had a real and total human nature, with all that that implies. In His human soul, our Savior had a true human personality, and in the Gospel narratives we are allowed to glimpse absolute human perfection.

Probably the most striking characteristic of Jesus' human personality is His love. Jesus showed forth the deepest love. He commanded His disciples to practice love (Jn 13:34). From her earliest days, the Catholic Church retains the memory of how Christ "went about doing good and healing all that were oppressed by the devil" (Acts 10:38). Jesus Himself spoke of His mission as one of mercy (Is 59:1; Lk 4:18). He gave Himself in love to people; He cured them (Lk 5:15); He fed them (Mk 8:2–6); He worked for them until He was exhausted enough to sleep through a storm at sea (Mk 4:35–39). Because of His loving service, He did not have any place to rest His head (Mt 8:20).

The love of Jesus was empty of self-seeking. He taught the value of service without compensation (Mt 5:46) and insisted on gratuitous generosity to the poor (Lk 14:12). His love was shown in His compassion for the hungry crowds (Mk 8:2) and for a friend who died (Jn 11:35). He was also compassionate toward the spiritually weak, such as the crowds who were like sheep without a shepherd (Mk 6:34).

Because of His love, Jesus was given to praising and comforting others. He praised Nathanael's purity (Jn 1:47) and His cousin, Saint John the Baptist (Mt 11:7). He praised the faith of the Canaanite woman (Mk 7:29), and He loved the rich young man who had kept the Commandments since his youth (Mk 10:20). He gave nicknames to His disciples, denoting their qualities: Peter (Mt 16:18) and sons of thunder (Mk 3:17). He consoled Peter with the thought of fishing for men (Lk 5:10) and promised James and John that they would drink from His cup (Mk 10:39). He assured Zacchaeus that he was a child of Abraham (Lk 19:9). He called His disciples by the tender title "little flock" (Lk 12:32) and little "children" (Mk 10:24) and promised they would not be left orphans (Jn 14:18). The "golden rule" that our Lord promulgated was a positive restatement of an ancient Jewish proverb (Tobit 4:16) found in the Jewish Talmud. Christ taught the golden rule (Mt 7:12; Lk 6:31) by both word and deed.

Jesus loved His enemies. He taught forgiveness in the Lord's Prayer (Mt 6:12) and in the number of times we are commanded to forgive (Mt 18:22), as well as in the Sermon on the Mount (Mt 5:44) and in the parable of the Good Samaritan (Lk 10:30). Although He opposed the Pharisees, He numbered some of them among His dearest friends, such as Nicodemus (Jn 3:1; 7:50) and Joseph of Arimathea (Mk 15:43). He cried over unrepentant Jerusalem (Mt 23:37) and called His betrayer "friend" (Mt 26:50). On the Cross He forgave with His words and with His life (Lk 23:34), and He inspired His followers to imitate Him in this (Acts 7:60).

Jesus loved people beyond the limits of His race and nation. He preached in the Canaanite city (Jn 4:22) and worked miracles for the pagans, for example, the Roman centurion (Mt 8:5), the Canaanite woman (Mt 15:21), and the cities of the Decapolis (Mk 5:19). It is clear that He intended the "good news" for all the world. The "field" (Mt 13:38) in which the word is sown is the whole "world", and His disciples are light and salt for the "earth" (Mt 5:13). On the Cross He draws all men to Himself (Jn 12:32) so that from east to west all will feast with Jacob and the other patriarchs in the kingdom (Mt 8:11). All must be made disciples (Mt 28:19), and this includes all nations as well as all creation (Mk 16:15).

Jesus had a special love for His closest friends: for Peter, James, and John (Mk 3:16), for Martha, Mary, and Lazarus (Jn 11:5), for the pure of heart (Mt 5:8), and for those who do the will of God (Mk 3:35). He had a particular love for children and those adults who assumed childlike dispositions (Mk 9:36; Lk 6:20; Mt 11:25).

Christ deeply loved sinners. He forgave the paralytic (Mk 2:5) and saved the adulterous woman's life (Jn 8:3–11). He showed mercy to the sinful woman (Lk 7:45), to the publican, Zacchaeus (Lk 19:5), and to the Samaritan woman (Jn 4:7). He selected the tax collector, Levi, as one of His apostles (Mk 2:14). He said that He came to call sinners (Mk 2:17) and to tell them how to be justified before God (Lk 18:9). He spoke with love about sinners in the parables of the prodigal son (better called the parable of the loving and forgiving father—Lk 15:11) and of the lost sheep and lost drachma (Lk 15:3–10).

The love of Jesus was effective and saving. He said that he did not love us simply for the sake of loving us, but rather He came to seek what was lost (Lk 19:10) and to be a servant to all (Mk 10:45), to sow the seed of the gospel (Mt 13:37), to have no fixed home (Mt 8:20), to be hated by His enemies (Mt 24:9), to suffer and die for many, and to rise from the dead (Mk 8:31).

True love, Christ taught, was not a matter of mere sentiment or feeling but rather was measured by giving and by sacrifice. Thus God measures His love by giving His only begotten Son (Jn 3:16), and Jesus shows God's love to us by laying down His life for His friends (Jn 15:13). There is no "greater love" than this. In instituting the Holy Eucharist, Christ again measured His love by sacrifice, because in this sign He is *given* and His blood is *shed* (1 Cor 11:23; Lk 22:19).

We who are members of the Catholic Church that Christ founded are commanded to measure our love by His. We are to love as He loved us (Jn 15:12). We must prove our love by keeping His commandments (Jn 14:15; 15:10) and by being true to His word (Jn 14:23). In this He Himself assists us by His grace and by His example. When we see Him, we see God (Jn 14:9), and God's other name is "Love" (see 1 Jn 4:8).

FEBRUARY 12, 1993

The Personality of Jesus

IV

It is erroneous and heretical to deny the divinity of Christ. Jesus is truly the second Person of the Blessed Trinity and possesses from all eternity

His divine nature. However, it would also be erroneous and heretical to deny the humanity of Christ. God Himself entered time and space and human history and assumed a real, true, and full human nature. In His human nature Jesus is like us in all things but sin (Heb 4:15).

In His human nature and, more specifically, in His human personality (without which one cannot, it seems, have a true human nature), our Lord showed a special relationship with God the Father. It is impossible to study the human personality of Jesus from the pages of the Gospels without noticing the elements of this relationship, elements that contribute to the utterly amazing picture of human perfection seen in the Divine Person of the Carpenter from Nazareth.

PUBLIC PRAYER

The relationship of Jesus to God the Father is seen most dramatically in the prayer life of Christ. He observed, first of all, Jewish liturgical activity. He made the usual religious pilgrimages to Jerusalem (Lk 2:42; Jn 2:13). He went to the synagogue on the Sabbath (Lk 4:31). He used the customary Jewish meal prayers (Mk 6:41). In answer to a question, He cited the morning and evening creedal song of the Jewish religion, the "Shema Israel" (Mk 12:29: "Hear, O Israel"). The prayer that bears our Lord's very name resembles in some ways the synagogue prayer called the "Qaddich". At the Last Supper He sang with His apostles the "Great Hallel" (Mt 26:30). On the Cross He prayed the psalms (Mk 15:34—Ps 22; Lk 23:46—Ps 31).

PRIVATE PRAYER

In all the great moments of His earthly life, our Savior engaged in private prayer. He prayed before He chose His apostles (Lk 6:12) and before He allowed Peter to make his profession of faith in His messianic mission (Lk 9:18). He prayed at the Transfiguration (Lk 9:28), for Peter before the Last Supper (Lk 22:32), during the Last Supper (Jn 17), and in the garden of Gethsemane (Mk 14:32). He often prayed before working His miracles, as when He uttered "Ephphatha" (Mk 7:34). He told His disciples that some devils could be cast out only by prayer and fasting (Mk 9:29). He prayed before He raised Lazarus from the dead (Jn 11:41) and before He sent the disciples out on their first missionary journey (Lk 10:1–2). He talked in prayer to His Father about His impending doom (Jn 12:27).

Jesus loved to pray in solitude. He fled from the crowds to pray frequently (Mk 6:46; Jn 6:15). He prayed early in the morning, before the day's work (Lk 4:42; Mk 1:35). He went into the wilderness alone to pray (Lk 5:16). The apostles noticed His love for prayer and asked Him to teach them to pray (Lk 11:1).

Our Redeemer seemed to detect God in everything. Sparrows, wildflowers, and our human hair reminded Him of God's providence (Mt 10:29ff.). Sun and rain reminded Him of God's mercy to the good and to evildoers (Mt 5:45). The sky reminded Him of God's throne, the earth of God's footstool, and Jerusalem of the "city of the great King" (Mt 5:34–35). Babies reminded Him of guardian angels (Mt 18:10). Parents reminded Him of God's love (Lk 15:11ff.), and a shepherd's joy, of God's joy (Lk 15:4), and the activities of kings, of His Father's activities (Mt 22:1).

FATHERHOOD AND TRUST

Our Lord's relationship to God was always filial. The New Testament records eight specific prayers of Jesus and, except for one time when He was citing a psalm (Mt 5:34), He always addressed God as Father. In the Old Testament tradition, there was some indication of Yahweh as the Father of Israel. Jesus expanded this usage, however, to embrace, at least potentially, all of humanity. God is the Father of all, and the Universal (or Catholic) Church, the mother of all. Christ instructed His followers to address God as "our Father" (Mt 6:9), and He Himself used a term of absolute intimacy, "Abba" (Mk 14:36). Even from His youth He understood God as His Father with Whose business He had to be occupied (Lk 2:49).

The Son was faithful to His heavenly Father. Faithful obedience is the only criterion for determining true love of God from spurious or false love. Jesus came to do God's will (Mt 26:39). He was sent for this purpose, and He conforms His human will to His divine will (Jn 5:30; Lk 22:42). Peter was a Satan (tempter) when he strove to persuade Jesus to abandon God's will (Mk 8:33), and the disciples remembered that zeal for God consumed Jesus (Jn 2:17).

Trust in God, too, marked the human personality of Christ. In the parables of the importunate friend (Lk 11:5ff.), the unjust judge (Lk 18:1ff.), and the child asking for bread (Mt 7:9), as well as in the express command to ask, seek, and knock, Jesus taught that faith and trust are vital in any relationship with God and, if they are adequate, can even move mountains (Mt 17:20).

OUR RELATIONSHIP WITH GOD

From His intimate union with God, both in His human and in His divine knowledge, our Lord told us many things to assist us in our relationship with the Father. He told us that God knows our needs before we ask Him (Mt 6:32) and that His heaven contains many mansions (Jn 14:2). He sent Jesus, His Son, and gives all things over to Him (Mk 12:6; Mt 11:27). He sends His Holy Spirit upon the Catholic Church (Jn 14:26), and He will come to dwell in the hearts of those who are followers of the Son. Indeed, the Son will come with Him to effect this indwelling (Jn 14:21). The special sonship of Jesus with the Father is shared by Him with others (Mk 3:35; Mt 12:50), but only with those prepared to pay the price of giving up earthly possessions and laying up treasures in heaven (Mt 13:45; 6:19).

Simplicity, humility, charity, prayer, confidence, and trust are the keys to the human personality of Jesus Christ. They help us gain, through the veil of His humanity, a glimpse of His divinity even now, after all these centuries since He walked the earth. When we approach Him in Holy Communion, we ought to beg His help in our work of inserting His personality into ours. What we hear and read about Him in the Gospels should nourish our outlook, attitudes, and life-style. Along with other "signs" it should convince us of the truth of Christ's claims and titles and help us to be better embraced by Him in Whom "we live and move and have our being" (Acts 17:28).

FEBRUARY 26, 1993

Presence of Jesus

Christ is present in a special way at every eucharistic celebration. As God, of course, He is omnipresent, everywhere by His divine knowledge and divine power, closer to us at this moment than the air we are breathing or the clothes we are wearing. In His Incarnation, moreover, He comes to be with us, His Chosen People of the New Testament, in a particular way when we "do in remembrance" His eucharistic command (Lk 22:19).

According to the Second Vatican Council, Christ is present at Mass particularly in four ways: in the very gathering of the faithful, in the person of the priest, in the reading of Holy Scripture, and, above all, under the Eucharistic Species.[1]

Jesus clearly taught that "where two or three are gathered" in His name, He Himself is present in a special way (Mt 18:20). At every Mass, even one where there are not many people present, the Church is "gathered together in His name". The very word "church" has the basic

---

[1] *Sacrosanctum concilium*, no. 7.

meaning of "assembly". Furthermore, the assembly of the faithful at Mass is not simply a haphazard grouping of people but a convoked and hierarchically ordered "meeting", an encounter between Christ and His Bride, the Catholic Church, made present in this locality and time. Especially in the principal Sunday Mass of a parish community should this reality of the presence of Jesus be recalled.

Also, it must not be forgotten that at every Mass the "Church Triumphant" is convoked, that is to say, the liturgy on earth is a pale reflection of the glorious liturgy going on at that same moment in heaven. The Second Vatican Council teaches, "In the earthly liturgy we share in a foretaste of that heavenly liturgy which is celebrated in the Holy City of Jerusalem toward which we journey as pilgrims." [2]

The Church Fathers and Doctors often refer to the priest as "another Christ". Priests, before everyone else, are conscious of their imperfections, weakness, and sins. They are not given to an attitude of "holier than thou". However, the magnificent dignity that comes to them through the sacrament of Holy Orders is undeniable. It is their vocation "to make Christ present", first of all in confecting the Eucharist, but also in all their life and ministry and in their very presence during Mass. The Second Vatican Council says Christ is "present in the person of his minister" at every Mass. [3]

The Council goes on to teach that Jesus at Mass "is present in his word, since it is he himself who speaks when the Holy Scriptures are read in church".[4] The Bible is the word of God in words of men. The Holy Spirit, God Himself, is its primary Author.

When read at Mass, the words of Scripture take on a "quasi-sacramental" aspect. This is especially true of the Gospel, which contains the very words of Jesus Himself. We stand for the Gospel (as when an important person enters the room), salute Christ Who is present ("Glory to You, O Lord. . . ." "Praise to You, Lord Jesus Christ"), the sacred text is kissed, and, at a solemn Mass, the Book of the Gospels (or Lectionary) is surrounded by candles and incensed.

The presence of Christ under the appearances of bread and wine is altogether different from His other "presences" at Mass. The Council of Trent expresses our faith in this matter: "In the most Blessed Sacrament of the Eucharist are the Body and Blood, together with the soul and divinity of our Lord Jesus Christ. Therefore, the whole Christ is truly, really, and substantially contained in the Holy Eucharist." It is by the conversion of the bread and wine into the Body and Blood that Christ becomes present in this Blessed Sacrament.

---

[2] Ibid., no. 8.   [3] Ibid., no. 7.   [4] Ibid.

The *Catechism of the Catholic Church* states, "The Eucharistic presence of Christ begins at the moment of the consecration and endures as long as the Eucharistic species subsist" (CCC 1377). The *Catechism* quotes the Council of Trent: "By the consecration of the bread and wine there takes place a change of the whole substance of the bread into the substance of the body of Christ our Lord and of the whole substance of the wine into the substance of his blood. This change the holy Catholic Church has fittingly and properly called transubstantiation." [5]

Pope Paul VI, writing about this abiding presence of Jesus, says, "Not only while the sacrifice is offered and the Sacrament is confected, but also after the sacrifice has been offered and the Sacrament has been received, as long as the Eucharist is kept in our churches and oratories, Christ is truly Emmanuel, that is, 'God with us'. Day and night He is in our midst, dwelling with us, full of grace and of truth." [6]

Saint John Chrysostom declared, "It is not man that causes the things offered to become the Body and Blood of Christ, but He Who was crucified for us, Christ Himself. The priest, in the role of Christ, pronounces these words, but their power and grace are God's."

Pope John Paul II says, "Jesus waits for us in this Sacrament of His love. Let us be generous with our time in going to meet Him."

OCTOBER 7, 1994

The Temptations of Christ

The three synoptic Gospels record the story of the temptations of Jesus (Lk 4:1–13; Mk 1:12–13; Mt 4:1–11), and the liturgy always presents an account of Christ's temptations in the Mass for the First Sunday of Lent. Saint Thomas Aquinas, relying on the testimony of many Fathers and Doctors of the Church, says that Jesus chose to undergo these temptations for four reasons.

First, He wants to help us in our own temptations, to strengthen us in our necessary struggle with the world, the flesh, and the devil. On the outcome of that lifelong effort depends our happiness for all eternity. Saint Gregory the Great said, "It was not unworthy of our Redeemer to wish to be tempted, since He came also to be slain. By His temptations He conquered our temptations, just as by His death He overcame our death."

---

[5] CCC 1376, quoting Council of Trent (1551): DS 1642.
[6] *Mysterium Fidei*, no. 67.

Second, Jesus wants to warn us that no one, no matter how holy, may think himself free or safe from temptation. Indeed, the closer we are to Christ, the more we are likely to be tempted by the devil. Saint Hilary said, "The devil above all strives to assail those who are most sanctified."

Third, Jesus suffered temptation in order to give us an example of how to overcome temptation, by prayer, fasting, and exercising free will to say "no".

Fourth, He was tempted so He could give us confidence in His mercy. In the Bible it is written, "We have not a High Priest who is unable to sympathize with our weaknesses, but one who in every respect has been tempted as we are, yet without sinning" (Heb 4:15).

The primordial calamity of the human race involved temptation and its victory over the first man. It is fitting that the undoing of this calamity should also involve temptation, with its defeat by Jesus, Who is the new Adam, the new Head of the human race.

In the account of the Fall of humanity (Gen 3:1), there was first a taunt with an enticement to pleasure. The "fruit" looked delicious, and the Father of Lies asked, "Did God say, 'You shall not eat of any tree of the garden'?" This was followed by a challenge to vainglory, "Your eyes will be opened." Finally, there was the appeal to pride, "You will be like God, knowing good and evil."

This same order of temptation was used by Satan in tempting Jesus. First, there was the taunt and enticement to pleasure in regard to bread. Then there followed the appeal to vainglory on the pinnacle of the temple and, finally, the appeal to pride in all the kingdoms of the world. We should not suppose ourselves immune to this same order of temptation. First, the devil lures us with pleasure. Then he moves on to entice us with the prospect of power. At last, he works to suggest to us that it is worthwhile to turn away from God for the sake of our possessions. Pleasure, power, and possessions are most often used by the enemy of our salvation to tempt us to sin. This is precisely why the threefold task of Lent (fasting, prayer, and almsgiving) is given us in order to strengthen our wills to resist.

One of the gravest dangers in all military operations comes from underestimating the strength of an enemy. The biggest folly of all, moreover, would come from being oblivious to the existence of an enemy. The fallen angels, with their sly cunning and the intelligence of their angelic nature, should not be underestimated. In our world today, the triumph of the devils often takes place because their very existence is doubted or denied by many. As Chesterton observed, it seems that the existence of original sin and its effects as well as the existence of the devils are articles of faith that are, for the most part, clearly demonstrable from what we can notice around us.

Saint John of the Cross said that no soul can overcome the strength of the devils without prayer, "nor will it be able to understand their deceits without mortification and humility". Saint Paul wrote (Eph 6:12), "For we are not contending against flesh and blood, but against the principalities, against the powers, against the world rulers of this present darkness, against the spiritual hosts of wickedness." Saint Macarius wrote, "It is impossible for a soul to cross the dreadful ocean of sins and keep God's commandments and be saved, unless it is aided by the Spirit of Jesus and borne along in the vessel of divine grace procured by humble prayer."

Francisco Suarez, a great theologian and spiritual writer, suggests that the story of how Jesus resisted the devil gives us a lesson on how to achieve victory in this vital area of our lives. The words of Christ in this episode show that He knew the Sacred Scriptures and used the word of God, that He cited the Commandments of God, that He trusted (in His human will) in God's promises, that He knew the snares of the devil and rejected him and his snares with authority and confidence, that He was, because of His forty days of prayer and fasting, totally immersed in humility.

To be tempted is our human lot. This is not directly willed by God but permitted by Him. Saint Bernard of Clairvaux said, "It is necessary that temptations should happen, for who shall be crowned except he that shall lawfully have fought, and how shall a man fight unless there be someone to attack him." Saint John Vianney said that the greatest of all evils is not to be tempted, because that means that the devil already looks upon us as his property and has no need to bother himself further. Saint Leo the Great said, "Virtue is nothing without the trial of temptation, for there is no conflict without an enemy, no victory without strife. Indeed, the Tempter, ever on the watch, wages war most violently against those he sees as the most careful to avoid sin."

On the positive side, temptations teach us to be humble. Resisting them can prove our fidelity, give us spiritual joy, increase our merits, deepen our virtues, reinforce our dependence on God, and fashion us for the glory that is to come. Following the example of Christ and relying on the strength of His grace, may Lent be for each of us a prelude to a definitive triumph over evil and sin.

FEBRUARY 23, 1996

Christ the King

On December 11, 1925, Pope Pius XI instituted the Feast of Christ the King. Originally celebrated on the last Sunday of October, the celebration was moved, subsequent to the liturgical reforms following the Second Vatican Council, to the last Sunday of the liturgical year. The purpose of the feast is to remind the People of God about Christ, our divine King, now reigning at the right hand of the Father, Who will come one day to judge the living and the dead.

The kingship of Jesus is part of almost every liturgical celebration, and thus it is appropriate that celebrating and adoring Christ as our King is the summary and completion of the liturgical year. At the Annunciation, Gabriel told the Blessed Virgin that Jesus would be "royal", possessing the throne of David and being king over the House of Jacob (Lk 1:32–33). The Magi came looking for the "king of the Jews" (Mt 2:2).

Throughout His earthly life Christ was acclaimed as "Son of David" or King; on Palm Sunday, the Church greets Him as did the children of Jerusalem, singing Hosanna to the King. On Good Friday in a special way we remember His nobility in answering Pilate's question: "So you are a king?" with "You say that I am a king" (Jn 18:37). The mockery and ridicule at the beginning of His Passion had to do with His claims to kingship (Jn 19:1–3, 15). The inscription on His Cross had to do with His kingship (Jn 19:19–22).

Never is Christ more thought of as King than at Easter, our greatest solemnity, which is complemented and completed by Ascension Thursday, another solemnity of Christ's kingship. Corpus Christi, too, is a solemnity of kingly majesty. Each feast of a saint throughout the year reminds us that Jesus is the King of martyrs and confessors and virgins and all holy men and women.

Saint Cyril of Alexandria says that Christ "has dominion over all creatures, a dominion not seized by violence nor usurped from anyone, but one that is His by His essence and by His nature".[7] Pope Pius XI wrote that since Jesus unites in His divine Person a total and complete human nature with His divine nature, in what is technically called the hypostatic union, He is not only to be adored as God by angels and men, but He is to be obeyed by angels and men as Man.[8]

Although Christ said His kingdom was "not of this world", His spiritual rule over the hearts and minds of His subjects and followers is

---

[7] Pius XI, *Quas Primas* (December 11, 1925), 13, quoting Cyril of Alexandria, *In Iuc. x.*
[8] Ibid.

intended to have a resonance in their lives and thus in the world in which they live and work. Saint Augustine of Hippo wrote that Christ became our King, "not to exact tribute, not to equip armies, not to subdue visible foes, but that He might rule over men's souls, counsel them about eternity, and lead to the kingdom of heaven those who would believe in Him, hope in Him, and love Him". In the Mass on the Solemnity of Christ the King, we pray about a kingdom "of truth and life, a kingdom of holiness and grace, a kingdom of justice, peace, and love".

It is clear from divine revelation that the Catholic Church, founded by Jesus, is the kingdom that He came to establish. However, it is His kingdom only in embryonic form. Thus, while the "kingdom of God is among you" (Lk 17:20), that is, already here in one sense, it is still necessary that we pray daily "Thy kingdom come" (Mt 6:10), for in another sense it is not yet here.

The kingdom of Christ has a twofold aspect, internal and external. The Church, like her divine Founder, has a part that is visible and a part that is invisible. We can see the visible head, the priesthood, the sacraments, sacramentals, and other signs and symbols. We can see the visible institutions and organizations of the Church. What we cannot see is the invisible Head Who is Christ now reigning in heaven or the Soul of the Church, God, the Holy Spirit, or the sanctifying grace and the supernatural virtues that invisibly unite us, who are exteriorly united in professing the same faith, worshipping the same way, and obeying the successors of the apostles in religious matters.

The most difficult task of a Christian is oftentimes the submission to Christ in our personal lives, showing Him obedience, loyalty, and constant love. If we as Christians are joined in Jesus in His Mystical Body, we must allow Him to direct and rule our households, our families, our activities, and our souls. The concept of "king" is not familiar or congenial to us Americans, egalitarian and democratic as we are. Our national history leads us to disdain the concept of royalty, and, speaking politically and materially, perhaps this is for the best. However, it would be a grave mistake to transfer this cultural bias of ours to the spiritual realm, where God's providence itself has established a monarchy.

In particular the celebration of Christ's kingship on the last Sunday of the liturgical year should fittingly prepare us for the next season in the liturgical cycle. We should already look ahead to the day when the prayer "Thy kingdom come" will be definitively answered and He shall come in power and majesty surrounded by the angels. Then in the heavenly Jerusalem, clad in our regal nuptial garment, we shall dine in glory and rule with Christ, our King, forever.

OCTOBER 19, 1993

The Holy Spirit

The *Catechism of the Catholic Church* lists eight places in which Catholics experience the Holy Spirit in the life of the Church. God, the Holy Spirit, is specially present in the Sacred Scriptures, for He is the One Who inspired the sacred writers of the Bible. The Holy Spirit is present in Sacred Tradition, the unwritten font of revelation, to which the Fathers of the Church bear witness. The Holy Spirit is present in the Magisterium, or teaching authority, of the Church and in the words and symbols of the holy sacraments. The Holy Spirit is present in the Church's official prayer and in the private prayer of Catholics, in the charisms and ministries of the Church, in the signs of apostolic and missionary life, and in the witness of the saints, in which He reveals His holiness and applies to souls the salvation won by Jesus in His death and Resurrection.

Catholics profess each Sunday their belief in the Holy Spirit as "the Lord and Giver of Life". These words derive from two ecumenical councils, that of Nicaea, held in A.D. 325, and that of Constantinople, held in A.D. 381. The third Person of the Holy Trinity, according to Pope John Paul II, is the "One in Whom the inscrutable Triune God communicates Himself to human beings, constituting in them the Source of eternal life".[9]

It was at the Last Supper that our divine Savior told the apostles about "another Counselor" (Jn 14:16) Whom the Father would send in answer to His very prayer. This other Counselor would be the "Spirit of truth" (Jn 14:17). Jesus is the first Counselor. Our Holy Father states, "The Holy Spirit comes after Him and because of Him, in order to continue in the world and in the Church the work of the Good News of salvation."[10] His function in regard to the Church is to teach, to "call to remembrance the teachings of Christ", and to "bear witness to Jesus" (Jn 15:26). He also will guide the Church "into all the truth" (Jn 16:13).

Seven weeks after the Passover of Jesus, on Pentecost Sunday, Christ's mission was fulfilled, as the *Catechism* puts it, "in the outpouring of the Holy Spirit, manifested, given, and communicated as a divine Person: of his fullness, Christ, the Lord, pours out the Spirit in abundance" (CCC 731). In fire and hurricane wind, Jesus kept His promise. Saint Basil wrote: "Through the Holy Spirit we are restored to paradise, led back to

---

[9] *Dominum et vivificantem,* no. 1.
[10] Ibid., no. 3.

the kingdom of heaven and adopted as children, given confidence to call God 'Father' and to share in Christ's grace, called children of light and given a share in eternal glory."

The first and greatest gift of the Holy Spirit is love. Since God is Love, it is the Gift of Himself (Rom 5:5). Love contains all the other gifts that are listed by the Prophet Isaiah: wisdom, understanding, counsel, knowledge, fortitude, piety, and fear of the Lord (Is 11:2).

God the Holy Spirit dwells inside the Catholic Church as a soul dwells in and animates a human body. When an individual is joined to Christ in the Church and in the invisible life of sanctifying grace, the Holy Spirit also dwells in a special way inside such a person (1 Cor 3:16), making him an actual "temple" of God. A consequence of such an intimate union with God is the possession of the "fruit of the Spirit", listed by Saint Paul: love, joy, peace, patience, kindness, goodness, faithfulness, gentleness, and self-control (Gal 5:22). Saint Cyril of Alexandria wrote: "For just as the power of Christ's sacred flesh makes those in whom It exists to be united in one Body, in the same way, the one and undivided Spirit of God, Who dwells in all, leads all into spiritual unity."

Our Holy Father, at the conclusion of his 1986 encyclical letter on the Holy Spirit (*Dominum et Vivificante*), wrote: "What is 'hard, he softens', what is 'frozen, he warms', and what is 'wayward, he sets anew' on the paths of salvation. Praying thus, the Church unceasingly professes her faith that there exists in our created world a Spirit who is an uncreated gift. He is the Spirit of the Father and of the Son: like the Father and the Son, he is uncreated, without limit, eternal, omnipotent, God, Lord. . . . [The Church] turns to him and awaits Him." [11]

By the Holy Spirit we are enlightened and strengthened. By Him we are made holy (Gal 4:4–7). It is through Him that Jesus pardons our sins in Confession (Jn 20:22–23). Just as the Holy Spirit brought about the Incarnation (Lk 1:35), thus in the so-called "Epiclesis" at Mass does He effect, through the words of institution spoken by an ordained priest, the presence of Christ in our midst in the Holy Eucharist. The *Catechism* states, "Through the Church's sacraments, Christ communicates his Holy and sanctifying Spirit to the members of his Body" (CCC 739).

The Holy Spirit was present at the baptism of Jesus (Jn 1:33–36). Christ spoke of the Holy Spirit to Nicodemus (Jn 3:5–8), to the Samaritan woman (Jn 4:24), and to others as well (Jn 7:37–39). May this gracious God, this Holy Spirit, Whom we have received in our Baptism and Confirmation, be with us always. May He come in a special way this next Pentecost Sunday to renew the face of the earth.

MAY 20, 1994

[11] Ibid., no. 67.

2

KNOWLEDGE OF GOD AND
DIVINE REVELATION

Knowledge of God

When he visited France some years ago, our Holy Father, Pope John Paul II, presided over a youth rally in Princes' Park in Paris. The rally was scheduled for one hour but lasted three. As the cheers for the Pope died away and as he was leaving the stadium, a youth clearly called out, "I am an atheist. What is faith?"

The Pope insisted that the youth be tracked down, and, improbable though it may seem, he was found by some priests who studied photographs of the event and who managed to meet with the young man some months later. They told him the Pope was concerned about him, was praying for him, and was sorry he had not been able to give him an immediate answer to his question. The young man replied that he had been so moved by the visit of the Pope that, immediately after the rally, he had gone to a bookstore and bought a New Testament, had read it carefully, and was now taking instructions in the Catholic faith. "Tell the Pope", he said, "that soon I will receive Baptism."

We exist, the catechism tells us, to know, love, and serve God in this world and to be happy with Him forever in the life to come. The first duty that defines our existence is to know God. We come to knowledge of His existence either through our natural, unaided human reason, which He created in us, or through His telling us about His existence in an extraordinary way, which we call divine revelation. Of course, it is not enough simply to know *about* God. We must strive to know God, personally and intimately, in Jesus Christ. This was obviously the experience of the young French atheist-turned-Catholic.

God did not simply leave us to our own devices when it came to knowing of His existence. Too often this knowledge would not be available to all people, distracted as many are by work or pleasure, undisciplined and untrained as many are in reflective and philosophical thought, and uninterested as many are in even the most vital and essential matters. Also, knowledge of God's existence, if not helped by divine revelation, can be mixed with serious errors. Human beings have a "natural propensity for religion", planted in each of them by God. If this is not resting in the one true religion, it shows itself in religious aberration, superstition, magic, and grotesque falsehoods. Finally, even were we to come to a knowledge of God's existence by our unaided human reason, this knowledge would often be misty, unclear, vague, and abstract. Thus, the First Vatican Council said that, although we have the power to know of God's existence "on our own", God took pity on us and revealed His existence.

As Pope Pius XII wrote: "Though human reason is, strictly speaking, truly capable by its own natural power and light of attaining to a true and certain knowledge of the one personal God Who watches over and controls the world by His providence, and of the natural law written in our hearts by the Creator, yet there are many obstacles which prevent reason from the effective and fruitful use of this inborn faculty." [1]

Just as it is logical and in accord with human reason to conclude from the existence of a computer to a computer manufacturer and illogical and unreasonable to doubt or deny the existence of some computer maker once we have encountered a computer, so Sacred Scripture tells us that human beings have the ability to discern the existence of a Creator from our encounter with creation (see Rom 1:20–21; Wis 13:1–9).

When one sees and experiences causality, one is logically led back to an uncaused Cause of it all. When one sees and experiences contingency and change, one is logically led back to the Necessary and Unchangeable. When one sees movement, one must eventually arrive at the existence of an unmoved and unmovable Mover.

As an artist leaves something of his personality and "self" in a masterpiece, so God has left something of His "personality" in His masterpiece, called creation. Although creation has been smeared and soiled by sin and its consequences, here and there, one can discern things that were not washed away by the flood or ruined by the Fall of Adam and Eve. Truth, beauty, goodness, freedom, unselfish love, all direct our thoughts to infinite Truth, Beauty, Goodness, Freedom, and Love. In creation we get a glance through a misty mirror (1 Cor 13:12), but what must the Reality be!

The macrocosm—the astronomical numbers of the stars and galaxies of the universe, their order and their laws—as well as the microcosm— the atomic and subatomic particles—along with the mystery of life, cry out to thinking humanity that just as computers "don't just happen", so

---

[1] *Humani generis*, no. 2.

even in the incomprehensible numbers of years the universe existed, it "didn't just happen". Someone "made it", and Someone "did it".

Thus, the Catholic Church teaches that "the one, true God, our Creator and Lord, can be known with certitude through His works, by the natural light of human reason." [2] However, she also teaches that "we need God's revelation even to enlighten us about those religious and moral truths which are not beyond human reason, so that in the present condition of the human race they can be known by everyone, without difficulty, with firm certitude, and with no admixture of error." [3]

People are religious by the nature God gave them. We all come from God and go toward God. We are not fully human until we are in a true relationship with the one true God.

Our conscience and our soul, "the seed of eternity that we bear in ourselves, irreducible to the merely material", call out to a thinking human being that God is the beginning and the end, "the Alpha and the Omega" (Rev 21:6) of all that exists. "In him we live and move and have our being" (Acts 17:28).

SEPTEMBER 24, 1993

No God or Know God

Sacred Scripture says: "The fool says in his heart, 'There is no God' " (Ps 14:1). The German poet Angelus Silesius wrote: "Creation is a book wherein who wisely reads can ever find the line that to its author leads." We know, too, that Saint Paul wrote that there is no excuse for atheism, for "what can be known about God is plain to them, because God has shown it to them. Ever since the creation of the world his invisible nature, namely, his eternal power and deity, has been clearly perceived in the things that have been made" (Rom 1:19–20). The Book of Wisdom says that all men are liars in whom there is no knowledge of God; who, from the good things that are made, could not know the One Who made them; or, from the masterpiece, cannot deduce the Master Workman (Wis 13:1).

NATURAL OR SUPERNATURAL KNOWLEDGE

Following the words of the Bible, the Fathers of the Church assert that God is knowable in a certain measure even outside of revelation. By

---

[2] First Vatican Council, *Dogmatic Constitution on Catholic Faith*, c. 2: DS 1786 (3005).
[3] Ibid.: DS 1785–86 (3004–5).

looking at the universe, a thinking human being can conceive some idea of God, along with some idea of His attributes, His power, His wisdom, His beauty, and His providence.

On the level of natural knowledge conscience, too, is an indicator of God's existence. An innate sense of good and evil that comes from the natural law points to a just Judge and a holy Lawgiver. The natural knowledge of God is weak and imperfect, compared to what we know about God from His talking to us in divine revelation. But natural knowledge and supernatural knowledge about God, His existence and His attributes, are not two opposed forms of knowledge; rather, both derive from God Himself and make up a continuity.

REVELATION

According to Athenagoras, only God can tell us about God. In a certain sense this is true. There is truth in the saying that God cannot be defined; otherwise He could be circumscribed with words, and, since He is unlimited in every way, He cannot be put into a test tube, a mathematical formula, or a genuine definition. Jesus told us that God is unknowable. "No one knows the Son except the Father, and no one knows the Father except the Son and anyone to whom the Son chooses to reveal him" (Mt 11:27).

We can describe God, of course, but we must always realize that our description falls short of even an approximation of reality. He is, in His existence and nature, truly ineffable and beyond all comprehension. Knowing of His existence and knowing something about Him, albeit in a defective and infinitesimal way, must be a work of grace.

God tells us in divine revelation, that is, in Sacred Scripture and Sacred Tradition, that He is all-kind, all-beautiful, all-just, all-merciful, omniscient, and everywhere, closer to us than the air we are breathing or the clothes we are wearing. We are beings, but He is Being. We are the many, but He is the One. He is identified with His attributes; that is, He is not only truthful, but He is Truth itself. He is infinite and eternal. He is absolute Perfection and not merely the source of holiness, but all-holy. He is all-wise and almighty. God tells us His other name is Love (1 Jn 4:16).

The total and complete transcendence of God is often a source of difficulty, since our finite human minds were made by Him to have a capacity for truth and an openness to Him, and yet He remained in a sense "out of our reach", until He Himself reached down to us in Christ Jesus. The poet writes: "As with my hand I cannot span the heavens or the earth below, so God Who is ere time began, my tiny mind I can't fully know."

Since change is a law of all we know in material existence, it is nearly impossible to grasp how God is absolutely unchangeable. Saint Teresa of Avila wrote: "Consider how quickly men change and how little one can rely on them. Therefore, hold fast to God, Who cannot change." God cannot grow in knowledge since He knows all things, including the past, the present, and the future. He also knows futurables, that is, "what would be if". (What you would be doing were you born in the year 2400 in China, the molecular structure of each body cell of each sparrow at that date, and so on.)

WE KNOW AND BELIEVE

The psalmist sings: "The heavens are telling the glory of God; and the firmament proclaims his handiwork" (Ps 19:1). Jesus tells us that our heavenly Father knows what we need before we ask (Mt 6:32). He will reward us according to our deeds (Rom 2:6). He is our Shepherd (Ps 23:1) Who will see to it that we lack nothing essential. He has numbered the hairs on our head (Mt 10:30), and He clothes us better than lilies or even Solomon, while He feeds us more abundantly than the birds of the air (Mt 6:26–34).

It is in the Incarnation, however, that the revelation about God, His existence and attributes, reaches its climax and completion. When God draws near to us in Christ Jesus, indeed, abides with us in a substantial and real way in the Holy Eucharist, we may be tempted to forget His total "otherness", and the power that flung into existence by mere act of the will a hundred trillion stars (and maybe more), while He deigns to bend down and touch our turbulent and sin-filled planet with divine condescension.

The Second Vatican Council said: "Through revelation, the invisible God (cf. Col 1:15; 1 Tim 1:17) out of the abundance of His love speaks to men as His friends (cf. Ex 33:11; Jn 15:14–15) and lives among them, so that He may invite them to be taken into fellowship with Himself." [4]

OCTOBER 1, 1993

Revelation

Jesus is the definitive and exhaustive Word of God (Jn 1:1). In Him God has given all He could; that is, He has given us Himself. The Word made flesh (Jn 1:14) shares our humanity and touches with the Godhead our

[4] *Dei Verbum*, no. 2.

human condition. Jesus is the Christ, the Messiah, the Anointed One. He is the visibility of God's forgiving Love. As God, He is Love (1 Jn 4:8). He is the image of the invisible God, the firstborn of every creature (Col 1:15). To see Jesus is to see the Father (Jn 14:9).

Our divine Savior not only embodies and enfleshes the Word of God, but He also speaks to us the "words of God" (Jn 3:34). Christ perfects revelation by being present to us and shows us God's revelation in His words and deeds, His signs and wonders, His death and rising, and His sending upon us the Holy Spirit of truth. This "testimony" of Jesus is the final proclamation of God's revelation, until He comes again.

This is why the Second Vatican Council teaches: "We now await no further new public revelation before the glorious manifestation of our Lord Jesus Christ." [5] In all that Christ tells us, through the work of the Holy Spirit, we have "the faith which was once for all delivered to the saints" (Jude 1:3).

In giving His revelation to humanity, God used a certain measure of continuity and gradualness. In the olden days, God spoke in a way that was fragmentary and intermittent. The content of revelation and the people addressed, as well as the mediators of revelation, were inferior to the excellence of the New Testament, the new revelation, which reaches its fulfillment in Christ, Who is simultaneously the Supreme Revealer and the Supreme Object of revelation. The Epistle to the Hebrews states: "In many and various ways God spoke of old to our fathers by the prophets; but in these last days he has spoken to us by a Son" (Heb 1:1–2).

Like the climactic *coda* of a great symphony, the Christ-event had an echo. This decisive intervention of God in human history was concluded when the echo died out. That is why public revelation ceased with the death of the last apostle, presumably Saint John. The constitutive phase of God's revelation is now concluded, until the Lord comes to judge the living and the dead. This, of course, does not exclude the possibility of private revelation, which can never contradict public revelation (Gal 1:8).

Private revelation need not be believed by all people, only by the person receiving such a revelation. Its authenticity is ultimately under the judgment of the authority of the Church Jesus established. Great care must always be exercised in giving any credence to alleged private revelations. Hallucinations, fraud, self-deception, and even the work of the devil often may be involved in various visions, happenings, and preternatural events. Much religious error and falsehood have come into the world through enthusiasms deriving from alleged private revelation.

---

[5] *Dei Verbum*, no. 4.

Jesus and His teaching are carried forward in history by His Body and Bride, the Catholic Church. The New Covenant, unlike the Old, is final. There is no successive Testament (1 Tim 6:14 and Titus 2:15).

However, the Catholic Church, which guards and preserves revelation, in both Sacred Tradition and Sacred Scripture, as the centuries succeed one another, grows in her understanding. As the Second Vatican Council teaches: "This happens through the contemplation and study made by believers who treasure these things in their hearts, through a penetrating understanding of the spiritual realities which they experience, and through the preaching of those who have received through episcopal succession the sure gift of truth."[6]

Although the constitutive phase of revelation is at an end, the understanding of revelation goes on. God did not simply reveal Himself, intervene in human history, and then leave it to His creatures to "carry on". God remains with His Church, as the Spirit of Truth, the Paraclete, Who recalls to our minds all that Jesus told us (Jn 14:26).

The transmission of divine revelation would be hopelessly impossible without the special presence of the Holy Spirit. In a classroom of about twenty-five youngsters, it is an entertaining exercise to whisper into the ear of one a single sentence and then ask that one to pass it on by whisper to the next child, and so on throughout the room. Invariably, the sentence comes out, when the last child has heard it, in a very garbled and even totally distorted form. If a single sentence in a few minutes in a room of only twenty-five children who speak the same language becomes so mutilated, we can imagine what could happen to the contents of divine revelation, which already have passed through twenty centuries and hundreds of languages and millions of human beings. Without the guidance of the Holy Spirit "to all the truth" (Jn 16:13), Christ's Church would be a lifeless Body exposed to "every wind of doctrine by the cunning of men, by their craftiness and deceitful wiles" (Eph 4:14).

Human response to God's speaking to us in revelation is called faith. This is a response that involves both belief and obedience. This response called faith is not simply a human action but a gift of God Himself, and God, speaking to us in Christ, is the direct Object of faith. First we believe Christ, and then we believe what He says.

The "obedience of faith" (Rom 16:26) is the response of our whole self to God Who speaks. This faith is not simply blind trust, but, filled with hope and crowned with charity, it is the giving over of our intellect and the totality of what and who we are to God Who comes down to us in Christ Jesus.

---

[6] Ibid., no. 8.

Sometimes the contents of divine revelation go by the name of "faith", as when we speak of the "Catholic faith" or the "deposit of faith". Let us often and lovingly profess our faith and give ourselves over to the gracious and condescending God Who reveals Himself and saves us in Jesus.

JANUARY 8, 1993

Tradition

Slogans can sometimes be illogical. Repeated often enough, they can enter into the mind-set of people who adopt them without reflection. One such slogan, coined by Martin Luther, is *"sola Scriptura"*, or "the Bible alone".

Except for writing upon the ground one time (Jn 8:8), Jesus is not recorded as having written anything. When our Savior founded His Catholic Church (Mt 16:18), He left no instructions to distribute Bibles; rather, He left a command to teach (Mt 28:20). The Bible itself tells us that faith does not come from reading but rather from hearing (Rom 10:17).

It would have made little sense for the apostles simply to distribute Bibles. This is, first of all, because there were no Bibles, the New Testament writings not having been compiled and authenticated by the Catholic Church until the fourth century. Second, the majority of the human race was (and still is) illiterate. Since the "good news" of Jesus is intended for every human person (Mk 16:15), Christ obviously did not intend to exclude those incapable of reading.

Third, until paper came into general usage in the thirteenth century and until Gutenberg, a Catholic, invented printing with moveable type in the fifteenth century, books were extremely rare and very expensive and, thus, accessible only to few people.

The Bible itself, for those who read it carefully and prayerfully, tells us that it does not contain all the truths of divine revelation. Saint John mentions the many "other signs" Jesus worked, which are "not written in this book" (Jn 20:30), and he tells us about "many other things Jesus did", so many "other things", in fact, that "the world itself could not contain the books that would be written" (Jn 21:25) to recount them.

Saint Paul explains that the truths of God's revelation come in two ways, by word of mouth and by the written word (2 Th 2:15). It is evident that the Scriptures to which Saint Paul alludes in his writings are the sacred books of the Old Testament (2 Tim 3:16), because it was only centuries later that all the New Testament books were separated from other spurious and fraudulent books, as well as from other pious but uninspired writings, and gathered into one volume by the Catholic bishops. Indeed, the number and names of the books of the Bible and the fact of their inspired character derive from Sacred Tradition, that is, from the oral, nonwritten part of divine revelation.

The *Catechism of the Catholic Church* instructs us that

> the Gospel was handed on in two ways: *orally* "by the apostles who handed on, by the spoken word of their preaching, by the example they gave, by the institutions they established, what they themselves had received—whether from the lips of Christ, from his way of life and his works, or whether they had learned it at the prompting of the Holy Spirit [*Dei Verbum*, no. 7]"; *in writing* "by those apostles and other men associated with the apostles who, under the inspiration of the same Holy Spirit, committed the message of salvation to writing [*Dei Verbum*, no. 7]" (CCC 76).

The *Catechism* goes on to say: "This living transmission, accomplished in the Holy Spirit, is called Tradition, since it is distinct from Sacred Scripture, though closely connected to it. Through Tradition, 'the Church in her doctrine, life, and worship perpetuates and transmits to every generation all that she herself is and all that she believes' [*Dei Verbum*, no. 8 §1]" (CCC 78).

Key figures in the preservation and transmission of Sacred Tradition are the Fathers and Doctors of the Church and the bishops. This, of course, is because genuine divine Tradition must be distinguished from merely human customs, some of which can be false and dangerous (see Mt 23). The Second Vatican Council teaches: "The sayings of the holy Fathers are a witness to the life-giving presence of this Tradition, showing how its riches are poured out in the practice and life of the Church, in her belief and in her prayer."[7]

Again, the *Catechism*, quoting the Second Vatican Council, tells us: " 'In order that the full and living Gospel might always be preserved in the Church, the apostles left bishops as their successors. They gave them "their own position of teaching authority" [*Dei Verbum*, no. 7].' Indeed, 'the apostolic preaching, which is expressed in a special way in the inspired books, was to be preserved in a continuous line of succession until the end of time' [*Dei Verbum*, no. 8 §1]" (CCC 77).

Neither Sacred Scripture nor Sacred Tradition is self-interpreting. As

[7] *Dei Verbum*, no. 8 § 3.

the Second Vatican Council notes, they are closely joined together. "For both of them, flowing from the same divine wellspring, in a certain way merge into a unity and tend toward the same end." [8] Both, therefore, are subject to erroneous interpretation. Their meaning is hardly clear and intelligible to all. This is why Jesus established a Magisterium, or authentic, living teaching authority, in His Church.

Consequently, the Second Vatican Council says: "It is clear, therefore, that Sacred Tradition, Sacred Scripture, and the teaching authority of the Church, in accord with God's most wise design, are so linked and joined together that one cannot stand without the others, and that all together and each in its own way under the action of the one Holy Spirit contribute effectively to the salvation of souls." [9]

OCTOBER 14, 1994

The Bible

"Ignorance of Scripture is ignorance of Christ", wrote Saint Jerome. The Second Vatican Council teaches: "The Church has always venerated the divine Scriptures just as she venerates the Body of the Lord." [10] And again the Council says: "The Church has always regarded the Scriptures together with Sacred Tradition as the supreme rule of faith and will ever do so." [11]

In the holy Bible God speaks to us in words of men. He condescends to us and clothes His revelation in the signs we call "words", which lead to that which we call "thoughts". The Council states: "As the Bride of the Incarnate Word and the Pupil of the Holy Spirit, the Catholic Church is concerned to move ahead daily toward a deeper understanding of the Sacred Scriptures so that she may unceasingly feed her children the divine words." [12]

The inspired words of God are always precious and valuable beyond human price, but they take on a special, almost quasi-sacramental value when Sacred Scripture is read in the liturgical assembly. Indeed, in the reading of the Gospel (where the very words of Jesus Himself are spoken), there is a "presence" of Christ at Mass. (A different kind of presence, and one inferior to that in the Blessed Sacrament, but a "real presence" nonetheless.) This is why we salute the Gospel announcement

[8] Ibid., no. 9.
[9] Ibid., no. 10 § 3.
[10] *Dei Verbum*, no. 21.
[11] Ibid.
[12] Ibid., no. 23.

by speaking directly to Christ: "Glory to You, O Lord" and "Praise to
You, Lord Jesus Christ", before we make the special sign of the cross,
asking that the holy words be always in our minds, on our lips, and in
our hearts. This is why, when the Gospel is announced, we stand (as we
do when someone important enters a room) and why at a solemn Mass
the Gospel Book is surrounded by candles and incense, and why the
book is so reverently kissed at the conclusion of the reading.

Because God speaks to us, however, in a human way, so that we may
receive His revelation, what He says to us needs to be interpreted correctly. The Bible is not a self-interpreting book, and the Bible itself tells
us this. We can also learn this fact from even a cursory glance at human
and religious history.

The interpretation of Sacred Scripture can be properly done only
against the backdrop of Sacred Tradition, out of which come the holy
books that make up the Bible, and this interpretation can be assuredly
authentic only when it is done by the teaching authority of the Catholic
Church, the Magisterium, which, the Second Vatican Council says, "has
been entrusted exclusively with this right".[13]

Useful for a better understanding of the Bible is some knowledge of
text, context, and *literary form*. The correct text and its meaning are more
difficult to come by than may be imagined at first glance. Take the
word "poke", for instance. If, in some sections of the United States, you
were to tell someone to "Give me a poke", you would be inviting a
punch, but, in other sections, you would be asking for a bag or a sack.
Or take the word "gay", for instance. One hundred years ago, it meant
"happy" or "jolly", but it means something altogether different in our
culture today. Now, if these variances can be present in a single country
and in a single language, how much more difficult it is when dealing
with ancient languages, spread over centuries and many countries. Add
to this the problem of dealing with translations of texts, versions, edi-
tions, and so forth, and you can see some of the difficulties in scriptural
interpretation.

Context, too, can be a problem. If I say "I will meet you at sunrise", I
am not making an astronomical statement. It is irrelevant to my meaning
whether I think that the sun rises or whether I know that the earth
rotates on its axis. The material error inherent in the expression does not
make the statement a formal error. Context can give or change meaning.
Material error inherent in forms of human expression takes nothing
away from the inerrancy of Sacred Scripture, which comes from the fact
that God, perfect Truth, is the prime Author of the Bible.

[13] Ibid., no. 10.

Finally, literary form is important to get to the meanings of words, including the words of Sacred Scripture. For instance, if someone from another era or planet, who nevertheless knew our language, were to come upon a newspaper clipping that said: "Bluejays Devour Tigers", he would be astounded or incredulous, unless he were familiar with our literary form of the sports page. Or if this same visitor were to read some poetry (for example, "My dear, I give you my heart"), he might be excused for thinking our customs very odd unless the literary form of the poem were known to him.

In the same way, the ancient world, in which the texts and contexts of the Bible were given to us, had literary forms with which we are often unfamiliar. Once a knowledge of text, context, and literary form is mastered, the problem of what do we mean by "meaning" arises.

None of this should scare us away from approaching the Sacred Scriptures often, listening to the readings in the liturgy attentively, and privately reading the Bible. We should thank God for the gift of His revelation and for the Magisterium of Christ's Church, by which this revelation is authentically guarded and interpreted. The best way to express this gratitude may be to resolve to read the Sacred Scriptures with more devotion and reverence and to listen to them in the holy liturgy with greater care, always remembering that we are dealing with the words of God in words of men.

SEPTEMBER 25, 1992

Who Wrote the Bible?

If someone with a minimum amount of literacy and training were to pick up a Bible and begin to page through it, he would find that it is composed of a series of "books", or parts, and that often these books or parts claim to have different authors. If one were to read the Bible in the original languages (Greek and Hebrew), it would be even more apparent that the books and parts came from various people. Some of the language is crude and harsh; some is elegant and polished. Some books contain a large and remarkable vocabulary, while others reflect an obviously limited literary capacity. What makes this collection of books special, and why are these authors chosen to be represented and not others?

The answer, of course, is that all of these books had more than human authorship. The Second Vatican Council says: "Holy Mother Church, relying on the belief of the Apostles, holds that the books of both the Old and New Testaments in their entirety, with all their parts, are sacred and canonical, because, written under the inspiration of the

Holy Spirit, they have God as their Author and have been handed on as such to the Church herself."[14]

The Second Vatican Council only repeats what the Church has always taught in her ecumenical councils. The Council of Florence states: "The holy Roman Church proclaims that one and the same God is the Author of both the Old and New Testaments." The Council of Trent says: "This Sacred Synod embraces all the books of the Old as well as the New Testament simply because God is the Author of both." While the First Vatican Council teaches: "If anyone denies that the books of Sacred Scripture, taken in full with all their parts, are divinely inspired, let him be anathema."

What this means is that every part of the Bible had two simultaneous authors, God and a human person. The interaction between these two authors we call "biblical inspiration", a term often misunderstood and misconstrued. Inspiration is not the same as revelation in a technical, theological sense, although the terms are often used interchangeably in ordinary speech. Everything in the Bible is inspired, but not everything is revealed. Some things could be known by the sacred author from experience, from knowledge gained from other people's experience, or from divine revelation given to others.

Some things revealed by God are mysteries and beyond our capacity to find out on our own (for example, the Blessed Trinity, the existence of angels). Some things are within the reach of unaided human reason but are still revealed by God, so they can be known by all, easily, and without fear of error (for instance, the existence of God, the necessity of virtue), while still other things are naturally knowable (for example, that there was a Hebrew king named David; that Peter, Andrew, James, and John came from Galilee). Yet, all of these things, insofar as they are contained in the Bible, are inspired in their being written for us.

The Sacred Scriptures are not written partly by a human author and partly by God but, rather, wholly by God and entirely, at the same time, by the human author. In this interaction between the Holy Spirit and the writer of Scripture, God used the person as His instrument. However, He did not use the author as a dumb or unthinking instrument (much as one uses a typewriter) or simply as a stenographer who takes His dictation.

The inspired writer, who is the instrument of the Holy Spirit, is used with all his abilities and faculties, including intellect and will, memory and experience, and training and education. The sacred writer writes exactly what God wants and just as God wants; yet what is written is

---

[14] *Dei Verbum*, no. 11.

(mysterious as it sounds) also exactly what the writer wants. God's inspiration is not simply approbation after the fact, nor is it "inspiration" in the ideological sense (as Julia Ward Howe was "inspired" to write the "Battle Hymn of the Republic" after seeing the Union Army in the Civil War), nor is it restricted to those parts of the Bible dealing with faith and morals.

When we read the Sacred Scriptures, then, as we should often find time to do, we should understand them as God's very words clothed in the words of men, telling us ultimately and fully about His Word made flesh, Who stands at the center of all revelation and is the reason for the Holy Spirit's work of inspiration.

When we listen to the Sacred Scriptures read in the liturgical assembly, when we are in a special way the convoked and assembled People of God, gathered to express and effect our unity in Christ, we should listen with the utmost attention and reverence. A letter from the pope or president or some other high personage would certainly command our attention and respect. How much more should we revere the very words of God Himself!

If God is the prime Author of the Sacred Scriptures, it follows that they are absolutely truthful, inerrant, and infallible. Saint Thomas Aquinas wrote: "Because the Scriptures come from the Holy Spirit, the holy writings cannot contain error." Saint Augustine tells us what must be our attitude in listening to or reading the Bible: "If you chance upon anything that does not seem to be true, you must not conclude that the sacred writer made a mistake. Rather your attitude should be: the manuscript is faulty; the version is not accurate; the translation is incorrect; or you yourself do not understand the matter."

Of course, various distinctions have to be made in any scientific analysis of the Sacred Scriptures. One must always distinguish material error (which is often inherent in the very nature of human words) and formal error. One must always defer to the triad of text, context, and literary form and ever keep in mind the place of Sacred Tradition and the Magisterium (official teaching office) of the Church in scriptural interpretation.

The Second Vatican Council says:

In Sacred Scripture, while the truth and holiness of God always remain intact, the marvelous condescension of eternal wisdom is clearly shown that we may learn the gentle kindness of God which words cannot express and how far he has gone in adapting his language with thoughtful concern for our weak human nature. For the words of God expressed in human language have been made like human discourse, just as the Word of the eternal Father, when he took to himself the flesh of human weakness, was in every way like men.[15]

As Saint Paul puts it: "All Scripture is inspired of God and is useful for teaching, for reproof, for correction, and for training in holiness" (2 Tim 3:16).

NOVEMBER 6, 1992

The Table of Contents

If we were to go back through the centuries in an imaginary time machine, we could find several interesting things on which many people do not often reflect. For instance, there were no Methodists, Lutherans, Episcopalians, Mormons, or Jehovah's Witnesses aboard the *Niña*, the *Pinta*, and the *Santa Maria*. The obvious reason is because those religions had not yet been founded in 1492. If the same time machine took us back to about A.D. 800, we would probably be surprised that no one was able to understand us, since the English language did not yet exist. If we were to journey back another six hundred years, we would probably be even more astonished to learn that there was as yet no Bible.

As was said earlier, Jesus was never recorded as having written anything (except on the ground, according to John 8:8). In the great commission (Mt 28:20), Christ gave the nascent Church the duty to "teach", not to distribute Bibles. He did this, first, because there were no Bibles. Second, Bibles would have been ineffective, for most of the human race was (and still is) illiterate. The Catholic Church existed for about twenty years before the first book of the New Testament was written (probably First Thessalonians) and about seventy years before the last was written. It was only several centuries later that all the books of the New Testament were gathered together and joined to the sacred writings of the Jewish People, and thus our present Bible was formed. The very word "Bible" (like the word "purgatory" or the word "Trinity", among others) is not found in the Bible.

Because of confusion caused by the circulation of heretical documents purporting to be inspired writings, sometimes attributed to the apostles or saints (gospels according to Philip, Thomas, Joseph, and so on) and because of other *apocrypha*, some uplifting, some fantastic, and some a bit of each, the authorities of the Catholic Church, in that part

---

[15] Ibid., no. 13.

of the world where the problem was most acute (North Africa), decided that a clearly delineated *canon*, or unchangeable table of contents, for the Bible had to be set forth, especially for the New Testament. So, a series of regional bishops' councils were held (in Hippo in 393 and in Carthage in 397 and again in 419) to set out authoritatively the "all and only" books in the Bible. This canon, or table of contents, for the Bible was approved by the pope (Pope Siricius) and by subsequent popes and ecumenical councils.

It is possible hypothetically to prescind from the inspired character of the New Testament books, for apologetic purposes, and use them only as reliable historical documents to verify the founding of the Catholic Church by Jesus (Mt 16:16ff.). Once one establishes this truth and sees this Church as endowed by Christ with the attributes of authority, indefectibility, and infallibility, one can then see how this Church's official teaching authority, or Magisterium, is capable of discerning which books are inspired by God and what is the nature of biblical inspiration. This is why Saint Augustine wrote: "I would put no faith in the Gospels unless the authority of the Catholic Church directed me to do so."

In point of time, our Lord founded His Church before the Holy Spirit inspired the books of the New Testament. The Catholic Church preceded chronologically the formation of the Bible, and it was the authority of our Church alone that determined which books were in the Bible and which were not. The early Christians, our Catholic ancestors, were certainly familiar with the Old Testament (or at least large parts of it), as the artwork in the catacombs attests. There is evidence that almost all the books of the New Testament were familiar to the Christian community by the year 125. Nevertheless, it was only in the second half of the fourth century that the Bible as we know it was gathered together and could be known by all Christians.

Unless one accepts from the testimony of Sacred Tradition the authority of the Catholic Church, it is impossible to establish with certainty the contents of the Bible and its inspired character. Some might say that the Holy Spirit immediately tells people when they read the Bible that it is inspired. But there is no evidence for this. Some might say that because the contents of the Bible are so sublime and lead to virtue it must be inspired. However, other spiritual compositions are also sublime (and claim divine inspiration, such as the Book of Mormon, the Koran, and the Upanishads), and although some parts of the Bible are magnificent and sublime, others are far from being that way. Some might say that reading the Bible is elevating and uplifting and that the Bible itself attributes its parts to prophets and apostles. On the other hand, many people read the Bible and experience no elation, and many biblical books were not authored by prophets or apostles.

The canon of Sacred Scripture can be known with the certitude of faith only through acknowledging the Catholic Church's right to teach. It is that same Church that is authorized by Christ to interpret the Bible correctly and to tell us that its authorship is not only fully and totally human but also fully and totally divine, coming from the Holy Spirit, God Himself.

When we listen to Sacred Scripture read in the liturgical assembly and when we read the Bible privately (as we ought to do often with prayer and devotion), we should thank God for the gift of His words, which can and should enter and transform our lives. We should also thank Him for the gift of the Magisterium of the Church, which has discerned "the wheat from the chaff", as far as inspired writings are concerned. It is this Magisterium that has kept us from what Saint Irenaeus describes as the "unimaginable multitude of perverse writings", which, as Saint Leo observes, "should not only be forbidden but completely suppressed and burned".

As a loving mother who warns her children when some sugary syrup may contain poison, the Church warns us that certain kinds of notes and commentaries and translations of the Bible may not be accurate and could even be erroneous and dangerous to our faith. Thus, before buying or using a Bible, we should always check the front of the book for the word *imprimatur*, followed by the name of a bishop. This is sort of a "truth in labeling" gesture to assist us, especially if we lack expertise in the field. Also, beware of unscrupulous Bible salesmen. A good Bible need not be fancy or expensive. As a matter of fact, we may be more inclined to read an inexpensive book more frequently than a ponderous tome encumbered with leather and pictures and the like.

God gives us His word to read and listen to. If we do not read it and listen to it, are we not being ungrateful for such a gift?

NOVEMBER 20, 1992

What Does Scripture Mean?

The New Testament has within it many powerful questions. A good exercise in Bible reading and meditation would be to go through its sacred pages and note carefully each question and every interrogatory phrase and think about them long and hard.

Two of the haunting questions of the New Testament are found in the eighth chapter of the Acts of the Apostles. Saint Philip, the deacon, asks the Ethiopian eunuch: "Do you understand what you are reading?" The Ethiopian replies with another question: "How can I, unless someone guides me?" In these two questions, as in other places, the Bible itself tells us that it is not a self-interpreting book. This, of course, contradicts with the very words of the Bible those who use "the Bible alone" (*sola Scriptura*) as a slogan they want to pass off as a thought.

How, then, can a person arrive at the *meaning* of the words of Sacred Scripture, words that are simultaneously those of God Himself and of a human author? To grasp the meaning or sense of the Bible, one must have a reasonable grasp of text, context, and (perhaps most of all) literary form. Since God in Sacred Scripture speaks to us in a "human way", we must ask ourselves what are the human forms of speech He sometimes uses? For instance, is this section or book of the Bible technical history, historical novel, fable, gospel, drama, correspondence, hymn, doxology, or catechesis?

The first and in many ways the primary meaning, or sense, of Sacred Scripture must be the *literal* meaning. What, under God's inspiration, is the "here and now" meaning of what the human author has written? Is this literal meaning *figurative* or *nonfigurative*? For example, when Jesus says about King Herod, "Go and tell that fox" (Lk 13:32), He is not implying that Herod was a quadruped. Certain numbers used throughout the Bible (seven, twelve, 144,000, and so on) have a figurative, nonmathematical meaning. On the other hand, when our Lord speaks of yeast, wheat, woman, fig tree, and so on, even in parables and extended similes, He is speaking nonfiguratively, as when He said: "This is my body" (Mt 26:26) or "The bread which I shall give for the life of the world is my flesh" (Jn 6:51).

A figurative use of words in human discourse can include such things as metaphor, hyperbole, synecdoche, irony, and sarcasm. God speaks to us in Sacred Scripture in plain language and in similes, but He also, since He speaks in "our" language, uses figurative speech in giving us His revelation.

In addition to the literal sense or meaning in the Bible, there is a *typical* sense or meaning. Saint Jerome says of the Bible: "The Old the New conceals, while the New the Old reveals." In this sense, one sees a *type*, or model, that later revelation makes clear, as, for instance, Melchizedek as a type of Christ (high priest, offers bread and wine, ancestry unknown) or the manna as a type of the Holy Eucharist (bread from heaven that is mysterious, that supports the Chosen People on their journey across the desert) or the crossing of the Red Sea as a type of Baptism (destruction of evil, salvation of the Chosen People through water).

Many commentators also insist upon a *fuller sense* (*sensus plenior*) in Sacred Scripture, a meaning that was unknown to the human author but known to God, who inspired the writing. For example, when Isaiah wrote of the "virgin" (*ha alma*, in Hebrew) who would conceive "Emmanuel", God intended a fuller sense for His words than Isaiah himself dreamed (see Mt 1:23).

Many of the Fathers of the Church, especially those from the famous School of Alexandria, which opposed the School of Antioch, also see an *allegorical* sense or meaning in Sacred Scripture. In speaking of Abraham's sons, Saint Paul is quite explicit that "this is an allegory" (Gal 4:24). The Fathers see an allegory for Christ in the sacrifice of Abraham, a father having his son carry a load of wood up a mountain on which he, the son, is to be sacrificed. Again, the Apostle of the Gentiles sees allegories in the rock, the cloud, and the water of Exodus (1 Cor 10:1–5).

Sacred Scripture also admits of an *accommodated sense*, when an entirely new meaning is given to the inspired words for liturgical or devotional purposes. When the Church uses the personification of wisdom in Ben Sirach to apply to the Blessed Virgin Mary, for instance, this is clearly an accommodated sense.

Besides using our human reason, however, to discover the meaning or sense of Sacred Scripture, we also must use the other instruments that God Himself gives us to accomplish this task. This includes divine revelation itself, which tells us of the unity of the Bible, with Jesus Christ as the central and unifying Force, of scriptural inerrancy, and of the impossibility of any contradiction between what is "in the Bible" and the truths taught by the Catholic Church. Since truth is one and God is its Author, there can be no contradiction between what is true in science, philosophy, history, and other human knowledge and in what God has revealed.

There also has to be a strong sense of Sacred Tradition in finding biblical meaning. It is from Sacred Tradition that the Bible comes and with Tradition that its meaning can be learned. The Second Vatican Council teaches: "Both Sacred Tradition and Sacred Scripture are to be accepted and venerated with the same sense of reverence and devotion."[16]

The principal means by which we can arrive at the true meaning of Sacred Scripture is, of course, to rely on the teaching authority, or Magisterium, of the Catholic Church, whether extraordinary (solemn definitions of faith or morals) or ordinary (teaching of the bishops in union with the Holy Father or of the Holy See alone). Using the principle called the "analogy of faith", the ordinary Magisterium of the

---

[16] Ibid., no. 9.

Church, in homilies, catechetics, liturgy, prayer, Church law, Church-approved organizations, and so on, gives us the meaning of Sacred Scripture, indeed, gives us the fullness of God's revelation, unmitigated and undistorted, down through the centuries, until He comes again to judge the living and the dead.

The Second Vatican Council teaches: "The task of authentically interpreting the word of God, whether written or handed on, has been entrusted exclusively to the living teaching office of the Church, whose authority is exercised in the name of Jesus Christ." [17]

The Council also says: "It is clear that Sacred Tradition and Sacred Scripture and the teaching authority of the Church, in accord with God's most wise design, are so linked and joined together that one cannot stand without the others and that all together and each in its own way, under the action of the one Holy Spirit, contribute effectively to the salvation of souls." [18]

OCTOBER 23, 1992

Private and Public Revelation:
The Other Revelations

Public revelation ended with the death of the last apostle, the last echo of the Christ-event, the definitive and final Word of God in human history. The faith has been delivered once and for all to the saints (Jude 1:3). After speaking in many and various ways in the past, God has, in these days, spoken through His Son (Heb 1:1–2), and we await no further new public revelation until the end of the world (1 Tim 6:14; Titus 2:13).

Where, then, do all sorts of other "revelations" fit into all this? Each year dozens of people claim to have visions and other supernatural events happen to them. In the history of the Church, there have always been saints and holy persons who have claimed to receive revelations. Even in our day there are claims of apparitions, as well as statues, icons, and pictures that bleed, weep, and sweat, rosaries that turn to gold, spinning suns, and so on.

These fall into the category called "private revelation". What should we know concerning private revelation? First of all, it is possible. The facts of history and the approval of the Church in many instances

---

[17] Ibid., no. 10.
[18] Ibid.

demonstrate this. Second, authentic private revelation offers nothing to the deposit of faith. True private revelation cannot in any way contradict what is in public revelation, nor can genuine private revelation propose anything new to be believed as divine and Catholic faith.

In any approach to private revelation, caution, such as that exercised by the authorities of the Catholic Church, is required. Many claims about private revelation are spurious, deriving from hallucinations, error, illusion, self-deception, or fraud. Before moving toward approval of some private revelation claims (such as at Fatima or at Lourdes or the visions of Saint Gertrude or Saint Margaret Mary or Saint Bridget), the authorities of the Church strive to be sure that there are no natural or psychological explanations for such events. Then, too, the possibility of demonic or diabolical activity must be examined and discounted.

Catholics are not required to give assent to what is contained in private revelations, even when they enjoy Church approval. We are required by God only to assent, without doubt or demur, to what He has said in public revelation. (Although most theologians would say that the one to whom private revelation is given must give his adherence and assent, unless he has less than moral certitude about the authenticity of the revelation.)

Of course, many Church-approved private revelations are simply new assertions of gospel truth. Thus it would be extremely imprudent to ignore the call to penance, for instance, that comes from Lourdes or the call to prayer that comes from Fatima, since we are called to prayer and penance in public revelation.

ORTHODOXY

Questionable claims about private revelation have been a source of great harm to the cause of Christ throughout ecclesiastical history. An overeagerness for the extraordinary and a craving for the marvelous and sensational have driven many people to the camp of hysteria and fanaticism and led to the loss of salvation for some.

Thus, authorities in the Catholic Church always are obliged to measure claims of private revelation against the criteria of Catholic orthodoxy. God cannot contradict Himself. If, for instance, someone claims for the Blessed Virgin Mary that Jesus instructed people to "adore her", such a claim is obviously contrary to the first commandment of the Decalogue, which demands that we give adoration (*latria*) to God alone. On the face of it, such a "revelation" must be considered false. Vulgarity, slang, error of fact, and similar components also rule out objective veracity for some alleged "private revelations".

TYPES OF PRIVATE REVELATION

In giving private revelation, God uses a variety of methods. Sometimes this kind of revelation can be a mere *internal locution*. At other times there can be the use of God's servants, the Virgin Mary, an angel, a saint, or a soul in purgatory. Revelations and visions can be an image in the eye of the beholder or on the brain or an actual "other something-out-there".

If God, Who knows the future, chooses to foretell future events for the benefit of some chosen souls, this contradicts neither sound theology nor sound doctrine. The difficulty, however, comes when discernment of real from false private revelation is not practiced. It is a sin (and can even be a mortal sin) to engage in fortune-telling or to guide one's life or one's actions by the "knowledge" of a fortune-teller. In the early years of the Church, religious beliefs based on secret knowledge known only to a select few were the basis of a large number of heretical sects that go by the collective name Gnostics (1 Jn 4:1).

Before giving adherence or money to any cause or shrine or activity connected with private revelation, it is always best to check with the authorities of the Church, especially with the local bishop. The Catholic Church, after all, is "the pillar and bulwark of the truth" (1 Tim 3:15).

Some alleged private revelations are openly disapproved of by the Catholic Church (for example, Bayside and Necedah). Some are still in the process of discernment, while other private revelations (for example, Knock and Guadalupe) enjoy Church approval.

Finally, to paraphrase Thomas à Kempis: When we go on pilgrimages to visit shrines or relics of saints, we must never forget that the God of all saints and the shrine of all shrines is ever on our altar in the Holy Eucharist.

JULY 30, 1993

3

LAST THINGS

Logical as Hell

In our time the word "damn" is used so often as an expletive, and car-
toonists make so many drawings showing the devil as a comic character,
that it is easy to forget the real possibility of eternal damnation. We live
in a civilization that values ease and comfort. We are generally people of
softness in sentimentality and life-style. Along with everything uncomfortable, the thought of the inferno is frequently put out of the mind of
modern man, who believes he has so many "more important" things to
think about.

The warning of Bishop Eusebius of Caesarea, which comes to us
from the fourth century, is appropriate even for our time: "Woe to him
who now treats hell as a matter for joking and first comes to believe in it
when he finds himself there." Jesus is our Savior, which means He came
to save us from *something*, namely, the consequences of our sins. He was
not joshing when He informed us that at the last judgment He will say
to those on His left: "Depart from me, you cursed, into the eternal fire
prepared for the devil and his angels. . . . And they will go away into
eternal punishment, but the righteous into eternal life" (Mt 25:41–46).
The Epistle to the Hebrews says: "It is a fearful thing to fall into the
hands of the living God" (Heb 10:31).

WHAT IS HELL?

Hell is the place or state where those who die without the possession of
sanctifying grace, God's friendship, are confined for all eternity. It is a
place and state of misery and torments whose pains are likened to that
of earthly fire. It is the opposite of heaven, which is light, happiness,
liberty, peace, rest, and joy that never ends, beyond all our imagining.
Hell is servitude and ugly darkness, with only hatred and ridicule among
all its inhabitants.

Human beings are made to possess God in love and vision. This is the
ultimate goal of human existence. The principal pain of hell comes from
being frustrated forever in the realization of that goal, seeing others in

happiness that is forever denied to the damned (see Lk 16:19–31). There is also the *pain of sense*, which is the vindictive punishment of unspeakable agony, proportionate to the evil in which one dies (see Mk 9:42–48).

Among the treasures God gave us in divine revelation is a warning about hell, its existence and its horror. Jesus said: "Fear him who . . . has power to cast into hell . . . fear him!" (Lk 12:4–5). God is everywhere. However, His presence in hell is due only to His justice and power.

God is all-merciful. Jesus Christ is the very mercy of God made visible. How can the eternal torture of hell be compatible with that divine attribute? We must meditate on a crucifix to get a better understanding of the divine mystery implied here. For God not only does not will us to go to hell (that is the reason for the Incarnation and why He warned us about the danger of misusing our gift from Him of freedom), but He also sent His only begotten Son to die on the Cross that we might be saved from hell (Jn 3:16–21).

The damned souls in hell are those who, while on earth, rejected God's proffered love and mercy. Mortal sin is preferring some created good to the Creator of all good things. Dying in such a state of "preference" means that God allows such a person to have his preference forever. God's *active* will is that all should be saved (1 Tim 2:4). Yet God's *permissive* will abstains from interfering when a human being freely rejects His pardon and love (Mt 2:41).

Frank Bigeart wrote: "So long as man is a free agent he must be free to reject the sovereignty of God and God will not compel him to accept it. Man can fight against his own perfection and choose to remain outside of the love of God. The power of choice can be lost forever, and this underlies the doctrine of hell. The will can be fixed in antagonism to God." In Christopher Marlowe's *Doctor Faustus*, Faust, who sold his soul to Satan, says: "Ah, Faustus, / Now hast thou but one bare hour to live / And then thou must be damned perpetually!" (5.2.131–33). In the same play, Mephistopheles says: "When all the world dissolves / And every creature shall be purified, / All places shall be hell that is not heaven" (2.1.124–26).

It is difficult for us creatures to realize that God owes us nothing and we owe Him everything. His boundless generosity gives us, undeserving as we are, a share in His life and eternal joy. If we throw this gift away, we have no guarantee that it will ever be offered again. To commit serious sin and, even worse, to persist in a state of serious sin is the ultimate act of ingratitude and foolishness on our part. We literally, in that case, play with eternal fire. It is not a wise game.

A limerick says: "There was young lady from Niger, who smilingly rode on a tiger. They came back from the ride with the lady inside, and the smile on the face of the tiger." Whittier wrote: "O Love ineffable, to turn aside from Thee is hell, to walk with Thee is heaven!"

NOVEMBER 5, 1993

The Intermediate State

"There is a purgatory and the souls detained there are helped by the prayers of the faithful, and especially by the acceptable sacrifice of the altar." The Council of Trent sums up in this one brief sentence the reality that God revealed to us, namely, that besides a place or state of eternal hatred and torment for those who die without sanctifying grace and a place or state of everlasting rest and joy for those who die justified and possessed of the righteousness of Jesus, there is an intermediate state or place, which we commonly name "purgatory". This is a place or state of temporary punishment for those who die guilty of unforgiven venial sins or who have not satisfied the justice of God for the sins they have had forgiven.

The Catholic Church, which speaks to us with the voice of Christ, her divine Founder, also tells us that the souls consigned to purgatory cannot help themselves but may be aided by the suffrages of the faithful on earth. As Cardinal Gibbons wrote: "The souls in purgatory are still exiles from heaven and fit subjects for divine clemency. They have not reached the term of their journey."

The souls in purgatory are sometimes called "poor souls", but they are also elect souls, for they are already saved, and their purgation and suffering are only temporary. Unlike us, who are still "on the way", the souls in purgatory are assured of salvation.

A CONSOLING DOCTRINE

Already in the Old Testament, God revealed the value of praying for the dead. In the Second Book of Maccabees (2 Macc 12:43–46) we read that it is a holy and pious thought to pray for the dead that they may be loosed from their sins. Also in the Bible, our Lord spoke about sins that could and could not be forgiven "in the age to come" (Mt 12:32), and Saint Paul talked about the fire that will try every man's work (1 Cor 3:13–15). Saint Paul himself prayed for a dead person (2 Tim 1:18).

Each time we recite the Creed, we profess that we believe in the communion of saints. This marvelous doctrine enables us to see ourselves as part of the larger family of God. The souls in purgatory and the blessed saints in heaven still are part of our community and we of theirs. Recently, a convert to our Catholic faith was reproved by some members of the Protestant religion from which she had converted for having pictures and statues of saints in her home. She calmly asked her former coreligionists if they had any family pictures in their homes. "Well," she said, after they answered affirmatively, "these are my family pictures." By prayer we can reach through the doorway called death and assist each other.

ANCIENT WITNESS

The testimony of Christian antiquity can be summoned to attest to the existence of purgatory and the value of praying for the dead. Earliest inscriptions on the tombs of the first Christians in the catacombs testify to requests and promises for prayer for the deceased.

In the second century Tertullian wrote that a faithful wife should pray for the soul of her deceased husband, especially on the anniversary of his falling asleep, and, if she failed to do so, she as much as repudiated her husband. Saint Cyril of Jerusalem said, "We pray for the priests and bishops who have fallen asleep, believing that the supplications which we present will be of great assistance to their souls while the holy and tremendous sacrifice is being offered up." Saint John Chrysostom wrote: "It was ordained by the Apostles that mention should be made of the dead in the sacred mysteries because they knew they would receive great benefit from this."

Saint Monica told her priest-son, Saint Augustine, shortly before she died: "Lay this body anywhere; let not the care of it disturb you in any way. This only I request of you, that you remember me at the altar of the Lord, wherever you may be."

ALL SOULS DAY

Christ has told us that nothing defiled can enter heaven and that we must one day give an account not only for our sins but for every "idle word". We should never minimize our sinfulness or the exacting severity of our final judgment.

The Church has defined neither the duration of purgatory nor the nature of the temporal punishment. However, great saints and mystics have speculated about these matters through the centuries, and there have been innumerable private revelations (which may or may not be true) about these issues. Saint Thomas Aquinas, for instance, thought the pain of purgatory was the intensity of the embarrassment one feels when standing sinful before the transcendence of God and the wounds of Christ. He also thought purgatory for some people could last until the end of time. Most theories hold the pain of purgatory analogous to the fires of hell, but without the hopelessness and eternity.

The annual commemoration of all the faithful departed, which we celebrate immediately after remembering all the saints in heaven at the beginning of each November, provides us with an opportunity to pray for our beloved dead and to remember that we are certainly bound to follow those "who have gone before us with the sign of faith". Our prayers for them, as Cardinal Gibbons says: "rob death of its sting, assuage the bitterness of our sorrow, reconcile us to their loss, keep us in touch with our absent ones who are living in another and better world, and preserve their memories fresh and green in our hearts". They call to us in the words of Tennyson: "Pray for my soul." Eternal rest grant unto them, O Lord. And let perpetual light shine upon them. May they rest in peace.

OCTOBER 29, 1993

Paradise

Every trip has a destination or a purpose. Rational persons always journey for some reason or to some place. The goal, the purpose, the end of human existence is union with God forever in happiness and bliss unending. The journey called life goes toward the Being from Whom all beings derive their essence and existence. God made and redeemed us so we can share His joy eternally (Jn 16:24).

Just as it is beyond the capacity of a pet goldfish to understand or appreciate the happiness we get from playing chess or traveling on a vacation trip or painting a picture or getting a raise, because a goldfish has a nature far beneath our own, so it is beyond our capacity to realize the happiness that God has planned for us, which is far beyond our natural ability to possess. God can and does raise us up to share His own nature. That is what sanctifying grace is (2 Pet 1:4).

When we speak of our union with God in heaven and the joy that will be ours to know as He knows and love as He loves, our earthly analogies fail. Our weak words and finite human experiences make it impossible for us to imagine what "no eye has seen, nor ear heard" (1 Cor 2:9).

Jesus told us to "rejoice and be glad, for your reward is great in heaven" (Mt 5:12). He told us also that heaven is not to be found in this world: "And when I go and prepare a place for you, I will come again and will take you to myself, so that where I am you may be also" (Jn 14:3). He will tell those on His right on judgment day: "Come, O blessed of my Father, inherit the kingdom prepared for you from the foundation of the world" (Mt 25:34). And He revealed to us that conditions in heaven are far different from those we are familiar with on earth. "They neither marry nor are given in marriage, but are like angels in heaven" (Mk 12:25).

Besides speaking of heaven as a "kingdom", our divine Lord also spoke of it as a banquet, a wedding feast, everlasting life, and a state of blessedness that consists of "seeing" God.

THE VISION

The primary happiness of heaven will consist in "seeing" God. The beatific vision, of course, has nothing to do with physical sight. Rather, it means a spiritual possession of God forever, God Who is perfect Love and Beauty. In heaven faith passes into sight, and, since we will see as we have been seen and "know even as we have been known" (1 Cor 13:12–13), faith will no longer exist. Hope, too, will pass away when the object of all possible hope is possessed. This is why the "greatest of these", love alone, will remain (1 Cor 13:13).

In the eternal vision of God all sadness and boredom, all evil and wickedness, all that is short of perfection will disappear and never return. Although freedom is part of heaven, the wills of the saints will never falter from being fixed on God's will, in which the blessed will find rest, peace, and the security of joy that cannot be flawed by monotony or any limit of time. Jesus told us that nobody will take our heavenly joy away from us (Jn 16:22).

OTHER JOYS

In addition to the happiness of "seeing" God, in which all other joy is reflected, we know that heaven also provides secondary or *accidental* joys. There is the joy of reunion with our loved ones who have gone before us with the "sign of faith". There is the security of knowledge beyond all our dreams and the sureness that our possession of happiness can never lessen but only increase. There will be the happiness of seeing our forgiven sins no longer as things of which we are ashamed but rather as manifestations of the gracious pardon and gratuitous mercy of God.

There will be the joy of "seeing" the human face and body of our Savior and visiting our Blessed Lady and the saints to whom we have talked in prayer in the course of our lifetime.

All earthly and material happiness that can be imagined or experienced will be possessed in superabundance by the blessed in heaven. Earthly pleasures sometimes cloy by being excessive or are marred by the knowledge that they cannot last, whereas the pleasures of heaven will not only exceed those we know in our world but will lack those defects and imperfections.

The inequality of beatitude in heaven will not be a source of the slightest twinge of envy. Rather, knowledge of the greater joy of some saints adds to the joy of all. As glasses varying in size and filled to the brim with liquid are all "perfectly filled" and yet some obviously have more liquid than others, so the souls of those who die possessed of "more sanctifying grace" than others will have more capacity for happiness. (It is not always wise to speak of grace in quantitative terms, but sometimes it is necessary, given the limitations of human expression.)

Saint Paul tells us that the blessed and saved differ from one another as "star differs from star in beauty" (1 Cor 15:41) and that those who sow in abundance will reap in abundance (2 Cor 9:6). He reminds us, as does Saint John, that each person will receive the reward of his labors (1 Cor 3:8; 2 Jn 8).

Let us walk on earth, as Christ's followers, with our thoughts in heaven. "Seek the things that are above, where Christ is, seated at the right hand of God. Set your minds on things that are above, not on things that are on earth" (Col 3:1–2).

NOVEMBER 12, 1993

Part Two

THE CHURCH

1

THE NATURE OF THE CHURCH
AND HER MISSION

Motherhood of the Church

Genealogical research is becoming a fascinating hobby for many people in our country. It is extremely interesting to find out something about our ancestry and where our family came from and who were the people from whom we descended.

THE FATHERS OF THE CHURCH

As God's family on earth, the Catholic Church, too, has a fascinating genealogy, which embodies much of her tradition and her early life. This is centered in a group of people called the Fathers of the Church, writers in the first centuries of Christianity who were distinguished by orthodoxy of doctrine and holiness of life. Reading the works of both the Latin and Greek Fathers of the Church is theologically important as well as spiritually uplifting.

Among the many themes and thoughts one can find in these patristic writings is the beautiful one of the motherhood of the Church. With tenderness and love these early spiritual ancestors of ours frequently spoke of the Catholic Church as "mother".

Tertullian wrote to the Christians in prison for their faith that "our Mother Church, from her maternal breasts, will provide enough spiritual milk to meet your needs." Saint Cyprian declared, "Our Mother, the Church, alone can give her children true wealth. The Spouse of Christ brings forth children spiritually for God. He alone can have God for a Father who first has the Church as his mother." Again he said, "Let no one draw Christians away from the Gospel of Christ. Let no one rob the Church of her children. Let them return to their mother, I mean to the Catholic Church."

Saint Augustine wrote, "The Church is a mother for us. It is from her that we were born spiritually. No one can find a paternal welcome from God if he scorns his mother, the Church." Saint Cyril of Jerusalem said,

"The Catholic Church is the proper name of the holy mother of us all, the spouse of our Lord Jesus Christ. She bears the seal and likeness of the Jerusalem above, which is free and which is our mother. She began by being barren, but now she has numerous children." Saint Augustine exhorted the heretics, "Come back to the mother Church, to the Catholic mother."

Tertullian wrote, "Adam prefigured Christ, and Adam's sleep represented the death of Christ, Who had to die the sleep of death so that the Church, the new Eve, the true mother of all the living, might come forth from the wound in His side."

Before he became a Catholic, Cardinal John Henry Newman studied the writings of the Fathers of the Church intensely. He said at that time, "In the triumphant zeal of this Church of the Fathers I recognized my spiritual mother. The self-conquest of her ascetics, the patience of her martyrs, the irresistible determination of her bishops, the joyous swing of her advance, both exalted and abashed me."

It is the Catholic Church that is our mother also. While the term "Holy Mother Church" may have assumed in the mouths of countless preachers something of the role of a trite expression, it still deserves our meditation and deepest respect. This is particularly true when we consider the obedience that we are bound to give to the Church. Mothers, as a general rule, command obedience in those things that are for the welfare of their children. Good mothers are never capricious, tyrannical, or cruel in what they demand of their offspring. And devoted children love and cherish their mothers and treat them with respect and deference.

The obedience that the Church asks of her children is simply to keep them better joined to her divine Spouse, Christ Jesus. What mother does not caution her children to avoid unnecessary exposure to dangerous and poisonous substances and situations? As our spiritual mother, the Church, too, with her laws and prohibitions, with her encouragement and exhortations, assists us to grow in God's grace and arrive at beatitude, that union with God which is our destiny.

WHY OBEY

Cardinal Henri de Lubac said:

> When a Catholic wants to expound the claims which the Church has on his obedience, he feels a certain embarrassment, or rather a certain melancholy. It is not that her title deeds are inadequate, but when taken in the dryness of the mere letter the

claims do not do justice to something which is . . . essential. He can comment on the illuminating complex of Scripture texts, point to the facts of history, develop arguments that are suitable to the occasion. But, when he has done all this, all he has done is to establish the fact that we ought to submit [and obey] as a matter of justice and our own good. . . . He has established an obligation, but he has not communicated an enthusiasm. He has not been able to convey the spontaneous leap of his own heart to obedience nor the joy he feels in submission.[1]

It is only when we see the Church as our true and loving mother that our obedience makes sense and changes from something extrinsic and difficult into a happy listening to the very voice of our Savior, Who said to His Catholic Church: "Who hears you, hears Me."

Preaching on the motherhood of the Church, Saint Bernard said, "O humility! O sublimity! Both tabernacle of cedar and sanctuary of God; earthly dwelling and celestial palace; house of clay and royal hall; body of death and temple of light; object of scorn to the proud and bride of Christ to the saved. Even if the labor and pain of her long exile may have discolored her, yet heaven's beauty adorns her." She is our mother, both human and divine, both visible and invisible, born in time and destined for eternity, a structured and hierarchical society that is the Mystical Body of Christ, the mystery of Jesus in time and space, the mystery of the union of God with us.

JANUARY 13, 1995

Our Name

The Bible tells us: "It was at Antioch that the disciples were called Christians for the first time" (Acts 11:26). Coincidentally, it was also from Antioch that the name of the "great" or "universal" Church, which Christ founded, came. Its first use in writing came from the pen of Saint Ignatius of Antioch, who suffered martyrdom in A.D. 110 and who wrote just before that to the Christians in Smyrna, saying: "Wherever the bishop is, there let the people be, for there is the Catholic Church."

The writing of Saint Ignatius seems to indicate that the term "Catholic" was already widely used from the earliest times. It was a common

---

[1] Henri de Lubac, *The Splendor of the Church* (San Francisco: Ignatius Press, 1986), 266.

term used universally by the Fathers of the Church from Saint Justin, Saint Clement, and Saint Irenaeus to Saint Jerome and Saint Pacian. As Cardinal John Henry Newman observed:

> It was the Church's everyday name, which was understood in the marketplace and used in the palace, which every chance comer knew and which the state edicts recognized. It was the one name which the various sects could neither claim for themselves nor hinder being enjoyed by its rightful owner, though, since it was the characteristic designation of the Church in the Creed, it seems to surrender the whole controversy between the two parties engaged in it. Balaam could not keep from blessing the ancient people of God, and the whole world, heresies inclusive, were irresistibly constrained to call God's second election by its prophetical title "Catholic" Church.

Saint Cyril gave a rule to his crowd of catechumens: "If ever you are sojourning in any city, inquire not simply where the Lord's house is (for the sects of the profane also make an attempt to call their dens houses of the Lord) nor merely where the church is, but ask where is the Catholic Church, for this is the peculiar name of the Holy Body, the Mother of us all, who is the Spouse of our Lord Jesus Christ." Saint Augustine said that if you were to ask any stranger where to find the "Catholic Church", he would not point to his own basilica or home but rather to the place where the true Church of Christ gathers. Saint Pacian, the Bishop of Barcelona, wrote in about 384: "My name is Christian, but my surname is Catholic."

> From the beginning [says Saint Epiphanius] we never heard of Petrines or Paulines or Bartholomeans, or Thaddeans, but from the first there was one preaching of all the Apostles, not preaching themselves but Christ Jesus the Lord. Wherefore also all gave one name to the Church, not their own but that of their Lord Jesus Christ. Since they first began to be called Christians at Antioch, this is the sole Catholic Church, having nought else for name, but Christ's being a Church of Christians, not of Christs, but Christians, He being One, they from that One being called Christians. None but this Church and her preachers are of this character.

Again, Saint Jerome, writing to Pope Damasus, said,

> Though your greatness terrifies me, your kindness invites me. From the priest I ask the salvation of the victim, from the shep-

herd, the protection of the sheep. I speak with the successor of the Fisherman and the disciple of the cross. I, who follow none as my chief but Christ, am associated in communion with your blessedness, that is, with the See of Peter. On that rock the Church is built I know.

To bear the name of Christ upon ourselves as "Christians", and to bear the ancient and beautiful name of "Catholic" upon ourselves as well, involves us in a great responsibility and lifelong undertaking. We must ever strive to be worthy of these exalted titles, for they are not simply external attachments but bespeak an underlying reality. We have not only been given the name of Christ when we were "christened", but, in the great sign or mystery called the sacrament of Baptism, we were plunged into His saving death and Resurrection. In Confirmation we were touched in a special way by the very Spirit of God through an oil that has a name like Christ's, sacred chrism. And we take our spiritual breath and existence from the greatest of all these sacraments, the very paschal mystery of our Savior and His substantial and most Real Presence as our supernatural Food and Drink and our abiding Guest.

How carefully we should recall the somber words of the Second Vatican Council: "All children of the Church should nevertheless remember that their exalted conditions results, not from their own merits, but from the grace of Christ. If they fail to respond in thought, word and deed to that grace, not only shall they not be saved, but they shall be the more severely judged." [2]

Let us pray that our most noble name will correspond to who we really are. Let us purge ourselves of any unworthiness that may still cling to a people who are indelibly sealed with the image of Jesus and whose mouths are purpled with His Blood.

SEPTEMBER 18, 1992

Unity

Jesus, our Divine Lord, spoke of "one flock and one shepherd" (Jn 10:16). In his First Epistle to the Corinthians, Saint Paul wrote that "we who are many are one body, because there is one bread, for we all partake of the one bread" (1 Cor 10:17).

Unity as applied to the Catholic Church has two aspects. First of all, it is a quality or mark that the Church possesses. It is one of the

[2] *Lumen gentium*, no. 14.

distinguishing characteristics of the institution that Christ founded. Saint Paul writes of "one body and one Spirit", and he also writes about "one Lord, one faith, one baptism" (Eph 4:6). This mark of the Church is what we profess to believe in each Sunday when we recite the Nicene Creed at Mass. This oneness is clear, by divine intention, in three basic areas: creed, cult, and code; that is to say, we are one in belief, one in worship, and one in ecclesiastical government. This oneness is God's will and God's gift.

On the other hand, there is the second aspect of unity, a reality that the Church does not yet possess, but still desires, yearns for, strives for, prays for, and works for. This is the "Christian Unity" for which we are asked to pray in a special way during the Week of Prayer for Christian Unity every January, from the eighteenth to the twenty-fifth of the month. This labor is also God's will and His gift.

Under its first aspect, unity is a gift from the Founder of the Catholic Church to His Bride and Body, of which He continues to be the Spouse and the invisible Head. It is closely related to the supreme Gift of Christ to His Church, Who is God the Holy Spirit. The Holy Spirit is the Love that unites the Father and the Son in the intimate and transcendent life of the Holy Trinity. He is bestowed by Jesus and the Father on the Church as her Soul and her Element of cohesion, origin, and expansion. The Holy Spirit gives the Church the animation that enables her to transcend the limits of space, time, and human particularisms. This gift of unity permits the Church to triumph over internal and external divisions, over the limits of history, over material wear and tear, over the prospect of growing old, and over the curse of death. The unity of the Church, which derives from the continuing presence of the Spirit of God within her, despite the sinfulness of many of her members, partakes of the indefectibility, infallibility, and authority of that Spirit's presence.

This unity of the Catholic Church is not merely an internal quality but also an external sign, by which an honest and sincere inquirer can discern the one true religion. It is not a superficial or indiscriminate unity, but a unity in complexity, which has been in the possession of the Catholic Church for twenty centuries, incorporating a multitude of human beings and producing a profound integration of personalities, reaching deep within humans to establish a solidarity among the members of the Church, however disparate and isolated, that transcends even the biological community, the blood bonds of family, clan, and nation.

The unity of the Catholic Church penetrates all human structures, never absorbing them or being absorbed by them. It imposes on the earth a new geography, reuniting all peoples scattered at Babel (Gen 11:1–9), regardless of race or color, language or culture, age or education, forming one body of Christ where there "does not exist among you Jew or Greek, slave or freeman, male or female" (Gal 3:28).

This unity, for which Christ prayed before His death (Jn 17:20–23) and which He gives to His Church and will continue to give until His Second Coming, is a unity in diversity, a universality in indivisibility, a unity that is not static but dynamic, for the Lord spoke of the "mustard seed" and of "yeast" (Mt 13).

The second aspect of unity is paradoxical. The Catholic Church already possesses unity in a way and a manner that is full and complete and that cannot be added to, yet she still lacks unity both internally and externally. Although she is and always remains one, there is something not essentially but integrally lacking in her oneness so long as there is on earth any child of Eve who is merely a potential rather than an actual member of this body of the new Adam. The fullness of the Mystical Body of Christ is not achieved until all human beings are reunited in Him, and this in accord with human nature, that is, visibly and invisibly, internally and externally.

While never essentially lacking any good thing, the Catholic Church is the poorer and is missing something unless and until all men and their gifts are joined to her. This is especially important in regard to other Christians, separated from her oneness because of past sins of schism, heresy, and apostasy, so often involving pride, anger, and hatred as well. While one sin does not justify another, and recognizing that human weakness often tries to find, in the sins of others, excuses and rationalizations for wicked conduct, we must remember, nevertheless, that some of the separation was occasioned by the sins of our Catholic forbears and perhaps by our own sins. It is also important to remember that the Second Vatican Council teaches "One cannot impute the sin of separation to those who at present are born into these communities and are instilled in them with Christ's faith. The Catholic Church accepts them with respect and affection."[3] Until all groups and churches, especially those called Christian, are united with her, there is something missing from the unity of the Church.

Even internally, while always one without uniformity, the Church sometimes suffers from wounds to her unity, lacking the perfect manifestation of that unity which the continuing presence of the Holy Spirit guarantees to her. Each day at Mass, throughout the world, we pray that God will give to Christ's Church "peace and unity". Our petition, of course, is part of the Eucharist, or gratitude, we owe to God for what He gave and gives us. It is an implicit request that He continue to bestow

---

[3] Decree on Ecumenism, *Unitatis redintegratio*, no. 3.

and actually to be the unity of the Church. However, it also implies that in the one Church there can be and de facto is the human tendency, a sad result of the effects of Adam's sin and ours, to offend unity, a tendency to disunity that not only involves the evil of schism and heresy but also involves defects in charity, in love, in order, in obedience, in humility, in hope.

The Church is simultaneously holy and filled with sinners. Her holiness, then, does not exclude the possibility of her members sinning. Each day we all must pray "forgive us our trespasses." While the Church is indefectible and in some ways impeccable, her members are not. Therefore, some of these sins can be against the Church's unity and its Source, God, the Holy Spirit and Christ the Head.

Let us thank God for our gift of the Catholic faith and for the unity of the Catholic Church. At the same time, let us remember that the Second Vatican Council teaches us that "the holy task of reconciling all Christians in the one and only Church of Christ transcends human energies and abilities."[4] It is prayer and absolute loyalty to the truth that God has revealed to us that can effect the unity of Christians more than any other efforts. As the Council states, our hope for this is "entirely in the prayer of Christ for the Church, in the love of the Father for us, and in the power of the Holy Spirit".[5]

JANUARY 15, 1993

Community Salvation

Revelation tells us that God has chosen to link the salvation of individuals to membership in a society. This flows from the social nature and the social instinct that God implanted in human nature when He created it. In communicating His life to the world, God was not content simply to draw to Himself a certain number of individuals separately from one another; instead, He founded a *Qahal*, a City of God, a People of God, a kingdom. By God's will, individual humans cannot attain to a supernatural level or develop themselves there unless they have a close bond with the community willed by Him.

The solidarity of human beings with each other in their relationship with God appears already in the first pages of the Book of Genesis. For the sacred author, the state of grace and friendship with God, which was to be the starting point of mankind's development, was to be transmitted to all humans by Adam. The solidarity of humanity in good and in evil

---

[4] Ibid., no. 24.   [5] Ibid.

is a fact willed by God. The Christian doctrine of original sin and of redemption is intelligible only if one admits as freely willed by God a "law of salvation in community".

The idea of salvation only in a community is applied in a manner still more visible to the religious society of Israel as God conceived it and brought it to reality in the Old Testament. Throughout Israel's history, God is seeking not so much to concern Himself with individuals as to form a People for Himself within which individuals can find salvation. This People was given the mission to safeguard the monotheistic faith, to prepare the environment in which the Messiah could appear, to furnish the first recruits for His messianic kingdom, and to be the starting point from which the kingdom would set out to conquer the world.

This People (the *Qahal Yahweh*) was called, separated, chosen from others, gathered together, and consecrated to God for this special mission. They were God's inheritance, His nation, the object and means of His promises. The society carried the individual, and he had religious value only in and through the religious society. One became a sharer in the messianic benefits, both present and future, only by being a member of the Chosen People, and one became a member by blood, by circumcision, and by observance of Jewish law (the Torah) and Jewish worship. The prophets (especially Jeremiah) reminded the Chosen People that this arrangement did not dispense them from individual moral effort, but even this individual effort had to be understood in terms of the community.

When the Messiah came, He carried out the plan of God, which had remained the same since the day of creation, "the law of salvation in community". This was a plan not merely to save individuals but to form a special people, a Church (the new and everlasting *Qahal Yahweh*). Jesus is the new Adam through Whom the human race is raised to a higher level than it could have attained if the old Adam had not sinned. Redeemed human beings are joined to Christ. Nobody can share the divine life without being really united to the Savior (Acts 4:12; Jn 15:4–6). Nobody can attain to this union except by entering the community formed by Christ to be His Body, His Bride, His People, His Church, His *Qahal* (Mt 16:18; Acts 2:37–39).

This Chosen People of the New Testament is not restricted to one race or to one blood, but by Christ's designation is "catholic" or universal, inviting all people of all time (Mt 28:19).

The Church is God's kingdom on earth, not in its fullness or completeness, but in its incipient and embryonic stage (Mt 13). She is the leaven in the dough of the world; the mustard seed, beginning small, yet later inviting the birds of the air to nest in her branches; a net gathering in the good and bad; a field having within both wheat and cockle.

The Catholic Church is a flock (Jn 10:7–18). Peter feeds it; Christ is its Good Shepherd, the Door of the sheepfold. The Church is the "little flock" put in danger by the hireling and the wolf. The Church is also the temple, a spiritual edifice of worship, containing the Spirit of God Himself (1 Cor 3:10–17; 1 Pet 2:5; 2 Cor 6:16; Eph 2:20–22).

The Catholic Church takes on a feminine character (hence we call her our holy Mother) in the symbol of the bride. In the Old Testament the People of God are spoken of in spousal terms. The New Testament continues and expands this image (Eph 5:23). The union of husband and wife in the sacrament of marriage is a type and a sign of the union of Christ and His Church. The Song of Songs of the Old Testament takes on this meaning in the light of the New Covenant. Therefore, the union of Christ and the Catholic Church is vital, life-giving, organic, self-sacrificing, exclusive, yet maintaining a relationship of authority in love.

The Church is also the Body of Christ (Rom 12:4–5; 1 Cor 12:27). Belonging to the Church is not simply like joining a club or a movement or an organization, but it is being joined in a real though invisible way to Jesus and through Him to all Catholics throughout the world.

These images of the Catholic Church teach us important lessons. The Church Christ founded has a Principle of order Who is Christ Himself. Jesus is the Vine, the Husband, the Cornerstone, the Head. He is apart from the Church and above her but at the same time part of her and her ordering Constituent. The Catholic Church is organically one in her very nature, but she consists of a multiplicity of elements (branches, stones, members). Within her there is a diversity of function and an inequality of dignity. She has within her an internal dynamism. The temple is still a building, although the foundation is sure and complete; the vine must still shoot forth branches and bear much fruit; the body must be built up in love; there are other sheep not yet in the one fold; the kingdom must still be coming.

Saint Paul uses yet another word for the Church. This word is *pleroma*, a Greek word that means "fullness" (Eph 1:23). The Church is the fullness or completeness of Christ that carries all Christians to heaven and manifests to all powers, both visible and invisible, the Wisdom of God that is contained in her. *Pleroma* means Christ and the entirety of those who are joined to Him and who receive their life and justification and sanctification from Him.

The Virgin Mary is the first disciple, the first member of the Church. She who was with Christ at His birth was with the Church at her birth (Acts 1:14). In consequence of this, Pope Paul VI has proclaimed her

"Mother of the Church". She is the archetype and symbol of the Catholic Church, the new Eve, the "Mother of all the living".

The Blessed Virgin Mary teaches us the lesson that the Second Vatican Council reiterates: "By her relationship with Christ, the Church is a kind of sacrament or sign of intimate union with God and of the unity of all mankind. She is also the instrument for the achievement of such unity and union."[6]

JANUARY 22, 1993

Truth and Charity

No teacher would be doing a correct job of teaching if he were to tell his elementary school students that it really does not matter if they hold that seven plus seven are fifteen, fourteen, twelve, or twenty, so long as they are "sincere". No parent would be less than utterly negligent if he were to tell the little children of the family that they should go to the medicine cabinet and try out the various things they find there, so that, when they grow up, they will know which things are good and which are bad for them.

INDIFFERENCE TO TRUTH

Indifference to truth can have horrendous consequences not only in math and parenting but also, and above all, in religion. Genuine love of neighbor is linked to truth, and it is certainly an offense against charity to allow people to persist in error to their peril when they can be assisted by truth. Religious truth exists and is knowable.

Consequently, it is a violation of reason and truth to adopt such slogans as "one religion is as good as another" or "it does not matter which church you belong to as long as you are sincere" or "try out different beliefs and find those that are suited to you" or "all churches and religions are basically the same."

Among the misconceptions sometimes held by people who claim to be following the Second Vatican Council, but who have never bothered to study carefully the documents of that ecumenical council, is the idea that the Council's Declaration on Religious Liberty (*Dignitatis humanae*) fosters or promotes religious indifference. The opposite is actually true. That declaration deals with freedom from governmental coercion in

---

[6] *Lumen gentium*, no. 1.

matters pertaining to religion but declares clearly: "[This Council] leaves untouched the traditional Catholic doctrine on the moral duty of men and societies toward the true religion and toward the one Church of Christ."[7]

The *Catechism of the Catholic Church* quotes the Second Vatican Council's stern words: "The Church is necessary for salvation" and again, "Hence, they could not be saved who, knowing that the Catholic Church was founded as necessary by God through Christ, would refuse either to enter it or to remain in it."[8]

In this area the Catholic Church is simply loyal to the teaching of her divine Founder. Jesus said, "He who does not believe shall be condemned" (Mk 16:16) and "Unless one is born of water and the Spirit, he cannot enter the kingdom of God" (Jn 3:5). Saint Peter, our first pope, said, "And there salvation in no one else, for there is no other name under heaven given among men by which we must be saved" (Acts 4:12). Without a doubt, this exclusiveness appears scandalous to people who, more and more, are infected with religious indifference. It is false charity and feigned love, however, that would be unconcerned with truth in matters pertaining to eternal salvation.

DAMNED?

Does this mean that all non-Catholics are damned? The *Catechism*, again quoting the Second Vatican Council, gives us the answer. "Those who, through no fault of their own, do not know the Gospel of Christ or his Church, but who nevertheless seek God with a sincere heart, and, moved by grace, try in their actions to do his will as they know it through the dictates of their consciences—those too may achieve eternal salvation."[9]

This teaching is also part of the doctrine of the Catholic Church over the centuries. It explains that the correct saying, "outside the Church there is no salvation", means that all who are saved are saved through Jesus Christ and through the Catholic Church, even though they may not know this. Certain kinds of faultless ignorance that cannot be overcome make it possible for people to be linked to Jesus and His Church in an invisible way.

This kind of invincible ignorance, however, does not excuse us from the constant duty to help others overcome their religious ignorance. Nor does it excuse us from what the *Catechism* calls "the obligation and

[7] *Dignitatis humanae*, no. 1.
[8] CCC 846, quoting *Lumen gentium*, no. 14.
[9] CCC 847, quoting *Lumen gentium*, no. 16.

sacred right to evangelize all men".[10] The *Catechism* also says of the Church, "according to another image dear to the Church Fathers, she is prefigured by Noah's ark, which alone saves from the flood" (CCC 845). Those who are linked to her despite (and because of) their ignorance are like people clinging by ropes to the outside of the ark, and we, who are aboard, must do all we can to bring them safely into the bark of Peter.

We must also remember that the Second Vatican Council says, "Very often, deceived by the evil one, men have become vain in their reasonings and have exchanged the truth of God for a lie and served the creature rather than the Creator."[11] Living and dying in this world without God, such human beings are exposed to ultimate despair.

The *Catechism* uses many images to teach these matters. It says, "To reunite all his children, scattered and led astray by sin, the Father willed to call the whole of humanity together into his Son's Church. The Church is the place where humanity must rediscover its unity and salvation. The Church is 'the world reconciled'. She is that bark which in 'full sail of the Lord's cross, by the breath of the Holy Spirit, navigates safely in this world' " (CCC 845).

Quoting the Second Vatican Council, the *Catechism* teaches, "The Church, further, which is called that 'Jerusalem which is above' and 'our mother' (Gal 4:26), is described as the spotless spouse of the spotless Lamb (Rev 19:7). It is she whom Christ 'loved and for whom he delivered himself up that he might sanctify her' (Eph 5:26)."[12] Let us never be indifferent to her, but proclaim her by our lives and words to the world and see this proclamation as our duty in both truth and charity.

JANUARY 20, 1995

Evangelization

Evangelization has been described as "loving people so much that our loving brings them to Christ and to His Catholic Church". During Lent it is particularly appropriate for all Christians to examine anew their conformity to the "Great Commandment" (Lk 10:25–28), whereby God insists that we love Him above all things and love our neighbor as ourselves. We cannot say that we truly love our neighbor if we have an abundance of food while he is starving, and we neglect to share our

[10] CCC 848, quoting *Ad gentes divinitus*, no. 7.
[11] *Lumen gentium*, no. 16.
[12] CCC 757, quoting *Lumen gentium*, no. 6.

riches with him. This applies even more to spiritual riches than to material food and goods.

In bringing the "good news" of Christ to our neighbors in our town, our country, and our world, it is quite clear that a serious responsibility rests upon every Catholic. The burden of evangelization does not apply merely to priests and religious, but, as Pope Paul VI and Pope John Paul II have reminded us, active participation of the whole Church is necessary in evangelization. Every believer is required to take an active part. In an address at Port-au-Prince, our Holy Father called for an effort in evangelization by the entire Catholic community in the world that would be "new in its ardor, its methods, and its expression".

THE PRINCIPAL AGENT

There can be no doubt that the principal Agent of evangelization is God Himself. The Holy Spirit makes announcing the "good news" of Jesus (His pardon, His love, and His redemption) a divine undertaking. However, the Catholic Church is the sign and instrument of this work of the Holy Spirit. Each and every member of the Church is charged and commissioned to evangelize.

The term "evangelization" was used in the recent past in Catholic circles to apply almost exclusively to missionary activity, which, in turn, seemed to be the job of those priests and religious who had a "missionary vocation". More recently this term has been used, as Father Avery Dulles observes, for catechesis and for pastoral and sacramental care of souls as well as for missionary proclamation. In his encyclical *The Mission of the Redeemer* (*Redemptoris missio*), Pope John Paul II said that evangelization has three areas of operation: first, proclamation of the gospel where Christ and the Church are not yet known; second, work among Christians who are seeking to put their lives more fully under the influence of the gospel; third, a renewed evangelization among lapsed, fallen away, and nonpracticing Catholics and among those who have allowed their faith to grow cold.

CHARACTERISTICS

In a speech to a group of American bishops in Washington, D.C. (November 1995), Father Dulles indicated several characteristics of evangelization as the recent popes have set them forth. The first characteristic is that evangelization is both "inward" and "outward", that is, directed both to us who are already in the Church as well as to the great majority of the human race who are not yet fully joined to the Body of Christ.

The second characteristic is that the evangelization involves every member of the Church, because the Universal Church is "in a state of mission". The laity especially are called upon to evangelize the world of politics, economics, culture, the sciences, art, and the media. The third characteristic is that freedom is involved. There must be no external coercion, but, at the same time, there must be a prayerful and vigorous presentation of the truth, which alone can truly make human beings free (Jn 8:32). In presenting this truth, we all must accompany it by the witness of our Christian lives. The example of believers will be decisive in the evangelization of the world.

The fourth characteristic of evangelization is dialogue. This does not mean that we doubt or conceal our religious convictions about the unique and exclusive truth of the Catholic faith. Nor does it mean that we gloss over or consider irrelevant the important differences in religion that distinguish us from non-Catholics. It does mean that we speak frankly and listen respectfully to the views and opinions of others. It means that we owe it to ourselves and to our success in evangelization to become well informed and articulate Catholics, able to explain our faith to others in a convincing way whether in polemics or in fraternal discussion.

INCULTURATION

The gospel of Christ must be brought to people where they are, and those who proclaim the gospel must do so with skill and with respect for human beings in their cultural milieu. The interaction of the gospel with culture has always been a delicate and difficult undertaking. On the one hand, faith does not necessarily mean a disdain for the human condition or for the world in which human beings live and work. It does not necessarily force people to abandon cultures or life-styles or their own personal or collective history. It is a mistake to impose a certain outlook or a certain culture on other human beings. Indeed, trying to do so breeds resentment and can be a serious obstacle to evangelization. It can also be an act of injustice disguised as an act of missionary effort.

At the same time, faith and the gospel definitely have the power to transform cultures, especially those aspects of culture which the intervention of God in human history in the Person of Jesus Christ shows to be incompatible with the divine will for our happiness in time and eternity and which violate the end or purpose for which the human race was created.

Current American culture definitely has aspects that constitute an obstruction to evangelization. There is its agnosticism, its materialism, its relativism, and its pragmatism. There is its false view of freedom, which thinks liberty means being able to do anything one is inclined to do instead of the ability to find and pursue and practice the truth, above all in religion. There is a continuing labor to eliminate all traces of religion from education and from all public life. There is the toil of the media to pander to the lowest instincts for purposes of greed and entertainment.

Notwithstanding these obstacles, however, we should make our Lent a time to reinvigorate our determination to carry out our baptismal and confirmation commitment to share the priceless treasure of our faith with our neighbors, loving our neighbors so much that we bring them to Christ and His Church.

MARCH 1, 1996

2

ROME AND THE PETRINE MINISTRY

Where Peter Is

The Eternal City, which rests astride the Tiber, is the repository of a large part of Western civilization. According to legend, Rome was founded and named after Romulus 752 years before the birth of Christ. By the beginning of the New Testament era, Rome had become the capital of the then-known world. Her eagles and her army, divided into the famous legions, ruled and controlled the *orbs terrarum*, while her roads, aqueducts, and other engineering feats joined with her laws and language to unite her vast empire.

Sometime in the sixth decade after Christ, Rome, then a thriving metropolis of approximately two million free men and one million slaves, acquired two new residents. One was a Roman citizen, although a Jew by ethnic origin, a tent maker by trade, who had spent the better part of thirty years as an itinerant Catholic bishop, priest, and missionary, spreading the teaching and saving grace of Jesus throughout the Roman Empire. He went by the name of Paul. The other was originally a Galilean fisherman, thoroughly Hebrew, yet now commissioned to be the Catholic bishop of Rome. He arrived in Italy coming from Jerusalem by way of Antioch. His given name was Simon Son-of-John, but Jesus had changed it to Rock (Cephas, in Hebrew; Peter, in Greek). Both Peter and Paul were destined to evangelize Rome, establish the Christian religion there on a stable basis, and bear witness to Jesus Christ by consecrating the soil of Rome with their blood, Peter dying on a cross and Paul by the sword.

THE AUTHORITY OF PETER

When Saint Peter arrived in Rome, he carried with him an enormous authority and a huge responsibility. Notwithstanding his all-too-human weakness, he had been given by the Son of God Himself the "keys of the kingdom of heaven" and the duty to bind and loose in such a way that heaven itself would be involved (Mt 16:18–19). As the Vicar on earth of Christ, Peter and his successors, the bishops of Rome, received the office of strengthening the brethren (Lk 22:32) and of feeding and tending the very flock of the Good Shepherd (Jn 21:15–17).

The prominence of Peter in the New Testament is undeniable. In every list of the apostles, there is a variance, except that in every list in the Gospels Peter is always mentioned first and Judas Iscariot is always mentioned last. The Book of the Acts of the Apostles shows that Peter's was the deciding view in the disputes that led to the apostolic Council of Jerusalem. It was Peter who decided, with divine guidance, the issue of whether or not to keep the Old Testament kosher laws, and it was Peter who preached on the first Pentecost Sunday, who presided over the election of Matthias to succeed the traitor Judas, and who was called upon to preach the various prominent sermons that marked the beginning of Christianity's spread throughout the world. The Acts of the Apostles also show Peter as a miracle worker, whose shadow was capable of conveying the healing power of Jesus to the sick and handicapped.

THE SUCCESSION

Peter's position as the chief of the apostles, not simply in honor but also in authority, was passed on to his successors in the See of Rome. The unbroken line of apostolic succession in Rome, from Peter to the present Pope, John Paul II, is historically unique and theologically of the greatest significance.

The *Catechism of the Catholic Church* states: "The *Pope*, Bishop of Rome and Peter's successor, 'is the perpetual and visible source and foundation of the unity both of the bishops and of the whole company of the faithful' [*Lumen gentium*, no. 23]. For the Roman Pontiff, by reason of his office as Vicar of Christ, and as pastor of the entire Church has full, supreme, and universal power over the whole Church, a power which he can always exercise unhindered' [*Lumen gentium*, no. 22]" (CCC 882).

The *Catechism* also says, "The Lord made Simon alone, whom he named Peter, the 'rock' of his Church. He gave him the keys of his Church and instituted him shepherd of the whole flock. 'The office of binding and loosing which was given to Peter was also assigned to the college of apostles united to its head' [*Lumen gentium*, no. 22 §2]. This pastoral office of Peter and the other apostles belongs to the Church's very foundation and is continued by the bishops under the primacy of the Pope" (CCC 881).

In ancient, pagan Rome, the chief priest was in charge of constructing and maintaining the bridges over the Tiber River. He was given the title of *Pontifex Maximus*. Later on, this title was appropriated by the

Roman emperors. In our day it is often applied to the pope, translated from the Latin as "Supreme Pontiff". Of all the designations of the Holy Father, however, the one that, since the ninth century, has been used most frequently is "servant of the servants of God".

Saint Patrick told the heathen Irish whom he converted to Christianity: "As you become children of Christ, so you must become children of Rome. As you are Christians, so you must be Romans." During the Ecumenical Council of Chalcedon, in the fifth century, the bishops gathered there shouted out together, after a letter from Pope Leo was read to them, "Peter has spoken through the mouth of Leo." Saint Hippolytus wrote: "We are all bound by God to profess the faith which is guarded by the Chair of Peter."

The Second Vatican Council teaches: "All the teaching about the institution, the perpetuity, the force, and the reason for the sacred primacy of the Roman Pontiff and of his infallible teaching authority, this sacred Synod again proposes to be firmly believed by all the faithful." [1]

Saint Ambrose, the Archbishop of Milan, said: "Where Peter is, there is the Church. And, where the Church is, there is eternal life." May we make this one of the principal mottoes by which we guide our lives.

FEBRUARY 17, 1995

Petrine Ministry

In an encyclical letter entitled *That They All May Be One* (*Ut Unum Sint*), our Holy Father, in writing about ecumenism from the Catholic point of view, expresses himself quite clearly about the place of Saint Peter and his successors through the ages. Pope John Paul II writes, "The Catholic Church is conscious that she has preserved the ministry of the Successor of the Apostle Peter, the Bishop of Rome, whom God established as her 'perpetual and visible principle and foundation of unity'[2] and whom the Spirit sustains in order that he may enable all the others to share in this essential good".[3]

The Pope goes on to say, "The Bishop of Rome is the Bishop of the Church which preserves the mark of the martyrdom of Peter and Paul: 'By a mysterious design of Providence, it is at Rome that [Peter] concludes his journey in following Jesus, and it is at Rome that he gives his greatest proof of love and fidelity. Likewise Paul, the Apostle of the

[1] *Lumen gentium*, no. 18.
[2] Ibid., no. 23.
[3] *Ut unum sint*, no. 88.

Gentiles, gives his supreme witness at Rome. In this way, the Church of Rome became the Church of Peter and Paul' ".[4]

On June 29 each year, we celebrate the Solemnity of Saints Peter and Paul. In the Liturgy of the Hours for that day, the song is sung: "Rejoice, O Rome, this day; thy walls they once did sign with princely blood, who now their glory share with thee. What city's vesture glows with crimson deep as thine? What beauty else has earth that may compare with thee?"

THE MISSION

When He founded His Catholic Church, Christ, of course, established the papacy for a specific mission and duty. Pope John Paul II teaches,

> As the heir to the mission of Peter in the Church, which has been made fruitful by the blood of the Princes of the Apostles, the Bishop of Rome exercises a ministry originating in the manifold mercy of God. This mercy converts hearts and pours forth the power of grace where the disciple experiences the bitter taste of personal weakness and helplessness. The authority proper to this ministry is completely at the service of God's merciful plan and it must be seen in this perspective.
>
> Associating himself with Peter's threefold profession of love, which corresponds to the earlier threefold denial (see Jn 21:15–17; 13:38), his Successor knows that he must be a sign of mercy. His is a ministry of mercy, born of an act of Christ's own mercy. This whole lesson of the Gospel must be constantly read anew, so that the exercise of the Petrine ministry may lose nothing of its authenticity and transparency.[5]

The Second Vatican Council was very clear in its teaching in this regard:

> In order that the episcopate itself might be one and undivided, Jesus placed Blessed Peter over the other apostles and instituted in him a permanent and visible source and foundation of unity of faith and fellowship. And all this teaching (from the First Vatican Council) about the institution, the perpetuity, the force, and the reason for the sacred primacy of the Roman Pontiff and of his infallible teaching authority, this Sacred Synod again proposes to be firmly believed by all the faithful.[6]

[4] Ibid., no. 90.
[5] Ibid., nos. 92–93.
[6] *Lumen gentium*, no. 18.

Sacred Tradition and the Gospels which derived from that Tradition all assign a most significant and special place to Saint Peter. In the Acts of the Apostles, he is clearly the leader and spokesman for the apostolic college (Acts 2:14; 2:37; 5:29).

The Gospel according to Saint Matthew shows how Christ gave to Peter not only his special name, meaning "Rock", but also the power to bind and loose in heaven and on earth, as well as the "keys" to the kingdom of heaven. At the same time, He gave Peter the assurance that the gates of hell or the "powers of death" would not prevail against the Catholic Church (Mt 16:17–19). The Gospel according to Saint Luke indicates how Jesus gave to Saint Peter the mission to strengthen his brethren, singling him out for a particular mission (Lk 22:32).

When I received the special letter (called a bull) that the Pope sent to me, naming me the Bishop of Lincoln, the title at the top of the letter said that he, Pope John Paul II, was the "servant of the servants of God". (This letter, or bull, can be seen in the archives located in the basement of our diocesan chancery office in Lincoln.) This title, "servant of the servants of God", was coined by Pope Saint Gregory I (also called Gregory the Great) and describes basically what the office of the Successor of Saint Peter really involves. In the Church, power and authority are related only to service, or else they are signs of something other than the kingdom of God.

In his encyclical on ecumenism, the Pope continues:

> With power and the authority, without which his office would be illusory, the Bishop of Rome must ensure the communion of all the Churches. For this reason, he is the first servant of unity. This primacy is exercised on various levels, including vigilance over the handing down of the Word, the celebration of the Liturgy and the Sacraments, the Church's mission, discipline, and the Christian life. . . . He has the duty to admonish, to caution, and to declare at times that this or that opinion being circulated is irreconcilable with the unity of faith. When circumstances require it, he speaks in the name of all the Pastors in communion with him. He can also—under very specific conditions clearly laid down by the First Vatican Council—declare *ex cathedra* that a certain doctrine belongs to the deposit of faith. By thus bearing witness to the truth, he serves unity.[7]

---

[7] *Ut unum sint*, no. 94.

Long ago, Saint Ambrose declared that "Where Peter is, there is the Church. And, where the Church is, there is eternal life." It is important for all of us always to be in "peace and communion" with the See of Peter, to thank God frequently for the gift of membership in the one, true Church founded by Christ, and to pray for the Successor of Saint Peter, the Bishop of Rome, the servant of the servants of God, His Holiness, Pope John Paul II. Finally, it is our obligation to share with others the treasure of our Catholic faith.

JULY 14, 1995

The Roman Curia

I

It is very difficult to imagine anything that numbers one billion. Even a million is a huge number. From time to time schoolteachers will have children try to gather a million bottle caps or something similar to show them how big a number a million is. If you tried to count to a billion, can you guess how long it would take you to do so? The total population of the United States is about two hundred and sixty million people.

The number of Catholics of the Latin Rite throughout the world is more than one billion. There are also about two hundred million Catholics of the Eastern Rites. (These should not be confused with the Eastern Orthodox, who are not united to us or to the Holy See.) To care pastorally for this flock of Christ, the successors of the apostles, that is, the bishops of the Catholic Church, number a few more than four thousand. The Chief Bishop, the Successor of Saint Peter, whom Jesus made the head of the apostolic college, has a serious responsibility not only for the Diocese of Rome but also for the entire People of God.

One can suppose what a difficult task rests upon the shoulders of our Holy Father, the Pope. In an ordinary year, when nothing too important happens, the Pope receives more than two hundred thousand letters in English alone. His correspondence numbers in the millions when many other languages are considered.

Over the centuries, as the Catholic Church has grown and the leadership task of the Bishops of Rome has become more demanding and more complex, the popes, out of necessity, have gathered around themselves a group of coworkers and assistants. These, taken together, have assumed the name "Roman Curia". Some of the structures of the Church are of divine origin. Christ Himself, for example, instituted the office of pope and the threefold Orders of bishop, priest, and deacon.

The Roman Curia is not of such divine origin but rather is a man-made construct, important and very useful for the discipline and good Church order of God's People, but open to any change that the Supreme Pontiff might choose to make. The Roman Curia is the complex of departments and institutes that assist the Roman Pontiff in the exercise of his supreme pastoral function for the good and service of the universal Church and of the particular churches, by which the faith and communion of the People of God are strengthened and the mission proper to the Church in the world is fostered.

The Bishop of Rome is perfectly free to use or not to use the Roman Curia, as he sees fit. He can change it or abolish it or ignore it as he might desire. The vast number of Catholics and the diversity of the Pope's responsibilities make it nearly impossible to imagine how he might carry out his duties without some help, however. The present structure of the Roman Curia, as it is now being used by Pope John Paul II, was set up in 1988 by an apostolic constitution issued by the Pope and entitled *Pastor Bonus*. The Curia includes a Secretariat of State, also called the Papal Secretariat, nine congregations (departments), three tribunals, twelve pontifical councils, seven offices, ten special commissions or committees, and twelve special institutions.

Some people misunderstand the Roman Curia and think that somehow this complexus of institutes and offices actually manipulates the pope, restricts his access to information, or otherwise unduly influences his works, words, or acts. I myself worked in the Roman Curia for eleven years and can assert from personal experience that seeing the Roman Curia in such a light is utter nonsense. Toiling in the Curia requires great dedication and sacrifice. Far from being the power-hungry obstructionists that they are sometimes portrayed as being, the people who work in the Roman Curia I found to be unselfish, humble, and docile to whatever wishes the Pope might express, and completely devoted to the cause of Christ and of His Vicar on earth.

It is true, however, that the Curia must sometimes, as part of its duty, take criticism for some things, deflecting such criticism from the pope. It is, after all, more "polite" on the part of some critics of the Pope to assign blame for things they do not like to "advisors" rather than to the Holy Father himself. Of course, like any purely human institution, the Roman Curia and those who labor in it are subject to mistakes, sins, errors, and shortcomings. Most of these, however, are inadvertent and unintentional.

Because in these days the Holy See is rather poor, those who work in the Roman Curia are not well paid. (Notwithstanding the famous quip of Pope John XXIII—in reply to the question: How many people work in the Roman Curia? He said, "About half of them!"—the people in the Curia are very hardworking.) Also, living in Rome sometimes can be uncomfortable and expensive. For these reasons, it had been difficult in recent decades to recruit people who were not citizens of Italy to work in the Curia. However, Pope Paul VI and Pope John Paul II worked very hard to change this situation and to internationalize the Roman Curia. Naturally, there are still many Italians working in the Vatican, and Italian is still the most widely used language there.

Today the people who labor in the Roman Curia, especially the priests and religious, come from almost all the countries of the world. The Pope, directly and through his Curia, carries on business and correspondence in almost seventy various languages on a regular basis and in many other languages on an occasional basis. It is a moving tribute to the "catholic", or universal, mark of the Church that our Holy Father is able to gather such a variety of collaborators around him who can work for Christ in a spirit of family harmony and charity.

JANUARY 12, 1996

The Roman Curia

II

Our Holy Father, Pope John Paul II, needs helpers to enable him to carry out his worldwide ministry of tending Christ's flock on earth (Jn 21:15–17). His task of "strengthening the brethren" (Lk 22:32) is too overwhelming for one man to carry out without the special support of God's grace and that of trusted collaborators. When he became the Successor of Saint Peter, in 1978, he found, as many popes before him had, a set of organizations set up to assist him, which goes by the name of the Roman Curia. As Bishop of Rome and Supreme Pontiff, the Pope reorganized this Curia in 1988 and continues to use it as an effective instrument of his policy and work.

Pope John Paul II wrote:

> It is evident that the function of the Roman Curia, though not belonging to the essential constitution of the Church willed by God, has nevertheless a truly ecclesial function, because it draws its existence and competence from the Pastor of the Universal Church. For the Curia exists and operates only insofar as it has a relation to the Petrine ministry and is based on it. Just as the Petrine ministry, as the servant of the servants of God, is exer-

cised in relationship to the whole Church and the Bishops of the entire Church, similarly the Roman Curia, as the servant of Peter's Successor, looks only to help the whole Church and her Bishops.[8]

Centuries ago, Pope Sixtus V wrote:

The Roman Pontiff, whom Christ the Lord constituted as the visible head of His Body, the Church, and appointed for the care of all the Churches, calls and rallies to himself many collaborators for this immense responsibility, so that he, the holder of the keys of the kingdom (Mt 16:19), may share the mass of business and administration among the Cardinals and other authorities in the Roman Curia and, by God's helping grace, avoid breaking under the strain of his duties and obligations.

BISHOP OF ROME

It is as the Bishop of Rome that the Pope succeeds the Prince of the Apostles. Therefore, besides taking care of the whole of the Catholic Church throughout the world, he has a constant local task, that of shepherding the Catholics who live in Rome and its environs. At the present time, the Eternal City is a metropolis with a population running into the millions. The pope rules and guides his Diocese of Rome through a cardinal vicar, who, in turn, is helped by a senior auxiliary bishop called a "vicegerent" and several other auxiliary bishops. The pope appoints a separate vicar general (usually an archbishop) to be his vicar for Vatican City.

Although in recent centuries the popes have lived close to St. Peter's Basilica, where the tomb of the Apostle Peter is located under the high altar, in the past they dwelt near the Church of St. John Lateran. It is the Basilica of St. John Lateran (not St. Peter's) that is the cathedral of the Diocese of Rome. Outside its front doors is inscribed the famous sentence, "This is the mother and head of all the churches in this city and in the world." After a pope is elected, there is a great ceremony in which he "takes possession" of his cathedral church.

Whenever Pope John Paul II is not away on Church business or taking care of his other responsibilities, he tries to celebrate Sunday Mass in a visit to one of the parishes in Rome. He tries to know his parish priests there, and he takes an active interest in visiting and caring for the Catholic schools and the other Catholic institutions in his local diocese.

---

[8] *Pastor Bonus*, June 28, 1988.

In 1993 he held a diocesan synod for Rome, and he personally involves himself in the governance of the Diocese of Rome.

THE HOLY SEE

The Pope, all the departments of the Roman Curia, and the Diocese of Rome constitute what is called "the Holy See". The Holy See is recognized as a supranational entity, enjoying particular rights and privileges that were codified in the Congress of Vienna at the beginning of the last century. The Holy See has always insisted on a measure of political independence and autonomy in order to enable it to work independently of national interests, to allow it to remain neutral and above national conflicts, and to ensure that the pope not be a citizen of any one country so that he can belong to all peoples of the earth.

For many centuries the popes were the civil rulers of the Papal States, located in central Italy, surrounding the city of Rome. Since 1929, however, the pope has been the sovereign of a tiny, independent nation of one hundred and nine acres located in the middle of Rome and known as Vatican City. This little country (with its own coinage, postage, and so on), together with a residence at Castel Gondolfo and several parcels of territory scattered about Rome, enables the pope to have the necessary freedom and autonomy to permit him to carry out his functions as the Supreme Pontiff of the Catholic Church.

Strictly speaking, ambassadors from various countries are accredited to the Holy See and not to the Vatican, just as the representatives of the pope to various countries and to international organizations are from the Holy See and not from the Vatican. However, just as we are accustomed by extension to use certain terms (for example, "The White House today announced . . ."), so, sometimes, it is permissible for journalists or others to substitute the term "Vatican" when, properly speaking, the term "Holy See" should be used.

In a letter to the bishops and priests of France in 1198, Pope Innocent III summed up the need for a Roman Curia:

> Although the Lord has given us the fullness of power in the Church, a power that makes us owe something to all Christians, still we cannot stretch the limits of human nature. Since we cannot deal personally with every single concern (the law of our human condition does not allow it), we are sometimes constrained to use certain brothers of ours as extensions of our own body, to take care of things we would rather deal with in person, if this were possible.

When we pray for our Holy Father at every Mass, let us also occasionally murmur a prayer for his coworkers in the Roman Curia.

JANUARY 19, 1996

The Roman Curia

III

THE SECRETARIAT

Among the various groups that assist our Holy Father as he carries out his heavy responsibilities to tend Christ's flock on earth (Jn 21:15–17) and to strengthen the brethren (Lk 22:31–32) is that part of the Roman Curia known as the Secretariat of State, or Papal Secretariat. It is presided over by a Cardinal Secretary of State, who visits with the Pope daily to learn his wishes and commands and carry them out.

The Secretariat consists of two sections. The first section takes care of what are called "ordinary" affairs, such as answering correspondence, translation work, preparation of documents, personnel matters in the Curia, and the preparation for and carrying out of papal trips and journeys. It also is the liaison with the various nunciatures and apostolic delegations throughout the world. The Secretary of State governs this section through a deputy called the "Substitute", who is an archbishop and who, in turn, has a deputy called the "Assessor", who is a monsignor.

The second section of the Secretariat deals with relations with governments and with international organizations, such as the United Nations and its affiliated organizations. It oversees all matters pertaining to treaties (called "concordats") between the Holy See and civil governments and takes care of ambassadors and diplomatic persons assigned to the Holy See by the various countries. This section of the Secretariat has a group of cardinals and bishops from around the world who meet regularly and advise the Pope on these matters. The Cardinal Secretary of State governs this section through his secretary, who is an archbishop, and he, in turn, is helped by the undersecretary, a monsignor. Both the first and the second sections have a large, multilingual, and multinational staff of priests, religious, and lay personnel.

NUNCIOS

The Pope has a personal representative (usually an archbishop) in just about every country. When such a representative is only for the Catholic

Church in a country, he is called an "Apostolic Delegate". If the Holy See has diplomatic relations with a nation, the Pope's representative to the civil government of that nation is called a "Nuncio" or "Pro-Nuncio". In 1815 the Congress of Vienna determined that a pope's representative in a country should be dean of the local diplomatic corps and take precedence over all other ambassadors. In countries where this formality is still observed, the Pope's ambassador is called the Nuncio. Otherwise, he is called the Pro-Nuncio. Nuncios are also sent by the Pope to various international organizations, such as the Organization of American States, the International Atomic Energy Commission, and the Council of Europe.

Most countries have ambassadors accredited to the Holy See. The Pro-Nuncio to our country resides in Washington, D.C. It is the duty of the Nuncio to keep the Holy See informed about the situation of the Catholic Church in a given country as well as about political, social, economic, and diplomatic conditions in that country, and to help the local bishops in their dealings with the Holy Father and the various organs of the Roman Curia.

CONGREGATIONS

The Pope has divided up the major portion of the Holy See's work among nine departments, which, by old custom, are called "congregations". Each congregation is presided over by a cardinal, who is called the prefect. He is assisted by an archbishop, the secretary. There usually are one or more undersecretaries, who are monsignors, as well as a staff of priests, religious, and lay people. Each congregation also has a group of "consulters", experts who can be priests, religious, or laymen and who are on call to provide expertise and advice when needed.

A congregation itself consists of a large group of cardinals and, usually, several bishops as well, from all over the world. Most congregations meet about once or twice a year, but the Congregation for Bishops and the Congregation for the Doctrine of the Faith meet much more often. The congregations act out of the vicarious power that the Pope bestows on them and can do no more or less than the Holy Father desires. He usually gives them executive, legislative, and judicial power in their area of competence. Sometimes the Pope reserves certain things to himself, however, and then the congregations can give him advice only if he seeks it. For instance, the Pope reserves to himself personally the decision about which priests are to be named bishops. The Congregation for Bishops (or the Congregation for the Evangelization of People or the Congregation for the Oriental Churches) presents names to the Pope and gives him its opinion about the priests on its lists, but the Holy Father makes the decisions personally. Between meetings of a congregation, the staff carries out its ordinary work and also implements what the congregations's plenary assembly, with the Pope's approval, has decided and ordered.

FEBRUARY 9, 1996

The Roman Curia

IV

The departments of the Holy See that assist the Holy Father in carrying out his essential task of tending the flock of Christ on earth (Jn 21:15–17) and his vital duty to strengthen the brethren (Lk 22:32) are called "congregations". A congregation is a group of cardinals and archbishops with a permanent staff, which possesses legislative, judicial, and executive authority insofar as the Pope bestows on them the power to act vicariously in his name. Congregations also serve as primary advisory groups for the Pope. There are presently nine such congregations.

THE CAUSES OF THE SAINTS

The Congregation for the Causes of the Saints is competent for everything that pertains to the beatification of servants of God and to the canonization of saints. It also is in charge of the preservation and authentication of all relics of saints and other relics. This congregation compiles the writings of those proposed for beatification and the facts about their lives, controls the local diocesan investigations and research, checks into alleged miracles attributed to the intercession of a deceased person, and brings all this information to a consistory (a gathering of all the cardinals of the world) so it can advise the pope whether to proceed with a beatification or canonization.

DOCTRINE

The Congregation for the Doctrine of the Faith assists the Pope in carrying out one of his most important responsibilities, that of promoting, fostering, and safeguarding the doctrine of faith and morals in the entire Catholic world. This department of the Holy See also is of great service to the Catholic bishops throughout the world, who, because they are the legitimate successors of the apostles, are the authentic teachers and doctors of the faith. New developments in the sciences and in culture are met in large measure by the studies promoted by this congregation.

Connected with the Congregation for the Doctrine of the Faith, through the presidency of its Cardinal Prefect, are the Pontifical Theological Commission and the Pontifical Biblical Commission, which consist of scholars from all over the world who regularly meet for study and to advise the Pope.

This congregation reproves doctrines opposed to the faith, as well as teachings, books, and principles that violate or endanger the faith. In its deliberations the congregation follows a new process-system, developed after the Second Vatican Council, that allows the authors of such doctrines and books to be heard and involves interested bishops of the territories in which these difficulties have arisen. This congregation is also involved in all matters pertaining to what is called "the privilege of faith" and in safeguarding the integrity and dignity of the sacrament of Penance.

THE ORIENTAL CHURCHES

The Congregation for the Oriental Churches assists the Pope in all matters pertaining to the Eastern Catholic Churches. Besides the membership of the Latin Rite (which is by far the largest numerically), there are many millions of Catholics throughout the world who belong to the Eastern Rites of the Church. Many of these rites are ancient and apostolic in origin, and their laws, liturgical practices, and customs, while different in many ways from the Latin West, enrich the Church in the diversity and spiritual richness they offer.

The Eastern Rites of the Catholic Church are not to be confused with the so-called Eastern Orthodox. These latter are separated from the See of Peter, dating from their schism in the ninth and eleventh centuries. Some of these separated groups have since returned to union with Rome, however, and those who have now fall under the competence of the Congregation for the Oriental Churches.

The Congregation for the Oriental Churches advises the Holy Father on the naming of bishops and patriarchs and on the dioceses and activities of Eastern Rite Catholics everywhere, even where their dioceses overlap the territory of Latin Rite dioceses. It may be interesting to know that there is in my diocese of Lincoln an Eastern Rite Catholic Church in union with the Holy See. This Ukrainian Rite Church celebrates the Byzantine Liturgy of Saint John Chrysostom and belongs to the Ukrainian Diocese of Chicago. Incidentally, a Latin Rite Catholic can attend Mass at this Ukrainian Catholic Church and receive

Holy Communion there. Attendance on Sunday fulfills one's Sunday obligation.

Most Eastern Rite Catholics are concentrated in the countries of the Middle East, in parts of India, and in various areas of Eastern Europe and Asia Minor.

BISHOPS

As the Successor to Saint Peter, the Bishop of Rome is the chief bishop of the whole Catholic Church. It is his duty to choose priests to be elevated to the episcopacy. The Congregation for Bishops provides most of the help he needs in this work, except for missionary territories and for the Eastern Rite Churches. This congregation not only suggests to the Pope priests whom he might name as bishops but also advises him about constituting dioceses, provinces, and regions in the Church and about uniting, dividing, or realigning them. It also takes care of military dioceses. For the United States there is a Military Archdiocese, and all Catholic U.S. servicemen and women and their dependents living with them, everywhere in the world, as well as all U.S. Catholic military chaplains, come under its jurisdiction.

The Congregation for Bishops also is in charge of approving the statutes for bishops' conferences throughout the world. For instance, here in the United States, the National Conference of Catholic Bishops and the United States Catholic Conference operate under statutes approved by this congregation.

Connected with the Congregation for Bishops are also some special agencies for particular pastoral needs, such as the Pontifical Commission for Latin America, which works closely with CELAM, the special conference of bishops for all of Latin America.

When viewing the panorama of departments that help the Pope in his work, one can get a slight view of the awesome responsibilities borne by our Holy Father. This should make us pray fervently for him at every Mass, especially when we hear his name mentioned in the Eucharistic Prayer.

APRIL 12, 1996

The Roman Curia

V

It is interesting to survey the various departments, or dicasteries, of the Holy See, which the Pope has established to help him in the exercise of his obligation to shepherd the People of God throughout the world. Such a survey enables one to see something of the complexity of the task that rests upon the Successor of Saint Peter in the See of Rome.

The congregations or departments of the Holy See are composed of cardinals and bishops from around the world, chosen by our Holy Father to be his helpers and advisors.

WORSHIP

The Congregation for Divine Worship and for the Discipline of the Sacraments has been given charge, by the Pope, over the liturgy of the Latin Rite, in those matters pertaining to the Holy See. Among these are the approval of translations from the Latin language of the various vernacular liturgies in the different countries. The congregation also moderates and promotes the sacred liturgy by means of documents, studies, and the like.

This dicastery also has the duty to safeguard the dignity of the sacraments and to decide various aspects of their valid and licit celebration. Like other congregations, it has the ability to issue various dispensations and favors that are not in the competence of local bishops. Recently, I obtained from this congregation authority to permit priests in the Diocese of Lincoln to offer Mass four times on Sundays and Holy Days and three times on weekdays, when this would be a necessity.

This congregation also decides issues involving marriages that have not been consummated. (A non-consummated marriage could be dissolved under God's law and Church law.) It also decides issues concerning Holy Orders, including reducing priests to the lay state. (A priest is a priest forever, but, by action of the Holy See, he can be made a layman canonically while remaining only ontologically a priest.)

EVANGELIZATION

The Congregation for the Evangelization of Peoples or for the Propagation of the Faith has been placed by the Pope in charge of the entire missionary effort of the Church. Dioceses, prefectures apostolic, and vicariates apostolic that are missionary in character have all their dealings with the Holy See through this dicastery. The Diocese of Fairbanks, Alaska, is the only diocese in the United States that remains under this congregation, although our entire country was considered missionary until 1908.

In mission territories, this congregation advises the Pope on the selection of bishops, on catechetical work, and on the sending of missionaries. It promotes the missionary vocation and missionary spirituality. In mission territories it coordinates all the work of bishops' conferences, synods, and councils. Its duty is to do all that is possible to spread the kingdom of Christ over the world.

Closely connected with this congregation are the great Pontifical Missionary Works: the Missionary Union of the Clergy, the Society for the Propagation of the Faith, the Society of Saint Peter the Apostle, and the Society of the Holy Childhood.

INSTITUTES

The Congregation for Institutes of Religious Life and for Societies of Apostolic Life is charged by the Pope to promote and supervise the practice of the evangelical counsels of poverty, chastity, and obedience in the Latin Rite, when they are practiced in approved forms of consecrated life. It takes care of all religious orders and communities of common life as well as all secular institutes. This congregation also takes care of all Third Orders and similar groups and organizations in the Church.

Some religious communities are of *diocesan right*, which means they come directly under the diocesan bishop and only indirectly under the Holy See. In our diocese the communities of the Marian Sisters of Lincoln and the School Sisters of Christ the King are of diocesan right. Other religious communities are of *pontifical right* and come directly under the Holy See. An example of such a community would be the Crosier Fathers and Brothers, in Hastings.

CLERGY

The Congregation for the Clergy has been placed by the Pope in charge of matters pertaining to the work and discipline of diocesan deacons and priests. It promotes the sanctity of the priesthood and helps bishops in their work of caring for the pastoral ministry of the faithful.

This congregation also promotes the preaching and teaching of the word of God in catechesis, approves national catechetical directories, supervises the Confraternity of Christian Doctrine, and issues norms for the instruction of children, youth, and adults. In addition, it is in charge of matters pertaining to the preservation and administration of the temporal goods of the Church and also treats such matters as questions regarding Mass stipends.

EDUCATION

For eleven years I was on the staff of the Congregation for Catholic Education. This department of the Holy See is charged by the Pope to take care of all Catholic seminaries throughout the world, except those in the Eastern Rites and those in mission lands. It only takes care of the academic (not the spiritual) formation of religious orders and communities preparing future priests. It also takes care of ecclesiastical and Catholic universities throughout the world and all secondary and elementary Catholic schools. Connected with this congregation is the Pontifical Work for Vocations, which fosters Church vocations throughout the Church.

When you think of these congregations, remember all the burdens our Holy Father must shoulder. Then be sure to keep him always in your prayers.

MAY 10, 1996

Great Reading

Recent popes, since the time of Pope Leo XIII at the beginning of our century, have been composing and publishing some of the most memorable religious documents in history. This activity seems to have reached its climax in the untiring and brilliant work of our present Holy Father, Pope John Paul II. Our Church and our world have been blessed with very significant publications, in fine English translations, of works of the Pope.

Also, we now have the *Catechism of the Catholic Church*, a monumental work, with a resonance that will last for centuries. It deserves to be on the bookshelf of every Catholic and needs to be read and studied with diligence by all the Catholic faithful who have at least a high-school education.

The Holy Father's book *Crossing the Threshold of Hope* has not only been a best-seller in secular terms, but it provides a glimpse into the very thought processes of Pope John Paul II, one of the most fascinating and interesting personalities of our era. The Pope used in this book the literary device of a journalistic interview to expound on questions that are unavoidably on the minds of many contemporary men and women, and this may account for the book's overwhelming popularity.

Of the Pope's magnificent encyclical letters, two of the more recent are distinguished by their power, authority, and relevance to the moral life of the world. The letter *The Splendor of Truth* is the most thorough treatment of moral theology that any pope has ever engaged in. It treats of a myriad of modern issues and confronts current confusion and errors with solid principles, clarity of doctrine, and the timeless truths of divine revelation and of the natural law.

The encyclical *The Gospel of Life* is especially applicable to our own country and our own time. Of all the encyclicals of this Pope, it is perhaps the easiest and clearest to read and understand. Whether we like it or not, the issues about which the Holy Father writes are issues that are as near to us as the voting booth, our home television set, and the taxes we all have to pay. He gives us guidance and direction to form our consciences not only about such matters as abortion and euthanasia but also about such things as human embryo and fetal research and what it means to vote for or support politicians who permit, foster, or allow abortion and euthanasia, even though they may claim to be "personally against" them. His remarks about the death penalty also should be studied and followed by all of us. It is difficult to imagine any Catholic who claims to be well informed about his religion who would not feel obliged to own a copy of *The Gospel of Life* and to read it conscientiously.

The Pope with ceaseless energy, despite his many sufferings and problems and his more than seven decades of life, continues also to publish a prodigious amount of letters, speeches, and other literary output. His regular audience talks are done in a masterful way, lending them to future publication.

The Holy Father often addresses *apostolic letters* and *apostolic exhortations* to all the faithful. Every year, for instance, he publishes a significant message for the World Day of Prayer for Peace, celebrated on January 1. He publishes a message for World Mission Day, for the World Day of Prayer for Vocations, and for World Communications Day. It is profoundly regrettable that so many people throughout the world, including, unfortunately, many Catholics, do not even know of the existence of these papal works, much less what they contain.

Of special importance to us all should be the apostolic letter of our Holy Father entitled *On the Coming of the Third Millennium*. In this letter he outlines the plans of the Catholic Church for the coming celebration of the year 2000, along with plans for the important years of preparation leading up to that "holy year". He explains his plans for "continental synods of bishops" throughout the world. The year 1997 will be dedicated to Christ our Lord. The year 1998 will be given over to God, the Holy Spirit, and 1999 will be the year of God, the Father.

With the invention of wireless broadcasting and various methods of sound reproduction and with the invention of the cathode tube and assorted methods of image construction and communication, reading has taken something of a back seat in our culture. This cannot but have the effect of impoverishing our time on earth. The writings of the Pope are especially valuable and even necessary for the whole Church, and this includes not only the clergy and religious but, more than ever, the laity, who are being called upon to exercise roles of growing importance and leadership in our Catholic community.

During the Ecumenical Council of Chalcedon, held in the fifth century, a letter from Pope Saint Leo I was read to the assembled bishops by the papal legate. When the reading was concluded, the bishops rose as a body and shouted, "Peter has spoken through the mouth of Leo." Saint Peter continues to speak to us today through the writings of his successor, Christ's Vicar on earth. We are the losers if we do not make a real effort to listen to what he has to say to us.

Saint Ambrose said, "Where Peter is, there is the Church, and where the Church is, there is everlasting life." There is no more effective way to know "where Peter is" than to read what the Pope writes and says. We make a big mistake if we derive our knowledge of what our Holy Father says and does only from the secular media. These media are part of the culture of unbelief and come from an attitude of hostility to Christ and to the Catholic Church. Both consciously and unconsciously, they frequently distort, slant, and even falsify information and news about our faith. Go to the source. Find out what the Pope says from the very words of the Pope himself. You will be spiritually the richer for the effort.

APRIL 28, 1995

Ad Limina Visit to Rome

I

The law of the Church requires that bishops pay a visit to Rome every five years. This is called the visit *Ad limina apostolorum*, which means "to the threshold of the tombs of the apostles". From very ancient times, Catholic bishops have been required on a quinquennial basis to pray at the tomb of Saint Peter and the tomb of Saint Paul in the Eternal City. In accord with the arrangements made by the Holy See with the National Conference of Catholic Bishops, I had occasion in 1993 to join the bishops of our region (Iowa, Missouri, Kansas, and Nebraska) and visit Rome for the purpose of the quinquennial *Ad limina* requirement.

Long before the *Ad limina* visit is made, bishops are required to submit to the Holy See a very large and detailed account of their diocese over the last five years. This very extensive document in triplicate is sent on several months ahead of the bishop's visit, so that the Holy Father and the departments of the Holy See have ample opportunity to study and summarize what the bishop has to report.

I left for the *Ad limina* visit on Saturday evening, May 22, shortly after I had had the enormous joy of ordaining two young men to the priesthood and six young men to the transitional diaconate in the Cathedral of the Risen Christ in Lincoln. My trip took me from Lincoln to Chicago, from Chicago to London, and from London to Rome. Because Rome is seven hours ahead of our time zone, I arrived in Rome in the evening of May 23. As has been my misfortune in past times, my luggage, unfortunately, did not keep up with me and only arrived in Rome the next day.

While in Rome, I stayed at the Pontifical North American College, which is located on the Janiculum Hill, a hill overlooking the Vatican hill, making St. Peter's and the offices of the Holy See very close to our residence. I found the bishops of our region already there. After taking some time to refresh myself and to adjust my biological clock to the new time situation, I offered Sunday Mass in the chapel at the North American College. That brought back for me many fond recollections, since I had been a seminarian at the North American College from 1957 to 1961, being ordained a priest in Rome in 1960. The Mass, of course, like my Mass every Sunday and holy day, was offered for all of the people of our Diocese of Lincoln.

The next morning, Monday, May 24, I joined the bishops of our region in making the first of the required *Ad limina* visits. This was to the tomb of Saint Peter, where we prayed for our respective dioceses and asked the Prince of the Apostles and the first pope to intercede with our Savior for the Church. We concelebrated Mass that morning in the Lithuanian Chapel, very close to the place where Saint Peter is buried. As I was celebrating Mass with the other bishops, I looked up at the beautiful icon of the Blessed Virgin that adorns that chapel and was surprised and happy to see that beneath were the words of my episcopal motto, "*Sub tuum praesidium*". Later on that same day, with all the other bishops of our region, I visited the Congregation for the Clergy. This department of the Holy See takes care of matters pertaining to the discipline of the diocesan clergy, matters pertaining to catechetics, and matters pertaining to the material goods and possessions of the Church. The

congregation was presided over by Cardinal José Sanchez, who is Fili-
pino in national origin. He was assisted by Archbishop Sepe, who is an
Italian in origin. Our discussions at the congregation with the Cardinal,
the Archbishop, and their staff members were long and fruitful. They
centered on such subjects as the clergy of our respective dioceses, matters pertaining to vocational recruitment and vocation work, particularly
with respect the diocesan priesthood, and matters regarding catechetical
and religious education work in our dioceses. We also touched upon
various issues pertaining to the material possessions and goods of the
Church.

The following day, after Mass in the chapel of the North American
Martyrs at the North American College, the bishops of the region went
to the Congregation for the Doctrine of the Faith. I was very happy to
visit that department of the Holy See, which has the duty of overseeing
matters of correct doctrine and morals throughout the Church. Cardinal
Joseph Ratzinger, the Prefect, was on retreat in Germany when we came
to the congregation, but we were warmly and cordially welcomed by
Archbishop Bovone and other staff members. We had long and fruitful
discussions about the situation of the faith in the United States and
touched upon various items of considerable importance, including developments in the translation into English of the *Catechism* (the translation appeared in 1994). The Archbishop was particularly keen to alert
the bishops to various aspects of doctrinal confusion and heterodoxy
that pose a danger to the Church universal and, in some instances, to the
Church here in our country. Some of these matters are, of course, in-
trinsic to the Church, and others are extrinsic or external to her structure. I was able on the same day, after our visit to the Congregation for
the Doctrine for the Faith, to enjoy a working lunch with Cardinal Anthony Bevilaqua, the Archbishop of Philadelphia, and Archbishop
Levada, the Archbishop of Portland, Oregon. I also had occasion to visit
many other American prelates who were in Rome at the same time,
including their Eminences, Cardinal Law of Boston and Cardinal
Hickey of Washington. Archbishop William Keeler, the Archbishop of
Baltimore and president of the National Conference of Catholic Bishops, was also in Rome at the same time and staying at the North American College.

JUNE 18, 1993

Ad Limina Visit to Rome

II

On Wednesday, May 26, 1993, the bishops of our region made a call to the Congregation for Bishops. There we had a delightful and extensive conversation with His Eminence, Cardinal Gantin, the Prefect, assisted by his secretary, Archbishop Justin Rigali, along with several American and English-speaking staff members. The Congregation for Bishops, of course, is the department of the Holy See that suggests to the Holy Father the names of priests who would be suitable candidates to the episcopacy. It is also the department of the Holy See that helps bishops in their labors and apostolic endeavors.

After our visit to the Congregation for Bishops, we went to the Hall of Pope Paul VI, which is sometimes called the "audience hall", where we joined our Holy Father, Pope John Paul II, in one-half of his usual Wednesday general audiences. On this particular Wednesday, the Holy Father was receiving people who spoke German, Polish, and Czech in Saint Peter's Basilica. In the Hall of Pope Paul VI, where we were present, he was receiving the people who spoke English, Spanish, French, Italian, Portuguese, and Japanese. We listened to the extremely beautiful discourse that the Holy Father delivered, his current catechetical theme in his Wednesday audience talks being about the priesthood of Jesus Christ. The Holy Father then invited all of us bishops who were present to join him in bestowing a blessing upon the thousands of people who were gathered in the hall.

At the same time that I was in Rome, one of our priests was also there, Father Thomas Kuffel, then a parochial vicar at Saint Mary Parish in Lincoln, soon to be the parochial vicar at Saint Mary Parish in Nebraska City. I was delighted to see Father Kuffel and to be able to invite him to join me at the general papal audience on Wednesday. Also while I was in Rome, I was able to have many long and delightful conversations as well as several enjoyable meals with Father John Folda, a priest from our diocese, appointed to study spirituality, living at the North American College and taking his courses at the Pontifical University of Saint Thomas (also called the Angelicum) in Rome.

On Wednesday afternoon, the bishops of our region went by bus to the Basilica of Saint Paul Outside-the-Walls. This is the place where the great Apostle of the Gentiles is buried. It is only a short distance from the spot where he suffered martyrdom for the faith, in the same year in which Saint Peter died in Rome. We concelebrated Mass together at the tomb of Saint Paul and listened to an eloquent homily given by one of the bishops. It is exceptionally moving to see the inscription on the tomb of Saint Paul; it comes from his Epistle to the Philipplians, "For me to live is Christ and to die is gain."

After we finished Mass and prayers of thanksgiving, we were transported to the Casa Santa Maria dell'Umilta, which is to say, the famous house on Humility Street, the section of the North American College that is the residence for student-priests from the United States doing graduate studies in Rome. There I was greeted by Father Folda, and, with the other bishops, I had a pleasant evening. The dinner at which we were present celebrated the end of the school year and the departure of many of the student-priests for their assignments in the United States. We were greeted by Monsignor Charles Elmer, the superior of the Casa, and by his superior, Monsignor O'Brien, the rector of the entire complex of the North American College.

On Thursday, May 27, I was able to celebrate Mass at the North American College once again. That day is the birthday of my deceased father, and whenever providence allows me, I say Mass on that day for the repose of his noble soul. It was on that day that the Holy Father invited the fifteen bishops from our region to have lunch with him. We were summoned to his apartment door at 1:30 and were admitted to his private quarters. He cordially greeted us and invited us to make a visit in his private chapel. After some prayers before the Blessed Sacrament, he led us into his dining room. There were just the fifteen of us bishops and the Holy Father at the table. The table in his dining room was adorned with beautiful flowers, as was his private chapel. He told us these bouquets of flowers were the work of the Polish Sisters who were his housekeepers. His valet, in a white jacket, and one of the Sisters served us our food at lunch. The Holy Father ate heartily and joined in extensive and interesting conversation, answering questions, asking questions, and talking about various topics that the bishops or he himself chose to bring up. Our lunch consisted of water and wine, with a first course of cantaloupe or melon and prosciutto ham. The main course consisted of a slice of beef with asparagus and carrots and boiled potatoes. Then we were given a platter with assorted cheeses, and finally the meal concluded with strawberries and ice cream. After lunch, the Holy Father again invited us to spend some time with him, praying in his private chapel, and then he accompanied us to the exit.

In the evening of May 27, a bus again took all of us bishops of Region IX to Villa Stritch, a house that the American bishops own in Rome, where diocesan priests who work in various offices in the Holy See might reside. I lived at Villa Stritch for eleven years, after I had lived for three years at the Casa Santa Maria dell'Umilta. This was when I was assigned as a staff member for the Congregation for Catholic Education. It was delightful to greet many of the priests at Villa Stritch, to renew old friendships, and to make some new acquaintances. Among the people at Villa Stritch was Archbishop John Foley, from Philadelphia, the president of the Pontifical Commission for Social Communications. Also visiting Villa Stritch at that time was Cardinal William Baum, former Archbishop of Washington, in charge of the Sacred Penitentiary Apostolic, which is not a prison but the department of the Holy See vigilant about matters pertaining to indulgences and the internal forum and consciences. Also there that evening was Cardinal Bernardin, Archbishop of Chicago.

JULY 2, 1993

Ad Limina Visit to Rome

III

Friday, May 28, 1993, was an exceptionally busy day. First, we bishops of Region IX were invited to concelebrate Holy Mass with our Holy Father in his private chapel at 7:00 A.M. We were allowed to bring along any priests whom we had with us. So I was able to invite Father Thomas Kuffel and Father John Folda to be with me as we joined our Holy Father in concelebrating the Holy Sacrifice of Jesus. Afterward, we had the opportunity to greet the Holy Father when his thanksgiving after Mass was concluded. It was a joy to be able to introduce Father Folda and Father Kuffel to him. I told the Holy Father that these two priests represented each and every one of the wonderful priests in my Diocese of Lincoln.

Later that morning I was summoned to a private audience with the Pope. After I was ushered into his study, the Holy Father with great cordiality had me sit at his desk with him, and we discussed at considerable length a large number of matters pertaining to the Diocese of Lincoln as well as to the Church in general. The Pope was obviously well briefed. He also, with his exceptional and phenomenal memory, recalled our relationship, which dates back to before his being elected the Successor of Saint Peter as the Bishop of Rome. I knew him when he was still the Archbishop of Krakow in Poland. In addition to some business and practical matters, we were able to enjoy some conversation on a personal and friendly basis. The Holy Father was gracious enough to assure me that he extends his apostolic blessing to all of my fellow workers and all of the priests and religious and lay people of the Diocese of Lincoln. I was happy to reassure the Holy Father of our absolute loyalty, obedience, and devotion to his person and to his teaching.

Sometime after my private audience with the Holy Father, all of us bishops of Region IX were invited together to join the Holy Father. On this occasion, he gave a formal discourse to us. He touched on the necessity of bishops' being vigilant about the intrusion of "New Age" or other kinds of foreign philosophies into the doctrines and teachings of the Church and on the need to emphasize proper eschatology, which is to say, that salvation has to do with the last things of death, judgment, heaven, purgatory, and hell. Lastly, he spoke about the issue of vocations, particularly about vocations to the religious life for young women and girls.

It was a very full day, that Friday, and it was made even more complete and full by the visits our bishops made to the Congregation for Catholic Education. There Cardinal Pio Laghi and his collaborators talked with us extensively about seminaries, Catholic universities and colleges, and Catholic schools at all levels, as well as about religious vocations and vocations to the priesthood. It was a joy for me to return to the department of the Holy See where I had spent eleven years working for Pope Paul VI, Pope John Paul I, and Pope John Paul II.

Later on that same day, the bishops visited the Congregation for Divine Worship and the Discipline of the Sacraments. Many issues pertaining to the liturgy and to the seven sacraments were discussed at considerable length, at the highest level, with Cardinal Antonio Javierre-Ortas, the Prefect of that congregation.

When I was with the Holy Father in the private audience, His Holiness was kind enough to invite me to join him in concelebrating the Mass for the vigil of Pentecost, on Saturday evening, May 29. The Mass was splendid, celebrated in St. Peter's Square before and with hundreds of thousands of people. I was able to join the bishops and archbishops and cardinals in celebrating Mass with the Holy Father to mark the conclusion of the Diocesan Synod before the Archdiocese of Rome. It was an occasion of particular beauty. The lovely and magnificent Square of St. Peter's, surrounded by the glorious colonnade of Bernini and the façade of the mighty basilica, made a particularly splendid setting for the invoking of the Holy Spirit on the whole Church and upon the whole world. The lighted candles held by hundreds of thousands of people in the great piazza added to the special beauty that marked Pentecost 1993 in Rome.

I stayed in Rome five days after the *Ad limina* visit had concluded. I was able to visit with the bishops from the other region that followed us, which is to say, the Catholic bishops from Kentucky, Tennessee, Alabama, Mississippi, and Louisiana. I was also able to visit and renew old friendships with the friends I had acquired in living those many years in Rome. These extra days also gave me an opportunity to visit more extensively with Father Folda, who was looking forward to assuming his duties as the new pastor in Syracuse and Avoca.

Thus concludes my account of the 1993 *Ad limina* visit of the Bishop of Lincoln to the Holy See and the threshold of the tombs of the apostles. I trust that this personal memoir will stimulate some of my readers to remember in prayer our Holy Father and the Bishop of Lincoln, named to this See a little more than a year ago by the Vicar of Christ on earth.

JULY 16, 1993

The East Coast Trip

The original plans for the Holy Father's trip to our country had called for all the American bishops to concelebrate Mass with him on October 8, at Camden Yards, the Baltimore Orioles' ballpark. Much to my surprise, however, I received some additional invitations to be with Pope John Paul II at the beginning of the month, and I was happy to be able to accept them.

Archbishop Renato Martino, the Permanent Observer of the Holy See to the United Nations in New York, invited me to be present on October 5, when the Pope addressed the General Assembly. Cardinal John O'Connor, the Archbishop of New York, asked me to be present at Evening Prayer, held at St. Joseph's Seminary in Dunwoodie, Yonkers, and also to concelebrate Mass with the Holy Father on the Great Lawn in Central Park and then to recite the rosary with him at St. Patrick's Cathedral and to dine with him at the Cardinal's home.

It is always an inspiring experience to be with Pope John Paul II and an uplifting joy, so I was happy to be able to extend my trip to the East Coast and make New York part of my travel plans. Unfortunately, I was unable to get in contact while there with the Wahlmeier family, who were also in New York and who joined the Holy Father for Mass in Brooklyn, since they had been chosen by the Knights of Columbus as the 1994 family of the year. Father David Bourek, their pastor in Hastings, was with them. It was a source of pride for me to have such a beautiful Catholic family representing so many of the values and ideals of our Diocese of Lincoln before a national audience and before our Holy Father. I saw them on television, but I did not take a direct part in the Pope's activities in Brooklyn and Newark. Of course, I had congratulated the Wahlmeiers on previous occasions.

AT THE UNITED NATIONS

After waiting to go through the security procedures in a pouring rain, I got to my seat in the impressive hall of the United Nations General Assembly. The president of the General Assembly and the Secretary General of the UN accompanied the Pope into the chamber, where he was greeted by enthusiastic applause. It seemed to me that almost every seat among the delegates was filled. I watched the reaction of such delegations as those from China and Cuba. They were very attentive to the Pope's words.

The talk of Pope John Paul II was masterful and delivered in the six official languages of the UN (French, English, Spanish, Russian, Chinese, and Arabic). The speech deserves study and attention from the whole human family. It defies summary because of its complexity and careful construction. He spoke about a common human patrimony, taking the risk of freedom, the rights of nations, respect for some differences, freedom and moral truth, the United Nations and the future of freedom, and the civilization of love.

A chartered bus with a police escort got me and a group of other bishops through the traffic jams, enabling us to be at St. Joseph's Seminary for Evening Prayer. We have some of our seminarians from the Diocese of Lincoln there preparing to become priests, and it was good to see them. Again our Holy Father gave a splendid discourse to the seminarians. He emphasized the gift and virtue of wisdom and how the seminarians are challenged to confront the wisdom of this world with the certainty of Christ's teaching and love, serving people when they become priests by joyfully sharing with them the "good news" of Jesus, Who is the eternal Wisdom of God.

IMPRESSIONS

The welcome at Newark International Airport, the prayer service at Sacred Heart Cathedral in Newark, the Mass at Giants' Stadium, and the Mass at Aqueduct Racetrack I watched on television. The saturation media coverage on the East Coast was most gratifying. Also I was happy to see that it was very favorable to the Pope and the Catholic Church, in contradistinction to what the national media usually present. Commentators were well informed and fair. The local newspapers were thorough in their coverage and balanced.

There were armies of police and other law-enforcement officers. The secret service was everywhere, and badges and other identification were always being demanded. I have never walked through so many metal detectors as I did in those three days I was on the East Coast.

I was deeply impressed by the Holy Father's remarkable strength and stamina, very unusual for a seventy-five-year-old man. He walked slowly and cautiously, and his left hand seemed to have a tremor (which, I was told, was a result of the assassination attempt several years ago), but his complexion and disposition were excellent. He spoke with clarity and unfaltering depth. I was fatigued long before he was, and he was the one presiding and using languages different from his mother tongue (a very tiring thing to do, as I can testify from experience). Weather and mishaps never daunted the Pope as he calmly carried out a most exceptional exercise in zeal for souls and for God's glory.

OTHER EVENTS

The Mass in Central Park, the Mass at Camden Yards, the rosary in St. Patrick's Cathedral were, of course, among the highlights of my trip.

After the rosary, on Saturday, October 7, the Pope visited with various New York politicians and other notables in St. Patrick's Cathedral and around Fifth Avenue. He also visited with groups of Muslim leaders and members of other non-Christian religions. He had visited with non-Catholic Christian leaders after the Mass in Central Park. At dinner there were fifty of us bishops and cardinals with the Holy Father. (We had spinach soup, veal, cooked vegetables and pasta, pie and cake. The Pope ate some of everything except the cake.)

After dinner the Pope went to talk with representatives of the Jewish community, and I, with the other bishops, got on another chartered bus and rode to Baltimore. I am thrilled at what this visit of the Pope accomplished and am convinced that it will continue to have a great and positive resonance in our land.

OCTOBER 27, 1995

New York and Baltimore

I enjoyed many outstanding experiences at the beginning of October, when I was privileged to be with our Holy Father during some of the time he was making his visit to the United Nations and his fourth pastoral trip to the United States as the Bishop of Rome. Among these experiences was my concelebrating Mass with him in Central Park in New

York and at Camden Yards in Baltimore. It was also a singular joy to be able to recite the holy rosary with him in St. Patrick's Cathedral in New York late in the afternoon of October 7.

The Pope regularly recites the rosary over the worldwide network of Vatican Radio. Consequently, his recitation of the rosary at St. Patrick's was broadcast over the world by Vatican Radio. The beautiful cathedral, a Fifth Avenue landmark, was jammed with invited guests and media people when we bishops were ushered into the sanctuary. There was a speech of greeting by Cardinal John O'Connor, the Archbishop of New York. After praying the rosary, the Holy Father spoke in reply.

The Pope knelt at a prie-dieu while praying. He said the Our Fathers, and Cardinal O'Connor led the Hail Marys. Various readers introduced the mysteries and the words from Sacred Scripture that served as a vehicle for meditation. After the rosary the Pope spoke especially to religious (nuns and religious brothers) and to Catholic families.

The Pope said, "There are two immediate things which the Catholic families of America can do to strengthen home-life. The first is prayer: both personal and family prayer. . . . The second suggestion I make to families is to use the *Catechism* to learn about the faith and to answer the questions that come up, especially the moral questions which confront everyone today." [9]

In speaking about prayer in families, our Holy Father said, "One prayer in particular I recommend to families, the one we have just been praying, the *Rosary*. And especially the Joyful Mysteries. . . . To use a phrase made famous by the late Fr. Patrick Peyton: The family that prays together, stays together." [10]

CENTRAL PARK, NEW YORK

Earlier that day the weather for the Mass on the Great Lawn had been soggy, wet, and cold. However, this had not diminished the enthusiasm or the turnout of a huge crowd. There were one hundred twenty thousand tickets given out, and all were used. There were other thousands of people who watched outside the grounds on gigantic TV screens. We bishops who were invited to concelebrate vested in an enormous tent that served as the sacristy. The ceremonies of the sacred liturgy, the music, the devotion of the tens of thousands of people, and the natural beauty of the surroundings were most moving to me. I was also happy

[9] John Paul II's address, "Foster the Life of Faith and Grace in Yourselves and in Your Children", was later published in *L'Osservatore Romano* 41 (October 11, 1995): 6, nos. 5–6.
[10] Ibid., no. 5.

to see some of our Lincoln seminarians as important ministers in the liturgy.

In the homily the Pope preached about the joyful mysteries of the rosary. He directed many of his remarks specifically to the immense numbers of young people who were present at the Mass. When speaking about the third joyful mystery, the Holy Father recalled a "song I used to sing in Poland as a young man, a song which I still sing as Pope, which tells about the birth of the Savior".[11] Then the Pope actually sang a verse from this Polish carol. He mentioned that it was a Christmas carol, much like "Stille Nacht", or "Silent Night". After his homily the people and choirs all joined in singing "Silent Night".

When the Pope spoke about the second joyful mystery, the visitation, he exhorted us to " 'visit' the needs of the poor, the hungry, the homeless, those who are alone or ill: for example, those suffering from AIDS".[12] He said:

> *You are called to stand up for life!* To respect and defend the mystery of life always and everywhere, including the lives of unborn babies, giving real help and encouragement to mothers in difficult situations. You are called to work and pray against abortion, against violence of all kinds, including the violence done against women's and children's dignity through pornography. Stand up for the life of the aged and handicapped, against attempts to promote assisted-suicide and euthanasia! *Stand up for marriage and family life! Stand up for purity!* [13]

BALTIMORE

A group of us bishops arrived by bus from New York in Baltimore in the early hours of the morning of Sunday, October 8. There we joined a large number of the United States hierarchy. There were about two hundred and forty American bishops present. The Pope, who had slept in New York at the home of Archbishop Renato Martino, the Permanent Observer of the Holy See at the United Nations, arrived later by plane and helicopter.

The weather was bright, sunny, clear, and pleasant. After a police-escorted bus ride to Camden Yards and the annoying but necessary security procedures, we awaited the Pope's arrival for Mass. Various choirs

---

[11] John Paul II, "You Are Called to Respect and Defend the Mystery of Life Always and Everywhere", *L'Osservatore Romano* 41 (October 11, 1995): 7, no. 7.

[12] Ibid., no. 6.

[13] Ibid.

and groups aroused excitement and fervor in the vast throng that filled the ballpark as we waited. Many of our Lincoln seminarians from Mount St. Mary's Seminary in Emmitsburg were present at the Mass (and later saw the Pope close up at his visit to the Seminary in Roland Park).

Enthusiasm and joy greeted the Holy Father's arrival. The liturgy was, once again, splendid, almost a vision of the eternal liturgy of heaven. The Pope spoke about the Catholic Church in our country. He exhorted parents, teachers, and us, his brother bishops, to guard the rich deposit of faith, guarding the truth which makes us free, "especially in view of the challenges posed by a materialistic culture and by a permissive mentality".[14]

One of the best ways we can show our gratitude for the visit to our shores of the Vicar of Christ on earth and the successor of Saint Peter would be to read carefully what he so eloquently and lovingly wrote and spoke to us during his visit.

NOVEMBER 3, 1995

---

[14] John Paul II, "Sometimes Witnessing to Christ Means Challenging Your Culture", *L'Osservatore Romano* 41 (October 1, 1995): 13, no. 8.

3

BISHOPS, PRIESTS, AND LAITY

The Episcopacy

As we approach the celebration of the Solemnity of Pentecost, it is useful to meditate on the various manifestations of God, the Holy Spirit, in the Church's life. Among the many people and places attributed to the work of the Holy Spirit is the order of bishops.

The Second Vatican Council teaches, "Bishops have been appointed by the Holy Spirit and are the successors of the Apostles as pastors of souls. . . . Through the Holy Spirit, Who has been given to them, bishops have been made true and authentic teachers of the faith, pontiffs, and shepherds." [1] That Ecumenical Council also says, "A diocese is that portion of God's People which is entrusted to a bishop to be shepherded by him with the cooperation of his priests. Adhering thus to its pastor and gathered by him in the Holy Spirit through the Gospel and the Eucharist, this portion of Christ's flock constitutes a particular church in which the one, holy, Catholic, and apostolic Church is truly present and operative." [2]

That same Council also says, "A bishop, marked with the fullness of the sacrament of Holy Orders, is the steward of the grace of the supreme priesthood, especially in the Eucharist, which he offers or causes to be offered and by which the Church constantly lives and grows." [3]

Saint Ignatius was a successor of Saint Peter as the bishop in the See of Antioch (after Saint Peter had moved from Antioch to Rome). He was martyred in Rome in the year 110. He wrote a series of letters between the year 107 and the year of his death. Some were written to Saint Polycarp, a young bishop in the Diocese of Smyrna (present-day Izmir, in Turkey). These letters of Saint Ignatius are very important because they tell us much about the attitudes and doctrines of some of the first successors of the apostles.

To the Catholics in Ephesus, Saint Ignatius wrote, "May you be obedient to your Bishop and to your priests and thus be sanctified in every

---

[1] *Christus Dominus*, no. 2.
[2] Ibid., no. 11.
[3] *Lumen gentium*, no. 26.

respect." To the Christians of Magnesia, he wrote, "I exhort you to do everything that God desires. Remember that the Bishop presides in the place of Christ, while the priests function as a council of Apostles."

To Saint Ignatius we attribute the first official use of the name of the Church that Christ founded. Just as the name "Christian" came from Antioch (see Acts 11:26), so also the name "Catholic" came from there. To the Diocese of Smyrna, Saint Ignatius wrote, "Where the Bishop appears, there let the people be, just as where Jesus Christ is, there is the Catholic Church." To those same people, he said, "Let no one do anything touching the Church apart from the Bishop. . . . It is well to revere God and the Bishop. He who honors the Bishop is honored by God."

The *Catechism of the Catholic Church* states, " 'The bishops, as vicars and legates of Christ, govern the particular Churches assigned to them by means of their counsels, exhortations, and example, but over and above that also by the authority and sacred power' [*Lumen gentium*, no. 27] which indeed they ought to exercise so as to edify, in the spirit of service which is that of their Master" (CCC 894).

The office of bishop (*episcopos* in Greek, which could be translated as "overseer") is plainly seen in the New Testament (Phil 1:1; 1 Tim 3:2; 1 Th 5:12; Titus 1:5). By divine institution, Catholic bishops are the true and legitimate successors of the apostles. This is a defined doctrine of our faith.

The *Catechism* also says, "Bishops, with priests as co-workers, have as their first task 'to preach the gospel of God to all men,' in keeping with the Lord's command [*Presbyterorum Ordinis*, no. 4; cf. Mk 16:15]. They are 'heralds of the faith, who draw new disciples to Christ; they are authentic teachers' of the apostolic faith 'endowed with the authority of Christ' [*Lumen gentium*, no. 25]" (CCC 888).

The *Catechism* remarks, "When Christ instituted the Twelve, 'He constituted [them] in the form of a college or permanent assembly, at the head of which he placed Peter, chosen from among them' [*Lumen gentium*, no. 19]. Just as 'by the Lord's institution, St. Peter and the rest of the apostles constitute a single apostolic college, so in like fashion the Roman Pontiff, Peter's successor, and the bishops, the successors of the apostles, are related with and united to one another' [*Lumen gentium*, no. 22]" (CCC 880).

Saint Augustine, himself the Bishop of Hippo, said, "The office of bishop implies work rather than dignity. . . and so no man can be a good bishop if he loves his title but not his task." Palladius, the fourth-century monk and Christian writer, said, "Every bishop must expect to labor much and suffer much tribulation." Saint Ambrose, the Archbishop of Milan, wrote, "If we examine the content of Holy Scripture, who will deny that it is a matter of faith that bishops are to judge emperors, not emperors, bishops? . . . There is nothing so fraught with danger before God and so base before men, as a bishop not declaring freely what he thinks. Who will dare to tell you the truth, if the bishop does not?"

Saint Cyprian, the third-century Bishop of Carthage, said, "The Lord, Who condescends to elect and appoint for Himself Bishops in His Church, will protect those chosen and appointed by His will, supplying them with vigor for restraining the insolence of the wicked and mildness for nourishing the repentance of the lapsed."

The sentiments of Saint Caesarius, the Bishop of Arles, I would like to make my own: "Pray, dearly beloved, that my episcopacy may be profitable for both you and me. It will be useful for me if I preach what I should, and advantageous for you if you practice what you hear. If I pray for you ceaselessly with perfect love and charity and you do the same for me, with the Lord's help, we shall happily reach eternal bliss together. May Christ deign to grant this."

JUNE 2, 1995

National Bishops' Meetings

Each year, the week before Thanksgiving, the news media focus on an important Catholic event that takes place in our country. This is one of the semiannual meetings of all the Catholic bishops of the United States. For some years the American bishops have been meeting twice a year. In the spring, usually in June, the meeting is held in various cities. In the autumn, however, the meeting always is held in Washington, D.C. In the last several years the meetings of the bishops have been televised live by EWTN, the Catholic television network founded and controlled by Mother Angelica.

Most of a bishops' meeting is held in the glare of the television lights. However, there usually are one or more executive sessions from which the press and the observers are absent. In general there are a large number of items the bishops are required to consider each time they meet. These can range from approving liturgical translations from the Latin to issuing statements on various contemporary matters. These items can even involve discussing the very structure of the gathering of bishops itself.

NCCB–USCC

The same American bishops actually operate, when they meet, as two groups. One is called the National Conference of Catholic Bishops

(NCCB). This is a canonical organization, consisting only of the bishops themselves, and is mainly concerned with matters that are almost exclusively ecclesiastical, such as priestly formation and vocations.

The other group is called the United States Catholic Conference (USCC). This is a civilly incorporated organization. In its committee structures it contains religious men and women and laymen and women, as well as the bishops. It is registered as a federal lobby and represents the bishops before the legislative and executive branches of our national government. When the bishops meet, they "change hats" during the meeting, sometimes acting as the NCCB and sometimes as the USCC. The USCC concerns itself with matters that basically overlap with secular concerns, such as education, immigration matters, federal regulations, and tax laws.

Among the issues currently being debated by the American bishops is the question of whether to retain this twofold structure or to simplify it by joining the NCCB and the USCC formally into one. As a matter of fact, the same staff members often serve both organizations, at least at the top executive level.

Of course, there can be no question but that a national bishops' conference is necessary. This was ordered by the Second Vatican Council, which, in its decree on bishops, stated:

> Episcopal conferences, already established in many nations, have furnished outstanding proofs of a more fruitful apostolate. Therefore, this most sacred Synod considers it supremely opportune everywhere that bishops belonging to the same nation or region form an association and meet together at fixed times. Thus, when insights of prudence and experience have been shared and views exchanged, there will emerge a holy union of energies in the service of the common good of the churches.[4]

HISTORY

The Second Vatican Council called these episcopal conferences "a kind of council in which the bishops of a given nation or territory jointly exercise their pastoral office by way of promoting the greater good which the Church offers mankind".[5] In the United States our Catholic bishops had been meeting for many years in the forerunner of the

---

[4] *Christus Dominus*, no. 37.
[5] Ibid., no. 38.

NCCB-USCC, which was called the National Catholic Welfare Conference (NCWC). This originated during the First World War out of what was called the National Catholic War Council.

Certainly, the idea of local bishops meeting together goes back to the earliest days of the Church. Following the example of the apostles, whose successors they are (Acts 1:15–26; 15:1–29), bishops' council meetings took place in various places to combat heresy and religious error, to enforce Church order and discipline, and to answer important pastoral questions.

In the history of the Catholic Church in our own country, there have been important meetings of the bishops of various ecclesiastical provinces, as well as plenary assemblies of all the U.S. bishops. These were usually held in Baltimore, our primatial see. It was these meetings that gave us the Baltimore Catechism and the naming of the Blessed Virgin Mary, under her title of the Immaculate Conception, as the patroness of our land.

Episcopal conferences, as such, have very limited authority over a very small number of matters. These matters have to be passed by a two-thirds vote of a bishops' conference and confirmed by the Holy See if they are to have validity. Of course, when Catholic bishops, either alone or gathered in a meeting, teach the authentic doctrine of the Church, all Catholics are bound to listen and obey. Under all circumstances, the bishops' views should be met with respect and docility. However, there is a legitimate debate as to whether the efforts of the bishops' conference to apply the gospel message to current events (for instance, the pastoral messages and letters on war and peace and on the economy) enjoy any more authority than individual bishops choose to give them.

When we hear about the meetings of the NCCB-USCC, we should pray fervently for our bishops, who need and depend upon our prayers for their apostolic work. We should also learn about what the bishops are doing and saying from sources of genuine and true information. Often the secular news media misunderstand, distort, misinterpret, and even misinform the public about these meetings.

OCTOBER 17, 1995

The Cardinals

The primary advisors, consultants, and assistants to the pope are the cardinals of the Holy Roman Church. It is usually the cardinals who are placed by the pope in charge of the various departments of the Roman Curia. The sacred college (or group) of cardinals is a man-made organization that has grown up over the centuries and has assumed an important role in the order and organization of the Catholic Church.

Jesus Christ, Who founded the Catholic Church, established certain constitutive elements in that Church, including the papacy and the arrangement of Holy Orders in the ranks of deacons, priests, and bishops. However, He left many other organizational arrangements and matters of Church order and discipline to the Church herself to set forth as time and circumstances might indicate.

Almost from the beginning, the Bishop of Rome, who is the Successor of Saint Peter and, therefore, the visible head of the Universal Church, relied on some of the chief pastors of the parishes in Rome for advice, counsel, and help. When the See of Peter became vacant by the death of a pope, the priests and people of Rome, along with the bishops from the neighboring dioceses, would gather together and elect a successor. As the centuries went on, this became too difficult and unwieldy because of the larger number of Catholics and the factionalism that such elections reflected. Consequently, since the time of the pontificate of Pope Alexander III (1159–1181), the election of the pope has been restricted to the chief pastors in Rome and to the neighboring bishops.

The college of cardinals has undergone many changes and developments over the years. However, the popes have all retained this institution, with various modifications, and have continued to use the cardinals as those empowered, when a pope dies, to elect his successor. This is the reason why, when the pope names a man a cardinal, he also names him the titular (or nominal) pastor of a church in Rome or else names him a titular (or nominal) bishop of one of the seven nearby dioceses, called the suburbican sees. Obviously, these dioceses and parishes actually have Italian bishops and pastors who take care of them directly on a day-to-day basis.

Nevertheless, when the Bishop of Rome dies, it is in their capacity as nearby bishops or as pastors in Rome that the cardinals gather together in a conclave (which means "with the key") to select a successor to Saint Peter. To become pope, the only qualification is that one be a male Catholic. Were someone elected who was not a priest, he would have to be ordained a priest and consecrated a bishop immediately. De facto, the cardinals have almost always in recent centuries chosen one of their own number as pope.

The number of cardinals has varied significantly throughout history. Current Church law states the number at one hundred and twenty under the age of eighty. The pope, of course, can dispense with such laws as he chooses. Since the time of Pope Paul VI, the cardinals entitled to vote for a new pope are only those under eighty years of age.

Over the course of time, the cardinals have varied in their ecclesiastical status. Some popes have named laymen to be cardinals, in addition to naming bishops, priests, deacons, or men in minor Orders. Pope John XXIII legislated that all cardinals had to have the rank of bishop, but our present Holy Father has made some exceptions to this rule and has nominated as cardinals some men who have remained priests and have not been named bishops.

There are three ranks of cardinals within the sacred college, cardinal bishops, cardinal priests, and cardinal deacons. The cardinals in each of these ranks are personally (for the most part) archbishops. There are six cardinal bishops, who are the titular heads of the suburbican sees. The senior cardinal bishop (besides being head of his own see) is always the titular Bishop of Ostia and the president of the sacred college of cardinals. The senior cardinal deacon is the one who announces to the world the name of a new pope. The junior cardinal deacon is the one who locks the doors from the inside at consistories and in the Sistine Chapel in conclaves.

The pope can and does name as cardinals whomever he chooses. He is bound by no rules or laws in this regard. In recent centuries it has become customary for the pope to nominate the archbishops of large and important archdioceses throughout the world, such as Milan, Vienna, Brussels, Armagh, Westminster, New York, Los Angeles, Madrid, Munich, and Prague. In our century there has been a noticeable effort on the part of the popes to internationalize the college of cardinals and to include significant numbers from the continents of Africa, Asia, and South America.

Papal nuncios or apostolic delegates to the larger countries in North and South America and Europe are often named cardinals and summoned back to work in the Roman Curia, although there have been exceptions. For instance, Cardinal William Baum, who was the Archbishop of Washington, became the Major Penitentiary in the Holy See. Cardinal Edmund Szoka was the Archbishop of Detroit but was named the President of the Prefecture for Economic Affairs of the Holy See.

The distinctive bright red color of a cardinal's robes is meant to remind him of his pledge to shed his blood if necessary in defense of the Holy See. (The color has given rise to the names of birds and of sports teams.) The word "cardinal" comes from the Latin word *cardo*, meaning "hinge". Pope Eugenius IV wrote, "As the door of a house turns on its hinges, so on the cardinalate does the Apostolic See, the door of the whole Church, rest and find support."

FEBRUARY 2, 1996

The Order of Presbyters

Thomas à Kempis in the *Imitation of Christ* remarks, "O how great and honorable is the office of the priest to whom is given the task to effect the consecration of the Lord of majesty in sacred words, whose lips praise Him, whose hands hold Him, whose tongue receives Him, and whose ministry it is to bring Him to others!" Saint Vincent Ferrer said, "The Blessed Virgin opened heaven only once, but the priest does so at every Mass." Saint John Chrysostom preached, "Speak not of the royal purple, of diadems, of golden vestments. These are but shadows, frailer than the flowers of springtime, compared with the power and privileges of the priesthood."

The sublime dignity of the priesthood should be a source of constant awe to all believers, especially at this time of the year, when young men, from our own families and parishes, called by God to the order of presbyters, find their vocations authenticated and vindicated in the sacrament of Holy Orders. The Catechism of the Council of Trent says, "They only can be certain they are called by God who have been called by the lawful bishops of the Church." Pope John Paul II, following the teaching of his predecessors and of the Second Vatican Council, writes that the share in Christ's priesthood received in Holy Orders differs not only in degree but in essence from that share in the same priesthood of Jesus which is possessed by all the baptized faithful. Thus the words about priests being "chosen from among men . . . and appointed on behalf of men" take on their full meaning (Heb 5:1).

The Epistle to the Hebrews contains words that are at the same time consoling and frightening to every priest. "He can deal gently with the ignorant and wayward, since he himself is beset with weakness. Because of this he is bound to offer sacrifice for his own sins as well as for those of the people" (Heb 5:2–3). Cardinal John Henry Newman wrote, "It seems that angels alone should be appointed to this high office of Catholic priest. Yet, God has sent forth for the ministry of reconciliation, not angels but men. He has sent not beings of some unknown nature and some strange blood, but men of your own bone and your own flesh. He has appointed sons of Adam, men like unto us, exposed to the same temptations."

Cardinal Suhard wrote, "You must never forget that priests are and remain men. God does not perform a miracle to wrest them from the human state." Saint Laurence Giustiniani said, "The priestly dignity is great, but great also is the burden."

Father Leo Trese once wrote, "Whatever his admittedly human faults may be, of this you can be sure regarding your parish priest: He does love his people and worry about them, because he can never forget that one day he must give an accounting to his Master for each of you."

Cardinal Cushing said, "Catholics should beg God to shield their priests from every danger, to drive far from them the onslaughts of the infernal enemy. They should ask each day that their priests may increase in virtue and that their imperfections melt away in the heat of divine love." As the old prayer for priests says, "Keep them and O remember, Lord, they have no one but Thee; yet they have only human hearts, with human frailty."

The *Catechism of the Catholic Church* asserts the universal and ancient belief of the Church that the ordained priest acts in the person of Christ. It quotes Saint Thomas Aquinas, "Christ is the source of all priesthood: the priest of the old law was a figure of Christ, and the priest of the new law acts in the person of Christ" (CCC 1548). Pope Pius XII wrote, "The minister, by reason of the sacerdotal consecration which he has received, is truly made like to the high priest and possesses the authority to act in the power and place of the Person of Christ Himself."[6]

The *Catechism* goes on to say, "The ministerial priesthood has the task not only of representing Christ—Head of the Church—before the assembly of the faithful, but also of acting in the name of the whole Church when presenting to God the prayer of the Church, and above all when offering the eucharistic sacrifice. 'In the name of the whole Church' does not mean that priests are the delegates of the community. . . . It is because the ministerial priesthood represents Christ that it can represent the Church" (CCC 1553).

The Second Vatican Council notes that presbyters "are consecrated in order to preach the gospel and shepherd the faithful as well as to celebrate divine worship as true priests of the New Testament".[7] Of course, their second great prerogative is to forgive sins, once again in the Person of Christ (Lk 5:20; Jn 20:23).

GRATITUDE

Father William Ryan remarks, "People must forever thank God for the priesthood. Thank Him that He has selected from among your sons and brothers men to appease His divine wrath by offering the perfect sacrifice, men of your own flesh and blood to bring you to God and God to

[6] *Mediator Dei*: AAS, 39 (1947), 548.
[7] *Lumen gentium*, no. 28.

you." Cardinal John Heenan said, "When we consider the gift of the priesthood which God has given to His Church, we know that the longest lifetime would be too short to express fully the gratitude we owe to our Almighty Father."

Cardinal Suhard said:

> Take care of your priests. Help them with their mission of authority and life. Your priests are poor. You must help them live. They have forsaken everything for God and for you, giving up a career comparable or superior to your own. Relieve them of those menial chores that take up their time and strength, much to the detriment of their interior life and ministry. Be generous in providing material assistance. This is partly an act of charity, but most of all it is strict justice. You must take the initiative in supporting the Church. It is not up to your priests to demand it. But, you must not confine your cooperation with your priests to material donations alone. You must create an atmosphere in your parish of spiritual affection for them.

Remember always the words of Saint Vincent de Paul: "Oh how great is a good priest!"

MAY 19, 1995

The Lay Vocation

I

From time to time it is a good exercise to read again what the Second Vatican Council teaches about the vocation to be a lay person in the Catholic Church. The best place to start would be the fourth chapter of the Dogmatic Constitution on the Church (*Lumen gentium*) and then go to the Decree on the Apostolate of the Laity (*Apostolicam actuositatem*), which the Council issued to supplement and emphasize that fourth chapter.

One of the points implicit in what the Council says is that being a layman in the Church is a specific vocation. It is not simply something that happens by default. The Council says, "The term laity is here understood to mean all the faithful except those in Holy Orders and those in a religious state sanctioned by the Church. These faithful are by baptism made one Body with Christ and are established among the People of God. They are in their own way made sharers in the priestly, prophetic, and kingly functions of Christ. They carry out their own part in the mission of the whole Christian People with respect to the world and to the Church."[8] This is the first time in history that an ecumenical council (and there have been twenty-one of them) ever precisely addressed the laity and defined them.

In examining and trying to understand the lay vocation, however, it is necessary to continue with the next chapter (chap. five) in the Dogmatic Constitution, which speaks of the universal call to holiness. Building on the vocation that Jesus gives to each of His disciples (Mt 5:48), this chapter situates the call to be a lay person in the wider vocation of every single Catholic to be holy.

It is quite interesting to notice that the Council places the lay vocation in temporal affairs and in the secular milieu. "The laity, by their very vocation, seek the kingdom of God by engaging in temporal affairs and by ordering them according to the plan of God. They live in the world, that is, in each and in all of the secular professions and occupations. They live in the ordinary circumstances of family and social life, from which the very web of their existence is woven."[9]

The *Catechism of the Catholic Church* says, "The initiative of lay Christians is necessary especially when the matter involves discovering or inventing the means for permeating social, political, and economic realities with the demands of Christian doctrine and life" (CCC 899). Pope Pius XII said, "Lay believers are in the front line of Church life; for them the Church is the animating principle of human society."[10] Saint Thomas Aquinas wrote, "To teach in order to lead others to the faith is the task of every preacher and of every believer."

The Council teaches, "The laity are called in a special way to make the Church present and operative in those places and circumstances where only through them can she become the salt of the earth. Thus every lay person, by virtue of the gifts bestowed upon him, is at the same time a witness and a living instrument of the mission of the Church herself, 'according to the measure of Christ's bestowal' (Eph 4:7)."[11]

While the Council rightly speaks of the secular sphere as independent in some ways from the religious, it was vehement about rejecting secularization. It said that the faithful laity "should learn to distinguish carefully between those rights and duties which are theirs as members of the Church, and those which they have as members of human society". Still they are required "to harmonize the two, remembering that all temporal affairs must be guided by a Christian conscience. For even in

---

[8] *Lumen gentium*, no. 31.
[9] Ibid.
[10] CCC 899, quoting Pius XII, Discourse, February 20, 1946: AAS 38 (1946), 149.
[11] *Lumen gentium*, no. 33.

secular affairs there is no human activity which can be withdrawn from God's dominion." [12]

It is certainly clear that those so-called Catholics who profess to be "personally against abortion, but . . ." are living in contradiction to the Second Vatican Council. The Council says, "While it must be recognized that the temporal sphere is governed by its own principles, since it is properly concerned with the interests of this world, that ominous doctrine must rightly be rejected which attempts to build a society with no regard whatever for religion and which attacks and destroys the religious liberty of its citizens." [13]

The Second Vatican Council teaches:

> With ready Christian obedience, lay people as well as all disciples of Christ should accept whatever their sacred pastors, as representatives of Christ, decree in their role as teachers and rulers in the Church. Let lay people follow the example of Christ, Who, by obedience even at the cost of death, opened to all men the blessed way to the liberty of the children of God. Nor should they omit to pray to God for those placed over them, who keep watch as having to render an account of their souls, so that this account will be rendered with joy and not with grief (Heb 13:17). [14]

There can be little doubt that the lay vocation involves some measure of tension and potential conflict. However, every worthwhile vocation, which contains something of Christian love, has some of these elements in it. The Council tells us:

> All their works, prayers, and apostolic undertakings, family and married life, daily work, relaxation of mind and body, if they are accomplished in the Spirit, indeed, even the hardships of life if patiently borne, all these become spiritual sacrifices acceptable to God through Jesus Christ. In the celebration of the Eucharist these may most fittingly be offered to the Father, along with the Body of the Lord. And so, worshipping everywhere by their holy actions, the laity consecrate the world itself to God, everywhere offering worship by the holiness of their lives. [15]

The call from Christ to be a lay person in the Catholic Church is truly a noble vocation. The Council says, "Each lay Catholic must stand

[12] Ibid., no. 36.
[13] Ibid.
[14] Ibid., no. 37.
[15] Ibid., no. 34.

before the world as a witness to the Resurrection and life of the Lord Jesus and as a sign that God lives."[16]

The Lay Vocation

II

How many times have you seen a sign that says: "No Entry—Employees Only"? The question may occur: Do such signs on doors allow Christ in or keep Him out? The answer rests with the lay people who go in and out of such entrances.

The universal call to holiness, which the Second Vatican Council reiterated with great emphasis,[17] was given by Jesus, our Divine Teacher, to all human beings, including not only the clergy and religious but also the laity. It is a vocation that invites all human beings to separate themselves from sin and be joined to God.

However, the universal vocation to holiness also includes a call to every member of the Catholic Church, the laity as well as the clergy and religious, to diffuse this sanctity or holiness and to share this gift with the rest of humanity. The laity, too, are called to be light (Mt 5:14) and salt (Mt 5:13) and yeast (Mt 13:33) to our world.

By the fact that they are joined to Christ by Baptism and strengthened by the Spirit of God in Confirmation, men and women who are called upon by God to live a lay life are simultaneously given by God a call to holiness and a vocation to the lay apostolate. With what care should conscientious Catholic lay people read and study the decree on the lay apostolate issued by the Second Vatican Council!

The Council teaches that lay people must not only share in the work of bringing the message and grace of Christ to mankind, but, in a special way, they have a particular mission to penetrate and perfect the temporal sphere with the spirit of the gospel of Jesus.

In union and coordination with the clergy and the religious, lay people must keep the goal of the Church's mission in mind as they go about their serious and important task of sanctifying the temporal order. This mission and goal is to give glory to God and effect the salvation of souls.

---

[16] Ibid., no. 38.
[17] See Mt 5:48; *Lumen gentium*, no. 40.

The temporal sphere, which is the special arena of the lay apostolate, includes family and home life, culture, economic affairs, business, industry, labor, commerce, agriculture, arts, the professions, political institutions—local, national, and international—government affairs, education, science, and the communications media.

There used to be a "seminary axiom", given to men preparing for the priesthood in times past, to the effect that unless a priest was bringing fifty converts into the Church each year and sending annually a boy to the seminary and a girl to the convent, he had little reason to congratulate himself. No priest, of course, could possibly accomplish such things without the cooperation and vigorous collaboration of the dedicated laity. What in times past was a "seminary" axiom retains its validity for the clergy even now, but it must be expanded to be an axiom for every Catholic layman as well.

Making converts and fostering priestly and religious vocations are far from exhausting the duties and privileges incumbent upon those given a lay vocation by God. To be effective in their work and mission in the lay apostolate requires that lay people be properly formed and trained—too often this is necessary because they do not know how or, even worse, do not know what Christ and His gospel stand for or teach.

A special closeness to the Catholic Church and her teaching authority places a Catholic in close touch with Christ, for the Church is His Bride and Body. To be any kind of apostle of Christ means being close to Him. As the Council says: "Since Christ in His mission from the Father is the fountain and source of the whole apostolate of the Church, the success of the lay apostolate depends upon the laity's living union with Christ. The perfect example of this type of spiritual and apostolic life is the most Blessed Virgin Mary." [18]

To assist lay people in carrying out their call from God to holiness and apostolic work, there are in the Church numerous lay organizations, groups, societies, movements, leagues, clubs, and the like. Frequently lay people find one of these associations or institutes quite congenial to their temperament and cultural level and are enabled by joining such organizations to carry out better what God has called them to do. In this regard the Second Vatican Council writes:

> The laity who in pursuit of their vocation become members of one of the associations or institutes approved by the Church should faithfully try to adopt the special characteristics of the spiritual life which are proper to these. All lay people should

---

[18] *Apostolicam actuositatem*, no. 4.

hold in high esteem professional skill, family and civic spirit, and all the virtues relating to social behavior, namely honesty, justice, sincerity, kindness and courage, without which there can be no true Christian life.[19]

Those doors with the signs on them that say: "Do Not Enter—Employees Only" should be a challenge and an opportunity for every Catholic layman. Do those doors admit Christ or exclude Him? The answer rests with the Catholic laity.

SEPTEMBER 4, 1992

[19] Ibid.

4

CREEDS AND COUNCILS

Creeds and Symbols in the Church

I

A writer recently commented on the recitation of the Creed at Catholic Sunday and solemnity Masses: "It is as if a freight train were going ever more rapidly downhill, word piling upon uncomprehended word until the bottom of the hill arrives." The same author laments that we Catholics often do not esteem the words of our Creed as the precious treasures they are, words that challenge us to affirm consciously what we believe, words that explain why we gather together to worship on Sundays, words that we are determined to live by and are willing to die for.

A prominent convert to our Catholic faith said that he never allows the anniversary of his reception into the Church to pass without reciting on his knees the words of the Creed. Many of our Catholic ancestors have endured terrible sufferings, even death, for the words that some of us treat lightly and thoughtlessly.

GIVING AND TAKING

Creeds are technically called by another word. These summaries and formulations of our faith, complete or incomplete as they may be, are called "symbols". Used as a synonym for "creed", the word "symbol" does not mean a sign of something but rather, deriving from the Greek word *symbolon*, it means two things joined together.

In olden days, when people made a contract, it was customary to take something valuable, such as a ring or a gold coin, cut it in half, and give half to each party to the contract. On special and solemn occasions both parties would put their halves together to show they were still parties to the contract.

This is basically why the term "symbol" is used in relationship to the creeds. The creeds have two aspects to them. In Latin one aspect was called *traditio*, or the handing over or giving over, and the other aspect was called *reditio*, or the giving back. In ancient times creeds always had these two aspects. One received the Creed and then gave it back. Converts were instructed in the Creed, and then the instructor asked questions to ascertain whether they were in possession of the requisite knowledge.

Students of creedal formularies divide Christian creeds into baptismal creeds, scriptural creeds, declaratory creeds, conciliar creeds (which are usually subdivided into antiheretical and catechetical creeds), and, finally, eucharistic, or worship, creeds. These categories are not compact and autonomous but interpenetrate each other. Thus, scriptural creeds can be baptismal, or declaratory creeds can be conciliar, and so on. There are all kinds of overlappings, since these are not exclusive categories.

BIBLE CREEDS

The first creedal formularies appear in the Bible. Restricting our vision to the New Testament for now, we can notice many places in Sacred Scripture where there are creedal statements. This is especially and easily noticed in the writing of Saint Paul, who included in his letters excerpts from early Christian hymns, which were often creedal hymns. (Much work remains to be done in exploring second- and third-century Christian hymnology.) Saint Paul in his First Epistle to Timothy, for example, writes about Jesus: "He was manifested in the flesh, indicated in the Spirit, seen by angels, preached among the nations, believed on in the world, taken up in glory" (1 Tim 3:16). Here one sees an early Christian hymn that is also a "creed".

Many authors believe that the earliest Christian creeds originated from elaborations of doxologies, which are words of praise that one gives to God ("Praise to the God and Father of our Lord Jesus Christ", and so on).

In his First Epistle to the Corinthians, Saint Paul writes, "I delivered to you . . . what I also received" [notice *traditio* and *reditio*], namely, that Jesus Christ suffered for our sins, that He rose from the dead, and was seen by more than five hundred brothers at one time (1 Cor 15:1–6). (For another instance of *traditio* and *reditio* in the same letter, see 1 Corinthians 11:23.)

Another example of New Testament creeds can be found in Saint Peter's sermons recorded in the Acts of the Apostles. These give a clear outline of the apostolic *kerygma*, or proclamation of the faith. The *kerygma* is a creedal statement that is meant to capture attention and state simply and directly the basis of faith: that Jesus was born and proclaimed by John the Baptist, that He suffered on the Cross, and that God raised Him up again.

The New Testament definitely shows evidence that, from the earliest times, the Catholic Church was in possession of creedal statements that were the required beliefs of her children. The Epistle to the Hebrews says explicitly: "Since then we have a great high priest who has passed through the heavens, Jesus, the Son of God, let us hold fast our confession" (Heb 4:14; also see Heb 10:23; 3:1). Saint Jude writes about the "faith which was once for all delivered to the saints" (Jude 3), which evidently refers to a creed.

Saint Paul presupposes in his letters that the early Christians had a very definite creed: "Hold to the traditions which you were taught . . ." (2 Th 2:15). He talks of the "standard of teaching" he imparted to his converts (Rom 6:17; also see Col 2:7; Eph 4:5).

FIRST BAPTISMAL CREEDS

It appears that the first baptismal creeds are also scriptural creeds, since they are in the New Testament. They are of a declaratory variety. In the Acts of the Apostles, the Ethiopian eunuch makes a declaration of belief before he is baptized, in answer to the question of Saint Philip (Acts 8:36–38), and Lydia makes a creedal declaration before Saint Paul baptizes her (Acts 16:14–15).

It seems that the famous phrase of Saint Paul "If you confess with your lips that Jesus is Lord and believe in your heart that God raised Him from the dead . . ." (Rom 10:9) is part of an ancient baptismal creed. The same can be said for a statement found in the Epistle to the Ephesians (Eph 1:13).

The Book of Revelation and the Epistles of Saint John and Saint Peter are other places in the New Testament rich with texts of early Christian creeds.

Whatever the stage of our Christian development, the creeds, especially the Creed recited at Sunday Mass, should be our object of study, our careful and heartfelt profession, and our rule and guide in life and death.

SEPTEMBER 3, 1993

Creeds and Symbols in the Church

II

Official summaries or formularies of belief are an essential part of Christian history and practice. From the earliest statements in the apostolic preaching cited in the New Testament through the development of baptismal questionnaires to creedal declarations and those creeds set out by ecumenical and regional councils, there is a long and interesting history.

So often we recite the Creed at Mass or at the beginning of our rosary devotions and do so without much thought for the seriousness of the words and without allowing those words to assume the normative aspect in our life they should have.

It may be asked why we did not simply remain with the earliest creedal statements. The answer is that new pastoral situations require a new approach. All creeds in the Catholic Church presume and include the official creeds that have gone before. When new questions are asked, however, or when new attacks are made on the integrity of our faith, it is obvious that a more complete and adequate response must be made in our creeds and symbols. The most recent official creed (the *Credo* of the People of God, composed by Pope Paul VI) includes and amplifies all the official creeds that preceded it.

BAPTISMAL CREEDS

The New Testament gives a strong indication that there was some kind of statement of belief required by candidates for Baptism (see Acts 8:36–38; 16:14–15; Eph 1:13). Four documents that we have from the second century indicate this as well. The document called the "Shepherd of Hermas" speaks about the name of Jesus and how the candidates for Baptism were instructed, presumably by a creed, in the meaning of the name into which they were to be baptized (Acts 8:16). The document called the *Didache* talks about the trinitarian formula of Baptism (Mt 28:19), which is evidently the basis of a creedal statement. Saint Justin Martyr writes about the "instruction" those to be baptized received while they were fasting and praying in preparation for the sacrament. Tertullian speaks about the questions that were asked of the candidates for Baptism to which they were required to make a "fuller reply" than what was laid down in the Gospel.

By the third century, the custom of administering Baptism in interrogatory form was established. Saint Hippolytus lists, around the year 217, the questions asked, which are similar to the words of the Apostles' Creed. Many Christian writers of the third century indicate that by the middle of the century a series of questions, based on the trinitarian formula of Baptism, was well established throughout the Church.

DECLARATORY CREEDS

Saint Ignatius, one of Saint Peter's successors as the Bishop of Antioch, wrote, in the year 116, something that looks very much like a creed. Saint Polycarp, the Bishop of Smyrna, also issued a creedal declaration, based on various phrases found in the First Epistle of Saint Peter. Very early in the fifth century (around the year 404) the Apostles' Creed as we know it (also called the Roman Creed) was in widespread use, especially in connection with the sacrament of Baptism.

Two hundred years before, Saint Hippolytus wrote about the creed handed over (*traditio*) by the bishop to the catechumens just before their Baptism and about the catechumens then giving it back (*reditio*) before they received the sacrament. The "discipline of the secret", necessary because of persecutions and infiltration of pagan informers into the Christian assembly, meant that the creed had to be memorized by the catechumens.

A legend grew up in the fifth century that the Roman Creed had been given to the Church by the apostles. It is true that the Roman Creed (now called the Apostles' Creed) was most likely originally set out in Greek, thus attesting to its antiquity. It is also true that writers such as Saint Justin and Tertullian and Saint Irenaeus spoke of a "rule of faith", or creed, that came from the apostles themselves. However, while some elements of the Apostles' Creed doubtlessly date from apostolic times, it seems clear that the words as we have them come from a later era.

Bishop Rufinus tells us that the Apostles' Creed was already ancient in the year 404, that it was widely used in Rome at baptisms, and that the people listened carefully and would not allow a single word to be changed, "although in other places certain prayers are added to exclude the new and false doctrines of various heretics".

Whenever we recite the great baptismal creed, that is, the Roman or Apostles' Creed, or whenever we renew our baptismal vows and promises, especially at the Easter Vigil, we should remember that we are doing much more than merely declaring our faith publicly. We are joining, in the unity of the Catholic Church, our brothers and sisters throughout the world and throughout the centuries in summarizing the immutable deposit of faith, "once for all delivered to the saints" (Jude 3).

SEPTEMBER 10, 1993

Creeds and Symbols in the Church

III

The first mark of the Church Christ founded is her oneness (Jn 17:11–19). Despite variety, diversity, and pluralism, the followers of Christ must be one. Of the various ways in which the Catholic Church is one (in government and in worship), the first is her unity in doctrine. She is the custodian of the deposit of faith, the fullness of divine revelation (in Sacred Scripture and Sacred Tradition).

This deposit of faith, confided in a special way to the authentic interpretation that can be given to it only by the successors of the apostles exercising their teaching authority, is manifested in the official creeds of the Church basically on two occasions, namely, when the faith is challenged by error or defect (heresy) and when there is a call to teach and catechize the faithful.

CONCILIAR CREEDS

From the time of the first ecumenical council in Nicaea, in the year 325, a custom arose for the council fathers in these gatherings to draw up a creed. This was a means by which the unity in faith of the bishops gathered in the council could be publicly proclaimed and a test of the orthodoxy of believers could be set forth. Not only worldwide meetings of bishops (ecumenical councils) were marked by creeds, but even regional and provincial gatherings set out creedal statements, often to reiterate the unity of the Church in doctrine. Sometimes creeds were connected with ecumenical councils but not directly ordered by them, as, for instance, the Creed of Saint Athanasius, the Creed of the Council of Trent, the *Credo* of the People of God.

Legitimate ecumenical councils (there have been twenty-one in the history of the Catholic Church) have incorporated the creeds of the previous councils into their own. In other words, once a creed is officially set out by the teaching authority of the Church, it never can be repudiated or recalled, since it manifests unchangeable doctrine in the deposit of faith. Often, however, there is a different focus or emphasis, especially when new errors, problems, denials, or doubts arise in the world in regard to Catholic teaching.

The Nicene Creed, for example, demanded that Catholics proclaim, as the eternal faith of the Church, that Jesus is "consubstantial" ("one in being") with God the Father, in answer to the heresy of Arius, who said the Word is a creature and not the Creator. The First Council of Constantinople, in the year 381, gave a fuller expression of faith to the Church by asserting more forcefully the divinity of the third Person of the Blessed Trinity. This is the origin of the Creed that we, in the Latin Rite of the Catholic Church, recite at our Sunday Masses. It is called the Nicene-Constantinople Creed.

CATECHETICAL USAGE

There can be no doubt that ecumenical councils and popes have constantly used the creeds as catechetical devices, structuring much of their instruction and religious education around creedal statements. It is not only to distinguish orthodox from heterodox doctrine that the official creeds have been used, but they are used as the skeleton of the catechism. This is clear even today in the *Catechism of the Catholic Church*, issued by Pope John Paul II. There the Creed, along with the Commandments, the Sacraments, the Lord's Prayer, and the virtues, is used as the basic foundation of the entire *Catechism*.

All Catholics, but especially parents and teachers, could profitably enhance their work with the young by themselves obtaining and studying the texts of the creeds themselves, especially the *Credo of the People of God*, by Pope Paul VI, the Athanasian Creed, the Creed of the Council of Trent, and the Anti-Modernist Oath. Parish priests can tell people where such texts can be found.

EUCHARISTIC CREEDS

In the fifth and sixth centuries the custom arose of incorporating the recitation of the Creed into the Mass. This was done in some areas of the world to warn people about erroneous and false doctrines and untrue religions that were rising here and there, as well as to strengthen the faith of Catholic people in the words of the Gospel, before receiving Holy Communion.

Since the words of the official creeds of the Church are considered by the Church herself as infallible statements of the faith, these summaries of our faith are very suitably recited by the liturgical assembly, convoked as it is by Christ and His Church, to worship the Father through Him in union with the Holy Spirit. In that recitation, now prescribed by liturgical regulations for Sundays and solemnities, we see and hear a manifestation of the unity of the Church in her fundamental beliefs. We proclaim in the words of the Creed our oneness with Christ and with each other in the Holy Spirit.

With what reverence ought we to receive not only the Creed we recite at Mass but all the official creeds of the Church! With what diligence ought those words to be respected, studied, and loved! We receive the Creed (*traditio*) from Christ and His Holy Spirit acting in the Church. When we say or sing its precious words (*reditio*), we activate the gift of supernatural faith we received at Baptism, we emphasize our unity in doctrine and belief, and we express our gratitude for the ineffable treasure of divine revelation.

SEPTEMBER 17, 1993

Councils

I

Citing the Second Vatican Council, the *Catechism* states: " 'The college of bishops exercises power over the universal Church in a solemn manner in an ecumenical council' (Code of Canon Law, can. 337 §1). But, 'there never is an ecumenical council which is not confirmed or at least recognized as such by Peter's successor' [*Lumen gentium*, no. 22]" (CCC 884). Following the example of the apostles (Acts 15:6–29), the bishops of the Catholic Church, who are the legitimate successors of the apostles, have gathered together from around the world for an ecumenical council twenty-one times since the days of Christ.

The most recent such gathering took place in the Basilica of St. Peter in the Vatican from 1963 to 1965 and goes by the well-known name "The Second Vatican Council". Traditionally, councils have been named after the locality in which they were held. In current Church law the convoking of such a council is the prerogative of the pope alone, and the latest of the twenty-one councils have all been brought together by the command of the Bishop of Rome. Earlier councils, however, were summoned sometimes on another basis, such as a call from the Roman emperor. Their work had no validity, of course, until or unless confirmed by the pope.

The historian Philip Hughes writes:

> The General Council is a purely human arrangement whereby a divinely founded institution functions in a particular way for a particular purpose. That divinely founded thing is the "teaching Church", the "Magisterium", that is, the Pope and the diocesan Bishops in communion with him teaching the faithful and world. This teaching is an activity of the Catholic Church

which is continuous, never ceasing, whereas General Councils have sat for at most thirty years. The Council is an exceptional phenomenon in the life of the Church, and usually it appears in connection with some great crisis in that life.

VATICAN II

The Fathers of the Second Vatican Council saw themselves as standing in the line of tradition of the previous general councils of the Church. They said, officially and explicitly: "Following in the footsteps of the Councils of Trent and of Vatican I, this present council wishes to set forth authentic teaching about divine revelation."[1] These kinds of phrases were used again and again in the Council's documents. In no sense did the Second Vatican Council intend to repudiate or change the teaching of the previous ecumenical councils. This year of 1995 may be a good time to remember this, since it is the 450th anniversary of the Council of Trent.

Sometimes, exercising its primacy in union with the pope, an ecumenical council enjoys the charism of infallibility. However, by explicit declaration of the pope, supported by the Fathers of the Council themselves, the Second Vatican Council did not claim this charism, except when reiterating the infallible teaching of previous councils and popes. The thrust of Vatican II, both under Pope John XXIII and Pope Paul VI, was that it was to be a pastoral and disciplinary council, concerned with working to apply better the perennial and unchanging doctrine of the Catholic faith to the conditions of our time.

OFFICIAL DOCUMENTS

The Second Vatican Council promulgated sixteen official texts in 103,014 official words. Unfortunately, these official texts and words remain largely unread even by many Catholics. More unfortunate still is the fact that much silliness, error, and nonsense is often falsely attributed to the Second Vatican Council. Even many of the "changes" in the Church, including some of those in the liturgy, while sometimes official and good and important, are unrelated to the Second Vatican Council.

Before, during, and after the Second Vatican Council, there was a sort of "para-council", consisting of lobbyists, journalists, experts, ecumenists, and assorted hangers-on. Some commentators and media types even to this day erroneously attribute to the real and genuine Second Vatican

---

[1] *Dei Verbum*, no. 1.

Council the productions of this "para-council". Under a rubric called "the spirit of Vatican II", much falsehood and confusion has managed to camouflage itself. Just like the inspired word of God itself in the Bible, the Second Vatican Council often can be read out of context and sometimes misinterpreted.

The solution to the problems resulting from such a situation is for informed Catholics to read and study the authentic work of the Second Vatican Council from the official texts. In modern official documents of the Magisterium, most notably the *Catechism of the Catholic Church*, the genuine spirit of Vatican II can be found and learned.

The official documents of the Second Vatican Councils have varied titles, indicating that they do not all have the same value. In studying this council, this fact should be kept in mind. The most important documents are the two *dogmatic constitutions*, one on the Church and the other on divine revelation. These are followed in dignity by two other constitutions, the Constitution on the Liturgy and the Constitution on the Church in the Modern World.

Next in importance are the *decrees* by which the Council intended to apply what it taught in the constitutions. Finally, of lesser significance, are what are designated *declarations*. This hierarchy of importance should be borne in mind by students of the Council's documents.

I was a student-priest in Rome during the last session of the Second Vatican Council and had the privilege of acting as an usher in the aula for some of the time. I also count it as a unique honor to have been present at the closing of the Council on December 8, 1965. That was an ecclesiastical event of this century, now drawing to an end, that will undoubtedly live in significance in the history of the Catholic Church until the Lord returns in the clouds in glory and majesty. It is an event worthy of our attention and study.

JANUARY 27, 1995

Councils

II

All the Catholic bishops of the world taken together are called the "college", or body, of bishops. Twenty-one times in the history of the Church the bishops constituting this body have gathered in one place at one time on official business. These gatherings are called ecumenical councils. The Second Vatican Council teaches us about such general Councils. The Dogmatic Constitution on the Church says, "This college has supreme and full authority over the universal Church, but this power cannot be exercised without the agreement of the Roman Pontiff."[2]

Ecumenical councils can issue a large variety of utterances. Some are solemn and even infallible (that is, inerrant) declarations about the contents of our faith, what is contained in divine revelation. Some are condemnations of religious and moral error. Some are pious exhortations, while others are disciplinary laws and decrees. When these latter coincide with the divine law, they are unchangeable, while when they are dealing merely with human laws, they are subject to change and variance. Some of the councils have issued all of these various kinds of utterances, while others have confined themselves to one or the other type of focus. Some councils were particularly keen on clearly defining the limits of the Church's boundaries and of her faith. Others had a different emphasis.

PRIMACY

Some teachings of our Catholic faith are difficult for non-Catholics to grasp, and many are wont to confuse the terminology used in expressing them. For instance, many non-Catholics (and some Catholics, too) do not know the difference between the doctrine of the virginal conception and birth of Jesus and His Mother's own immaculate conception. This is also the case with the terms "primacy" and "infallibility".

The pope and an ecumenical council, when it is in session and joined to him and operating under his approval and authority, exercise primacy in the Catholic Church, that is, they operate with the authority bestowed on them by God the Holy Spirit (Mt 18:17–18; Jn 20:21–22). Catholics must give them obedience and reverence and follow their commands.

Not every legitimate exercise of primacy in the Church, however, enjoys the benefit of infallibility. Infallibility is a special gift that God has given to the Catholic Church to keep her from teaching error in doctrine and morals. Sometimes primatial declarations of popes and ecumenical councils are made in a solemn way that shows they are linked profoundly to the revelation God has given to the Church to preserve unmutilated and free from all error. Thus they are irreformable and come under the charism of infallibility. At other times utterances made from the position of primacy by popes and councils require our obedience and acquiescence but are not beyond further refinement and change by these authorities themselves.

---

[2] *Lumen gentium*, no. 22.

INFALLIBILITY

Throughout history, ecumenical councils have made declarations and adopted positions that are infallible. This means that God Himself guards such conciliar actions from mistakes and error. This does not mean that ecumenical councils can add or subtract anything from God's revelation. Public revelation has ended with the last echo of the Christ-event, because in Jesus God spoke His final, definitive, and exhaustive Word, until the Lord returns to earth. Sacred Scripture and Sacred Tradition, as transmitted by the Magisterium of the Catholic Church, are God's word, and this, like God Himself, is unchangeable. Infallibility is neither inspiration nor a new revelation.

The charism or gift from God of infallibility does not have anything to do with the moral worth of those who occupy a position of authority in the Church, either as pope or as bishop. Nor does it involve the prudence or pastoral suitability of certain ecclesial actions or words. It does rest upon the Bishop of Rome when he speaks *ex-cathedra* about faith or morals and also upon the moral unanimity of the believing Church, that is, when all the Catholics throughout the world believe the same doctrine or moral teaching. (Obviously, this has nothing to do with other kinds of believing than that about faith and morals. There may have been a time when most Catholics thought the world was flat!)

The gift of infallibility also rests upon bishops, not individually, of course, but when they teach (with, under, and never against the Bishop of Rome) the same doctrine or moral instruction all together, either scattered throughout the earth or gathered in an ecumenical council. There is, in such a case, a special action of God that prevents them from teaching false or incorrect doctrine or morals, something different from what God Himself has said.

Every Catholic believes that when the Church Christ founded is engaged in her task of teaching His truths she is preserved from teaching falsely. This is because those who are her official teachers, the successors of the apostles, have this promised divine guidance (Mt 28:18–20) both when teaching the same thing over the planet and when gathered in one place in an ecumenical council.

As Cardinal John Henry Newman expressed it, "Every Catholic holds that the Christian dogmas were in the Church from the time of the Apostles; that they were ever in their substance what they are now; that they existed before the formulas were publicly adopted, in which, as time went on, they were defined and recorded, and that, such formulas, when sanctioned by due ecclesiastical acts, are binding on the faith of Catholics and have dogmatic authority."

The *Catechism* says, "To proclaim the faith and to plant his reign, Christ sends his apostles and their successors. He gives them a share in his own mission. From him they receive the power to act in His Person" (CCC 935).

5

CATECHISM, CATECHETICS, AND CATHOLIC EDUCATION

Recommended Reading

Too often Catholic people in our country receive information about their own religion from the secular media exclusively. They are restricted in their news intake to media sound bites, which are, at best, deficient and, therefore, distorting and, at worst, misrepresenting and deceiving. In their eagerness to be "fair", the media often find, for every authoritative Catholic teaching, some dissenter or other claiming to be "Catholic". Uninformed Catholics sometimes are misled into thinking that such dissent actually represents a substantial segment of the Catholic population, or that one can continue to be a Catholic in good standing while refusing to accept certain doctrinal or moral teachings of the Church.

Some organizations are very good at fomenting such distorted views. For instance, Planned Parenthood, an inherently evil organization founded by the hateful racist Margaret Sanger, often tries to pretend that one could support or belong to its wicked group without giving up membership in the Catholic Church.

A GRAND ENCYCLICAL

The encyclical *The Splendor of Truth*, a panoramic view of current moral theology by our Holy Father, deserves an "eyes-on" view by all Catholic adults, who should not allow the secular media to do their thinking for them. It is a sublime document, which, however, is not easy reading. It requires thought and concentration.

The Splendor of Truth (*Veritatis splendor*) is addressed to the Catholic bishops of the world, but, obviously, it is intended to be read by everyone. Some of the great themes that it treats are the relationship of morality and faith; the relationship of freedom, conscience, and law; and the relationship of liberty, tradition, and the teaching authority of the Catholic Church.

What makes the encyclical unique is best expressed in the words of our Holy Father himself: "This is the first time, in fact, that the Magisterium of the Church has set forth in detail the fundamental elements of this teaching, and presented the principles for the pastoral discernment necessary in practical and cultural situations which are complex and even crucial."[1] Another unique feature of this document is its treatment of dissent, which it says is "opposed to ecclesial communion and to a correct understanding of the hierarchical constitution of the People of God."[2]

From a biblical perspective, from a theological and traditional perspective, and from a pastoral perspective, this document of the Pope cries out to be read. Ask your parish priest where to obtain a copy. You will be the spiritually richer for the time you spend with it.

THE CATECHISM

The *Catechism of the Catholic Church* is another treasure that every thinking Catholic should want to read and study with the greatest care. It was a best seller in its English edition even before publication. On the first day of its publication in French, more than four thousand copies were sold in the Paris airport alone!

Not just parents and teachers but all Catholics will profit immensely from owning and studying the *Catechism*. Like the encyclical just mentioned, this is not a document one simply curls up with on cold winter nights (it is more than eight hundred pages in length!), but it will serve as a standard and authoritative Catholic reference work for years to come.

The *Catechism* is divided into four basic sections. The first and largest section has to do with what we Catholics believe. This part is structured on the twelve articles of the Apostles' Creed. Following our faith is our worship and our means of sanctification, and, therefore, the second part deals with the seven sacraments. Belief and worship have consequences in how we live and act. Hence, the third part is based on the Ten Commandments of the Decalogue. It is this section that the media show interest in, because of "new sins".

There are no "new" sins, of course. However, in applying perennial and absolute moral principles and values to new cultural situations, the *Catechism* treats of issues that previous catechisms did not confront. Answers to many questions can be found, including such things as a treatment of the death penalty for criminals, the ethics of evading taxes, and

[1] *Veritatis splendor*, no. 115.
[2] Ibid., no. 113.

so on. As Pope John Paul II writes: "The contents are often expressed in new ways in order to respond to the questions of our age."

The final part of the *Catechism* treats the life of prayer and virtue, building on the skeleton provided by the seven petitions of the Our Father. Prayer should not only be fundamental to Christian existence, but it should accompany our reading of the *Catechism*.

Adult Catholics certainly want to take their faith seriously. The content of that faith would be much better understood if each Catholic were to take in hand the encyclical *The Splendor of Truth* and the *Catechism* and give some serious and quality time and attention to both.

In the end, both of these documents have to do with a person, the Person, as Pope John Paul II writes, "of Jesus of Nazareth, the only Son of the Father, full of grace and of truth, Who suffered and died for us, and Who now, after rising from the dead, is living with us forever".

OCTOBER 8, 1993

A Best Seller

It is very seldom that a book makes the best seller list even before its publication. However, that was the situation with the *Catechism of the Catholic Church*. It is a bestseller in German, Italian, French, and Spanish. In the United States, publishers did an initial press run of five hundred thousand copies in English, with more than two hundred fifty thousand copies presold.

There can be no doubt that the *Catechism* should occupy a place of honor in every Catholic household, right next to the family Bible. However, the *Catechism* should not just gather dust on the bookshelf but should be read and reread carefully and thoughtfully, along with that family Bible. It is a formidable book, of 803 pages and almost thirty thousand references. But it is written in plain, uncomplicated language that can be grasped by anyone of average intelligence.

There are a large number of books and commentaries on the *Catechism*. Some are good and some are bad. The best idea is for adult Catholics to procure a copy of the *Catechism* for themselves and read it, not allowing so-called experts or so-called theologians to do their thinking for them. Our Holy Father, Pope John Paul II, says that this new *Catechism* is meant to "guard the faith carefully". The Pope himself approved the text of this *Catechism* on June 25, 1992, and wrote the apostolic constitution entitled *The Deposit of Faith* that inaugurated it on October 11, 1992.

Just as the well-known Baltimore Catechism was a national adaptation of the 1566 Catechism of Pope Saint Pius V, so many national and local catechisms will be based on this new large, or major, *Catechism*. This *Catechism* follows the ancient catechetical structure, using four parts: the Creed, the sacraments, the Commandments, and the Our Father. As our Holy Father writes: "In reading the *Catechism of the Catholic Church*, we can perceive the wonderful unity of the mystery of God, his saving will, as well as the central place of Jesus Christ, the only-begotten Son of God, sent by the Father, made man in the womb of the Blessed Virgin Mary by the power of the Holy Spirit, to be our Savior. Having died and risen, Christ is always present in His Church, especially in the sacraments; He is the source of our faith, the model of Christian conduct, and the Teacher of our prayer."[3]

The chronically ill and care givers for the sick often complain about the quality of some of the religious reading provided in our times, reading of sometimes questionable orthodoxy and soundness. The *Catechism* will provide the answer to an often asked question: What does the Catholic Church really believe and hold? The Pope tells us that this *Catechism* is a "valid and legitimate instrument" and also is a "sure norm for teaching the faith".[4]

The *Catechism* will provide hours of fine spiritual reading, which can be recommended to the infirm and the homebound. It would be beautiful if those who are dedicated to concern for the sick would themselves volunteer to read from this book to those who may be handicapped or otherwise unable to use this volume themselves. Members of the Apostolate of Suffering may want to offer some of their pains and sorrows to God for the intention that this *Catechism* will have a lasting and beneficial resonance in the life of Christ's Catholic Church.

The *Catechism* itself says:"Because she is our mother, [the Church] is also our teacher in the faith" (CCC 169). Archbishop Levada writes: "In the Catechism the Church intends to make a presentation of all and only that which she regards as the patrimony of Catholic doctrine about faith and morals, which the Christian faithful need to believe and practice as Catholics."

[3] John Paul II, *Fidei Depositum*, no. 2.
[4] Ibid., no. 3

The *Catechism of the Catholic Church*

It is named, simply, *Catechism of the Catholic Church*. Already published and a bestseller in French, Spanish, German, Italian, Portuguese, it will be available in English next June 22, in bookstores all over the English-speaking world. (The paperback price will be $19.95.) Printers in the United States have scheduled an initial press run of 400,000 copies.

Every thinking Catholic adult will want to have a copy of this *Catechism*, not simply to own, but to read and study. It is a compendium of the Catholic faith and should rank next to the Holy Bible itself on family bookshelves. Pope John Paul II said: "The Catechism explains [once more the fundamental and essential contents of Catholic faith and morality] in the light of the Council as [they are] believed, celebrated, lived, and prayed by the Church".[5] Again, he said that this *Catechism* is a "sure and authentic reference text for teaching Catholic doctrine".[6]

This is the first new catechism issued by the Holy See since the *Roman Catechism* was issued by Pope Saint Pius V in 1566. (This is often called *The Catechism of the Council of Trent*.) Although the Holy See has issued some important catechetical documents in recent years, most notably the apostolic exhortation of our Holy Father entitled *Catechesi tradendae* and the *General Catechetical Directory*, no catechism has been published by the Apostolic See for centuries.

There is a timeless and unchanging element in our Catholic faith. As Cardinal John Henry Newman puts it: "Every Catholic holds that the Christian dogmas were in the Church from the time of the apostles; that they were in their substance what they are now; that they existed before the formulas were publicly adopted, in which, as time went on, they were defined and recorded; and that such formulas, when sanctioned by due ecclesiastical acts, are binding on the faith of Catholics and have dogmatic authority."

In the autumn of 1985, however, at a meeting of the international synod of bishops in Rome, Cardinal Bernard Law, Archbishop of Boston, suggested that the time had come for a new and definitive catechism for the entire Church, which could promote unity among Catholics in the face of confusion in some minds brought about by modern culture and "changes" in the Church and which could serve as an authoritative witness to the oneness of Catholic belief and practice throughout the world. This suggestion was passed on to the Pope, who

---

[5] John Paul II, "Catechism Is Truly a Gift to the Church", *L'Osservatore Romano* 49 (December 9, 1992): 1.

[6] John Paul II, *Fidei depositum* (October 11, 1992), no. 3.

set up a commission, headed by Cardinal Joseph Ratzinger, to formulate this catechism. The bishops of the Universal Church were all consulted, and the finished product was ultimately approved by the Holy Father and promulgated by an apostolic constitution on October 11, 1992.

This *Catechism* is not meant to be a textbook for children or youth. Available, valuable, and extremely important for all Catholics, its 803 pages are directed mainly to bishops, priests, catechists, teachers, and parents. It is what tradition calls a "large" or "major" catechism, which is to serve as the basis for local and national "small" or "minor" catechisms.

The Baltimore Catechism is an example of a minor catechism. It was drawn up and issued by Cardinal Gibbons of Baltimore in 1885 at the behest of the United States Catholic bishops who met in 1884 in the Third Plenary Council of Baltimore. It was based on the *Roman Catechism* of 1566. The U.S. bishops decided to put it into a question-and-answer format. It had the advantage of solid orthodoxy and offered a good skeletal outline of the Catholic faith. Its major disadvantages are its failure to answer some modern questions in the light of the faith, its arrangement, and its pedagogical defects. It served a great purpose, however, and trained rather well many generations of American Catholics.

The *Catechism of the Catholic Church* will be the basis for future local and national catechisms, as was the *Roman Catechism* for the Baltimore Catechism. It is a benchmark and solid anchor in these times when sometimes even good and well-instructed Catholics find themselves confused by discordant voices that occasionally come even from misleading teachers and clergymen.

The *Catechism* follows the traditional catechetical structure, which appears to date from the time of the apostles. There are four headings: the Apostles' Creed, the sacraments, the Ten Commandments, and the Lord's Prayer. Thirty-nine percent of the text is devoted to the Creed, that is, what Catholics must believe; 27 percent to the Commandments, that is, how Catholics must act; 23 percent to the Mass, the sacraments, and the Church, that is, where Catholics encounter and are joined to Christ; and 11 percent to prayer.

Bishop Christoph Schönborn, the Auxiliary Bishop of Vienna, and the general editor of the new *Catechism*, said: "*The Catechism of the Catholic Church* is to serve the guardianship and the transmission of the deposit of faith. The Church has the duty, but also the right to express the fullness, the riches, and the beauty of 'the faith that was once and for all entrusted to the saints' (see Jude 3)."

The *Catechism*: A Privileged Gift

The *Catechism* owes its remote beginnings to the conscientious concern of the Church's pastors over the last several decades that the mission Jesus gave to the Catholic Church He founded be faithfully carried out.

In January 1983, in Paris, Cardinal Joseph Ratzinger reminded his listeners in a catechetical conference that "catechesis, the handing on of the faith, has been from the beginning a basic responsibility of the Church, and it must continue to be so for as long as the Church continues to exist. . . . What pertains to the very essence of the faith is this injunction (Mt 28:19; Lk 16:16–17) that it is to be handed on."

It was to a series of these catechetical conferences, in which the Archbishops of Dublin, Krakow, Brussels, and Paris took a prominent part, that the germ of the idea for a new and comprehensive summary of the Catholic faith in a new catechism can be traced. The difficulties and crises in catechetics were worldwide in scope by then, and the pleas of bishops, priests, parents, religion teachers, and catechists culminated in a set of documents from the Holy See and finally, at the suggestion of the Archbishop of Boston, in the *Catechism of the Catholic Church*.

SYMPTOMS OF CRISIS

Religious ignorance, catechetical semiliteracy, and moral and doctrinal illiteracy are not confined to the borders of our country. Throughout the world, as Cardinal Ratzinger observed, "the question of salvation is not raised in terms of God, Who does not even figure anywhere in the question. Rather, it is raised in terms of man's accomplishments, as he strives to become his own master builder, the designer of his own destiny."

Dissent and confusion have seeped even into some ecclesiastical circles. Pope Paul VI himself said that smoke from hell has come into the Church under her door and over her threshold. The family, the basic cell transmitting Christian knowledge and culture, is often on the verge of disintegrating. The classic supports of Christian society are being broken down. All of this is reflected in and nourished by the mass media.

Sometimes parents and teachers, themselves the products of impoverished, degenerate, and defective catechetical training, do not see the seriousness of the obligation to have children and youth continue their Christian education beyond the sacraments of initiation, through high school years, and into college.

The *Catechism* is not some simple panacea for the present ills of society and of the Church. However, if it is read and seriously studied, it will be and will remain an invaluable tool to help (as the *Catechism* itself states) "deepen the understanding of faith. In this way it is oriented toward the maturing of that faith, its putting down roots in personal life, and its shining forth in personal conduct" (CCC 23).

As our Holy Father observes, the *Catechism* unites us with God's revelation as contained in Sacred Tradition and Sacred Scripture. He says: "This compendium of Catholic faith and morals is a *privileged gift* in which we have a convergence and collection in a harmonious synthesis of the Church's past, with her tradition, her history of listening, proclaiming, celebrating, and witnessing to the Word, with her Councils, doctors, and saints."[7]

The Pope also says: "The *Catechism of the Catholic Church* is a qualified, authoritative instrument. . . . [Its] publication . . . must certainly be counted among the major events of the Church's recent history. It is *a precious gift* because it faithfully reiterates the Christian doctrine of all times: it is *a rich gift* due to the topics treated with care and depth; it is *an opportune gift*, given the demands of the modern age. Most of all, it is *a true gift*, which presents the Truth revealed by God in Christ and entrusted by him to his Church."[8]

We would show ourselves deeply ungrateful to God if we were to ignore such a gift, which is precious, rich, opportune, and true. I sincerely hope that every adult Catholic will procure a copy of this *Catechism* and will study it with a sincere and open mind.

When the Second Vatican Council concluded in 1965, few Catholics carefully read and studied the documents of the Council. As a matter of regrettable fact, few are familiar with these documents even today. Rather, Catholics were enveloped by a "shadow council" of commentators, experts (mostly self-proclaimed), and "theologians" (often self-designated). This shadow council, which often spoke of the "spirit of Vatican II", is largely responsible for a great amount of erroneous religious doctrine that is spread abroad in our time.

I strongly recommend that you leave aside for now all the commentaries and penumbra of the new *Catechism*. (Some current books and articles are good, but many of them are bad.) Obtain a copy of the

---

[7] John Paul II, "Catechism Is Truly a Gift to the Church", *L'Osservatore Romano* 49 (December 9, 1992): 2, no. 5.

[8] Ibid., 1, no. 4.

Catechism and read it for yourself. Do not let others try to tell you what it says. Say a prayer to the Holy Spirit as you read all 803 pages on your own.

APRIL 22, 1994

Reading the *Catechism*

The month of June is always special in the calendar of the Catholic Church. It is the month when great feasts are celebrated: Corpus Christi, the Sacred Heart of Jesus, the Birthday of Saint John the Baptist, the Solemnity of Saints Peter and Paul.

June 1994 is the month in which the *Catechism of the Catholic Church* became available in English. Our Holy Father has called the *Catechism* one of the most significant documents issued by the Catholic Church in the twentieth century.

This *Catechism* should be of interest to every thinking, adult Catholic. It is directed to bishops, priests, religion teachers, catechists, and others directly involved in "Church work", but it is also intended to be read and studied by all Catholics. It is a magnificent and coherent presentation of our Catholic faith, done in fullness and clarity.

The media, especially, but not exclusively, the secular media, have already begun in many instances to distort and sensationalize the *Catechism*. Consequently, the first rule in reading the *Catechism* should be to read it without being distracted and deflected by the lack of focus that so many news reports and commentaries have had and will have about it.

The second rule for reading the *Catechism* is to treat it as a cohesive whole, although the individual parts lend themselves to particular treatment. One part of the *Catechism* is always linked with other parts. The third rule is to receive the *Catechism* in the light of prayer and faith, indeed, in the light of the living Sacred Tradition the Church possesses, Tradition that, along with Sacred Scripture, constitutes the fonts or sources of revelation. The fourth rule for correctly receiving the new *Catechism* is to do so in the context of supernatural love.

The *Catechism* itself quotes the previous *Catechism of the Council of Trent*: "The whole concern of doctrine and its teaching must be directed to the love that never ends. Whether something is proposed for belief, for hope or for action, the love of our Lord must always be made accessible, so that anyone can see that all the works of perfect Christian virtue spring from love and have no other objective than to arrive at love." [9]

---

[9] CCC 25, quoting the *Roman Catechism*, Preface, 10.

Cardinal Joseph Ratzinger, in introducing the *Catechism*, remarked:
"The catechism must be read as a whole. It would be an erroneous reading of the pages on morality if they were to be separated from their
context, namely, from the profession of faith and the teaching on the
sacraments and prayer." [10]

Father Giuseppe Segalla, of the Pontifical Theological Commission,
mentions the importance of seeing the contents and unity of the use of
the whole Bible in the *Catechism*. Sacred Scripture is used in the *Catechism* in the "living tradition of the whole Church", and not only in the
sense of "apostolic Tradition". [11] Also, each dogma of our Catholic faith
that is presented in the *Catechism* must be seen in the context of the
"analogy of faith", which is the coherence of the truths of the faith with
one another.

The four major sections of the *Catechism*, based on the Apostles'
Creed, the Sacraments, the Commandments, and the Lord's Prayer, constitute a unified body of teaching. They are interconnected and locked
together, but, for purposes of study and reading, they can be treated
separately. However, some of the richness of the presentation will be lost
if their union with each other is not perceived.

Historical notes and complementary doctrinal expositions are
printed in small type and can be omitted by readers who are less interested in a specialized viewpoint. Also in small type are a large number of
what Cardinal Ratzinger calls "brief, poignant texts" taken from the Fathers of the Church, the sacred liturgy, the teaching of the Church's
Magisterium, and Church history. [12] These are meant to assist the reader
in understanding something of the completeness and beauty of our
Catholic faith.

At the end of each section of the *Catechism* is a part titled "In Brief",
which summarizes the section and makes it easy to review and memorize relevant items. It is on these summaries that local catechisms and
catechisms for children and youth will be constructed in the future.

The truly "Catholic" nature of the work is seen also in the balanced

---

[10] "Catechism Has Aroused Great Interest", *L'Osservatore Romano* 50 (December 16,
1992): 4.

[11] "Catechism Presents Scripture as Revelation of God's Salvific Plan", *L'Osservatore
Romano* 23 (June 9, 1993): 9–10.

[12] Ratzinger, "Catechism", 4.

citations from both the Latin and the Greek Fathers of the Church, as well as in the testimony from many holy women, including Saint Catherine of Siena, Saint Teresa of Avila, and Saint Thérèse of the Child Jesus.

Pope John Paul II tells us that this *Catechism* is to serve to educate people in what the Catholic Church professes and proclaims. It is a gift for all. Even more, it is something that we Catholics can offer to anyone who asks us the reason "for the hope that is in [us]" (1 Pet 3:15).

JUNE 17, 1994

Catholic Schools

Not as well known as they ought to be are the words of the Second Vatican Council regarding Catholic schools: "As for Catholic parents, this Council calls to mind their duty to entrust their children to Catholic schools when and where this is possible, to support such schools to the extent of their ability, and to work with them for the welfare of their children."[13]

The Council also "earnestly entreats pastors of the Church and all the faithful to spare no sacrifice in helping Catholic schools to achieve their purpose in an increasingly adequate way and to show special concern for those who are poor in the goods of this world or who are deprived of the assistance and affection of a family or who are strangers to the gift of faith."[14]

PARENTS ARE PRIMARY EDUCATORS

The Catholic Church has always taught that parents are the primary and principal educators of their children. The Second Vatican Council said nothing new when it proclaimed: "Since parents have conferred life on their children, they have a most solemn obligation to educate their offspring. Hence, parents must be acknowledged as the first and foremost educators of their children. Their role as educators is so decisive that scarcely anything can compensate for their failure in it."[15]

It is to assist parents in carrying out their responsibilities in the formation and education of their children that the Church has, at enormous cost and effort, erected a Catholic school system. However, Catholic

[13] *Gravissimum educationis*, no. 8.
[14] Ibid., no. 9.   [15] Ibid., no. 3.

schools, according to the Second Vatican Council, are not erected by the Church only to assist parents but also by virtue of the very mission of the Church herself:

> The office of educating belongs by a unique title to the Catholic Church, not merely because she deserves recognition as a human society capable of educating, but most of all because she has the responsibility of announcing the way of salvation to all men, of communicating the life of Christ to those who believe, and of assisting them with ceaseless concern so that they may grow into the fullness of that same life.[16]

PUBLIC SCHOOLS

In a pluralistic democratic republic, such as our country is, a well-educated citizenry requires a good public school system. There are many dedicated persons involved in public education, and their work and witness deserve, in many instances, praise and gratitude. However, many conscientious parents and other people of goodwill question whether the total government monopoly on education is desirable or responds to the basic demands of social justice.

Originally, public schooling in the United States was largely a Protestant enterprise. Instruction, atmosphere, attitudes, and even textbooks were heavily Protestant and often anti-Catholic. Obviously, this posed a threat to the faith and salvation of Catholic students.

In recent times, however, public schools have become totally secularized. Education that is fundamentally Christless and Godless offers an even more basic threat to the faith and salvation of Catholic students. Indeed, such nonreligious and, in many cases, antireligious instruction, atmosphere, attitudes, and even textbooks provide a flawed, incomplete, and deficient education.

A SPLENDID TRADITION

Sometimes the lack of availability of Catholic schools makes it impossible for parents to make use of such facilities. The Council states that those "who are being trained in schools which are not Catholic" must be persons who are specially assisted by parents and priests and lay people to learn their faith and practice it with regularity and devotion.[17] But this is clearly second best for Catholic children.

---

[16] Ibid.   [17] Ibid., no. 7.

It seems to be a particular injustice to assert that parents have the "right" to send their children to Catholic schools while, at the same time, through a lack of tuition tax credits, education vouchers, and other constitutional means, making it utterly impossible from an economic standpoint for parents to exercise that right.

So, Catholic schools in our country carry on. They follow a splendid tradition, and, despite sometimes desperate economic straits, their accomplishments are remarkable, surpassing public school results in almost all academic fields by every objective measurement or standard. Most of all, they labor not only to impart religious and catechetical instruction in a more complete way than could be offered by other means but also to impart to the students, in an atmosphere of Christianity, the rudiments of Catholic culture and tradition, the opportunity to approach the Mass and the sacraments and other means of grace on a daily basis, and the principles of Christian morality with the accompanying value system of Catholic truth. Perhaps most surprising of all is that this is accomplished with a per-pupil cost far lower than the system that is supported by government-enforced taxation.

The Church, too, has certain parental rights and duties. The Second Vatican Council says: "As a mother, the Church is bound to give to her children the kind of education through which their entire lives can be penetrated with the spirit of Christ, while at the same time she offers her services to all peoples by way of promoting the full development of the human person, for the welfare of earthly society and the building of a world fashioned more humanly." [18]

The Council tells us too that the Catholic school has (or ought to have) certain

> distinctive purposes. It aims to create for the school community an atmosphere enlivened by the Gospel spirit of freedom and charity, to help the child in such a way that the development of its personality will be matched by the growth of that new creation it became in baptism, and to relate all human culture eventually to the news of salvation so that the light of faith will illumine the knowledge which the student gradually acquires of the world, of life, and of mankind.[19]

AUGUST 13, 1993

---

[18] Ibid., no. 3.   [19] Ibid., no. 8.

Catholic Education

There were some raised eyebrows in our part of Nebraska when the Newcomen Society, a group dedicated to the cause of private enterprise, decided recently to honor the Catholic schools of the Lincoln Diocese. Our schools here, of course, are part of the most comprehensive and extensive system of private education in our country and, perhaps, in the world. In the speech I was asked to deliver at the special Newcomen Dinner, I tried to emphasize how the schools of the Lincoln Diocese are linked historically to the tradition of Catholic schooling in our land that existed long before our national Constitution and our Declaration of Independence.

Catholic schools existed in the colonies and in the lands that were later annexed to us for the simple reason that initially there were few or no alternatives. Even after free, compulsory public education was adopted throughout the early United States, public schools were often heavily Protestant in their textbooks, teaching, graduation exercises, and prayers. Frequently this included bitter anti-Catholicism. Because public schools constituted a danger to the Catholic faith, especially for immigrants, bishops and pastors were anxious to provide Catholic schools to the extent possible for the Catholic people. In fact, the matter was codified by the American bishops gathered in Baltimore in the last century, when they ordered that each parish should have a parish school attached to it.

With the impact of continuing Protestant divisions and the formation of new sects, of growing cultural and political pluralism, of less overt forms of anti-Catholic discrimination, and of Supreme Court decisions forbidding anything religious in the public schools, the Protestant character of American public schools has gradually eroded, and the system has evolved into something that seems to be basically Godless and areligious.

It should be mentioned that many good and believing people are involved in public education and are striving by word and witness to do their best in their professional lives. However, it has been declared by the courts to be against the U.S. Constitution to pray aloud in public schools, to assert the existence of God or to say anything about God, to teach the Ten Commandments, or to teach anything about Jesus Christ our Savior. Public schools appear to be required to teach a doctrine that is contrary to our Catholic faith, namely, that religion is a purely private affair that must be excluded from public discussion and merely practiced internally.

Conscientious Catholic parents realize their most serious obligation to provide for the religious education of their children. Parents must answer to God someday for the souls as well as the bodies of their children. Many of these parents want the schools that their children attend to reflect their family beliefs and values. Indeed, they see a grave peril to the faith of their children and an enormous obstacle to their own duty to be the primary and inalienable educators of their offspring if their children are placed in a godless educational environment that may be not only nonreligious but, in some instances, actually hostile to the true faith. Such parents obviously see the need for a strong and progressive Catholic school system.

Parents, too, find in Catholic schools a precious help in transmitting to their children their Catholic heritage and culture. They find in these schools dedicated partners in the whole educational enterprise. They find in them academic excellence even in the secular and profane subjects, as well as an atmosphere of discipline and a love of teaching and learning.

In addition, Catholic schools supply the dimension of supernatural grace. Holy Mass and the sacramental life of the Church are the channels of divine life that students in Catholic schools have at their disposition, in a way that pupils in other systems lack. Jesus Christ and His gospel are the driving force and the dynamic center of life and learning in a truly Catholic school. Catholic schools are not simply private schools with some religion classes attached. They are beacons of light in our enveloping national darkness of greed, dishonesty, sexual immorality, family breakdown, and destruction of human life.

Catholic schools are human institutions, deriving from the Catholic Church, which is of divine origin. As human institutions, they are subject to improvement and growth. The Second Vatican Council teaches: "While the Catholic school fittingly adjusts itself to the circumstances of advancing times, it is educating its students both to promote effectively the welfare of the earthly city and to serve the advancement of the reign of God. Their purpose is to have their graduates become, by living an exemplary, apostolic life, the saving leaven of the human family." [20]

The Second Vatican Council goes on to teach: "As for Catholic parents, this Council calls to mind their duty to entrust their children to Catholic schools, when and where this is possible, to support such schools to the extent of their ability, and to work along with them for the welfare of their children." [21]

AUGUST 26, 1994

---

[20] *Gravissimum educationis*, no. 8.   [21] Ibid.

6

CHURCH LAW AND PRECEPTS

Church Law

Besides the natural law and the divine positive law, there are two kinds of human law. These are Church law and civil law. Law, along with conscience, is the criterion of morality, law being external and objective, while conscience is internal and subjective.

So long as human laws are not unjust or impossible to observe, and so long as they are properly promulgated, they bind us to obedience, albeit with differing degrees and manner of obligation.

Sometimes laws overlap. For instance, some of the divine positive law is also natural law. There are also many civil and ecclesiastical laws that overlap each other and overlap natural and divine laws. For instance, laws forbidding incest, in both Church and state, are often repetitions of natural law. Again, the divine positive law requires that we "keep holy the Lord's Day", and Church law tells us how we do this (by participating in Mass and abstaining from unnecessary servile work) and tells us which day is the "Lord's Day" (the first day of the week). Again, state laws against drunken driving simply overlap natural and divine positive law, reflected in the fifth commandment of the Decalogue.

Every human society has the right to regulate itself internally. It is impossible to call a lawless or disorganized group a "society". Jesus, Who founded the Catholic Church, intended her to be a society with the basic qualities of human societies, including order. Church order requires law and its corollaries, obedience, justice, authority, enforcement, and sanctions. Because the effects of original sin abide in humanity, these corollaries will always be necessary for a human society.

Moreover, her divine Founder gave to His Catholic Church the gift of authority, indeed, of His own divine authority. Christ said, "He who hears you, hears me" (Lk 10:16), and again, "As the Father has sent me, even so I send you" (Jn 20:21). He gave to Peter and his successors the power of binding and loosing (Mt 16:19) and the same power to the rest of the apostles and their successors (Mt 18:18). If someone does not hear the Church, Jesus instructs us to treat him as a heathen or a tax collector (Mt 18:17).

Our Savior, then, gives to His Church the right to make and enforce laws. From her beginning, the Church has exercised this right for the good and the salvation of those entrusted to her maternal care. The lawgiver for the Universal Church is the chief bishop, the Bishop of Rome, either alone or with his fellow bishops in an ecumenical council. The legislator for an individual diocese is the bishop, the successor of the apostles designated to shepherd a portion of Christ's flock.

CANON LAW

Church law is codified in a publication called the Code of Canon Law. There is also an Oriental Code of Canon Law for the Eastern Rites of the Catholic Church. The most recent revision of the Code was issued by the Holy Father in January 1983 and became operative on the First Sunday of Advent that same year. There are 1,752 canons, or laws, in the current Code.

Some Church laws are meant for good order. Some are also meant for our salvation. Jesus gave the custody of the sacraments He instituted to His Catholic Church. Hence, many canons have to do with legal or licit activity as well as valid material and action in regard to the sacraments. Our Redeemer designed some elements as structurally basic to the Catholic Church, such as the existence of deacons, priests, and bishops, while other elements are man-made and historically conditioned, such as the existence of monsignors and cardinals.

Some canons are exhortative in nature, but many bind us in conscience and under pain of sin, sometimes even mortal sin. Pope John Paul II said, "By their very nature canonical laws are to be observed."[1] Some superficial minds do not understand the nature of the norms. They may say, "How can eating a little piece of meat on Fridays in Lent be so bad as to put one in jeopardy of salvation?" But it is the disobedience, not the meat, that is the serious matter.

PRECEPTS OF THE CHURCH

In catechetical instruction, it is usual to group the treatment of Church law under the title of the "precepts of the Church", normally listed as six in number: to attend Mass on all Sundays and holy days of obligation, to fast and abstain on the appointed days, to confess our sins at least once a year, to receive Holy Communion at least once during the Easter

[1] John Paul II, *Sacrae disciplinae leges* (January 25, 1983).

Season, to support the Church financially, and to obey the other laws of the Church, especially those regarding Matrimony.

Canon law, however, is far richer and more detailed. There is no reason why a reasonably intelligent Catholic should not have more than a passing acquaintance with the laws of the Church. Reading the Code of Canon Law can be "heavy going" but also very enlightening. Copies of the Code in English can be purchased in most Catholic bookstores.

Our Holy Father writes: "The Code of Canon Law is extremely necessary for the Church. Since the Church is organized as a social and visible structure, it must also have norms: in order that its hierarchical and organic system be visible; in order that the exercise of the functions divinely entrusted to it . . . may be adequately organized; in order that the mutual relations of the faithful may be regulated according to justice based upon charity, with the rights of individuals guaranteed and well-defined; in order . . . that common initiatives undertaken to live a Christian life . . . may be sustained."[2]

May God give us always the grace to be absolutely obedient to Christ's Church and ever to hear in her voice the sound of His own.

MAY 14, 1993

Lost Sabbaths

One of the changes that distinguishes the New Testament from the Old is the celebration of the Lord's Day on the first day of each week. The Old Testament related that, after creation, God "rested", or sabbathed, on the seventh day (Gen 2:2–3). However, using the power of binding and loosing, which Jesus gave to the Catholic Church that He founded (Mt 18:18), the Lord's Day, the day of rest, was moved in the New Covenant to Sunday (Rev 1:10; Acts 20:7; 1 Cor 16:2). It is clear that Christians are no longer obliged to keep the seventh day (Col 2:16; Gal 4:10). However, Christians are still required to observe the third commandment of the Decalogue.

Writing between A.D. 107 and 110, Saint Ignatius of Antioch said: "Let every friend of Christ keep the Lord's Day as a festival, the resurrection day, the queen and chief of all days of the week, the day on which our life sprang up again and victory over death was obtained." In the earliest days of the Church there was only one feastday, Easter, and every Sunday was considered a "little Easter".

Saint Justin Martyr, who wrote in A.D. 120, said: "Sunday is the day

[2] Ibid.

on which we hold our common assembly, because it is the first day on which God, having wrought a change in darkness and matter, made the world, and Jesus Christ, our Savior, on that same day of the week, rose from the dead."

Sunday is the day that marked the "beginning of creation". It is also the day of the week on which the greatest events in human history happened: Christ rose from the dead, and the Holy Spirit came down upon the Catholic Church on Pentecost. It is certainly a sin, and sometimes even a serious sin, for Christians to see Sunday as "just another day". Unfortunately, the degeneracy of our post-Christian civilization makes the observance of the Lord's Day more than difficult for many Catholics.

Still, Christians who are constrained to nonobservance of Sunday should long for and desire to observe the weekly "little Easter" with their whole parish community. Those who are able "to keep holy the Lord's Day" should surely and joyfully do so. Sunday must be, first of all, a day of worship and spiritual growth. A "day of rest" does not mean a day of inactivity. Holy Mass must be not just a part of the week, but the *heart* of the week. Anticipated Mass on Saturday evening must be seen as part of the Sunday celebration (calculated like the Jewish Sabbath—from sundown the day before). Above all, Sunday should be a weekly day for the family and for the Christian community, a day to "take delight in the Lord".

Our divine Lord spoke and acted strongly against Sabbath scrupulosity (Mt 12:1–13). He taught us that "the sabbath was made for man, not man for the sabbath" (Mk 2:27). At the same time, He made it clear that we must keep the third commandment (Mt 5:17–20).

Some servile work is necessary on Sunday. One can think immediately of medical personnel, fire fighters, law enforcement officers, mothers cooking meals, dairy farmers milking cows, and military personnel on duty. Genuine demands of justice and charity take precedence over other Sunday obligations. Emergencies (weather-related agricultural problems, storm damage requiring some extra efforts) can excuse one from the Christian duty to abstain from unnecessary servile work on Sundays. Also, people sometimes are allowed to work on Sundays so that others can enjoy a Sabbath rest (for instance, restaurant employees, golf course workers, television operators). It occasionally happens that business owners can suffer irreparable damage if their competitors are open on Sundays and they are not.

On the other hand, mere consumerism and convenience are not valid excuses to shop, plow, cultivate, wash the car, do the family laundry, cut the grass, paint the house, or allow regular business, industry, and commerce to operate "as usual" on Sunday. Only if such things are genuinely impossible on other days of the week could they be permitted to Christians on a Sunday without their committing a sin. Dedicated and devout Christians not only should carefully observe Sunday as a special day for the Lord but should do all in their power to see to it that human society makes it possible and even easy for followers of Christ to give this one day each week to God.

The Book of Chronicles in the Bible quotes the Prophet Jeremiah about retrieving the lost Sabbaths (2 Chron 36:21). Sunday should be kept holy by setting it aside, hallowing it, or making it special (cf. Rom 14:5–6). It should be for every Catholic household a day of "honor", when Catholics honor the Lord Himself by "honoring" His day. Participation in Sunday Mass must be seen each week not only as a Christian duty and a Catholic obligation but also as a welcome and beautiful privilege.

Many Catholics enrich their lives by making each Sunday truly a "little Easter", a day of quiet and relaxation, a day of family fun and enjoyment, a day of hospitality and friendship, a day of household prayer and Scripture reading, a serene day to contemplate the things of eternity, a day that is a window by which to view heaven itself, a Day of the Lord.

MAY 6, 1994

Holy Days

For Catholics who know and love their faith, attendance at Holy Mass is a great privilege and a joyful opportunity to participate in the very redemptive act of Christ Himself. For such Catholics, speaking about an "obligation" to attend Mass is as uncomfortable as speaking about the "obligation" of a husband to kiss his wife.

However, for other Catholics, who may not yet have achieved such an outlook, Church laws are necessary to specify a certain amount of necessary, minimal attendance at Mass. This is why the laws of the Catholic Church oblige Catholics over the age of seven, under pain of mortal sin, to assist at Mass on the fifty-two Sundays in the year (or on Saturday evenings) and also, in the United States, on six holy days.

In 1991, before I was appointed a bishop, the United States bishops voted to remove the obligation to attend Mass for three of the holy days when they occurred on either a Monday or Saturday. These are: the Solemnity of Mary, Mother of God (January 1); the Assumption of Mary (August 15); and All Saints Day (November 1). For the remaining three holy days—Christmas (December 25), Ascension Thursday (forty days after Easter), and Immaculate Conception (December 8)—and when January 1, August 15, and November 1 fall on a day of the week other than Monday or Saturday, Catholics are still obliged, under penalty of serious sin, to attend Mass.

The principal motivation for the bishops' action, as I understand it, was the great shortage of priests in certain parts of our country, especially in the West, and the vast distances, requiring some elderly priests to travel hundreds and hundreds of miles on "holy day weekends" to accommodate people with Mass. In any event, the Holy See confirmed the vote of the bishops, and this new arrangement came into effect in our country in November 1992. Of course, the holy day obligation can be satisfied by Mass the previous evening, just as the Sunday obligation can.

Even when the obligation for everyone to share in Mass on a holy day is not present, the liturgical solemnity is still celebrated, and, when Mass is available, it is assumed that devout Catholics will try to attend, although they are not required by law to do so.

When our country gained its independence, the Catholic Church laws of England governed the Catholics of the early United States. In 1776, English Catholics had thirty-four annual holy days of obligation. This seems excessive to us now, but it must be remembered that Saturdays in those times were ordinary working days. The holy days, added to the Sundays of the year, were originally meant as a humane gesture to give laboring men and women a compulsory rest from their toils. Of course, by 1776, the Protestants of England and the early United States paid no attention to these Catholic holy days.

At the Third Plenary Council of Baltimore, in 1884, the Catholic bishops of the United States voted to reduce the number of holy days of obligation in our country to the six we presently have. The Holy See granted this derogation from the general law of the Church, and this was continued even after promulgation of the 1918 Code of Canon Law, which listed other holy days (some of which in our country were moved to the nearest Sunday), such as the following: Epiphany, Corpus Christi, Birthday of Saint John the Baptist, Feast of Saint Joseph, and Feast of Saints Peter and Paul. The action of the Holy See was not unique in regard to our country, since other national groups of bishops made similar requests, which were also granted; for instance, the Irish bishops asked that in Ireland the Feast of Saint Patrick, rather than the Feast of Saint Joseph, be a holy day.

The current law of the Church states: "On Sundays and other holy days of obligation the faithful are bound to participate in the Mass; they are also to abstain from those labors and business concerns which impede the worship to be rendered to God, the joy which is proper to the Lord's Day, or the proper relaxation of mind and body" (canon 1247 of the Code of Canon Law).

The usual answer to the question "What is a holy day of obligation?" is: Holy days of obligation are those important solemnities of our Lord, of the Blessed Virgin Mary, and of other saints in the Roman calendar that Catholics are obliged to observe by participating in the celebration of the Eucharist and abstaining from unnecessary servile work. They are similar to Sundays in matters of festivity and observance because of their special meaning and significance.

Actually, there are twenty-four solemnities in the current liturgical calendar of the Latin Rite. "Solemnity" is the name given to the highest type of feastday in the liturgy. Only six of these are holy days in the United States. Conscientious Catholics, even those who are unable to attend daily Mass, should strive to participate in Mass on at least some of the nonobligatory solemnities, such as the Annunciation or the Sacred Heart of Jesus.

In the early days of the Church there was only one "solemnity", and that was Easter. Each Sunday was considered a celebration of Easter. This is why even today Canon Law states: "Sunday is the day on which the paschal mystery is celebrated in light of the apostolic tradition and is to be observed as the foremost holy day of obligation" (canon 1246).

JULY 29, 1994

7

IN THE DIOCESE AND PARISH

The Bishop's Mail

In the twelve years I spent as pastor of a fairly large parish, I received a huge amount of mail each day. However, that experience did not prepare me for the even larger amount I regularly receive as a bishop. I enjoy receiving mail, and I try conscientiously to work my way through what I daily receive, although my success in this task is somewhat uneven, and I find myself apologizing more than I would prefer for my tardiness in answering letters.

The large amount of advertising and commercial mail is a never-ending source of amazement for me. The old-fashioned door-to-door salesman of a few years ago seems to have given way to the computerized address-o-graph, as many companies and enterprises sell their wares and services by mail. While the famous Sears catalogues have gone the way of the corner drugstore, there are many imitators and descendants of that undertaking.

Twice a day, Monsignor Timothy Thorburn, the chancellor of our diocese, carries into my office an armload of mail, and I set to work going through it all, wishing most days that I had taken a few speed-reading courses in my younger years.

As iron filings are attracted to magnets, so it seems that various types of unbalanced people are moved to write to bishops. From all over our country and abroad, I receive mail from people who have odd causes and purposes to promote. An astonishing number of these people claim to have had private revelations of various sorts. Messages from our Lord, from the Blessed Virgin Mary, and from angels and saints seem to be directed to bishops. Many of these messages, unfortunately, are difficult to distinguish from hallucinations and often contain erroneous doctrines, internal contradictions, and general linguistic and content incoherence.

Apart from these religious types of communications, there are many other varieties, including those trying to convert bishops to different kinds of religions and churches, to political causes of the extreme left and right, and to a spectrum of social justice and political issues. I try to

163

give this type of correspondence some attention but, obviously, not too much.

The Second Vatican Council says: "Every layman [they mean the women too] should openly reveal to the pastors of the Church his needs and desires with that freedom and confidence which befits a son of God and a brother in Christ. An individual layman, by reason of the knowledge, competence, or outstanding ability which he may enjoy, is permitted and sometimes even obliged to express his opinion on things which concern the good of the Church."[1] For this reason, I do carefully read and consider letters sent by laymen and laywomen. If these letters are polite and courteous, of course, they are more welcome, even when they contain complaints, bad news, or strongly stated points of view.

Anonymous letters, naturally, receive very little or no attention. If they are hate-filled or threatening or are signed with a false name or give a false return address, they can be turned over to federal postal authorities for investigation.

Sometimes some very fine people are capable of making unreasonable demands on a bishop or of presenting excessive expectations. Occasionally, the local or parish perspective about persons and matters is not complete, and these things take on a different look from the bishop's vantage point on the diocesan level.

Understandably, people tend to write letters more when they are upset, angry, or dissatisfied, but it is nice to receive an occasional letter that is positive about a priest or about some aspect of our diocesan life. When disagreement with a priest, nun, school principal, or church employee is involved, it is always better to follow the teaching of Jesus (Mt 18:15–17) and bring the matter to the bishop's attention only after having brought it first to the attention of the party who has "sinned against you". Sometimes it is necessary for me to point out to complaining people that I do not have a closet full of substitute priests whom I can send to them when they have a disagreement with their local priest. It might be a question of "this priest or no priest". Incidentally, the priests of our diocese are the finest, and complaints against them are truly few in number.

A number of complaining letters to me contain threats. The most common are those that threaten to cease contributing to the support of the Church if this or that is not done. These threats are quite insulting, because, of course, I would never make important pastoral decisions based on financial contributions. The obligation that we have by divine law and Church law to contribute to the support of the Church benefits

---

[1] *Lumen gentium*, no. 37.

everyone, including the poor, as well as the cause of Christ. If we do not fulfill this duty, we are the ones who are hurt the most.

Threats to quit the Church or abandon the faith incline me to question whether people making such threats even have the faith to begin with. Having lived in Rome for many years, where our Christian martyrs gladly suffered the confiscation of their property, saw their children slain before their eyes, endured unspeakable torture, and underwent horrible death rather than abandon their Catholic faith, makes one somewhat impatient with people who think their threat to give up their eternal salvation by spiritual suicide over a relatively trivial matter has some significance.

I welcome your letters, whether they contain good news or bad news. It is joy to be in touch with the people of our diocese by mail, to study their proposals and learn their views. Make your communications short and clear for better and quicker attention. Remember that the Second Vatican Council teaches that it is your right, and perhaps even your duty, to communicate sometimes.

MAY 5, 1995

Friendly Parishes

In the second meeting of the National Conference of Catholic Bishops that I attended, in Washington in November 1992, the United States bishops issued a rather important document entitled "Go and Make Disciples". It is a national plan for applying to our country the splendid apostolic exhortation of Pope Paul VI, from 1975, *Evangelii nuntiandi* (*Announcing the Good News*).

EVANGELIZATION

Evangelization means loving people into the kingdom. It means obeying the command of Jesus (Mt 28:19) to "go therefore and make disciples of all nations". Every Catholic who is baptized and confirmed no longer has any option in the matter. He is obliged to be an evangelizer, one who spends time and effort to bring the "good news" of Jesus to others.

"Go and Make Disciples" lists three goals explaining our national American plan for evangelizing:

I. To bring about in all Catholics such an enthusiasm for their faith that, in living their faith in Jesus, they freely share it with others;

II. To invite all people in the United States, whatever their social or cultural background, to hear the message of salvation in Jesus Christ, so they may come to join us in the fullness of the Catholic faith;

III. To foster gospel values in our society, promoting the dignity of the human person, the importance of the family, and the common good of our society, so that our nation may continue to be transformed by the saving power of Jesus Christ.

At present in the United States there are about sixty million of us practicing Catholics. There are also about seventeen million fallen-away Catholics (or "inactive" Catholics, as the current saying goes). There are about seventy-eight million Protestants, divided into various denominations, as well as about fourteen million non-Christians (of which Moslems are the largest group, followed by the Jews). There are also eighty-two million Americans who are called "unchurched", that is, they belong to no religion at all. Obviously, there is a grand amount of hard work awaiting us all in the field of evangelization. Where can we start?

Although our evangelizing work must not stop there and remain there, our own parish is usually a good place to begin. It is amazing how many non-Catholics find themselves in a Catholic church in the course of a year. They are brought there sometimes by special occasions, such as weddings, funerals, baptisms, and graduations. More often than we realize, non-Catholics drop in for Sunday Mass, sometimes merely out of curiosity.

It is to these non-Catholic neighbors, friends, or strangers that we must show ourselves on the parish level to be smiling, friendly, hospitable, and welcoming. All of us, priests and laity, must take a genuine interest in such "walk-ins", not just as potential converts to our faith with whom we want to share the treasure and riches of our Catholicism, but also as they are in themselves. It is not enough just to invite them afterward for coffee and doughnuts in the hall, but we must get to know them, invite them to visit us in our homes, and be ready and eager to talk about our faith with them, explaining, for instance, customs and ceremonies they may find strange and unappealing at first glance.

Non-Catholics are known to lament at the "cold reception" they sometimes receive in Catholic churches when they visit them. Occasionally they encounter surly and unsmiling ushers, indifference on the part of people in the pews, and sometimes even a perception that they are not welcomed by the priest himself.

Without violating the atmosphere of silence and reverence that should pervade our churches because of their consecrated character and, even more, because of the presence of Christ in the Blessed Sacrament, I believe we all can do better in becoming a more welcoming community. If you notice non-Catholic visitors in church, be sure to greet them with a smile, share a missalette or hymnal, point out the order of the Mass to them, and introduce them to the priest after Mass.

Not only non-Catholic visitors should be met with the warmth of genuine Christian love and hospitality, but our fellow Catholics, especially those who are recent converts to "the fullness of Christianity which is found only in the Catholic Church" should be the objects of our concern and interest. There are probably more people in our parishes suffering from a sense of loneliness and isolation than we can imagine. Evangelization must touch them too.

ORGANIZATIONS

Every parish should have some group actively working in the area of outreach, extension, census, and information. Existing parish groups and organizations can often divert some of their focus and efforts in that direction, while others, such as the Legion of Mary, can even have that as their primary emphasis. The pastor of the parish, of course, has the main responsibility and authority in this area, but most pastors do and should welcome volunteer assistance. Most parish RCIA programs always seem to be in need of volunteer help. Ask your pastor if you can make sure your parish is clearly identified by means of highway signs and outside signs. Help to promote a "come home for Christmas" or "reconciliation for Easter" program in your parish. Volunteer, when needed, to be a greeter or usher. Get the message of the Catholic Church into the local media. Make sure that all your non-Catholic friends and neighbors and townspeople know that yours is a friendly and welcoming parish family.

No parish should allow itself to be outdone in charity and kindness and in the fostering of social justice. If your parish is not growing in numbers, perhaps it is not because of simple demographic decline but because we Catholics are not the friendly evangelizers Christ has commissioned us to be. Our Holy Father, Pope John Paul II, recently said, "To be Christians means to be missionaries, to be apostles. It is not enough to discover Christ, but you must bring Him to others!"

JULY 28, 1995

Good Shepherd Sunday

In its decree on priestly formation, the Second Vatican Council speaks in a most serious way about the duty of promoting vocations to the priesthood and to other forms of special consecration. It says, "The task of fostering vocations devolves on the whole Christian community, which should do so in the first place by living in a fully Christian way. Outstanding contributions are made in this work by families which are alive with the spirit of faith, love, and reverence, and which serve as a kind of introductory seminary, and by parishes in whose pulsing vitality young people themselves have a part."[2]

To keep us aware of our collective responsibility as a Catholic community for vocations, the popes, for the past three decades, have sponsored an annual World Day of Prayer for Vocations. The custom has been to have this celebration on the Fourth Sunday of Easter, which is traditionally "Good Shepherd Sunday". Thinking of Christ as the Good Shepherd is an appropriate time to reflect on the need for a sufficient number of shepherds in the Church to tend and feed the flock of Jesus on earth, to keep His chosen ones from harm, and to bring us all to the eternally green pastures of heaven. Pope John Paul II writes, "Only living Christian communities are able carefully to welcome vocations and then accompany them in their development, as mothers attentive to the growth and happiness of their offspring."[3]

PRAYER FOR RELIGIOUS VOCATIONS

There can be no doubt that prayer is the most essential component of any community's vocational efforts. Our Savior Himself made this very clear when He told us, "Pray to the Lord of the harvest that He might send laborers into His harvest" (Mt 9:38). God Himself, Who is perfectly free, chooses to "depend" upon our prayers for our priestly and religious vocations.

When people occasionally want additional priests or different priests in their parish or complain because they lack religious sisters in their parishes and schools and bring such laments to me, I often wonder whether they, individually or as a parish community, have ever really prayed, with the utmost seriousness that the situation requires, for vocations, as well as for the perseverance and holiness of those called by God.

[2] *Optatam totius*, no. 2.
[3] John Paul II, Message for World Day of Prayer for Vocations, *L'Osservatore Romano* 50 (December 13, 1995): 3, no. 2.

The Second Vatican Council teaches that "primary consideration" in vocation work must be given "to the traditional means of joint effort, such as persistent prayer and Christian mortification".[4] Pope John Paul II said, "I [invite] you, dear brothers and sisters, to commit your communities to the Lord in prayer, so that united according to the example of the first Christian community in an assiduous listening to the Word of God and in the invocation of the Holy Spirit, with the aid of the Virgin Mary, they may be blessed with an abundance of vocations to the priestly and religious life."[5]

After bishops, priests, deacons, and religious, the important instruments that God uses as actual graces of vocational discernment certainly are parents. Through unselfish love in wholesome family life, Christ often whispers His call to children and youth. Generous parents, who are highly honored to have a son or daughter called by the Lord to a life of special consecration to Him and special service to His People, can be crucial in nurturing the possible vocation of one of their offspring.

Our Holy Father also singles out catechists "who often have direct and prolonged contact with children, adolescents, and young people, above all during their preparation for the sacraments of Christian initiation [Baptism, Confirmation, and First Holy Communion]. To these also is entrusted the task of explaining the value and importance of the special vocations in the Church, thus helping to bring it about that believers live fully the call which God is addressing to them for the good of all."[6] The Second Vatican Council said, "Teachers and all others, especially Catholic societies, who in any capacity provide" for the training of young people "should strive so to develop those entrusted to them that these young people will be able to recognize a divine calling and willingly answer it."[7]

Special mention should be made of the invaluable service to the work of fostering vocations provided by some wonderful Catholic lay organizations, such as the Serra Club, the Knights of Columbus, the Diocesan Council of Catholic Women, and the Bishop's Lay Committee for Vocations.

OBSTACLES TO RELIGIOUS VOCATIONS

Nobody can doubt that there are some serious obstacles in today's culture to vocational discernment and perseverance. External to the

---

[4] *Optatam totius*, no. 2.

[5] John Paul II, Message for World Day of Prayer for Vocations, *L'Osservatore Romano* 50:4, no. 6.

[6] Ibid., no. 5.

[7] *Optatam totius*, no. 2.

Church is the atmosphere of consumerism, materialism, and hedonism. Noise, distractions, and constant sense stimulation militate against a prayerful and recollected spirit, in which alone one can find the direction that God is suggesting for a life. Disdain for decency and purity, to say nothing of holy virginity and consecrated celibacy, make a gift of oneself to God with an undivided heart something more difficult to manage than in other times. Within the Church, too, there are sometimes scandals and human imperfections, which pollute the soil in which a vocation can be found and made to grow.

None of such obstacles, however, is insurmountable. In addressing today's young people, the Successor of Saint Peter says: Be not afraid. Be generous in giving your life to the Lord. "God is the Lord of history and of the universe. Let grow in you the desire for great and noble projects. Place at the use of your communities the talents which Providence has lavished on you. The more ready you are to give yourselves to God and to others, the more will you discover the authentic meaning of life." [8]

On the World Day of Prayer for Vocations, but also on all the other days of the year, make certain to pray in a special way that God will continue to bless His Church with numerous and holy vocations to the priesthood and religious life.

APRIL 26, 1996

The Altar

Since the altar is the most important furnishing in a Catholic church, the two aspects of its meaning should occasionally be considered. The altar is simultaneously the "stone" of sacrifice, on which the mystery of the Cross is made present at each Mass, and the table of the Lord, on which His sacred meal is prepared and at which this banquet is eaten at each Mass, recalling His Last Supper with His apostles the night before He died.

This is why the *Catechism of the Catholic Church* states: "The *altar*, around which the Church is gathered in the celebration of the Eucharist, represents the two aspects of the same mystery: the altar of sacrifice and the table of the Lord" (CCC 1383).

Theologically, the altar can be considered as God's representative, clothed with God's majesty and sanctity. It is the altar that receives the sacrificial gifts that are offered and is the "agent of change" in regard to

[8] John Paul II, Message for World Day of Prayer for Vocations, no. 5.

those gifts. This is why Jesus was so emphatic in viewing the altar as far more significant and important than any purely human gift that could be laid upon it. "You blind men! For which is greater, the gift or the altar that makes the gift sacred?" (Mt 23:19).

Indeed, in Christian tradition, the altar, seen as an "ambassador of God", is viewed as a prime symbol of Christ Himself. The *Catechism* says, ". . . the Christian altar is the symbol of Christ himself, present in the midst of the assembly of his faithful, both as the victim offered for our reconciliation and as food from heaven who is giving himself to us. 'For what is the altar of Christ if not the image of the Body of Christ?' asks Saint Ambrose. . . . 'The altar represents the Body of Christ and the Body of Christ is on the altar' " (CCC 1383).

Consequently, the altar is generally accorded the utmost respect. It is "clothed" in fine linen not only as a "tablecloth" but also a sign of the deepest respect for a symbol of our Savior. When a permanent altar is consecrated, it is anointed with sacred oil, because "Christ" means "the Anointed One", the Messiah. Altars are surrounded by lights and flowers and should always be bowed to out of reverence.

IN THE CATACOMBS

Visitors to the catacombs often notice the special niches over some of the tombs. Frequently these niches have paintings depicting the Last Supper or the *agape*, or love feast, that marked early Christian gatherings. It seems clear from the archeological evidence available that from the first years of the Church's history, Mass was offered over the tombs of martyrs, using the top of the tomb as an altar table. The *Acts* of the martyrdom of Saint Lucian, who suffered on January 7, 312, at Nicomedia, present an excellent example of Mass offered on the top of a martyr's tomb.

Later on, in the Western part of the Church, the translations of martyrs' bodies from the catacombs to the churches inside the walls of cities became the occasion for the widespread practice of placing the relics of martyrs, or a portion of such relics, under or in the altar stone. For centuries it was required that altar stones contain the relics of martyrs. Today this is not obligatory but still is widely practiced. In the Greek, or Eastern, part of the Church, such relics are sewn into a special cloth called the *antemensium*, on which Mass (or the Liturgy, as it is called) is celebrated.

Kissing the altar is seen as a sign of the utmost reverence for Christ, Whom the altar represents, Who is the Cornerstone, the spiritual Rock. It is also a sign of respect for the saints whose relics the altar may contain. Ancient Hebrews always kissed the threshold when entering the temple in Jerusalem and, when passing by, always "threw a kiss" toward the temple.

INCENSING

The Book of Psalms sees clouds of incense billowing upward as a symbol of our prayers ascending to God (Ps 141:2), and the Book of Revelation shows its bowls of incense as the sign of the prayers of the saints (Rev 5:8). Early Christians meditated often on the second gift of the Magi (Mt 2:11) and saw in the blessed incense a sacred object, a vehicle for divine purification and protection. It is to purify and protect that people are incensed at Mass, the celebrant and sacred ministers as well as all the faithful assembled together and thus constituting God's holy People, duly convoked and summoned before Him.

At a solemn Mass the altar is incensed to purify and protect but most of all to express respect and reverence. The crucifix near or on the altar is incensed as well as any reliquaries or special icons near the altar. However, it is the altar itself, as a symbol of the Redeemer, that receives the incensation at the beginning and at the presentation of gifts during a solemn Mass. This is done to express dramatically the sacred and important character of the altar.

When the Blessed Sacrament is present on the altar, either during a solemn Mass at the Consecration or during a service of Benediction, incensing has only one purpose, to express adoration and worship of the sacrament of Christ's Body and Blood.

Throughout the Old Testament altars were erected to God. Now, in the New Testament, we worship in "spirit and truth" (Jn 4:23). Therefore our altars are not only in Jerusalem and Samaria but are erected wherever God's priests and people are gathered through the Holy Spirit in the name of Jesus.

SEPTEMBER 23, 1994

Appeals to Our Charity

As the calendar year draws to a close, we are more likely than at other times to find our mailboxes stuffed with all sorts of appeals to our charity and generosity. There can be little doubt that many of these appeals are authentic and, perhaps, worth responding to. But the question is: Which ones?

Some of these appeals are slick and carefully crafted to make us feel sad or guilty. Some are more crude, while others appeal to our kindness. Sometimes these appeals are or claim to be "Catholic" or "Christian" or otherwise "religious". They often take on a dunning character and occasionally are accompanied by unsolicited "gifts" (such as rosaries, Christmas seals, cards). Morally we have no obligation to return unsolicited gifts that may come with such appeals. Unless the gift was clearly a mistake on the part of the sender, we may keep what is sent or throw it away, no matter how many dunning letters we receive or how much guilt the sender tries to foist on us. Because the word "Catholic" or "Catholics" appears on something is no guarantee that what is involved is anything truly Catholic. Indeed, it might involve something anti-Catholic.

As a general principle, we should never send money to any cause or appeal unless we know, with reasonable certainty, where the money is going. Mailing lists, nowadays computerized, are a big business. Firms sell these at great profit. They are taken from magazine subscription lists, bank and government files, and so on. They can be very particular (for example, Catholic widows with an income over thirty thousand dollars). Sometimes advertising firms are hired that use psychiatrists and marketing experts to work on their persuasive appeals.

If an appeal strikes us as worthy of our charitable concern, it is always good to learn more about it before contributing. It may represent a genuine need, but, on the other hand, there may be other needs more urgent and more profound.

Another principle that should guide us in our reply to appeals is the limitation of our resources. Parents, for instance, are not obliged to give their children a college education (although many try to help with such things) or to provide their families with luxuries. However, there are necessities that parents are required to strive to provide for their families, and it would be wrong to give away as charity what is due to others in justice.

A question that is often asked is in regard to various "Mass enrollments" or cards from groups that promise (presumably in exchange for a contribution) that someone will be "remembered" in hundreds or even thousands of Masses. Is this the equivalent of or even "better" than donating a Mass stipend to the parish priest? While even the appearance of simony must be avoided in the use of Mass stipends, it must be said that these things are far from equal, for the Mass stipend is by far the better. It is certainly worthwhile to be "remembered" at Mass, but a Mass stipend is of a far different and higher nature than such "enrollments" or cards.

It should be noted, however, that we do have obligations in justice as well as in charity. Catholic social teaching instructs us in the duties of stewardship. Although we have no obligations in regard to "mail mendicants", we are obliged to support the Church, and this centers in our parish and in our diocese. To support our parish and our diocese is not only a duty but a privilege and an honored and fulfilling way of life. In doing this, we are "lending" to God, Who repays the "loan" with "interest" beyond all price. Our parish is also an excellent site for discharging our other obligations in justice and charity, since it can be the focus of diocesan and national collections, which clearly indicate the destination of our contributions.

How much should we give? In the Old Testament God demanded from His Chosen People 10 percent of their gross income. The famous "tithe" is not obligatory in the New Testament, although many conscientious people strive to use that as a measuring rod for the fulfilling of their responsibilities. When other responsibilities intrude, some families find this beyond their reach. Many Catholic families, however, designate a portion of their income for carrying out their duty to support the Church and for charity. A sum of 6 percent is most usual, designating 3 percent for the parish and 3 percent for other appeals (charities, religious Orders known to the giver, disease alleviation, and so forth). Some people like to give the first hours of work each week to God and designate what their labor earns in those hours for the Church.

When it comes to supporting the Church, we American Catholics cannot congratulate ourselves very much. Many other Americans are more generous in supporting their religious convictions than we are. Not only Jews, Mormons, and Seventh Day Adventists, but many Lutherans and Fundamentalist Protestants give a proportionately higher share of their incomes to their churches and contribute more heavily on a per capita basis than we do. In many instances they also, like us, support a private school system. While we must be careful in regard to appeals, we cannot slacken that support for our parish and our diocese which God and our faith demand of us.

It is amazing that someone who would not think of leaving less than 15 or 20 percent as a restaurant tip or who expects the famous COLAs (cost of living allowances) to follow the inflationary curve thinks nothing of giving to God at Mass each weekend a pitiful pittance, perhaps as little as he has given for years. The widow's mite was only a penny, but most parishes are not filled with poor and destitute widows. If some families were to examine what they actually spend for cosmetics, alcoholic beverages, tobacco, and so on and then to look at their church contributions realistically, they would find that they could and should make a significant improvement in the latter.

May God give us a strong sense of responsibility in the use and management of this world's goods, which He has entrusted to our care, so that, when the time comes when we can be stewards no longer and must "leave it all behind", we can give Him a good account of our stewardship.

NOVEMBER 13, 1992

Part Three

THE LITURGICAL YEAR

1

ADVENT

Maranatha

People working in the field of Christian archaeology and paleontology all affirm that the early Christians attended Mass with the priest and altar facing the people, and with the priest's back to the people. They did this with seeming indifference, since their basic concern was that the altar and priest be facing east. Churches, altars, and even the burial of the dead were always "oriented".

Deep in the consciousness of God's People were the words of Jesus about the lightning flashing from east to west as a symbol of His Second Coming (Mt 24:27). In the Eucharistic Sacrifice they saw not only the past brought forward, that is, the death and Resurrection of Jesus made present, but also the future anticipated, that is, the Second Coming of Christ, also made present. In word and sacrament, in sign and symbol, the reality of the Parousia was simultaneously "not yet" but also "already here". With joy the Christians prayed "Thy kingdom come", while they remembered the words of Jesus: "The kingdom of God has [already] come upon you" (Lk 11:20). Christ Himself said: "The hour is coming, and now is, when the dead will hear the voice of the Son of God" (Jn 5:25).

It is impossible to understand the Catholic liturgy without an understanding of the Advent of Christ. This season of the year, called Advent, is not simply some pious playacting, awaiting the arrival anew of the Baby Jesus on Christmas. It is much deeper and much more serious than that. We live historically between the two great "comings" of Christ: His first in poverty and humility as our Savior and His second in glory and majesty as our Judge. The season of Advent is meant to focus our attention on where we stand in the stream of history.

Although we know not the day or the hour (Mt 24:36), not even the angels know that, we do know for sure that Christ is coming again. He Himself exhorts us to be ever watchful (Mt 24:37–51). It is this anticipation of the eschaton that should mark our lives as it did those of our ancestors in the Catholic faith. The world and the universe as we know it are going to come to an end. Perhaps this will be in the next few minutes, perhaps in millions of years. During the season of Advent, we prepare for Christ's Second Coming by remembering how God prepared His world and His people for the First Coming. The anticipation and emptiness of the Christless centuries, the prophecies, the hopes, the fears, and the longing and waiting are useful to us in our present historical condition. In reliving what has gone before, the Church teaches us to "wait in joyful hope for the coming of our Savior Jesus Christ".

In Advent we prepare, of course, for the rebirth of Christ by grace into our souls on Christmas. But this season is also a time to prepare for His Second Coming "on the clouds of heaven in power and majesty". There are other comings that can help us in this preparation: His coming in the person of our neighbor, in the person of the needy and poor; His coming in the "gift" of sickness and pain; and, most of all, His coming in Holy Communion, substantially under the appearance, or *accidents*, of bread and wine.

The "end times", or eschaton, are described in Sacred Scripture often in terms of a literary form called the *apocalyptic* style of writing. This type of literature is replete with symbolic portents in the sky and the heavens, tribulations and destruction on earth, and so on. The great poem "Dies Irae" perhaps sets out the best in synthetic form what the Bible says about the eschaton. When meditating on the "end", words like "fearful" or "awesome" come frequently to mind (see Lk 17:22–37; Rev 15–20).

Through the centuries many semiprominent figures have dabbled in end-of-the-world speculation. Some of these were rogues and religious frauds, while others were simpleminded people speaking or writing out of ignorance. Some people still treat the Bible as if it were a book of riddles to be figured out by the more clever. Jesus told us clearly that no one knows when the end will come, not even "the Son" (Mt 24:36), in His human knowledge (although in His divine knowledge, as God, He knows all things). Misunderstanding what the Book of Revelation says, there are, even in our day, rapturists and millenniallists (see Mk 13:21–22).

The most important element in the prophecy and prediction of Christ about the end of the world was His promise that He would come again. It is on this that the early Christians focused their attention, and so should we. The flames, brimstone, falling stars, and astronomical catastrophes should be consigned to the background of our thoughts, while Christ Jesus, coming to recognize us and claim us, should be in the forefront of our consideration. While His enemies and those in the embrace of sin ought to be fearful of the awful Judge of the living and the dead, we should remember that we are the "elect" for whose sake the days are being "shortened" (Mk 13:20).

When we affirm each Sunday at Mass that we believe Jesus "will come again in glory to judge the living and the dead and of His kingdom there will be no end", we are announcing our Advent hope. Instead of "have a nice day", the early Christians greeted each other with the phrase "Maranatha", which, roughly translated, means "Come, Lord Jesus", words that conclude the last book of the Bible. In that hope they lived, and they always died "in the hope of rising again". How often that phrase is found on the tombs of the saints and sepulchers of the martyrs in the catacombs!

In the frenzy of Christmas holiday activity, it is easy to overlook the serious adult purpose and meaning of Advent. It is wonderful to fill children with a knowledge of how the coming of Christ was anticipated as He was awaited from the fall of Adam to the time of His birth in Bethlehem. But we must also remind ourselves that we are still in a state of anticipation. Saint Paul tells us that at Mass we not only recall the past but also anticipate the future. "For as often as you eat this bread and drink the cup, you proclaim the Lord's death until he comes" (1 Cor 11:26).

Not so much in fear and dread, but rather "in joyful hope" ought we to look forward to His coming again, at Christmas by grace and at the end of time in majesty. We must become and remain close to Him, His disciples, His followers, His brothers and sisters (Mk 3:35). The season of Advent (a Latin word meaning "coming") is our annual opportunity to "orient" ourselves anew. "Look up and raise your heads, because your redemption is drawing near" (Lk 21:28).

DECEMBER 4, 1992

The "Threes" of Advent

There are basically three things that encompass the object of Advent, this first part of the liturgical year: longing, repentance, and intimacy with God. For this reason there is another set of threes to assist us in our approach to the attitude that is expected of us. This set consists of the Prophet Isaiah; the precursor of Christ, Saint John the Baptist; and the Immaculate Virgin, Saint Mary, the Mother of Jesus, the Mother of God.

Our longing is represented by the prophets of the Old Testament, in particular by the Prophet Isaiah. More than a thousand years of prophetic utterance prepared the Chosen People of old for the decisive and final intervention of God in human history. Prophets, of course, did more than foretell the future. As a matter of fact, that was one of their minor duties. What they did (and still do for those who listen to them) was to recall the covenant of God to the People who had made a league or treaty or testament with Him, to stimulate hope in the promises of God, to inspire their listeners and readers to live by that hope, and to instruct the People to whom they were sent to internalize their formal and external religious practices.

The entire Old Testament is a *pedagogue* to Christ. It tells of His ancestors in the flesh: Adam and Noah, Abraham and Isaac, Jacob and Judah, Ruth and Jesse, David and Solomon. It tells of those who prefigured and predicted His coming: Joseph and Moses, Saul and Joshua, Ezekiel and Jeremiah, Micah and Amos, Judith, Daniel, and Job. This pedagogue is summed up in Isaiah, in his messianic promises (Is 2:1–19), in his "servant songs" (see Is 42:1–7), and in his prediction of glory (Mt 12:17–21).

Our longing for Jesus to be reborn by grace into our souls at Christmas and our longing for His return at the end of time are assisted by our recollection of the centuries of expectation that preceded His First Coming in Bethlehem. However, our longing has little purpose if it is not accompanied by repentance. For this we are given the Advent figure of the Baptizer, the cousin of our Savior in the flesh, His forerunner and herald. He was sent by God to bear witness to the Light (Jn 1:6–7), and he called himself the voice in the desert (Jn 1:19–35). He was the "friend of the bridegroom" who even now prepares us for the wedding banquet of heaven (Jn 3:22–36). He was the last and greatest prophet of the Old Testament (Mt 11:11) and doorway into the New Covenant (Mt 11:1–10). Saint John the Baptist calls out to us from the pages of the Gospels every Advent to turn anew to the ultimate things, the final goals and ends of life, to "prepare the way for the Lord", leveling valleys and lowering hills.

Standing as Elijah (Mt 17:11–13), Saint John reminds us that Christ comes only to those who await Him in penance and humility. Martyred for his moral courage (Mt 14:1–12), he teaches with more than words that God's economy and our salvation engage our free will and that there is a cost to discipleship. Eating locusts and honey, dressed in camel hair and leather, he proclaims to us in Advent that Christ, for Whose birthday we are preparing, must "increase, but I must decrease" (Jn 3:30).

Longing and repentance, though, are directed toward something sublime, that is to say, intimacy with God. It is Mary, full of grace (Lk 1:28), *Theotokos*, who is given to us in this season, not only to pray for us but also to remind us of our own intimacy with the divine. She was overshadowed by the Holy Spirit so that she can rightly be called "blessed"

(Lk 1:48). Her blessedness is a foretaste of our own. She provided the human framework in which God chose to touch our universe, our planet, our humanity, our innermost selves. He came initially, not in thunder and might, but as our Emmanuel, "God with us". In the image of Caryll Houselander, Mary is the "reed of God" on which He played the melody of His infinite love to a world awaiting rescue from sin and the hopelessness and misery that are its consequences.

Mary's cooperation with grace enabled her for nine months to be the place where heaven touched earth. In those months especially she gave to God Himself the human flesh He chose to use to redeem us. She gave Him eyes to look with compassion, feet to carry the "good news", hands to touch and heal. Beneath her immaculate heart His Sacred Heart was formed. Intimacy with God is the purpose of our Advent longing and repentance. We too, as Christians, are called upon to carry Christ as Mary did, to provide Him with hands to touch and heal, feet to carry the "good news", eyes to look with compassion, and hearts with which to love.

These weeks and days before Christmas are often filled with bustle and extra work. Some of this is unavoidable. But, by longing for Christ, preparing for Him with appropriate repentance, and striving to deepen our intimacy with Him, we can make Advent a season of peace and calm, of self-examination and reflection. The mists and darkness of our Northern Hemisphere's winter, penetrated with the light of the candles on our Advent wreaths, should help us to recall that a day is coming that will never end, the "Day of the Lord". Jesus is truly coming again, by grace on Christmas and at the end of our lives and at the end of time. Only those will receive His embrace who have longed for Him, repented, and achieved a high degree of intimacy with Him. In Advent He tells us our duty in one word: "Watch" (Mk 13:37).

Jesus asked the question: "When the Son of man comes, will he find faith on earth?" (Lk 18:8). This is certainly the Advent question that should haunt our consciousness each year as we "wait in joyful hope for the coming of our Savior, Jesus Christ". By the "threes" of Advent— longing, repentance, and intimacy with God—we can answer our divine Lord in the affirmative. Isaiah, John the Baptist, and the Blessed Virgin Mary can help us formulate our response.

DECEMBER 11, 1992

The Coming

There is perhaps no season of the year that, for us Christians, combines so diverse an emotional outlook, an outlook that is almost contradictory, as does Advent. On the one hand, it is the time when, once again, we must think of the *dies irae*, the day of wrath and day of mourning, when the books will be opened and the just Jesus will come, not this time as our Savior, but rather as our Judge. He will come amid the portents of apocalyptic calamity (Mt 24:23–31). On the other hand, there will be "new heavens and a new earth" (2 Pet 3:13), where the tears will be wiped away from our eyes and there will never again be any death or pain (Rev 21:1–4).

Because Christmas is such a glorious and happy feast, there is a strong temptation to anticipate it. Sometimes this anticipation, especially in the form of early Christmas parties, inclines us to forget the nature of the preparatory season. Advent, however, is important to our spiritual outlook and a Catholic preparation for the proper celebration of our Lord's Nativity. Our celebration will be happier and spiritually richer if we use the weeks before Christmas as the Church intends us to: to reflect on the coming of Christ, His coming to be born again by grace in our souls on Christmas and His coming at the end of time in the clouds of heaven.

Before the general judgment at the end of world, there is a particular judgment for each person who dies (Heb 10:26–27). This moment of death, the decisive moment of our entire human existence—since the state in which we die will determine our eternity—is truly an anticipation of Christ's coming at the end of the world, when the universe as we know it will be destroyed.

Then too, every time we receive our Lord in Holy Communion, we anticipate His coming. He comes to us in sign and symbol, which conceal the substantial reality of His presence in the Holy Eucharist. In the divine Eucharist, Saint Paul tells us, "we proclaim the Lord's death until he comes" (1 Cor 11:26). Although we "wait in joyful hope for the coming of our Savior, Jesus Christ", at every Mass, we also enjoy His coming in anticipation of the final Advent of the Lord at the end of time.

Our Redeemer also anticipates His final coming by coming to us in the course of our lives in the person of our neighbor, especially our family members, beggars, the uncongenial, enemies, children, the elderly, the sick. He told us that what we do to them, we do to Him (Mt 25:40).

If we are alert, we can discover many anticipations of the final coming of Christ in our lives. He comes, for instance, in sickness and tribulations that are accepted without anger or impatience. He comes in prayer and in temptations that are resisted. He comes in Sacred Scripture and Sacred Tradition. He comes in the teaching of the Catholic Church, His Bride and Body. He comes with His pardon and pity in our Advent and Christmas confessions. He comes to us in the duties we must perform and the obedience we are asked to render to lawful authority.

Historically, we live between the two great comings of Christ: in the Incarnation, when He came in history as the gentle Savior, and at the eschaton, when He will come in awesome majesty and glory. We use the historical recollection of the preparation in the Old Testament for the first coming of Christ to help us in our preparation in the New Testament for His Second Coming.

When we gather around our Advent wreaths, we keep in mind what Cardinal John Henry Newman wrote: "We are looking for the coming of the day of God, when all this outward world, fair though it be, shall perish; when the heavens shall be burnt and the earth melt away. We can bear the loss, for we know it will be but the removing of a veil. We know that to remove the world which is seen, will be the manifestation of the world which is not seen. We know that what we see is a screen hiding from us God and Christ and His Saints and Angels. And we earnestly desire and pray for the dissolution of all that we see, from our longing after that which we do not see."

Advent should be a period of joy for every Catholic household. In particular it should be a time for children to learn about the deeper meaning of the coming solemnity of Christmas. For adults it ought be a time of peace and calm, given to self-examination and interior reflection. There should be Advent songs, stories, pictures, and, most of all, attendance at Advent Masses, and not just on Sundays. For children and adults it ought to be a season of longing, joy, and holy seriousness.

Although in our Northern Hemisphere, Advent is the darkest time of year, it is preeminently the time when we must heed the words of Jesus: "Watch, therefore, for you do not know on what day your Lord is coming" (Mt 24:42). As Saint Peter tells us: "Therefore, beloved, since you wait for these, be zealous to be found by him without spot or blemish, and at peace" (2 Pet 3:16). Jesus Himself said: "Surely I am coming soon" (Rev 22:20). What can we do during Advent except to reply as the Bible does with its closing words: "Amen. Come, Lord Jesus!"

NOVEMBER 26, 1993

Clean for Christmas

Thomas à Kempis in the *Imitation of Christ* wrote: "With the recurrence of the principal feasts our practice of virtue should take on new life. . . . At each feast we should make our good resolutions as if we would no longer celebrate the next year's one on earth but in heaven, keeping the one eternal festival with the friends of God. . . . Then if God should extend the number of our days on earth, we ought to feel ourselves not yet sufficiently adorned for the feast, not yet worthy to share in the tremendous glory to be revealed in us at the appointed time. Therefore, the remaining days must be used to prepare still more for our journey home."

Fastidious housewives clean their homes meticulously for Christmas. Before decorations go up and company arrives, houses are usually scrubbed, dusted, and vacuumed with exceptional care. How important it is that our souls be prepared for Christ's coming! Indeed, He is truly coming to be born within us by grace on Christmas morning, just as He is coming at the end of our lives and at the end of time to judge us. If Love is to be our Christmas guest and now, in the season of Advent, is "on the way", cleanliness of soul should be a preoccupation that takes precedence over shopping and partying.

A strange man who dwelt in the desert, wore camel's hair, and ate grasshoppers and wild honey (Mk 1:6) would hardly qualify as an example of antiseptic behavior. Yet, in Advent more than in any other time, the figure of the precursor and cousin of our Lord is presented to us in our liturgical tradition, and, odd as it may seem, he is presented to call us to cleanliness, cleanliness of soul. His message in ancient times and for today is "repentance" and "forgiveness of sins".

Saint John the Baptist, by his holy example, teaches us that humility before God and God's Messiah is an absolute prerequisite for genuine repentance, without which we cannot approach the Solemnity of the Lord's Nativity in spiritual cleanliness. From across the centuries the last and greatest prophet of the Old Testament exhorts us to "decrease" while Christ "increases" within us (Jn 3:30).

As we approach the Advent and Christmas Confession, which should be an essential part of every Catholic's annual Christmas preparation, we are encouraged by the liturgy to have the call of Saint John the Baptist to *metanoia* (change of life) continually ringing in our ears (Mt 3:7–10; Lk 3:7–9). Joy and peace, the characteristic gifts of Christmas, will not be possessed except by those who are interiorly cleansed by the forgiveness of God given in the sign and symbol called the sacrament of Penance.

Those who do not avail themselves of the sacrament of Reconciliation will not be able adequately to receive the rebirth of the Christ Child in their souls on Christmas, nor will they be able to recognize and be recognized by Jesus when He comes at the end of life and the end of time.

Cardinal John Henry Newman wrote:

> This in particular is a time for purification of every kind. When Almighty God was to descend upon Mount Sinai, Moses was told to "sanctify the people," and bid them "wash their clothes". . . much more is this a season for "cleansing ourselves from all defilement of the flesh and spirit, perfecting holiness in the fear of God" [see Ex 19:10–12; 2 Cor 7:1]; a season for chastened hearts and religious eyes; for severe thoughts, and austere resolves, and charitable deeds; a season for remembering what we are and what we shall be. Let us go out to meet Him with contrite and expectant hearts; and though He delays His coming, let us watch for Him in the cold and dreariness which must one day have an end. Attend His summons we must, at any rate, when He strips us of the body; let us anticipate, by a voluntary act, what will one day come on us of necessity. Let us wait for Him solemnly, fearfully, hopefully, patiently, obediently; let us be resigned to His will while active in good works. Let us pray Him ever to "remember us when He cometh in His kingdom;" to remember all our friends; to remember our enemies and to visit us according to His mercy here, that He may reward us according to His righteousness hereafter.[1]

Father Bede Frost wrote: "Love, the Revealer—are you prepared for that . . . for seeing what God truly is and what you are? Love, the Illuminator—can you bear that Light? Love, the Forgiver—but have you forgiven? Love, the Peace-bringer—but Who brings a sword, for peace may reign only when the war with self within and evil without has been fought and won."

Saint John the Baptist is no "reed shaken by the wind", but He is, in the words of Father Parsch, "a man of steel and granite, a man of rock on whom Christ can build. We must be the same, strong in faith, unshakable in obedience and in dedication to God's will. Only this type of Christian prepares the way of the Lord."

Pope Saint Leo the Great said:

---

[1] John Henry Newman, *Parochial and Plain Sermons*, bk. 5, serm. 1 (San Francisco: Ignatius Press, 1997), 965–66.

Let every man prepare himself for the coming of the Lord, lest
he be found at the coming enslaved to luxury and absorbed in
worldly cares. Everyday experience proves that excess of drink
dulls the keenness of mind and excess of food saps the vigor of
one's heart. Remembering the coming of Christ will encourage
the virtue of temperance and free us to dwell on the wisdom of
God. When the tumult of earthly cares is stilled, to us will come
delight in holy meditation and in the contemplation of everlasting joys.

DECEMBER 3, 1993

Preparation

Clutter is most often an undesirable distraction from the focus of anything. This can certainly be true of Advent, a season of longing, waiting,
watching, and yearning for the coming of Christ. Somebody cleverly
wrote: "If I could do whate'er I wish to do to make complete your
gladsome Christmas Day, I would not bring one single thing to you, but
I would come and take some things away."

Preparing for the coming of Jesus in grace on Christmas and at the
end of our lives and the end of the world is indeed a serious undertaking. Material and, even worse, spiritual "clutter" in this season can be an
undesirable distraction from our preparation for His coming. Sometimes
a glance at antiquity can assist us to regain our focus when contemporary customs cloud the purpose and meaning of Advent.

EXPECTATIONS OF THE ANCIENT WORLD

The ancient heathen world gave many hints of a messianic expectation.
In the famous speech of Hermes in the Prometheus myth, he says:
"Look not for any end to your curse, until some god appears to accept
upon his head the pangs of your sins vicarious." In his second dialogue,
Alcibiades says: "When the one comes who will tell how we are to conduct ourselves before God, I am ready to do all that he desires, but I ask,
when will he come?"

In his "Morals", Confucius wrote: "The holy one must come from
heaven who will know all things and have power over heaven and
earth." Cicero quotes a Sybil who said: "A king will come who must be
recognized for salvation." Suetonius said that "Nature has been in labor
to bring forth a person who will be king of the Romans", and Tacitus

said: "Mankind is generally persuaded that the ancient prophecies of the East will prevail, and it will not be long before Judea will bring forth one who will rule the universe." Classical scholars often enjoy searching for and finding numerous messianic indications in ancient literature.

EXPECTATIONS OF THE HEBREWS

Chesterton once said "How odd of God to choose the Jews", but choose them He did. A prime function as His Chosen People of the Old Testament was to keep alive in humanity the expectation and hope of redemption and deliverance. That which began as a tiny glimmer of hope in the catastrophe of Eden (Gen 3:15) was fanned into a glowing flame through the centuries until the fullness of time arrived (Gal 4:4).

Modern research seems to indicate that there were possibly three messiahs expected by the Jewish people in the intertestamental period. Undoubtedly, they expected a prophet like Moses (Dt 18:15) and a king in the line of David (Rev 22:16), but now we have learned that it seems they also expected a special high priest, such as Aaron and Melchizedek (Ex 29:4–9). It is unclear whether, in Jewish thought, these messiahs were expected to be separate persons or one person. We know, of course, that whatever their expectations, the Jews never suspected that God, Yahweh Himself, Elohim, would become incarnate and be, in a way they never imagined, Priest, Prophet, and King.

More than two thousand years of prophecy played an important part in fanning the flame of Hebrew anticipation of a messiah (a "Christ" or "Anointed One"). The physical lineage and descent of the "Expected One" was rather clearly delineated, from Sem through Abraham and the Patriarchs to Judah and the family of Jesse that came from Boaz, Obed, and Ruth. Even His native town was indicated, as we well know (Micah 5:2).

The entire prophetic corpus of the Old Testament points to Jesus, including all of Jeremiah, Isaiah (especially the "Emmanuel Book", that is, chapters 7 to 12), Daniel, Proverbs, Wisdom, the Psalms, Zechariah, Malachi, Job, Joel, Amos, Habakkuk, Nahum, and Sirach. Yet, the sad words are spoken every Christmas morning at Mass: "The world was made through him, yet the world knew him not. He came to his own home and his own people received him not" (Jn 1:10–11).

CHRISTIAN EXPECTATIONS

Undoubtedly, "spiritual clutter" blinded our world and those who should have been watching and yearning for the First Coming of Christ. Their lack of preparation and a suitable welcome for that First

Coming are meant to serve us as lessons as each Advent we prepare for His Second Coming. Perhaps the noise of parties prevented all but the humble shepherds from hearing the angels sing (Lk 2:13). People were warned, but they were still unprepared. We have been warned. Are we prepared?

This season is supposed to be a time of memory and hope. Cardinal Joseph Ratzinger tells us that it is memory that awakens hope. "It is the beautiful task of Advent to awaken in all of us memories of goodness and thus open the doors of hope." Our memories are not just personal but also collective, the memories of the human race. It is especially at Mass that the "memorial of Christ" is supposed to excite our hope as His coming at the end is anticipated in His real and true "coming to us" in the Holy Eucharist.

A soldier in the army of Alexander the Great was reported to him for cowardice. The Emperor asked the man his name. "Alexander", was the reply. The Emperor said: "Either change your name or change your behavior." We are called "Christians". To be worthy of that name we must obey the injunction of Jesus: "Watch, therefore—for you do not know when the master of the house will come" (Mk 13:35).

DECEMBER 10, 1993

Joyful Hope

What does "Advent" mean? Of course, it derives from the Latin expression *"Adventus Domini"*, "the coming of the Lord". In ancient liturgical practice, this season was not just the beginning of the liturgical year, but it was also the end of the liturgical year, because it was not only the time for preparing to commemorate the birth of Jesus in Bethlehem, but it was also, and more importantly, the season to prepare for the return of Christ in glory at the end of time.

The *Catechism of the Catholic Church* says: "When the Church celebrates *the liturgy of Advent* each year, she makes present this ancient expectancy of the Messiah, for by sharing in the long preparation for the Savior's first coming, the faithful renew their ardent desire for his second coming [Rev 22:17]" (CCC 524). This is the time of the year when we Catholics are expected to pray with greater fervor the petition in the Lord's Prayer, "Thy kingdom come." It is the season when the words of the priest at Mass take on renewed importance: "We wait in joyful hope for the coming of our Savior, Jesus Christ."

FIRST COMING

By living again the longing and desire of the peoples and centuries that preceded the First Coming of Jesus, the Church helps us ready our souls for His Second Coming. The *Catechism* teaches: "The coming of God's Son to earth is an event of such immensity that God willed to prepare for it over centuries. He makes everything converge on Christ: all the rituals and sacrifices, figures and symbols of the 'First Covenant' [Heb 9:15]. He announces him through the mouths of the prophets who succeeded one another in Israel. Moreover, he awakens in the hearts of the pagans a dim expectation of this coming" (CCC 522).

All the world's preparation for the First Coming of Christ reached a climax in the work of the cousin of Jesus, Saint John the Baptist, the last and greatest of the Old Testament prophets (Lk 1:76; Mt 11:13). Speaking of John the Baptist, the *Catechism* states, "By celebrating the precursor's birth and martyrdom, the Church unites herself to his desire: 'He must increase, but I must decrease' [Jn 3:30]" (CCC 524).

PAROUSIA

Certain Hebrew words have been taken over into our contemporary vocabulary of prayer, words such as "Alleluia" or "Amen". A similar word (more Aramaic than Hebrew) was quite common among the early Christians, *Maranatha* (1 Cor 16:22; Rev 22:20). *Maranatha* basically means "Come, Lord" or "May the Lord come." It was used as a prayer or a greeting or an exclamation by the first Catholics. Our ancestors in the Catholic faith also used the word "Parousia" (for example, 1 Cor 15:23; 2 Pet 3:4) to indicate the Second Coming of Jesus, the ingathering of the elect, the last judgment, and the end of the world. Their use of the term *Maranatha* showed their longing for the "Parousia".

Although the "day of the Lord" was predicted to be preceded and accompanied by apocalyptic events (2 Pet 3:10), a day of wrath (Rom 2:5; Rev 6:17) and a day of judgment (Mt 10:15; 1 Jn 4:17), the early Christians were not frightened about its imminence because they saw it also as the time for the consummation of God's purpose, the victory of Christ and His Church. It is the time when Christ will come on the clouds in triumph and majesty (Lk 21:27) and be manifested, seen, and revealed (Lk 17:30).

OUR ADVENT

This Advent season is preeminently a time to prepare ourselves for the coming of the Lord. He comes to us to be reborn by grace in our souls at Christmas each year in order that we may be ready to "greet Him when He comes again". For He is certainly coming at the end of our lives and at the end of the world to be our judge. He comes to us daily in the guise of the poor and the hungry (Mt 25:40). He anticipates His final return to earth by coming to us in word and sacrament at every Holy Mass. Unless we recognize and greet Him when He comes even now to visit us, we shall find ourselves unable to recognize and greet Him when He comes in glory.

We are nearing the end of our millennium and the beginning of the third millennium of Christianity. We know, however, that a thousand years for the Lord are just as one day (2 Pet 3:8). Perhaps the Lord will come again in glory at the millennium, or perhaps He will delay for many more millennia. No one knows when the coming of the Lord will happen (Mk 13:32), but we are absolutely certain that sooner or later it will occur.

Our Savior Himself reminds us, "But take heed to yourselves lest your hearts be weighed down with dissipation and drunkenness and cares of this life, and that day come upon you suddenly like a snare" (Lk 21:34).

Getting ready for Christmas should mean more than just preparing for a worldly celebration. Our spiritual preparation for our Redeemer's special coming in grace to our souls on Christmas Day must give to this Advent season an element of sobriety and seriousness, for such a preparation is the antecedent to the more serious preparation that should be ours for the Second Coming of our Lord.

As we light the candles on our Advent wreaths, as we try to attend daily Mass as often as possible, and as we strive to fill our minds and hearts with Advent sounds, stories, and songs, we should remember how Jesus told us to prepare for His coming, "But watch at all times, praying [constantly]" (Lk 21:36). Let part of that prayer always be *Maranatha* as we look forward to the fulfillment of all of God's promises and the joyful hope that is ours.

DECEMBER 2, 1994

The Intruder

Once, at a formal Christmas party at the home of some people I knew (women in evening dress and men in tuxedos . . . some even in formal wear), one of the sons of the family, a twenty-year-old, arrived for the party wearing jeans, sneakers, and a dirty sweater. Everyone politely tried not to notice how improperly dressed the young man was, but there was a sense of awkwardness as all shook his hand and he joined the party for dinner.

This incident comes to mind in this season of Advent, when the whole Church is preparing to celebrate Christmas, and we are busy buying, selling, wrapping, decorating, and feasting. Then, in stark contrast, the sacred liturgy places in our midst the austere and even frightening figure of Saint John the Baptist. At first appearance, he seems so out of place, dressed in camel hair, eating grasshoppers and wild honey, and talking about repentance.

THE MESSENGER

Since Saint John the Baptist heralded the public mission of Christ, why would he be significant at this time in the Church year? The reason, of course, is that his preaching, his life, and his person were important for God to prepare human history for the entry of Jesus on its stage. In our own day he continues to be the forerunner of our Savior's coming to us in grace. Just as he prepared the Jewish people for Christ by calling them to repentance and conversion, so he continues to prepare us, the Chosen People of the New Testament, for Christ's coming at Christmas by grace and for His coming at the end of our lives and at the end of time.

Saint John the Baptist was the immediate precursor of Jesus, sent to prepare the way for Him (Acts 13:2; Mt 3:3). He was the last prophet of the Old Testament, surpassing them all in importance (Lk 1:76). He welcomed Christ even while in his mother's womb (Lk 1:41), and later he pointed Him out as the Lamb of God (Jn 1:29).

Hebrew tradition very strongly looked forward to the return to earth of the Prophet Elijah, whose coming again was to be the signal that the Messiah would soon arrive. Jesus called John the Baptist "Elijah" (Mt 11:14; 17:11–13).

The son of Elizabeth and Zechariah, John the Baptist was a man of stern morals (Mk 6:17–19) but also a man of immense humility (Jn 3:30). Seven times we find in the New Testament a reference to the One Who is to come after John the Baptist (Mt 3:11; Mk 1:7; Lk 3:16; Jn

1:15, 27, 30; Acts 13:25), and we always see John's protestation of unworthiness in His regard. John announced that he was only the "friend of the bridegroom" and that the bridegroom "must increase" while he, John, "must decrease" (Jn 3:29–30).

THE MESSAGE

Without a doubt, the Church proposes for our meditation before Christmas the words of Saint John the Baptist. His moral correctness, noble humility, and courageous martyrdom teach us what attitude and dispositions should be ours as we "wait in joyful hope for the coming of our Savior, Jesus Christ". However, beyond his personal example, his message is also an important conditioner for our souls as we look forward to greeting Christ on His solemn birthday, when He comes to us in a special way, and as we prepare to recognize and welcome Him when He comes at the end of world.

John's words are simple, clear, and direct. He proclaimed a coming judgment in which the righteous would be separated from the wicked, as chaff is from good grain. This judgment must be seen as imminent and immediate, with the axe already laid to the root of the tree. He reproved hypocrisy and those who did not allow their religious beliefs to influence their lives and conduct. He vigorously urged his listeners to make a change of life (repentance) in order to avoid a coming punishment, a punishment that, for all its delay, is certain to arrive some day.

For sincere Christians who want to make Christmas more than just a worldly celebration filled with hedonism and consumerism, the words of Saint John the Baptist have a timeless quality, making them especially valid for our annual pre-Christmas consideration. His words teach us not so much to flee from the current way we celebrate Christmas but rather how to infuse our celebration with that spiritual dimension that permits us to make sense of all that we do at this time of the year.

The main duty that God gave to John the Baptist, however, was to point out Christ (Jn 3:25–30) once Jesus appeared. He did this by the way he lived and died, by the totality of his message, and by his specific words. His baptism of water, he told all who heard him, was only a prelude to a future baptism with fire (Mt 3:11).

Particularly during Advent are we Catholics called upon to point out Christ to our world. Saint John the Baptist summons us each year to prepare not only ourselves but our fellowmen for the coming of Christ. He continues his prophetic duty throughout the ages by his annual "intrusion" through the liturgy into our lives. He reminds us of our obligation to preach by the example of our lives what Christmas and the coming of Christ are all about. We must share with him the task of putting humility, penance, repentance, and joyful expectation into our own lives and thereby influencing others to do the same in their lives.

When we allow ourselves to listen to Saint John the Baptist each Advent and to let his words touch our deportment, we shall play, as he did, the role in the purposes of God that providence has eternally determined for us. Thus we shall find true peace and a genuinely merry Christmas.

DECEMBER 16, 1994

"As We Wait . . ."

A wise observer has noted that nature seems to have a twofold annual cycle. In the winter there is darkness, and then out of it comes light. In the springtime there is death, from which comes life. This rhythm of nature seems to correspond to that of the liturgical year. The Christmas cycle represents a transition from darkness to light, and Christmas, Epiphany, and Candlemas are feasts of light. In the Easter cycle, life is victorious over death in Christ and in all His brothers and sisters. Of course, one liturgical cycle not only fades into the next, but they interpenetrate each other in many ways.

For years experts have debated about when the liturgical year begins. Usually it is seen as beginning on the First Sunday of Advent. However, there are those who argue that Advent really represents also the end of the liturgical year, when Christians contemplate once again with great seriousness the end of the world and the Second Coming of our Savior, when He will come on the clouds of heaven to judge us (Lk 21:27). Here too there is interpenetration of two liturgical aspects. On the one hand, there is this consideration of the Parousia and the end of time. On the other, there is a remembrance of the First Coming of Jesus, a preparation for His annual birthday, a reliving of the centuries of anticipation that preceded His birth in the flesh in Bethlehem, and a looking forward to a rebirth of Christ in our souls by grace.

There are really three dimensions to this period of time before Christmas: past, present, and future. Christ came once at a definite place and time. He will "come again in glory to judge the living and the dead". However, in a real sense He has not left us orphans (Jn 14:18) but abides with us continuously. He remains in His Body, the Catholic Church. He remains in His holy word found in Sacred Scripture and Sacred Tradition. He remains in the person of His ordained priests. And He remains with us most substantially and really in the Holy Eucharist.

Between His First and Second Coming, our Redeemer lives with us in grace and mystery. In Advent the Church not only prepares to welcome Him anew at Christmas and to greet Him at the time of His triumphant return to earth, but she rejoices even now in her possession of Him and in His presence. Every Mass is celebrated "as we wait in joyful hope for the coming of our Savior, Jesus Christ". The Mass is not merely a rehearsal for greeting Him at the end of time, but, under the veil of the Sacrifice and the Sacrament, it is an authentic anticipation of His Second Coming at the same time that it is another reenactment of His First Coming.

Each year in Advent, we Christians, indeed all of mankind, are summoned to prepare the way of the Lord in our hearts and in our world and to listen to the voice of the One Who is even now in our midst, Whose sandal strap none of us is worthy to unfasten. Because humanity is rapidly coming to an enormously important milestone in our measurement of the journey of human history, namely, the end of this century and the beginning of the next, as well as the end of this second millennium of Christianity and the beginning of the third, the season of Advent in the next few years should take sharper focus in our consciousness and our lives than it hitherto has.

In telling us to prepare in a special way for the coming third millennium, our Holy Father, Pope John Paul II, mentions that "the solar year is . . . permeated by the liturgical year, which in a certain way reproduces the whole mystery of the Incarnation and Redemption, beginning from the First Sunday of Advent and ending on the Solemnity of Christ the King, the Lord of the Universe and Lord of History." [2] In his apostolic letter entitled "As the Third Millennium Approaches", the Pope reminds us that the dying year of 1995 and the coming year of 1996 are to be part of the "antepreparatory stage" of the jubilee celebration.

During these months, in preparation for the celebration of the year 2000, the Pope asks us all to study again the call of the Second Vatican Council commissioning us to point out "with fresh vigor to the men and women of today that Jesus Christ is the 'Lamb of God who takes away the sins of the world' (Jn 1:29)". [3] He requests that we "humbly heed" anew the "rich body of teaching" of the Second Vatican Council. The Holy Father urges that we start even now to toil toward the forgiveness of our sins and work toward a conversion of heart. He mentions the need to repent of past errors and instances of infidelity to the

[2] John Paul II, apostolic letter *Tertio Millennio Adveniente* (November 10, 1994), no. 10.
[3] Ibid., no. 19.

gospel of Jesus; to be sorry before God for our inconsistency and slowness to act, when our Creator expected us to put our beliefs into action; and to be more than passive in our relationship with Him and with our fellow human beings.

According to the timetable of the Pope, the year 1997 will be devoted to reflecting on Jesus Christ, the Word made flesh. The year 1998 will be given over to the Holy Spirit and His sanctifying presence within the community of Christ's disciples. The year 1999, the third and final year of preparation, will be dedicated to God the Father, from Whom the Lord was sent and to Whom the Lord returned (Jn 16:28). The whole of Christian life will be seen as a pilgrimage to the home of our Father (Mt 5:45; Lk 15:11–32).

It is difficult to imagine a better time to begin to prepare for the new millennium than the season of Advent, when we annually prepare ourselves for the coming of our Master. To make those coming preparatory years spiritually successful, we must first make these antepreparatory years a time of intense spiritual growth. Individually and collectively, our human race is invited by God each year to pass once again from darkness to light, from death to life. As we gather our family and our household around our Advent wreath this year, let us all remember what we have received from God and what we already possess, "as we wait in joyful hope for the coming of our Savior Jesus Christ". "Come, Lord Jesus!" (Rev 22:20).

DECEMBER 1, 1995

An Advent Saint?

Astronomers tell us that there are in the universe things called "black holes": imploded stars with a gravity so intense that they literally suck into themselves all surrounding matter. In a certain sense, Christmas has such an intense gravity, for it seems that almost all the surrounding feastdays are joined in one way or another to the annual celebration of our Savior's birth.

Every adult realizes that Saint Nicholas, whose feast is celebrated on December 6, has long ago been absorbed into Christmas celebrations. In some parts of the world, Saint Lucy too has become an important part of Christmas. The solemnity of the Immaculate Conception and feasts such as those of Saint John Kanty, Saint Francis Xavier, and Saint Ambrose have also been gathered into the Christmas perspective.

The feastdays after Christmas are deliberately made part of the celebration of the Nativity of Jesus, including those of Saint Stephen, the protomartyr; Saint John, the Beloved Disciple; the Holy Innocents; Saint Thomas Becket; Saint Sylvester; the Holy Family; and Mary, Mother of the Redeemer.

By virtue of an English Christmas carol, a saint whose feast is celebrated on September 28 each year has also been joined in popular imagination to our celebration of Christ's Nativity. This is, of course, good King Wenceslaus. According to the legend related in the Christmas carol, it was "on the feast of Stephen" that the saint and one of his pages noticed a very poor man and decided to bring him some Christmas cheer in the form of food and fuel. Finding it hard to walk through a blizzard to the poor man's home, the page is invited by the saint to follow in his footsteps, which, to the page's amazement, are miraculously warm and comfortable.

In many ways the canonization of Saint Wenceslaus represented for the people of Bohemia the beginning of their national identity. He became a beloved figure not only in the folklore of the Czech lands but, like Saint Nicholas, in that of all of Europe. It is understandable how many legends and stories have grown up around his memory as the centuries have gone on.

There can be no doubt that Saint Wenceslaus was indeed a heroic figure in the history of central Europe. He was the Duke of Bohemia in the tenth century and a martyr for the Catholic faith. In those years of barbarism, among the Slavic tribes that migrated from the steppes of Asia, dukes in Western Europe were considered the equivalent of kings. It is hard to imagine the savage inhumanity of the Slavs when they were in their uncivilized condition. To these tribes came the great missionaries, Saints Cyril and Methodius. They devised a written language for the people and developed a dictionary. Most of all, they converted large numbers to Christianity.

Among those baptized by Saint Methodius was Borivoj, Duke of Bohemia, the grandfather of Wenceslaus. Along with his wife, Saint Ludmila, Borivoj became a devout Catholic. Both Borivoj and Saint Ludmila struggled to promote the Catholic religion among their heathen people. They built the first church in Prague and raised their son and heir, Ratislav, as a good Catholic gentleman. Most of the people remained pagan, and Ratislav, for political reasons, married a pagan woman named Drahomira. Because her daughter-in-law was heathen, Saint Ludmila took over the education of Wenceslaus.

After Borivoj and Ratislav died, Drahomira, as regent, took over the country and bitterly persecuted the Catholic Church. She banned all Christian education and banished all the priests. She arranged to have Saint Ludmila strangled, and she began to educate Wenceslaus' younger brother, Boleslas, as a pagan. Boleslas was mentally unbalanced. When Wenceslaus came of age, he took over the country and restored the Catholic faith. His prayer life centered on the Blessed Sacrament, and he devoted himself to helping his poor and sick subjects. He maintained peace with the German emperor, Henry I, and obtained from him a relic of Saint Vitus for the cathedral in Prague. He studied the lives of the saints, prayed for hours each day, and attended daily Mass with great fervor.

Drahomira, more out hatred for the Catholic faith that Wenceslaus professed than for political reasons, encouraged Boleslas to kill his brother. She found support for her plot from some of the pagan Bohemian nobles, who were anxious to embark on wars of conquest, which Saint Wenceslaus refused to undertake. Wenceslaus was stabbed on his way to Mass one morning by Boleslas. As he fell by the church door, the last words of Saint Wenceslaus were, "Brother, may God forgive you."

It may seem farfetched to call Saint Wenceslaus a saint of Advent. Yet, his life teaches us many important lessons that can be most useful as we prepare to welcome Jesus in a new birth by grace in souls at Christmas and prepare to welcome Him at the end of our lives and at the end of time. Saint Wenceslaus avoided gloom and despair, always being joyful and cheerful. It is in "joyful hope" that we must await the coming of Christ. He was always close to Christ in the Blessed Sacrament, devoted to the example of the saints, and constantly prayerful. How could we do better in this holy, pre-Christmas season than to follow his example?

Of course, Saint Wenceslaus was anxious throughout his life to assist the poor, the hungry, the homeless, the sick, and the downtrodden. Christmas, for all of us, especially for children, should be an occasion to consider what we can give rather than what we will get. Advent is surely the season to remember "it is more blessed to give than to receive."

DECEMBER 8, 1995

2

CHRISTMAS

The Solemnity of Birth

The great night approaches when, the holy liturgy tells us, "the angels are singing on earth; the archangels are rejoicing; and the just exult." In God's design, the principal events of redemption seem to occur at night, in the darkness, away from the eyes of the curious. The slaying and eating of the paschal lamb, the Passover, happened at night. Jesus instituted the Holy Eucharist, the sacrament of His sublime love, at an evening supper. He rose from the dead "while it was still dark" (Jn 20:1). Also, Sacred Tradition has it that His birth occurred "while gentle silence enveloped all things, and night in its swift course was now half gone" (Wis 18:14).

At Christmas we think of a triple birth of Christ. The first is that which happens even now in the awesome grandeur of eternity, the everlasting begetting of the Son by the Father. This is the birth we speak about when we recite the Creed and say: "God from God, Light from Light". Before this mystery, which surpasses all that is finite, a human mind simply stands in fear and recognizes this as unfathomable, an event in the total and absolute oneness of God in the timeless night of eternity itself.

The second birth of Christ we celebrate is that which happened in the fullness of time (Gal 4:4), the historical event, when God Himself, the eternal Word, entered our world and our history. The Roman Martyrology specifies the precise time: It happened 2015 years after the birth of Abraham, 1510 years after Moses and the exodus, 1032 years from the anointing of David as king, in the sixty-fifth week of the prophecy of Daniel, in the 194th ancient Olympiad, 752 years after the founding of the city of Rome, in the forty-second year of the reign of Octavian Augustus, in the sixth age of the world, when all the earth was at peace.

These first two "births" of Jesus are mystically and really made present on our altar at Christ's Mass (hence "Christmas"). But there is a third birth that even more profoundly affects us. It is the reason why the first was revealed and why the second took place. This third birth is His spiritual birth by grace in our souls. It is glorious to remember that, for all eternity, in the very bosom of the Most Blessed Trinity, each of us was thought of by God, chosen by the Father, just as each of us was thought of by His divine Son, there in the manger in Bethlehem. The newborn Christ Child came to make us His brothers and sisters, to share His life and, ultimately, His happiness. All our celebration of Christmas is meaningless unless this third birth of Jesus is not only recalled but effected in our souls. Year after year the holy night of Christ's Nativity must be the night of our own spiritual rebirth.

The solemnity of Christ's birth should, of course, include a deep consideration of the human and miraculous event of historical record. Who could not be profoundly moved by the poverty, the humility, the utter simplicity that concealed the "fulcrum of the human story"? There in that place called "House of Bread" (this is what the Hebrew word "Bethlehem" means), the world's Bread came to be broken for us. There, where heaven touched earth and eternity entered time, angels sang in the skies, shepherds needed them to find a Lamb, a new Mother remained a virgin, and the hands that made the sun and the stars were too small to reach the heads of the animals in the stable.

An inn that night had no room, and so the supreme paradox was recorded forever. As Chesterton put it, in that "older place than Eden, the taller town than Rome, the place where God was homeless so all men might come home", the drama of human redemption reached a significant milestone. The hosts of heaven trembled in wonder at the indescribable love, while the object of that love, for the most part, ignored and still ignores the event and the Person that exceed all exaggeration. "He came to his own home and his own people received him not" (Jn 1:11).

Perhaps, like the shepherds in the fields, we cut no special swath in the story of our race. But, if we celebrate appropriately and knowingly the triple birth of our Savior on the "great night" of holy Christmas, like them we can see and understand what has been told us concerning this Child (Lk 2:17), and we can say with the Beloved Disciple: "We have beheld his glory, glory as of the only Son from the Father" (Jn 1:14), full of grace and truth, "and from his fullness have we all received, grace upon grace" (Jn 1:16).

The expectations of mankind were realized on the first Christmas night. Thousands of years of anticipation were summed up at that special time: "the sonship, the glory, the covenants, the giving of the law, the worship, and the promises; to them belong the patriarchs, and of their race, according to the flesh, is the Christ, who is God over all, blessed forever. Amen" (Rom 9:4–5). Until Christmas all creation groans and travails in pain (Rom 8:22). But, then the angels sing.

Once, a few days before Christmas, a telephone call came to a rectory. A woman wanted to know what was the earliest time she could attend Mass in order to satisfy her obligation. The reason for the inquiry, she stated, was that her family wanted "to get church over with, so they could have real Christmas sooner". The woman's desire to have her family attend holy Mass on a day of obligation was commendable, but her question surely makes one wonder what she considered "real Christmas". Too often, even today, the inn has no room for Him.

Christmas should be for us a spiritual celebration above all. "Real Christmas" should put all the folklore, customs, entertainment, family traditions, and the like into proper perspective as things that are useful only so long as they lead us to the triple birth of our Savior, when Omnipotence was in bonds, and Fire was in ice, and Transcendence was in immanence, and God became Man, and "the Word became flesh and dwelt among us" (Jn 1:14).

DECEMBER 18, 1992

Christmas Symbols

Often we put up our annual Christmas decorations without reflecting on why we do so or on the history of what we are doing or on its deeper meaning! Christmas is a beautiful time of the year, and our decorations add to its beauty. However, it would be more than useful to instruct ourselves and our children on what is behind it all.

The date of Christmas itself, experts tell us, was settled about the year 320, almost as soon as the Catholic Church emerged from the catacombs. The date coincided with the pagan celebration in honor of "*sol invictus*" (the unconquered sun), a celebration called the *saturnalia*. As with so many of our dates and customs, the Church "baptized" a previous heathen undertaking, making it over into a Christian reality. Humanity in the Northern Hemisphere for centuries considered the winter solstice to be a special and mysterious time, when the sun seemed to be bent on disappearing and then returned to begin making days longer once more. The farther north people lived, the greater the mystery to primitive minds. Hence, there were Stonehenge and the "yule" orgies of the Druids. Christians saw Jesus as the "unconquered sun" and called Him the "Sun of Justice".

The exact day or year of Christ's birth is unknown. When the Scythian monk Dionysius Exiguus (Dennis the Little) invented the calendar we use to make the Christian era, he fixed the date of Christ's birth at least four years too late, since it is certain He was born before the death of Herod the Great, which we now know took place at the end of March or the beginning of April in 4 B.C. The Church set the arbitrary date of December 25 as Christmas in the first year of the Christian era.

TREES AND WREATHS

The use of trees for decorations is an ancient teutonic practice, probably deriving from some animistic religious views. When the practice of bringing trees indoors began is uncertain, but early Catholic missionaries to the Germans "baptized" this pagan practice and used the *tannenbaum* as a catechetical tool. They used it to teach about the tree of life and of knowledge in the Garden of Eden transformed into the tree of salvation that is the Cross of Jesus. They also used the evergreen as a symbol of the fidelity of God, since the firs and balsams were "faithful in their greenery even in the coldest time of year". Christmas trees were confined in their use largely to northern Europe for many centuries. It was only in the nineteenth century that the English-speaking world began to use them, stimulated by the Germanic culture of Queen Victoria.

Wreaths are a symbol of eternity—a circle that has no beginning and no end. Often they were used to adorn tombs, and, in some parts of the world, they are so associated with death that they are not used as Christmas decorations. In Italy, for instance, some people were appalled when well-meaning American friends sent them a Christmas wreath for a present. Nonetheless, the eternity of God, as well as our own eternal destiny as a result of the Incarnation, is appropriately symbolized by the Christmas wreaths. When the wreaths were made with holly, the red berries on the leaves were seen by Christians in the past as reminders of Christ's blood shed to redeem us, a reminder by extension that is also given by red ribbons and bows.

SONGS AND MORE

Carols, songs, and hymns, of course, are related to our liturgical celebration and serve as a reminder of the song of the angels (Lk 2:13). The lights are symbols of Christ, the Light of the World, Who came on Christmas into our darkness (Jn 1:9), Who was called the "Light" by Simeon (Lk 2:32), and Who called Himself the "Light of the World" (Jn 8:12).

Although many depictions of the Nativity of Christ can be dated from the earliest manifestations of Christian art, the extensive use of the Christmas crib or creche is attributed to the ingenuity and creativity of Saint Francis of Assisi, who made a "living crib", including live animals, in 1223. Catholic homes should always have a prominent Christmas crib to replace or to complete the Advent wreath that Catholic families ought to use each year.

Poinsettia plants, since they resemble a star and frequently are bright red in color, were used by Franciscan friars in Mexico to decorate Christmas cribs and scenes. Their beauty and appropriateness for the season struck the United States ambassador to Mexico, Doctor Joel Poinsett, who in 1836 imported the "flower of the holy night", with the red Christmas bracts, into our country and bestowed his own name on the plant.

Local and ethnic customs have continued to enhance and enrich the celebration of Christ's Mass. The holy bread of the Polish (*Oplatki*) and the straw beneath the table and the tablecloth on Christmas are part of what the Holy Father uses in his personal celebration in Rome. For many people it would be unthinkable to celebrate the birth of Jesus without certain customs, activities, and foods. Many of these are founded in legends and practices that are supremely evocative and Christian.

GIFTS

The exchanging of gifts is probably the most widespread of Christmas practices. Surely it symbolizes the giving by God to us of the Gift of His Son. Particularly when children are the receivers of gifts do we remember that He became a little Child for our sake. (It is important, however, frequently to remind children that "It is better to give than to receive" and that there are needy and hungry children for whom we ought to be concerned and with whom we should want to share our good fortune.)

Gifts are involved in this season also because we remember that the mysterious Magi did not arrive in Bethlehem empty-handed but gave to Christ their expensive and symbolic presents. We, too, as we prepare for Christmas each year, should once again give to "the newborn King of the Jews" the gold of our faith, the incense of our prayers, and the myrrh of our sacrifices. May the generosity of God, fondly remembered each Christmas, be the inspiration under His grace for our generosity to Him and to those of His creatures made in His holy Image.

DECEMBER 17, 1993

The Nativity

Some years ago a submarine was disabled on the continental shelf off the east coast of the United States. Divers were able to go down to the ship and arrange for an oxygen line to be put into the hull. As this was being done, the men inside the ship tapped a message to the rescuers they heard working outside. The message was simple: "Is there any hope?" We can imagine their joy when the reply was tapped back: "Yes, there is hope!"

THERE IS HOPE

It is the annual celebration of Christ's birth that gives a similar message to our forlorn world: "Yes, there is hope!" Cardinal Joseph Ratzinger wrote: "If we are to be continually lighting candles of humanity, giving hope and joy to a dark world, we can only do so by lighting them from the light of God Incarnate."

Each Christmas we remember, in the words of Cardinal John Henry Newman, that "He, who is the everlasting Light, became the Light of men; he, who is Life from eternity, became the Life of a race dead in sin; he, who is the Word of God, came to be a spiritual Word, 'dwelling richly in our hearts,' an 'engrafted Word, which is able to save our souls;' He, who is the co-equal Son of the Father, came to be the Son of God in our flesh, that He might raise us also to the adoption of sons, and might be the first among many brethren."

FIRST LOVE

The love that derives from hope and that should be characteristic of Christmas, in our families, our parishes, and all of human society, is only a response to divine initiative. Saint John wrote: "In this is love, not that we loved God but that he loved us and sent his Son to be the expiation for our sins" (1 Jn 4:10).

Richard Crashaw describes Christmas: "Welcome all wonders in one sight! / Eternity shut in a span, / summer in winter, day in night, / Heaven in earth, and God in man. / Great Little One, whose all embracing birth / lifts earth to heaven, stoops heaven to earth." It is this paradox about which Saint Alphonsus asks: "Who would have ever thought of it if God had not thought of it and done it?" It is this incomprehensible love that causes all who ponder Christmas to be utterly amazed with an astonishment that lasts a lifetime.

The background against which the wonder of the Incarnation is seen is truly surprising: a Mother who remains a virgin, a village carpenter who is the guardian of the Savior, shepherds who listen to angels to find a Lamb, and wise men who follow a star to find Wisdom. There is a silent night when a heavenly choir sang, and the hands that made the sun and the stars were too little to touch the heads of cattle around the manger.

God did not desire to "cast off forever the work of His hands" and so "for us men and for our salvation, He came down from heaven." "Thus", says Pope Saint Leo the Great, "the Son of God entered this lowly world coming down from His heavenly throne without departing from His Father's glory. Although invisible in His own nature, He became visible in our nature. The impassible God did not disdain to become a man subject to suffering. The immortal God did not shrink from the laws of death."

Pope Pius XII said: "With the birthday of the Redeemer, the Church would bring us to Bethlehem and there teach us that we must be born again and undergo a complete reformation. That will happen only when we are intimately and vitally united to the Word of God made Man and participate in His divine nature, to which we have been elevated."

The Fathers of the Church delight in repeating that Christ descended that we might ascend. He came down that we may go up. This is the mystery of Christmas, which begins in mercy and ends in sanctity.

OUR RESPONSE

"Beloved, if God so loved us, we also ought to love one another" (1 Jn 4:11). To the utter and total love of God represented in Christmas (Lk 2:1–20), humanity can only reply with that which brings us closest to God, namely, love (1 Jn 4:8). "Some people", writes Caryll Houselander, "learn to love the whole world through the love of God. For them the way of sacrifice is direct and informed with joy. Others learn to love God through loving one another."

Unfortunately, our world is so often only "culturally Christian", and the observance of Christmas is reduced to mere sentiment. This Christmas, like so many others perhaps, can simply pass with no effect on our lives or on our world. True love of God and love of neighbor should lead us to greater simplicity, innocence, and truth in the year ahead. "Let our characters be formed upon faith, contemplation, modesty, meekness, and humility."

Let us make this Christmas different and special. As Newman puts it: "Let us come to church joyfully, let us receive Holy Communion adoringly, let us pray sincerely, let us work cheerfully, let us suffer thankfully." By our lives and witness we can and must "tap out" a message to all the world: "Yes, there is hope!"

DECEMBER 24, 1993

Christmas History

Could a battleship ever fit into your bathtub? Could a skyscraper be located in your living room? Would you ever think of sharing the life of some of your garden insects? The absurdities suggested by such questions are precisely the reason why the modern world finds so incomprehensible the true meaning and significance of Christmas. Beyond all power of human imagining, God Himself, Whom the universe cannot contain, entered the human race to share our weakness, suffering, and death.

He came to us at an exact place, Bethlehem of Judea, and at a precise time, when Octavian Augustus was emperor and Quirinius was governor of Syria. Many modern people find that this offends their sensibilities, this immersion of God in historical particularity. Thus Christmas constitutes a scandal for them. If they celebrate, it is done with noise and distraction, rather than with prayer and contemplation.

The *Catechism of the Catholic Church* tells us: "Jesus was born in a humble stable, into a poor family. Simple shepherds were the first witnesses to this event. In this poverty heaven's glory was made manifest" (CCC 525). Surely, this merits our deepest love and most profound prayer.

Cardinal Joseph Ratzinger observes that what is at stake at Christmas is the core of Christianity. Is Christianity just another sect or something really new, faith in the Incarnation of almighty God? Was Jesus of Nazareth simply a great religious man, or in Him had God Himself actually become one of us? Can God be so mighty that He can make Himself small, so mighty that He can really love us and enter our lives? Christmas is not mind-defying absurdity but an overwhelming reality surpassing our capacity to comprehend.

There is an enormous distinction between us and our garden insects. However, that difference is nothing compared to the infinite distance between us and our Creator. Yet, on Christmas, with angels singing, heaven standing in awe, and the night in the midst of its course, God's Word leapt from His eternal throne to bridge that distance and become flesh (Wis 18:14; Jn 1:14).

OUR ATTITUDE

Cardinal John Henry Newman gives us, in his eloquent style, the appropriate attitude for us Catholics as we celebrate the solemnity of our Lord's Nativity. He says:

Let us . . . approach Him with awe and love. . . . Let us come to
the Sanctifier to be sanctified. Let us come to Him to learn our
duty, and to receive grace to do it. At other seasons . . . we are
reminded of watching, toiling, struggling, and suffering; but at
this season we are reminded simply of God's gifts towards us
sinners. . . . This is a time for innocence, and purity, and gentleness, and mildness, and contentment, and peace. . . . This is not
a time for gloom, or jealousy, or care, or indulgence, or excess,
or licence:—not for "rioting and drunkenness," not for "cham-
bering and wantonness," not for "strife and envying" (Rom
13:13) . . . ; but for putting on the Lord Jesus. . . .

May each Christmas, as it comes, find us more and more like
Him, who at this time became a little child for our sake, more
simple-minded, more humble, more holy, more affectionate,
more resigned, more happy, more full of God.[4]

THE WONDER

Metaphrastes, a Father of the Church, wrote of Christmas: "Had He
wished, He might have appeared moving the heavens, shaking the earth,
hurling down lightnings. But, not in this way did He come. He wished
to save and not condemn and from the beginning to tread under foot
the foolish pride of men. So He not only became man, but He became a
poor man and chose a poor mother, who had not even a cradle wherein
her newborn baby could lie."

Saint Bede the Venerable said of the wonder of Christmas: "He that is
the Bread of angels reclines in a manger, that we, as sanctified beasts,
might be fed with the grain of His flesh. For he found that men had
become beasts in their souls and so is placed in a manger that we, changing our animal way of living, may be led back to that wisdom which
befits our humanity, reaching ourselves out to that heavenly Bread for
the life of our souls."

Pope Saint Leo the Great, in one of his famous Christmas sermons,
observes, "At Christmas lowliness is assumed by majesty, infirmity by
power, mortality by immortality. To pay the debt of our present state, an
inviolable Nature is united to our suffering, and true man and true God
are welded into the unity of one Lord. Such a birth befitted Christ, Who
is the Power of God and the Wisdom of God. He is joined to our lowliness, yet remains far above us in His divinity.

---

[4] *Parochial and Plain Sermons*, bk. 5, serm. 7 (San Francisco: Ignatius Press, 1997),
1020–21.

The poet Richard Crashaw wrote, in words we know so well, "Welcome all wonders in one sight, eternity shut in a span, summer in winter, day in night, heaven in earth, and God in man, great little One, Whose all-embracing birth lifts earth to heaven and stoops heaven to earth."

A recent song says, "That night when in the manger lay the holy One Who came to save, mankind turned in the sleep of death and dreamed there was no grave." Another carol sings, "What lovely Infant can this be, that in the little crib I see? So sweetly on the straw He lies, He must have come from paradise." What we say every Sunday let us say with special fervor on Christmas: "For us men and for our salvation, He came down from heaven. . . ."

DECEMBER 23, 1994

Christmas in Rome

Out of the dim mists of memory can come the recollection of many Christmas celebrations of the past. I have personal memories in a special way of those in which I found myself in the Eternal City, the famous city on the Tiber. The first time I spent Christmas away from my family and home, indeed, away from my country, was in 1957. I was a first-year theology student at the North American College in Rome, studying at the Gregorian University.

I remember the lack of "build up" toward Christmas. The lack of shopping frenzy, along with the lack of cold, snow, and Christmas street and house decorations, was something of a shock. (Alas, commercialism has now caught on in Italy too.) There was a series of Christmas shops in the Piazza Navona that sold Christmas decorations and sweets, and we homesick seminarians would, of course, pay regular visits there. Our college residence and our personal quarters were duly and beautifully decorated with what we were able to find at the Piazza Navona.

In 1957 Pope Pius XII was still reigning. (He had less than a year to live.) However, he was elderly and frail, so he celebrated Midnight Mass in the Sistine Chapel. This was a quasi-private celebration for the diplomats accredited to the Holy See, not for the general public.

We seminarians were awakened for Midnight Mass at the college by the smell of incense and by the sound of someone knocking on our door, saying (in Latin), "Christ is born today; let us go to worship Him." To this we responded, "Thanks be to God." The college chapel in its Christmas splendor greeted us with warmth and beauty. I sang in the seminary choir, which gave an hour-long concert of Christmas carols and hymns. (The range of my voice has been severely limited in subsequent years by the smoke of cigars and the words of countless sermons.)

The Solemn Pontifical High Mass was celebrated by Archbishop Martin O'Connor, the rector. The participation of the more than three hundred seminarians from all parts of the United States made the grandeur of the occasion all the more beautiful.

After Mass we enjoyed hot chocolate and special Christmas baked goods, including the famous *panetone*, Italian Christmas cake. Then we exchanged gifts with the men in our *camerata* (the small group of seminarians assigned to live in a certain section of the building) to remind ourselves of God's Gift of Himself in Christ, given to us on that first Christmas in Bethlehem. Then we caught a few hours' sleep.

Just as dawn was breaking, we hurried over to the Church of Saint Anastasia, at the foot of the Palatine Hill. To see the light of Christmas Day beginning over the ruins of the Imperial Forum was a moving sight as we arrived at the church. In those days, since there was no electricity at Saint Anastasia, we each carried a candle. The second Mass of Christmas, at dawn, was celebrated there in candlelit magnificence, with the monks from San Anselmo providing the schola, singing Gregorian chant in its prayerful and contemplative tones.

After that Mass at dawn, we went to the Basilica of Saint Mary Major for the Mass during the day. In that great Marian church are kept the relics that for centuries have been venerated as pieces from the manger in which Jesus was placed after His birth. The Mass was celebrated by the cardinal archpriest and was glorious in every respect.

Seminarians are notorious for being always hungry. We were no exceptions in that regard. After the Mass at Saint Mary Major, we had a wonderful American-style breakfast at a hospice run by a group of German nuns. Still wiping the remains of the ham and eggs from our mouths, we then hastened to St. Peter's Square for the Mass there with tens of thousands of people, a Mass celebrated in the presence of the Pope by the cardinal archpriest of St. Peter's Basilica. After Mass, from the central loggia, Pope Pius XII delivered his Christmas message (it was to be his last one) and then gave his blessing. For centuries, the pope's blessing on such occasions has been called "*Urbi et Orbi*", that is, to the city of Rome and to the world.

When we returned to the North American College (we had done all our traveling by foot and thus had covered about ten miles over all), the sisters who did our domestic work had a wonderful, multicourse Christmas dinner prepared for us. After dinner, exhausted, we were grateful for the opportunity to take siesta. For me, however, this was a special time to make a long-distance phone call to my home and to talk to my mom and dad. (Long-distance calls to and from Italy in those times were something of an ordeal, since the Italian telephone company lacked certain aspects of modern efficiency.)

Afternoon tea is a very agreeable European custom. The special aspect of our Christmas tea was the chance it gave us seminarians to exchange experiences with each other and to remark on various national and local Christmas customs. Later, a light supper was just the right touch to prepare us for our evening Christmas program. The choir again sang American Christmas songs, and with skits and playlets the seminary community concluded its celebration of Christ's Nativity in the year of grace 1957. Evening prayer and night prayer, celebrated with solemnity, as seems possible only in a Catholic seminary, brought my first Christmas in Rome to a pleasant end.

Over the decades many celebrations of Christmas in a variety of places on earth have been recorded in my memory. The memory of the first Christmas I spent in Rome, however, occupies a prominent place in my mind. The painful separation from family and familiar surroundings was somewhat mitigated by the wonder and newness of what I had experienced. That memory always brings to mind the words of Chesterton, who wrote about the "older place than Eden, the taller town than Rome, the place where God was homeless, so all men could come home".

DECEMBER 15, 1995

Love beyond All Telling

Among the various paradoxes of Christmas is that of the helplessness of the Almighty. The God of omnipotence made Himself helpless, while remaining all-powerful. The Creator of the stars and the planets chose to clothe Himself in a human nature, to shut Himself up in Mary's womb, and to sleep, as an infant, in the hay of a manger.

Father Hubert Dunphy observed that, as a baby, He

had to depend completely on His mother for everything. The Creator Who clothed the world in nature's splendor, Who cloaked the craggy mountains with capes of ermine snow, Who smothered whole countries with the splashing color of tropical flowers, Who streaked the sun's dawning with heaven's own pastels of green and blue and rose and stained the sunset with streams of His own bright red blood, this God Who dressed the world let Himself be dressed in swaddling clothes by one of His own creatures.

The paradox of Christmas continues in our own modern times. Therese Ickinger says:

> Greed has exploited it. Avarice ever buys and sells Christ in a thousand different treacheries. Yet, to it all, the eloquent stillness of the Child, the beautiful face of His Mother are answer enough to the world's profanities. Let vanity wear her emerald eyes. Let ambition build a throne of alabaster. Let talent boast and knowledge preen her purple plumes. Let strength array its arms of might, charms beguile, wealth secure. Love comes in straw, a ragged Prince with a court of oxen, breathing low the ancient anthem of life. Love comes in whispers, a presence which invites without urging, a reality which compels by appeal.

The most significant event in human history, the birth of the incarnate and transcendent God, took place in an animal shed and cave, while the world was totally absorbed in its own petty distractions. The Emperor Augustus had closed the doors of the temple of Janus for the third time. Caesar's power was unchallenged. The whole known world was at peace.

In the Holy Land, Herod the Great, subordinate to Augustus but still a king in his own right, was bringing to a close his tyrannical and monstrous thirty-three-year rule by murdering two of his sons and seeking permission from Augustus to kill a third. Neither Herod in his house in Jericho nor Augustus in his palace on the Palatine Hill in Rome had even the slightest suspicion that some rustic shepherds had been listening to angels sing and that some beasts had joined a humble Jewish carpenter and his wife to witness the birth of the eternal King of heaven and earth.

Abbot Ricciotti notes that "poverty and purity were the reasons why Jesus was born in a stable, the poverty of His legal father who did not have enough money to secure a private room among so many competitors in Bethlehem for the census, and the purity of His virgin Mother who wished to surround His birth with reverent privacy."

Monsignor Aloysius Coogan wrote:

> Could nature talk to us on the beautiful night of Christmas as stars twinkle in the heavens, she would say to us that which is small in you, you are magnifying and that which is great in you, you are minimizing. Your destiny lies beyond the stars, beyond the moon, beyond the earth. Your short span of earthly exis-

tence is so unimportant as compared to your eternal destiny that you are foolish to take anything too seriously in this life except the salvation of your immortal soul.

If the animals at Bethlehem could speak to us today, they would surely tell us that we should spend our lives on earth giving glory to God on high, as the angels still do in heaven, and fostering God's "shalom", peace on earth, that is, reconciliation of ourselves and our world with our Almighty Father.

As we genuflect on Christmas while reciting the words of the Nicene Creed, professing our faith in the Incarnation, the hypostatic union of God and humanity, we ought to try to remember the humility of our Savior, "Who, though he was in the form of God, did not count equality with God a thing to be grasped, but emptied himself, taking the form of a servant, being born in the likeness of men" (Phil 2:6–7).

The gift of Himself is so special that only God could have thought of it. Father Dunphy observes:

> When you receive Jesus in the Eucharist on Christmas, thank Him for this best of gifts. And if God is so infinitely generous as to surrender Himself to us, can we not abandon ourselves absolutely and without reserve to Him? Do not hold back one small fragment of yourself, reserve nothing for human pride and sensuality. Do not permit the devil or the world or sensual appetites to take title to one molecule of your being, but give yourself without condition to the God Who has given everything to you. This is the best Christmas present you can give God and, incidentally, the best you can give yourself.

The seventeenth-century poet Robert Southwell wrote, "God is my gift, Himself He freely gave me. God's gift am I, and none but God shall have me."

As Therese Ickinger observes, there can be no real Christmas without the Mass, which is the greatest miracle of all, the prolongation of the Nativity in time and space. "It is hidden from the eyes of skeptics, for were it seen, the world would waste away in glory. Faith alone can perceive it. It is at once Christmas and Calvary, the hope of the huddled cave and the triumph of the empty tomb." The Holy Eucharist is, like Christmas, love beyond all telling.

DECEMBER 22, 1995

3

LENT

The Goal of Lent

Very few people set out on a journey with no destination in mind. Pointless travel is quite unusual. Each year the Church makes a journey called "Lent", a forty-day period of mortification and self-denial, of intensive prayer and devotion, and of special efforts in almsgiving and unselfish generosity. Before we embark on this annual trip, it seems prudent and important to keep in our mind the ultimate goal.

The journey goes from ashes to glory. The somber and frightening yet realistic reminder that we are dust and will return one day to the dirt from which we are made (Gen 3:19) recalls the curse that our human race bears from Adam's sin and from our own. However, Ash Wednesday is only the first step in Lent. As the season advances, we are expected to progress in the areas of penance until we reach the last weeks before Easter. In those final days of Lent, our meditation on the Passion and death of Jesus is meant to draw us closer to the mystery of the Cross.

The triumphant finale to Lent is the Solemn Easter Vigil, when the climax of the liturgical year occurs in a foretaste on earth of our destiny to share in Christ's victory forever in heaven.

Our Lenten journey was foreshadowed by the forty-year trek of the Israelites across the desert to the promised land. In another way it relives the forty-day fast in the desert by Jesus, in preparation for His successful battle with the temptations of Satan and the beginning of His public ministry. In its turn, our Lenten journey symbolizes and recapitulates our journey across the desert-called-life to the blessed joy and peace of our true homeland, heaven, where we are to enjoy the vision of God's face eternally.

Our Lord was clear about our need to do penance. Unless we do penance, He told us, we would "likewise perish" (Lk 13:5). The preparation for Easter, the greatest of all our solemnities and feasts, provides us with an opportunity to obey this requirement of our religion.

Penance must be both external and internal (Mt 6:1–18), and this is, obviously, because, as human beings, we are composed of matter and spirit, body and soul. Fasting, extra time and effort in prayer, and more than usual kindness and help to the needy will enable us to acquire a renewed self-mastery, while at the same time giving us a way to repair the damage we have done to ourselves and others by our sins.

In his retirement after the Civil War, Robert E. Lee was convinced the world was becoming "soft". When a young mother approached him to ask his advice about rearing her son, he said: "Teach him how to make sacrifices." As we approach the end of this century, how much "softer" our world is than it was at the time of Lee's advice, the close of the last century!

Lent is an excellent time to demonstrate, for instance, that our household and family "rule" the television set and not the other way around . . . or that personal self-control in eating and drinking and smoking and recreating can still exist in our lives . . . or that serious religious reading, study, and prayer are able to constitute important values in our life-style and that we have the courage and fortitude to persevere in them for a month and a half.

In one of his great Lenten sermons, Cardinal Newman laments that most people are guided in their lives mainly by pleasure and pain and rarely by reason, principle, or conscience. As a result the world appears to them to be made for pleasure, and the vision of Christ's Cross "is a solemn and sorrowful sight interfering with this appearance. . . . The world is sweet to the lips, but bitter to the taste."

However, he goes on to say: "They alone are able truly to enjoy this world, who begin with the world unseen. They alone enjoy it, who have first abstained from it. They alone can truly feast, who first have fasted; they alone are able to use the world, who have learned not to abuse it; they alone inherit it, who take it as a shadow of the world to come, and who for that world to come relinquish it."

Pope Saint Leo the Great called Lent "the greatest and holiest of fasts", the "mystic days, appointed and consecrated for the purification of soul and body". He points out how even "the hearts of religious people can be defiled by the dust of worldly things". Therefore, in prayer, fasting, and almsgiving, we find the correctives and cleansing agents that, under God's grace, enable us to redeem the faults of other times and to restore us to the devotion and reverence that will permit us to celebrate the Passover of the Lord worthily.

Newman said: "The Cross will lead us to mourning, repentance, humiliation . . . but all this will only issue, nay, will be undergone in a happiness far greater than the enjoyment which the world gives." All our pains, he remarks, those we impose on ourselves and those that come to us unbidden, are, because of our sins, a foretaste of hell, but "by the sprinkling of His blood" they are changed into a preparation for heaven.

Holy Season

On a tombstone somewhere the somber verses are written: Remember man who passes by, as you are now so once was I. And, as I am, one day you'll be. Prepare, O man, to follow me. Beneath this message some wag wrote a graffito: To follow you is not my intent, until I learn which way you went!

The coming of Ash Wednesday each year invites us all to recall our personal mortality and to think more deeply about our eternal destiny. The blessed ashes and the grave words that accompany their being placed on our heads are meant to summon us, at least briefly, each year to ponder more seriously the purpose of our existence and the ultimate goal of our being.

What makes our Ash Wednesday and the holy season of Lent that it commences something more than merely an occasion for morbid pre-occupation with death is the knowledge that, in our forty days of prayer, fasting, and almsgiving, we are following Christ as a penitent and as a warrior, and at the end of it all we find not death and decay, but resurrection and life immortal.

At the conclusion of Lent, it is Easter innocence that is to be the result of the work of this season. In the case of catechumens, it is the innocence that comes from their Baptism or from their being received into the Catholic Church and their first Confession. For those of us already baptized, it is the innocence that derives from our Easter Confession, our self-denial and reparation for our past sins, our self-mastery obtained under God's grace by our penance and mortification, and our renewal of our baptismal vows at the Easter Vigil.

Lent is the springtime of the Church year. It is the joyous time when the Church makes her final preparation for the harvest of souls, ripe for Baptism, dying with Jesus in the blessed waters and then rising with Him to new life. It is also the time for the second baptism for us sinners, the painful baptism of penance, a baptism made bearable, however, and even happy by the sacraments of Reconciliation and Holy Eucharist.

FASTING

Christ, the divine Soldier Who enters into conflict with the devil, also gives us an example of proper penitential exercises by His prayer and fasting in the desert. As Cardinal John Henry Newman observes: "He has blessed fasting as a means of grace, in that He has fasted; fasting is only acceptable when it is done for His sake. Penitence is mere formality,

or mere remorse, unless done in love. If we fast, without uniting ourselves in heart to Christ, imitating Him, and praying that He would
make our fasting His own, would associate it with His own, and communicate to it the virtue of His own, so that we may be in Him, and He
in us; we fast as Jews, not as Christians."

God enjoined fasting on the Chosen People of the Old Testament.
Indeed, many of the great figures of the time before Christ were noted
for their fasting. Moses fasted before receiving the Old Law. Elijah fasted
before his fiery ascent to heaven. Daniel fasted and, like Jesus after His
fast in the desert, had angels, sent from God, to minister to him.

Our Redeemer maintained fasting as a rule and demand of the gospel. We, the Chosen People of the New Testament, are therefore required to fast in order to make reparation for the damage we have done
to ourselves and to others by our sins, to strengthen our willpower in
matters that are legitimate so as to be better able to resist temptations to
those things that are illicit, and to share Christ's Cross so we may eventually share His victory.

"Fasting", of course, should have a bodily or material component,
whether it is fasting from food (the traditional fast) or from television or
from some other pleasurable activity. However, most important is the
interior disposition that accompanies our fast (see Mt 6:2–18). There
should always be a spiritual aspect, such as fasting from criticism, anger,
gloom, sloth, and envy. Fasting will be meritorious only if accompanied
by extra prayer and special kindness to our neighbor, which can take the
form of courtesy and a few more smiles at home and at work as well as
generosity to the poor and needy and to the Church.

FORTY DAYS

In calculating sacred time, the number forty seems to have a special biblical significance. It was forty days and forty nights that the rains fell at
the time of Noah and his family in the ark. It was forty days and forty
nights that Moses stayed on the mountain before he was given the law.

The Israelites had to spend forty years wandering in the desert before
they were permitted to enter the promised land. Our Lord spent forty
days and forty nights fasting and praying before beginning His public life
(Mt 4:2). It is in imitation of Him that the Church gives us this annual
"retreat" of forty days (Sundays do not count) to prepare ourselves for
our greatest feast and solemnity, Easter.

This imitation of Jesus is what He Himself has commanded. He said,
"If any man would come after me, let him deny himself and take up his
cross and follow me" (Mt 16:24). Saint Paul teaches, "But far be it from

me to glory except in the cross of our Lord Jesus Christ, by which the world has been crucified to me, and I to the world" (Gal 6:14). The forty days of Lent provide us with an opportunity to fulfill the command of Christ in regard to penance. He said if we did not do penance we would "likewise perish" (Lk 13:5).

Cardinal Newman wisely instructs us, "Nothing is so likely to corrupt our hearts and to seduce us from God as to surround ourselves with comforts, to have things our own way, to be the center of a sort of world which ministers to us." This coming holy season of Lent will give forty mystical chances to each of us to avoid that peril and to unite ourselves more closely to our Savior.

FEBRUARY 24, 1995

Antidote to the Three P's

The English language enjoys many peculiarities, one of which has to do with the title we use for the great period of pre-Easter preparation. Other languages use such terms as "*Quadragesima*", which refers to the "forty-day" aspect of that period of time, but we use the old Anglo-Saxon expression "Lent", which means "springtime". Each springtime the holy season returns in which we prepare, under God's grace, to celebrate the paschal mysteries in an appropriate way.

Tradition says that there are three areas of temptation that bedevil our human journey toward eternity. These are pleasure, power, and possessions. In a certain sense all sinful temptations can be put under one of those categories, the three P's. Although these categories of temptation are found in every age group, customary wisdom indicates youth as the time of life when the temptation to pleasure is the strongest, middle age for power, and old age for possessions.

It is precisely to assist us in confronting the three P's that the holy season of Christian "springtime" offers us the three traditional Lenten activities of fasting, prayer, and almsgiving. To control our urges toward pleasure, our drive toward power, and our striving for possessions, we have an annual opportunity to share the desert experience of our Savior (Mt 4:1–11), to answer Christ's call to repentance (Mk 1:15), and dutifully to carry our cross as Jesus commands (Lk 9:23). Lent prepares us for Easter and enables us to make instruments and tools of pleasure, power, and possessions, rather than allowing them to become our masters or our goals. In the somber words that accompany the placing of the ashes on our heads, we have a serious reminder of what should be the priority of our lives, to save our souls, even at the price of the "whole world" (Lk 9:25).

Pope Paul VI wrote: "By divine law all the faithful are required to do penance."[1] He echoed the explicit teaching of Jesus that unless we do penance we will "likewise perish" (Lk 13:5). Mortification and self-denial are necessary to make reparation for sins, our own sins and those of others; to exercise our often flabby willpower, so to prevent our will from becoming atrophied; and to recognize in our created fragility God's holiness and majesty.

Gathering spiritual strength from His forty days of fasting and prayer in the desert, Jesus taught us by example as well as by His verbal instruction how to resist the temptations represented by the three P's. Surely the diabolical temptation to make bread out of stones (Lk 4:1–4) was a temptation to pleasure; that to fling Himself from the temple's pinnacle (Mt 4:5–7) and yet remain unharmed was unquestionably a Satanic temptation to power; while the urging of the devil to accept "all the kingdoms of the world" in exchange for violating the first commandment of the Decalogue could hardly be other than a temptation to possessions (Mt 4:8–11).

Fasting, prayer, and almsgiving should be a vital part of our yearly determination to prepare for the renewal of our baptismal innocence, the culmination of our Lenten exercises. The holy water of the Easter Vigil will welcome the newest members of Christ's Church into God's official family, but it also represents the freshness of a springtime that should touch all of us anew with risen Life, provided that the season of Lent is the time of grace that our Lord and His Church intend it to be.

To use again the ideas of Pope Paul VI, the exercise of bodily mortification, far removed from any form of stoicism, does not imply a condemnation of the flesh, which the Son of God deigned to assume. On the contrary, it aims at the liberation of the human being who often finds himself, because of concupiscence, almost chained by his own senses. Our asceticism, which strives to follow the example of Christ Himself, must be something special, because it should be motivated by a desire to participate in the sufferings of Christ, His Passion and death. Without this participation, Wednesday's ashes remain only the debris of burnt palms, rather than a prelude to the flowering of glory and happiness that should be the effect of that springtime called Lent.

The apostles, the Fathers of the Church, and the supreme pontiffs through the ages have condemned with the very words of Jesus (Mt 6:1–9) any form of penitence during Lent that is simply marked by

---

[1] Apostolic Constitution on Penance, *Paenitemini*, chap. 3.

formalism, pharisaism, or pure extrinsicism. Our Lenten works of fasting, prayer, and almsgiving must be ever accompanied by internal conversion, interior recollection, and works of charity that remain known
largely only to ourselves and to God, Who sees all things. However, we
are composed of bodies as well as souls. We are not merely "imprisoned
spirits", and therefore our internal dispositions must be interiorized versions of external acts.

While Lent ought to see us doing something "special", we should
also remember that true penance involves persevering faithfulness to the
duties of our state in life, the acceptance of the difficulties arising from
our work, and a patient bearing of the trials of earthly life and the inse-
curity that pervades it. So, then, in the alms we decide to give, let us
include a few gratuitous smiles; in our fasting, let us include abstinence
from gossip and bad speech; and in our Lenten prayer, let us include a
measure of deeper fervor. May fasting, prayer, and almsgiving be the
contradiction and antidote to our temptation to the three P's.

FEBRUARY 19, 1993

The Acceptable Time

In olden times and in Catholic cultures, there arose spontaneously
among ordinary people an impulse to celebrate a bit before the austerity
and penance of Lent were begun. Consequently, Shrovetide took the
form of Mardi Gras (fat Tuesday) or *Carnevale* (farewell to meat). The
self-denial of Lent in ancient days was severe both because of Church
laws and because of the desire of the Christian faithful to make amends
for sin, to share Christ's fast of forty days in the desert, and to participate
more fully and consciously in His suffering and death.

Today for the most part we live in a permissive culture of pleasure and
softness. The mortification of Lent, indeed, even Lent itself, is largely
unknown or ignored by large segments of the population. Even Christians often treat Lent and its importance with lightness and unbecoming
casualness. Yet, human nature being what it is, the pre-Lenten celebrations of Mardi Gras and Carnival are ironically still undertaken by
people who frequently have not the slightest notion why these celebrations are held.

There is no reason why Catholic households should not stand over
and against this current neglect of Lent. The call to repentance is certainly needed more today than ever before. The need for reparation for
sins (ours and those of others), the necessity of building up our willpower, and the command of our Savior Himself (Lk 13:5) should urge

us to take seriously the implications of the ashes that are placed on our heads on Wednesday.

Lent is the springtime of the Church, the time when she prepares the womb of her baptismal font to give birth to her new children, who will die with Christ and be buried with Him in the water and then rise with Him to new and everlasting life. It is the season when she prepares for the greatest and most important of her feasts and solemnities, Easter.

This is also the time when we, the children of the Church, must undergo our annual "baptism of penance", the painful and uncomfortable season when we are to cooperate with God's grace in a special way to regain our baptismal innocence, so that Easter will find us purified of our imperfections and once again prepared to share in the triumph of Jesus because we have shared in His Cross. Notwithstanding the self-discipline that Lent requires of us, it is, even for us penitents, a time of particular happiness as we draw closer to our Redeemer by our extra prayer, our fasting, and our almsgiving.

Lent provides a fine time to help us recognize and escape the chains of our addictions. Most of us are slaves, more than we might suspect, to television, to certain kinds of food or drink, to any number of persons and things. Resonating in our hearts during Lent should be the words of Saint Paul that we hear so solemnly every Ash Wednesday, "Now is the acceptable time; behold now is the day of salvation" (2 Cor 6:2).

It can be quite useful from time to time to consult the Fathers and Doctors of the Church. Their writings and works continue to have considerable value even for the people of our time. There can be no doubt that they unanimously treated Lent as a time of the year that must be taken seriously.

Saint Ambrose said, "He who fasts at other times will receive pardon, but he who does not fast during Lent will be punished. Anyone who cannot fast should be more charitable toward the poor in an attempt to do penance for past sins." Saint Basil noted, "Through lack of mortification we humans were expelled from Paradise. Let us fast, then, that its gates may be once more opened to us."

Saint Thomas Aquinas said, "Fasting cleanses the soul, raises the mind to God, subjects one's flesh to the spirit, renders the heart contrite and humble, scatters the clouds of concupiscence, quenches the fire of lust, and kindles the true light of chastity."

Sacred writers observe that Jesus wanted His followers to do penance after His own earthly life was over (Lk 5:34-35). It is clear that fasting and penance were part of what has always characterized the Church from the beginning (Acts 13:2-3; 14:22; 27:9).

Two very ancient documents that may even antedate some parts of the New Testament are the *Didache* and the *Pastor of Hermas*. Both of them indicate that the earliest Christians practiced penance and fasting regularly. They state that it was a Christian custom to eat or drink nothing on all Wednesdays and Fridays until Mass was celebrated, shortly after sunset. The first ecumenical council of the Catholic Church, the Council of Nicaea (325), ordered that all Catholics should observe forty days of penance in preparation for Easter. Since Sundays were not considered suitable days for fasting and penance (because all Sundays, even those during Lent, are celebrations of Christ's Resurrection), Lent was determined to begin on Ash Wednesday, so that there would be forty days of mortification to recall the fast of Jesus before His public life and the forty years the Chosen People of the Old Testament spent wandering in the wilderness before they were allowed to enter the promised land.

Pope Saint Leo the Great taught that to our penance and fasting in Lent we must join generous almsgiving, purity of conscience, an end to pride and the spirit of revenge, mildness and humility, renewed efforts at prayer, and a silent and docile listening to the word of God.

FEBRUARY 16, 1996

Foreshadowings

I

Many Americans are uninterested in history and, as a consequence, are unlearned in history. However, we Catholics, whether we find it congenial or not, must be a people familiar with history, since the phrase we recite each Sunday at Mass, "suffered under Pontius Pilate", anchors our faith in history. During this season of Lent, our preparation for Easter demands some historical reflection or else it will not take on the dimensions that it should.

HISTORICAL REFLECTION

Charles Dodd wrote, "The conviction remains central to the Christian faith that at a particular point in time and space, the eternal entered decisively into history. An historic crisis occurred by which the whole world of man's spiritual experience is controlled. To that moment in history our faith always looks back. . . . Above all, in the sacrament of the Eucharist the Church recapitulates the historic crisis in which Christ came, lived, died, and rose again, and finds in the Eucharist the efficacious sign of eternal life in the kingdom of God."

In the paschal event, which is to say, in the dying and rising of Jesus, one finds the key that unlocks the mysterious meaning of all human history (Rom 16:25; Col 1:26). Holy Thursday, Good Friday, and the Easter Vigil are not simply a historic commemoration of what God did for humanity in Christ, but these are occasions when we actually live again what happened once and for all long ago. To participate in these mysteries requires that we try to understand something about how God, over many centuries, prepared the world for them.

Saint Paul wrote, "I would not have you ignorant, brethren, that our fathers were all under the cloud and all passed through the sea, and all were baptized into Moses in the cloud and in the sea, and all ate the same supernatural food and all drank the same supernatural drink. For they drank from the Rock which followed them, and the Rock was Christ" (1 Cor 10:1–4). Saint Paul does not want us to be ignorant about the meaning of these historic happenings, which obviously have an important and prophetic meaning even for us modern Christians. Lent is preeminently the season of the year when we must labor to overcome our ignorance about these things.

Over many eons of time God Himself prepared to undo the damage caused by the first Adam. When the obedience surrounding the tree of the Cross was to repair the disobedience surrounding the tree of the knowledge of good and evil (Gen 2:17), God wished this to be done by a New Adam. To prepare for His death and Resurrection, God intervened in human affairs: in the flood, the tower of Babel, the call of Abraham, the birth and sacrifice of Isaac, the sale of Joseph, the slavery of Egypt, the call of Moses, the exodus and the wandering in the desert, and the entry into the promised land. We must know in a profound way the elements of this fascinating story to appreciate truly our participation in the liturgy of Holy Week and Easter. Father Clifford Howell wrote, "Let us learn from the past that we may profit from the future. . . . If we are to understand all that Christ did for us and all that He is doing for us now, then we must learn the lessons of these signs and wonders of the past . . . for they were explanations given in advance."

THE DELUGE

The story of the great flood (Gen 6–9) represents an important foreshadowing of our coming celebration of Easter. Easter is a great "water feast" (along with Pentecost and Epiphany). Just as the waters of the flood wiped sin off the planet Earth, so the water of Baptism (and also the annual "baptism of our Lenten penance") wipes away sin. The torrents of rain that composed the flood are a *type* of the pouring and sprinkling of Easter water in the liturgy of the Great Vigil.

The water of the flood not only destroyed wickedness but also saved the eight people in the ark. So the water of Baptism not only destroys sin but saves (1 Pet 3:21–22). The ark has ever been a symbol of the Catholic Church. Thus, Baptism links us to the Church and makes us her members and gives us the possibility of a new and everlasting life.

Upon emerging from the ark with his family at the end of his ordeal, Noah offered a sacrifice of thanksgiving to God, Who, in turn, made a pact, or covenant, with Noah, immortalized in the rainbow. The allegorical meaning is clear. We too make a sacrifice that is called "thanksgiving" (Eucharist), and, as the words of consecration indicate, this sacrifice too involves a "new and eternal covenant", the perpetual assurance of God's friendship. When we are at the Easter Vigil on Holy Saturday night, we should not forget about the deluge when we see the water and the sacrifice that are present.

ABRAHAM

Adventure and travel (Gen 11–25) certainly mark the history of Abraham, whom we call, in the liturgy, "our father in faith". Pope Pius XI said, "Spiritually, we are all Semites." Of course, this is because we are the spiritual descendants of this great patriarch (Gal 3:7). Called out of the city of Ur of the Chaldees, Abraham was the one chosen by God to be the founder of the Chosen People of the Old Testament and the remote ancestor of the Messiah.

God made a treaty, or covenant, with Abraham and arranged that it be sealed in blood, the blood of circumcision. This mark and this blood set off the Chosen People as having a special relationship with God. During Lent and especially during the coming Holy Week we should remember the words of Jesus, "This cup which is poured out for you is the new covenant in my blood" (Lk 22:20). We, the Chosen People of the New Testament, are set apart by the mark of our Baptism and the Blood of the Eucharist (1 Pet 2:9–10). There is no better time to recall this than now.

MARCH 8, 1996

Foreshadowings

II

Lent is a special time of the year when conscientious and devout Catholics prepare themselves to participate in the mysteries of redemption, especially in the Sacred Triduum (Holy Thursday, Good Friday, and the Easter Vigil). This participation demands a knowledge of the wonders and signs of the Old Testament in order truly to share in the paschal mystery in a complete and wisdom-filled way.

MELCHIZEDEK

One of the interesting personalities in the Old Testament, who first is mentioned in the Abraham story (Gen 14:18), is the king and priest named Melchizedek. His name appears only twice more in the Bible (in Psalm 110 and in Hebrews 7). He is called the King of Salem (which means "city of peace", hence, Jeru-salem), and he makes an unusual thanksgiving sacrifice out of bread and wine to honor a victory of Abraham over some bedouin chiefs (or kings) who had assaulted Abraham's nomadic camp and carried off his nephew Lot as a hostage. It is clear that Melchizedek is a *type* of Jesus, Who is also a Priest and a King, Who offers a thanksgiving sacrifice (Eucharist) in forms of bread and wine. At our Holy Thursday Mass especially should we recall Melchizedek, whose priesthood is "for ever" and who is likened to "the Son of God" (Heb 7:3).

SACRIFICE OF ISAAC

One of the dramatic and poignant episodes in the patriarchal history of Abraham (Gen 11–25) relates how in his old age and that of his wife, Sarah, he was able to father a son, Isaac. This was part of the covenant, or agreement, made with God, promising Abraham a huge progeny. All the hopes of the family rested with this boy. Suddenly God demanded that Abraham kill him, this only son, as a sacrifice to God.

Abraham prepared immediately to obey God. He took Isaac to Mount Moria; had him carry up the mountain, on his back, the wood on which he was to be slain; bound him; and was about to kill him (James 2:21) when he was stopped by an angel sent from God, who explained that God was exacting a test of Abraham's obedience and faith. Since Abraham had passed the test, he was forbidden to go through with the sacrifice. It is particularly on Good Friday that we are called upon to remember Isaac as a *type* of Christ. Jesus, too, is the only begotten Son of His Father. He, too, carried up the mountain called Calvary (could this be the same mountain previously called Moria?) the wood on which He was to be sacrificed by the will of His loving Father.

What God wanted to elicit from Abraham was, of course, faith (Rom 4:3). It is particularly on Holy Saturday, at the Easter Vigil, that the faith of Abraham should be recalled as we renew the faith that is concretized in our baptismal vows, promises, and commitments. Faith is intrinsically linked to Baptism, the faith of the Church, and—when we are old enough to make an act of faith—our personal faith. The Easter Vigil is, above all, the celebration of our Baptism and our faith.

JOSEPH

One of the most striking figures or *types* of Jesus found in the Old Testament is that of Joseph, one of the twelve sons of Jacob, or Israel. Joseph was the grandson of Isaac. He was sold into slavery by his brothers for pieces of silver. His garments were stained with blood (to deceive his father about his fate). He was falsely accused of a crime he did not commit. His virtue and God's providence arranged that he attain great power in Egypt, where eventually he was called "the Savior". Furthermore, he fed his starving people with bread sufficient for all.

The parallels with our Redeemer are obvious. Christ feeds His people with "Bread from heaven". He was betrayed by His brethren (and is betrayed by us when we commit sins). He was sold for pieces of silver by Judas but attained power and dominion by His glorious Resurrection. His garments are stained red with the purple of His precious Blood (Rev 19:13). How true is the saying of Saint Jerome regarding the relationship of the Old Testament to the New! He said, "The Old the New conceals, while the New the Old reveals."

EXODUS

No foreshadowing is more singular for Holy Week and Easter than that of the liberation of the Hebrews from the slavery of Egypt. A fuller understanding of our redemption and salvation is not possible without a reasonable grasp of the Passover and exodus. It is only in the context of the exodus events that sense can be made out of the liturgy of the Sacred Triduum.

Once Joseph had established his family in prosperity in Egypt, the Hebrew race and nation flourished as the years passed by. But then came "a Pharaoh who knew not Joseph", and thus slavery and attempted genocide ensued. Lent is an excellent time to read again the second book of the Bible and to understand it in terms of our annual celebration of Holy Week and Easter.

After a series of plagues and crises, God, through Moses, told each Jewish family to kill an unblemished lamb, sprinkle its blood on the doorposts of their house, and eat the roasted lamb with unleavened bread in a ceremonial meal, while His angel would go through the land killing the firstborn male of humans and beasts, but "passing over" the houses marked with the lamb's blood. This disaster convinced the Pharaoh to let the Hebrew slaves have their freedom. The "Passover", or Pasch, was to be celebrated annually by the Hebrews in a special seder banquet, its ceremonial repeated in every detail to recall their deliverance.

It is in Holy Week, for which we are preparing all through Lent, that these important historical events are remembered in the context of the New Testament. Jesus, the spotless Lamb of God, was slain to save us from slavery to sin and death forever. (We sing at the Easter Vigil to God: "To ransom a slave You gave up Your Son!") Our ceremonial meal (Holy Mass), the seder meal of the New Testament, does not only commemorate but actually makes present the very Passion and death of Jesus.

MARCH 15, 1996

Easter Gift

There is a story about a farm boy whose father gave him a goose to raise. But through neglect and foolishness, he allowed his goose to die. Terrified of his father, he spent two weeks of agony wondering how he could conceal his errors from him. Finally, when he could stand it no longer, he confessed what he had done. Instead of giving him the scolding and spanking he expected, his father smiled at him and said that he had known for two weeks what the son had done, and he had merely been waiting for him to own up to his faults. The father arranged for the lad to do some extra chores around the farm to make up for his wrongs. The boy said that in his whole life he had never felt an embrace more satisfying than the hug his dad gave him when that episode was all over.

GOD'S EMBRACE

God is our loving Father. He knows our sins, failings, faults, and shortcomings, but he is always ready to embrace us with a hug of forgiveness, provided we are truly sorry, are resolved not to sin again, and have the courage to own up to our errors before Him. Jesus, hanging on the Cross, has, in the words of Saint Francis of Assisi, His head bent to kiss us, His arms extended to embrace us, and His heart cut open to receive us. On that Cross He won from His heavenly Father for us pardon, peace, understanding, and forgiveness. Then, on the evening of the very day He rose from the dead, He poured His forgiveness into His Church to distribute to contrite sinners down through the ages, until He comes again (Jn 20:22–23).

It is through the sign or sacrament of Easter night that Christ touches our souls with His absolution and tells us, with the same voice that He told the woman taken in adultery: "Neither do I condemn you; go, and do not sin again" (Jn 8:11). In the *Catechism of the Catholic Church*, this mystery, or sacrament, goes by the names "sacrament of conversion", "sacrament of Penance", "sacrament of confession", "sacrament of forgiveness", and "sacrament of Reconciliation" (CCC 1423–24).

Saint Thérèse of Lisieux said: "If my conscience were burdened with all the sins it is possible to commit, I would still go and throw myself into our Lord's arms, my heart all broken with contrition. I know what tenderness He has for any prodigal child of His who comes back to Him." Saint Joseph Cafasso said, "This is a Friend Who will not terrify you, Who will not abandon you. Hope in Him and heaven is yours." Saint Alphonsus wrote, "When you commit any sin, repent of it at once and resolve to amend. If it is a grievous sin, confess it as soon as possible."

God alone forgives sins (Mk 2:7). Jesus Christ, in His human nature, has power also on earth to forgive sins (Lk 7:48), and He has given this power to the priests of the New Testament (Jn 20:21–23). The Council of Trent says that by the very words of our Redeemer, "all of the Fathers have always understood that the power of forgiving and retaining sins was communicated to the apostles and their lawful successors for the reconciling of the faithful who have fallen after baptism."

This season of Lent is meant to be a true springtime for our souls. We ought to use the opportunity that it gives us to return to the practice of frequent and devout confession. It would be folly to be preparing ourselves for Easter without making the best use of the precious Easter gift our Lord has bequeathed to His Church, the sacrament of Reconciliation. The *Catechism* states:

Christ instituted the sacrament of Penance for all sinful members of his Church, above all for those who, since Baptism, have fallen into grave sin, and have thus lost their baptismal grace and wounded ecclesial communion. It is to them that the sacrament of Penance offers a new possibility to convert and to recover the grace of justification. The Fathers of the Church present this sacrament as "the second plank [of salvation] after the ship-wreck which is the loss of grace" (CCC 1446).

Saint Isidore said, "Confession heals, confession justifies, confession grants pardon of sin. In confession there is a chance for mercy."

SORROW FOR SINS

Not even God will forgive our sins if we are not sorry for them. Confession and all that accompanies that sacrament would be worthless unless we approach our forgiving Lord with true contrition in our heart. The *Catechism* says, "Among the penitent's acts, contrition occupies the first place. Contrition is 'sorrow of the soul and detestation for the sin committed, together with the resolution not to sin again'" (CCC 1451).

The Lenten season gives us many opportunities to contemplate the suffering and death of Jesus on Mount Calvary. Consequently, it is a preeminent time of the year to work, under God's grace, to arouse in our hearts contrition for our sins. When the principal motive for our sorrow is the love of God and the realization of how we have responded to that love, our contrition is perfect. Perfect contrition remits venial sins and takes away mortal sins, if we are determined to go to Confession with those sins as soon as possible.

When the motive of our sorrow arises from the ugliness of our sins, fear of our eternal damnation, and fright of the penalties of our sins, our contrition is good but imperfect. Such contrition, which is also a gift of God, can lead us to sacramental absolution and to peace with ourselves, with the Church, and with God.

Pope John Paul II says, "Contrition and conversion are even more a drawing near to the holiness of God, a rediscovery of one's true identity which has been upset and disturbed by sin, a liberation in the very depth of self and thus a regaining of lost joy, the joy of being saved, which the majority of people in our time are no longer capable of experiencing."[2] Saint Francis de Sales wrote, "Who will dare to measure, by the greatness of his sins, the immensity of that infinite mercy which casts them all into the depths of the sea of oblivion, when we repent of them with love?"

MARCH 17, 1995

---

[2] *Reconciliatio et paenitentia*, no. 31.

The Cross

As the liturgical year goes toward its climax, the celebration of the dying and rising of Jesus, that which should loom largest in Christian thought is the instrument that God's providence chose to be the symbol representing what divine love effected in our regard. That sign and symbol, of course, is the cross.

CONSTANTINE

Legend tells us that before the battle at the Milvian Bridge, the Emperor Constantine saw in a dream a glowing cross in the sky, surrounded by the words: "In this sign you shall conquer." The Emperor ordered a cross to be placed on all the banners and on the shields of his soldiers, and the next day, October 27, 312, his army decisively defeated the forces of his foe, Maxentius. Eusebius, the historian, says that Constantine himself told him that he was convinced that the cross brought about his victory there on the Saxa Rubra, the bank of the Tiber, and consequently he decided to become a Christian.

Constantine's mother, Saint Helen, was already a Christian and probably had a significant influence on his decision. He was baptized only on his deathbed. Nevertheless, he not only issued the Edict of Milan in 313, freeing Christians from persecution in the Roman Empire, but he had a lifelong devotion to the Cross of Christ. In particular, he supported the expedition of his saintly mother to the Holy Land, where, it is said, she found the remains of the true Cross of Christ on Mount Calvary.

One of the great archeological treasures still kept in the ruins of the ancient Roman Forum is the triumphal arch that Constantine erected to commemorate his victory at the Milvian Bridge. The words can still be made out on the arch after all these centuries: "In this sign you shall conquer."

By providential irony, God chose to undo the damning calamity of the primordial Fall of the human race in a way that reversed that dismal and melancholy event with its opposite occurrence. In the Garden of Eden there was the head of the human race, called "Adam" or "the Man", and there was a woman. The event centered on a tree named "the tree of the knowledge of good and evil". Above all, there was disobedience (see Gen 3).

On Golgotha, there was a new head of the human race, a new Adam (Rom 5:12–20); there was another woman (notice that Jesus called her "woman": John 19:26); and, above all, there was obedience (Jn 4:34).

Of course, there was another tree, the Cross. The conquest of Constantine "in" that sign was a mere hint of the redemption that God brought about through that "sign", a conquest that has a resonance not only in human history but in the halls of eternity. As the song says: "Tree all beauteous, tree all peerless and divine, not a grove on earth can show us such a flower and leaf as thine."

Not only a Roman Emperor from the pages of history but we ourselves can and should conquer "in" the sign of the Cross. In our temptations, in our battles with evil, with pain, with doubt, with despair, with hatred, and with all that is negative in our lives and in our world, the Cross is the means and instrument of victory. Our Lord invites us to share the Cross (Mt 10:38), but only temporarily in suffering and sorrow and then forever in triumph and glory. This is an invitation that is especially keen in the weeks immediately before Easter. The shadow of the Cross on our imagination during the next weeks is a necessary prelude to a paschal feast of genuine joy.

Thomas à Kempis wrote: "Jesus has many lovers of His heavenly kingdom, but few are willing to bear His cross. He has many who desire His comfort, but few to share His tribulations. He finds companions for His table, but few for His abstinence. All want to rejoice with Him, but few are willing to suffer with Him. Many follow Jesus in the breaking of His bread, but few there are who are willing to drink the chalice of His passion." May we, during this passiontide, be numbered among the few.

LIFE FROM DEATH

When all seemed hopelessly dreary, when all that was heard were the tears and laments of family and friends, when the Lord Himself groaned and wept in sympathy, when all seemed lost because of the four-day-old corpse and the grave and stone upon it, Christ overcame death and restored Lazarus to his sisters and to life (see Jn 11). This is truly the story of every soul that confronts the Cross. Every encounter with this instrument of our salvation, in whatever form it takes, has the capacity to change misery and agony into happiness and joy, provided that it is bravely embraced, courageously carried, and ever united to His Cross in obedience and resignation. For Christ and His Cross deal with death only for a short time, while He and His Cross give life that lasts forever.

On the Cross Jesus was cursed for our sake (Gal 3:13), and there He satisfied divine justice in our regard, proving to us the horror of our sins and the infinity of God's love. At all times, but especially in the weeks before Easter, we must, like Saint Paul, be "crucified with Christ" (Gal 2:19). We should make our own the sentiments of the Apostle of the

Gentiles: "But far be it from me to glory except in the cross of our Lord Jesus Christ, by which the world has been crucified to me, and I to the world" (Gal 6:14).

It is common to hear afflicted people say: "What did I do to deserve this?" As we make the sign of the cross and follow the Stations of the Cross, in preparation for Easter, let us imagine our Lord asking that same question of us: "What did I do to deserve this?" Let us look at our sinfulness and His love and exclaim in the ancient words: Hail, holy Cross, our only hope.

MARCH 26, 1993

Passiontide

As Lent draws to its final weeks, we are invited annually to meditate especially on the redemptive suffering and death of Jesus. His dying and rising are the central facts of our holy religion. In His act of saving us, we are astonished not only by the realization that God Himself became one of us and, in total and complete innocence, was cruelly tortured and put to death but also by the astounding truth that He did this out of obedience.

OBEDIENCE

Because of the effects of original sin and our own sins, innocent persons often suffer unjustly and horribly. The mystery of evil will remain with us until we are able to understand it in the perspective of God after our death. Innocent babies sometimes die in agony. We see on television or read in the newspapers about innocent victims of human malice and depravity, just as we see natural disasters such as earthquakes and hurricanes killing and maiming the innocent. What stands out about the death of Christ is not simply His innocence in the face of His condemnation and execution but His foreknowledge of His Passion (Lk 9:51) and His willing obedience to God the Father, bringing His human will into perfect conformity with His divine will (Mt 26:39). His obedience became a substitute for all human disobedience (Rom 5:19).

The suffering and death of Jesus on Golgotha was a priestly act (Heb 10:4–10). Why did God the Father exact this kind of sacrifice from His divine Son on our behalf? This certainly was not necessary, since God could have redeemed us with a mere thought or even the slightest gesture of His incarnate and only begotten Son. Insofar as God has revealed His reasons to us, the saints and doctors of the Church say the sacrifice

on Mount Calvary was enacted to emphasize the horror and consequences of sin as well as to demonstrate infinitely overwhelming divine
love.

LOVE

The *Catechism of the Catholic Church* says, "It is love 'to the end' (Jn 13:1)
that confers on Christ's sacrifice its value as redemption and reparation,
as atonement and satisfaction. He knew and loved us all when he offered
his life [cf. Gal 2:20]" (CCC 616). Genuine love is not measured by
sentiment, emotion, passion, or desire, although, because we are human
beings with bodies as well as souls, these things often accompany love.
True love is measured by giving and sacrifice.

Saint Thérèse of Lisieux said, "Look at Jesus on the cross. See His
adorable face, His glazed and sunken eyes, His wounds. There you see
how He loves us." Gregory Dix said, "Calvary is not just an historical
accident. It is not something that might not have happened if Pilate had
been a braver man or Judas a trustier man, or Caiaphas a holier
man . . . the wages of sin is death (Rom 6:23) and Jesus comes to pay
the wages that men have so laboriously earned."

Archbishop Fulton Sheen observed, "The only recorded time in the
history of our Lord that He ever sang was the night He went out to the
Garden of Gethsemane and His death." It is clear that He went to His
terrible death with the thought of each of us in His Sacred Heart, a
thought of love for us.

The *Catechism* says: "By embracing in his human heart the Father's
love for men, Jesus 'loved them to the end,' for 'greater love has no man
than this, that a man lay down his life for his friends' [Jn 15:13]. In
suffering and death his humanity became the free and perfect instrument of his divine love which desires the salvation of men. Indeed, out
of love for his Father and for men, whom the Father wants to save, Jesus
freely accepted his Passion and death" (CCC 609).

SIN

Although it sometimes camouflages itself as love, sin is, in reality, the
opposite of love. Masking selfishness and egoism with some kinds of
emotions and passions that have a certain superficial resemblance to the
usual companions of love, we human beings often requite the love of
Jesus, manifested on the Cross, with disdain, ingratitude, and repudia-
tion. Archbishop Sheen says, "Sin in all its forms is the deliberate evic-
tion of love from the soul. Sin is the enforced absence of divinity."

Since sin is so common and usual in our modern day and since it is depicted so casually, openly, and approvingly in the media, we are quite apt to forget its horrible evil and its eternally deadly consequences. This is why especially every year toward the close of Lent we should concentrate our thoughts on our crucified Savior.

More than other times of the year should we, in the last weeks before Easter, remember that Christ "was put to death for our trespasses" (Rom 4:25) and that "while we were yet sinners, Christ died for us" (Rom 5:8). He laid up in the bank of pardon and life a deposit for us of infinite worth. Under the help of His grace, it is our duty to allow Him to touch us in His holy sacraments with His healing and love from that bank deposit. "In him we have redemption through his blood, the forgiveness of our trespasses according to the riches of his grace" (Eph 1:7).

The ultimate consolation for us sinners, however, is to recall the first words that Christ spoke after the hammer and nails had done their work: "Father, forgive them, for they know not what they do" (Lk 23:34). These words, of course, apply not only to His executioners and enemies, but to every contrite sinner.

Why should we meditate on Christ's suffering and death at this time of the year? The answer is simple: to remember His love in the face of our sins. Archbishop Sheen says, "It is so easy to lose Christ. He can be lost by a little heedlessness. A little want of watchfulness and the divine presence slips away. But sometimes a reconciliation is sweeter than an unbroken friendship." Saint Bernadette said, "Let the crucifix be not only in your eye but also in your heart." Let us keep this in mind as go to make our Easter Confession this year.

MARCH 31, 1995

4

HOLY WEEK

The Week Called Holy

The ancient calculation of the date of Easter (the first Sunday after the first full moon after the vernal equinox) reminds us that the holiest feastdays of our religion are about to be celebrated. In signs and figures beneath veils of symbols, the Cross and Resurrection of our Savior have been gradually impressed upon our consciousness by our participation in Lent. Now, as the season of Lent draws to a close, in a way that is more clear and open, the central mysteries of our faith, the Passover of the Lord of history, will be recalled and made present in a drama at once sublime and simple.

The holy liturgy gives us the figure of Jesus suffering and dying for us, but it also presents to us our role, not only to offer tearful sympathy and sorrowful lamentation, but also to prepare for victory and joy and participation in glory.

More than at any other time of the year, Holy Week should be a period of our lives when we annually set aside as much of our worldly affairs and occupations as possible to participate in the re-presentation of the saving mysteries of Christianity in the liturgical actions of Christ's Bride and Body, that is, His Church.

In the procession with palms on Palm Sunday, in the evening Mass of the Lord's Supper on Holy Thursday, in the sharing in the Liturgy of the Passion and Death of Jesus on the Friday we have named "Good", and, most of all, in the great Solemn Vigil of Easter and its concluding Mass of the Resurrection ought we to find, not merely a pious reenactment of bygone happenings, but a "true presence" of our divine Redeemer and a profound appreciation of the gift of His Cross. It is in Holy Week most of all that, in the overwhelmingly eloquent words of Cardinal John Henry Newman, we can see His Cross as the measure of the world:

> Go to the courts of princes. . . . Consider the form and cere-
> monial, the pomp, the state, the circumstance, and the vain-
> glory. Do you wish to know the worth of it all? Look at the
> Cross of Christ.

Go to the political world: see nation jealous of nation, trade rivalling trade, armies and fleets. . . . Survey the various ranks of the community, its parties and their contests, the strivings of the ambitious, the intrigues of the crafty. What is the measure? the Cross.

Go, again, to the world of the intellect and science: consider the wonderful discoveries which the human mind is making, the variety of arts to which its discoveries give rise . . . the pride and confidence of reason. . . . Would you form a right judgment of all this? look at the Cross.

Again: look at misery, look at poverty and destitution, look at oppression and captivity; go where food is scanty, and lodging unhealthy. Consider pain and suffering, diseases long or violent, all that is frightful and revolting. Would you know how to rate all these? gaze upon the Cross.

Thus in the Cross and Him who hung upon it, all things meet; all things subserve it, all things need it. It is their centre and their interpretation. For He was lifted up upon it, that He might draw all men and all things unto Him.[1]

It is difficult to improve upon the words of this famous and holy convert to our faith. He sums up quite well an important aspect of Holy Week. Jesus assured us that we would have sorrow but that our sorrow would be temporary (Jn 16:22). Ultimately, the meaning of Holy Week is that happiness is the ending of the human story (1 Cor 2:9). The apparent defeat of Christ upon the Cross is in reality a great triumph. When the "Holy Strong One" is fastened with nails, when the "Holy Immortal One" dies, and when the "King of Ages" is crowned with thorns, we approach in the liturgy the final irony of Christianity.

The history is all too plain to us: the betrayal of Judas, the denial of Peter, the cowardice of Pilate, the malice of the chief priests and scribes and Pharisees, the fickle crowds, and, above all, the love unutterable. Each year in Holy Week we are again invited to weep with Mary, to be vigilant with the Beloved Disciple, to be grateful for the Eucharist and the priesthood, to mourn our sins, to see in the bloody sweat, the lash of the scourge, and the jab of the lance our own doing, our sins and their horror, contrasted with God's pardon and love made visible on a hill called "Skull Place".

As Lent itself is a journey from ashes to glory, so Holy Week is a

---

[1] *Parochial and Plain Sermons*, bk. 6, serm. 7 (San Francisco: Ignatius Press, 1997), 1240–41.

journey from palms to splendor. We progress in this week from the winepress of God's wrath (Rev 14:19), which spatters the garments of God's Word (Rev 19:13) to the promise of the Alpha and Omega, the King of kings and Lord of lords (Rev 19:16; 21:6), that when the last chapter of humanity is completed, it will have no crying or pain but smiles and laughter forever.

As Cardinal Newman wrote: "The Cross will lead us to mourning, repentance, humiliation, prayer, fasting; we shall sorrow for our sins, we shall sorrow with Christ's sufferings, but all this . . . will issue . . . only in a happiness far greater than the enjoyment which the world gives— though careless worldly minds indeed will not believe this, ridicule the notion of it, because they have never tasted of it." In this coming Holy Week, let us "taste of it".

APRIL 2, 1993

A Special Week

This entire season of Lent leads up to the special week we Christians call "holy". It is a dreadful commentary on how removed our culture is from a Catholic outlook that we treat Holy Week not much differently from any other. Entertainment, sporting events, and commercial life go on as if God had not come to earth to be incarnate and to die for our sins and rise for our justification. Devout Catholics, however, will never want to make Holy Week anything but a very special time of the year, clearly distinct from the other fifty-one weeks.

It is in the sacred liturgy that the great events of our salvation are made present, pushing aside the veils of time and space and allowing Christ Himself to touch us in signs and symbols, in word and sacrament. Jesus in the liturgy "distributes" the redemption that He won on the Cross and in the garden of the Resurrection. Consequently, every Catholic household will want to be present, or, at a minimum, have a family member present, at the Chrism Mass (which in our diocese is celebrated on Monday of Holy Week in the cathedral), at the Solemn Mass of the Lord's Supper on Holy Thursday, at the Liturgy of the Passion and Death of Jesus on Good Friday, and, most of all, at the Solemn Easter Vigil and the glorious Solemn Mass of the Resurrection on Holy Saturday evening, the climax and most magnificent part of the whole liturgical year.

Holy Week, of course, is ushered in on Passion, or Palm, Sunday. Palm branches (or olive tree branches or some similar fronds) are blessed before Mass, the Gospel narrative of Christ's triumphal entry into Jerusalem is solemnly sung or recited, and a great procession is held. The drama of the distribution of palms and the procession lead to the Mass itself, celebrated in red vestments, a reminder of the precious blood of Jesus, shed to save us. The centerpiece of the first part of the Palm Sunday Mass is the reading of the narrative of the Passion of Christ according to one of the synoptic evangelists.

THE CHRISM MASS

The sacred liturgy, as we well know, is not just "ceremonies" or "entertainment" or "services". The externals indicate an underlying internal reality. What is visible in the liturgy is meant to make present that invisible realm of grace and "spirit" that true Catholics see "with the eyes of faith".

Normally the blessing of the holy oils at the Chrism Mass takes place on Holy Thursday. However, in dioceses such as Lincoln (which is spread out over more than twenty-three thousand square miles) permission is given to have this Chrism Mass earlier in the week. Thus it is held in our Lincoln Diocese on Monday in Holy Week.

At this Mass in the cathedral (where all Catholics are invited to witness and participate), the unity of the Catholic priesthood is emphasized, this priesthood that Jesus instituted in the sacrament of Holy Orders on the first Holy Thursday. During this Mass the bishop blesses the oil of the sick (used in the sacrament of the Anointing of the Sick and in the blessing of bells), blesses the oil of catechumens (used in the sacrament of Baptism), and consecrates the sacred chrism, pouring the perfume "balm" into the olive oil. (Chrism is used in Confirmation, Holy Orders, and the consecration of altars and churches. It is the most sacred of the three holy oils.)

It is from this Chrism Mass that these oils are taken to each parish in a diocese, so that "mystically and spiritually" the high priest of the diocese (the bishop) is present in all sacramental administration. At the annual Chrism Mass the priests of a diocese renew again their priestly vows and commitments. Every Catholic, even those not able to be present at the Chrism Mass, should pray in Holy Week for their priests.

MAUNDY THURSDAY

Every Mass commemorates the Last Supper of Jesus, but the Mass on Holy Thursday evening has a very special significance in this regard. In a most affecting way, when Catholics gather in their parish churches on that special night, they are again in the upper room with the Savior, where the ineffable mystery and sacrament of the Holy Eucharist was instituted. They hear again Saint Paul's moving account of the institution of the Blessed Sacrament, and in the Gospel they hear Saint John telling about the breathtaking humility of Jesus in washing His disciples' feet. They see their pastor, in humble imitation of the divine Redeemer, follow His example, vividly calling to mind their own duty to "serve rather than be served".

No one who could possibly help it would want to be absent from church during the Sacred Triduum. Who will not be touched by the eucharistic procession after the Holy Thursday Mass to the altar of repose? Which Catholic worthy of the name will not spend some time before the Blessed Sacrament on Holy Thursday evening, thanking Christ for the gift of His body and blood, for His sacrifice, for His abiding and substantial presence with us, for His priesthood, without which we cannot have the Eucharist?

It is on Holy Thursday evening that Christ's Church remembers most vividly His agony in the garden, His arrest and trial before the Sanhedrin, and the beginning of His humiliation and sorrows.

Speaking of the altar of repose on Holy Thursday evening, Saint Ephraem said: "O blessed spot, your narrow room may be set against the whole world. That which is contained in you, though bounded by a narrow compass, fills the universe. Blessed is that dwelling place in which, with holy hand, the Bread was broken. In you the Grape which grew on Mary's vine was crushed in the chalice of salvation."

MARCH 11, 1994

Good Friday

On Friday, April 1, 1994, there will be no Mass offered in any of the Catholic Churches of the world in the Latin Rite. This is not an "April Fool" joke, but a fact. The reason, of course, is that April 1, this year [1994], is the Friday of Holy Week, the Friday that we Christians call "Good". By very ancient custom, on Good Friday there is no unbloody and glorious re-presentation of the death and Resurrection of Jesus in Holy Mass so that on this one day of the year the whole Church can concentrate especially on remembering the historical, bloody torture and death of our divine Lord on Mount Calvary.

Of course, there is celebrated in all Catholic churches the "Solemn Liturgy of the Passion and Death of Christ", in the course of which Holy Communion, using the Sacred Hosts consecrated on Holy

Thursday evening, is distributed. Every Catholic who can do so will undoubtedly want to be present and to participate in the Divine Liturgy of Good Friday.

The Solemn Liturgy on Good Friday consists of four parts. The entire liturgy on that day is marked by somber restraint. The bells, which had been "put to rest" on Holy Thursday evening, are not rung. The organ, except to support singing, is not played.

The first part is a service of the Word. After a beautiful opening prayer, there is a reading of one of the "servant songs" of the Prophet Isaiah (Jesus is the "Servant" spoken of, the Paschal Lamb of the New Testament), a reading of a passage from the Epistle to the Hebrews (telling us that what Christ did on the Cross was a supreme act of *priesthood*), and the reading of the Passion of Christ according to Saint John. This is followed by a homily and by a collection for the Holy Land.

The second part is a series of "bidding prayers", also called "general intercessions" or "prayers of the faithful". These, on Good Friday, are more special and solemn than at any other time of the year. The third part is the veneration of the cross, the ceremony that in Catholic England was called "creeping to the cross". The veiled cross is brought into church and solemnly and slowly unveiled. As priests, ministers, and people venerate the cross, the meaning of Good Friday is brought vividly to the attention of all, by the atmosphere and, most of all, by the music.

Unveiling the cross dates from the centuries when the cross was often a *"crux gemmata"*, that is, a cross encrusted with jewels to remind everyone of the Resurrection. Such a cross was veiled during Passiontide so that the suffering of Jesus could be better recalled. During the veneration of the cross, the "reproaches" are often sung: "O my people, what have I done to you? Wherein have I offended you? Answer me!—Holy God! Holy Strong One! Holy Immortal One, have mercy on us!"

The fourth part is the Holy Communion service, with the Our Father and a very brief conclusion and closing prayer. Simplicity and silence attend the end of the service. From then until the Easter Vigil, churches are bare and quiet (except perhaps for some popular devotions proper to the occasion, such as Stations of the Cross, prayers to the five wounds, prayers at the tomb of Christ, and devotions to the sorrowful Mother).

Many people make it a point to do something special on Good Friday. Among such special things is a custom of silence, or not talking, especially from noon to 3 P.M., the hours when Jesus hung on the cross. Besides fasting from food and abstaining from meat, as Church law prescribes for us, many families fast from television or radio on Good Friday. People who find themselves unable to participate in the liturgy frequently visit a church to venerate the cross privately and to make the Way of the Cross.

Throughout the day on Good Friday, devout Catholics will remember how our Lord voluntarily, for love of us, endured the ridicule, the trial before Pilate and Herod, the mockery, the whipping and scourging, the thorns on His head, the nakedness and shame, the fever and insects, the gall and vinegar in His mouth, the iron nails and the spear (Jn 19:34).

Wounding the main human nerve centers can cause the most excruciating pain. The nails in Christ's wrist must have partially severed the median nerve and remained in contact with it for three hours. The whole ordeal of crucifixion is an experience that ancient writers call "indescribable pain", culminating in a type of asphyxiation.

Jesus made a certain Friday forever "Good" to show us the horror of sin, our sins and the sins of the world. "Having canceled the bond which stood against us with its legal demands; this he set aside, nailing it to the cross" (Col 2:14). Jesus also died in agony to show us the infinite love of God (Jn 15:13). He went to His Passion in total obedience (Phil 2:5–10). Those who killed the Son of God, of course, were not just people of long ago but each of us sinners by our evil. Yet He died forgiving and pardoning us (Lk 23:34).

MARCH 18, 1994

The Great Vigil

In the early days of the Catholic Church, it was almost always the custom to have "vigils", that is, to pray during the night, to listen to readings from the Bible, and to watch until near dawn, when the holy sacrifice of the Mass would be offered. Early Christians saw in the dawning of the sun a symbol of the rising of Jesus from the tomb and of His Second Coming. This ancient custom is still preserved on our greatest feasts, in Midnight Mass at Christmas and in the Great Easter Vigil.

Even if it were totally impossible to participate in the liturgies of the Sacred Triduum, no Catholic should ever want to miss the opportunity to "make" the Easter Vigil each year. It is lengthy, but not excessively so, and it must be, for it is a vigil. The Vigil begins in total darkness and commences with the blessing of the new fire and the Easter candle, as Catholics gather in their parish churches on Holy Saturday evening. The breath of springtime in the air is made more beautiful by the *candelora* that follows.

The liturgy on earth is a pale reflection and reminder of the eternal liturgy of heaven. So the Easter Vigil gives us a glimpse in sign and symbol of the glory of eternity.

When the church is lighted and all the personal candles are lit, the *Exsultet*, or Easter proclamation, is sung. This theological poem of outstanding and uplifting beauty is followed by the "vigil part", many readings from Sacred Scripture, interspersed with prayers, to tell us how the Resurrection is linked with creation, the exodus, the waters of olden prophecy, and the like. While the altar candles are lit, the *Gloria*, rarely heard since Lent began, is sung again amid pealing bells proclaiming Easter joy.

After we hear Saint Paul give us his annual and powerful Easter message, as he has for centuries, the *Alleluia*, suppressed completely since Ash Wednesday, sounds once more in our church and in our hearts. In clouds of incense, the "good news" of Christ's Resurrection is read out in the Gospel narrative.

After the homily, the entire Church Triumphant, the saints of God, are invoked as the font is prepared. The water is blessed, and "birth in water, fire, and the Holy Spirit" takes place before our eyes, when the newest members of Christ are joined to Him in Baptism and made our brothers and sisters in the Catholic Church. Each member of every parish should pray at this time for the neophytes and for the conversion of the entire world to Christ. Then the converts are confirmed, and all present stand and renew their baptismal vows and promises, reestablishing the "new and eternal covenant" broken or soiled so often in the past by sin. The sprinkling with the new Easter holy water links us mystically to the newly baptized and to our own Baptism, perhaps of long ago.

As the Solemn Mass of the Resurrection continues, the dying and rising of Jesus are made present in our midst. The risen Christ gives the special joy of His sacrifice and His Easter peace to those present. His triumph becomes ours, especially in our Easter Holy Communion. While the new converts receive Him for the first time, we come to Him with the innocence that His forgiveness imparts, to be joined to His risen life of grace, the promise of our future happiness and our own future resurrection.

It is a tradition in many places for people to take home vials and jars of the new Easter holy water and to use it to bless their homes anew, while they place the palms from Palm Sunday near their family crucifixes and holy pictures.

Earlier in the afternoon of Holy Saturday another charming and holy custom is sometimes observed. Families bring baskets of Easter food to church so that the parish priest can bless them. The family repast after the Easter Vigil or the family breakfast on Easter morning consists of blessed food. Often the blessed food includes the Easter eggs, ham, sausages, or other foods that were fasted from in Lent and Easter candy, cakes, breads, butter lambs, and other foods that family traditions dictate as part of Easter feasting.

The date of Easter is calculated as the first Sunday after the first full moon after the vernal equinox. It is appropriate that the Solemnity of the Lord's Resurrection be observed in springtime in the Northern Hemisphere, when nature seems to awaken from the sleep of winter, symbolizing the warmth of God's love as it saved humanity in the paschal mystery from the death and doom that would otherwise be our lot. The appearance of a resurrection in nature reminds of the real and true Resurrection of our Savior.

It is appropriate, too, that we begin our remembrance and participation in His Resurrection at the "Great Vigil", so, like the holy women, we can set out for the empty tomb "while it is still dark" (Jn 20:1; Mt 28:1). The Jewish day officially began at sundown of the day before. Thus the "first day of the week" (Mk 16:2) is already under way when we see that "new fire" struck from flint and hear the words that will greet us at the entrance to heaven one day: "The Lord has risen indeed, and has appeared to Simon!" (Lk 24:34). Alleluia!

MARCH 25, 1994

Foreshadowings

III

To make our participation in the liturgy of Holy Week, especially in the liturgy of the Sacred Triduum, more understandable, it is vital to have some grasp of the shadows, figures, and *types* of the Old Testament. These illustrate the realities of the New Testament, and it is these realities that are made present in the signs and symbols of the liturgy. Of all the episodes of salvation history in the Old Testament, the Passover has some of the highest allegorical significance.

Jesus Christ is the sinless and guiltless Paschal Lamb of the New Testament, Whose Precious Blood redeems and saves us. Just as the Hebrews were required annually to celebrate and commemorate their liberation and exodus in the seder meal, so we Christians in the Holy Eucharist remember and celebrate our salvation, in a sacrificial banquet that is more than mere commemoration but is in reality the actualization of the saving event of Jesus' suffering, death, and Resurrection.

In their journey to the promised land, the Hebrews came to the brink of disaster at the Red Sea. Their miraculous crossing, followed by the destruction of their enemies, was a distinct foreshadowing of our passing through the liberating waters of Baptism. This is why the narration of the deliverance of the Jews at the Red Sea must always be one of the prophecies read at the Great Easter Vigil each year.

As they left the Red Sea area and crossed the desert in their trek to the promised land, the Hebrews were fed by God with the "bread from heaven", a clear and precise prefiguration of the Holy Eucharist (Jn 6:31–33; Ex 16:15), which, of course, is the "Manna of the New Testament" and is given only to those who have passed through the waters of Baptism.

It does not take much reflection to note how much of the forty-year journey of the Jews to the "land flowing with milk and honey" was designed by God to be a *type* of His future Church. The Chosen People had to build God a house for worship and put an altar in it. Some men were to be consecrated as priests and wear certain garments when officiating at the altar. There was incense to be burned, and there were holy oils to be used. There were to be vessels made of precious metals, and there were times and places set aside for the adoration and worship of God.

The significance of all these foreshadowings was hidden for centuries, but their meaning has become clear in "these last days" (Heb 1:2). Our Lord knew the time had come for His passover and journey to the Father (Jn 13:1). His passover makes possible our passover. It is particularly in the Sacred Triduum that we Christians celebrate our passover with new signs and wonders: water (Deluge, Red Sea—Baptism), oil (Aaron—Confirmation), bread and wine (Melchizedek, manna—Eucharist). A careful reading of the Old Testament will show a large number of foreshadowings whose meaning is obvious as we attend and share in the liturgies of Holy Week. We recall the sacrifice of Isaac, the selling of Joseph, the singing of David, and so on. Pope Pius XII wrote that in the sacred liturgy "the work of our redemption is continued and its fruits are imparted to us."

The *Catechism of the Catholic Church* tells us:

> "The wonderful works of God among the people of the Old Testament were but a prelude to the work of Christ the Lord in redeeming mankind and giving perfect glory to God. He accomplished this work principally by the Paschal mystery of his

blessed Passion, Resurrection from the dead, and glorious Ascension, whereby 'dying he destroyed our death, rising he restored our life.' For it was from the side of Christ as he slept the sleep of death upon the cross that there came forth 'the wondrous sacrament of the whole Church'" [*Sacrosanctum concilium*, no. 5, § 2]. For this reason, the Church celebrates in the liturgy above all the paschal mystery by which Christ accomplished the work of our salvation (CCC 1067).

As we study and participate in the rites and in the liturgical and biblical texts of the liturgies of the Sacred Triduum, we should strive to understand them in terms of the history of salvation. As the Chosen People of the New Testament (1 Pet 2:9–10), we should view ourselves, especially in Holy Week, in the light of the Chosen People of the Old Testament. Theirs were "the sonship, the glory, the covenants, the giving of the law, the worship, and the promises" (Rom 9:4). Now these and much more have come down to us as a totally undeserved legacy. Speaking of the Sacred Triduum of Holy Thursday, Good Friday, and the Easter Vigil, our Holy Father, Pope John Paul II, said, "We lack words to express the depth of the mystery which opens up before us."

Saint John Chrysostom notes that we call Holy Week "great" "because in it many ineffable good things come our way: war is concluded, death is eliminated, curses are lifted, the devil's tyranny is relaxed, his pomps are despoiled, the reconciliation of man with God is achieved, heaven is made accessible, human beings are brought to resemble angels, things at odds are united, the wall is laid low, the bar is removed, the God of peace brings peace to things on high and things on earth." Father Pius Parsch observes that "special study is needed to pray the psalms, lessons, and prophecies of the Sacred Triduum with full understanding." This study is truly worth the effort. It is not very difficult to try to learn something of the foreshadowings of our faith and our Church and in this way to learn more profoundly the reality of redemption and salvation that we now live.

Commenting on Christians' activity during Holy Week, Saint John Chrysostom said: "We show by our behavior the regard we have for that week. After all, since the Lord has regaled us with such magnificent goods, how are we too not obliged to demonstrate our reverence and regard . . . ?"

MARCH 22, 1996

The Way of the Cross

People who visit the Holy Land during Holy Week especially look forward to walking the "Way of the Cross", that is, to go along the Via Dolorosa, the street Jesus walked carrying His Cross to Mount Calvary. Almost always, when they return from their pilgrimage, such people remark about the lack of devotion they encounter along the Via Dolorosa, with merchants hawking their wares, with donkeys piled high with back packs, with crowds pushing and shoving. So many people continue to ignore Christ, just as they did almost two thousand years ago, when He first made His sorrowful journey to redeem our human race on Golgotha.

Yet, it is not necessary to make a pilgrimage to the Holy Land to discover Holy Week, along with its central figure, our divine Savior, ignored. In much of the world, particularly in the de-Christianized West, religious indifference has anesthetized the consciousness of the public to the realities of our redemption, making Holy Week, for many, "just another week of the year".

There is no reason why we Catholics should succumb to such a deplorable attitude. Our spiritual life and perspective should induce us to make this coming Holy Week a time of intense prayer and a time for devout and frequent participation in the sacred liturgy.

FIGURE OF CHRIST

In Holy Week above all we should keep before the eyes of our mind and imagination the image of the crucified One. Cardinal John Henry Newman remarks that "upon the cross itself we discern in Him the mercy of a Messenger from heaven, the love and grace of a Savior, the dutifulness of a Son, the faith of created nature, and the zeal of a Servant of God." We ought to reflect upon "our Lord's sufferings, voluntarily undergone and ennobled by an active obedience, themselves the center of our hopes and worship, yet borne without thought of self, towards God and man".

In His Passion and death Jesus was truly the Suffering Servant predicted by the Prophet Isaiah (Is 53:11), bearing our sins in His own body and soul (Rom 5:6–11). However, our Lord was not simply an innocent One Who endured His painful death passively. On the contrary, He freely gave up His life for our salvation (Jn 10:18) and did this out of perfect and complete obedience to His heavenly Father (Phil 2:8), conforming His human will totally to His divine will. Saint

Peter wrote, "He himself bore our sins in his body on the tree" (1 Pet 2:24).

It is part of the irony of history that Christ, Who was a carpenter in His earthly adult life, Who knew and worked with wood and nails, should die to open for us the gates of heaven by being fastened to wood by hammered nails. It is paradoxical, by divine providence, that the Fall of humanity occurred in connection with a tree and disobedience, and so, the undoing of that Fall was designed to occur in connection with a tree and obedience.

Saint Rose of Lima said, "Apart from the cross, there is no other ladder by which we may get to heaven." In the sacred liturgy, the Church venerates the Cross with the words, "Hail, O cross, our only hope." Especially on the Cross, "God was in Christ reconciling the world to himself" (2 Cor 5:19). The Council of Trent said, "His most holy passion on the wood of the cross merited justification for us", and the *Catechism* teaches, "The cross is the unique sacrifice of Christ, the 'one mediator between God and men' (1 Tim 2:5)" (CCC 618). Saint Madeleine Sophie Barat said, "Calvary is the one place on earth which is nearest to heaven." Saint Bernadette remarked, "Let the crucifix be not only in my eyes and on my breast, but in my heart."

Cardinal Newman observes, "The great and awesome doctrine of the cross of Christ, which we now commemorate, may fitly be called, in the language of figure, the heart of religion. . . . In like manner the sacred doctrine of Christ's atoning sacrifice is the vital principle on which a Christian lives and without which Christianity is not. Without it, no other doctrine is held profitably." To some, the Cross of Jesus was an absurdity or a stumbling block (1 Cor 1:22–23), and so it remains even today in our contemporary culture. When confronted with the reality of Christ and the gift of salvation, our world in large measure still clamors for Barabbas (Mt 27:21). During Holy Week, those of us who are disciples of Jesus, however, should try to put into our lives the words of the Apostle of the Gentiles, "I have been crucified with Christ; . . . who loved me and gave Himself up for me" (Gal 2:20).

Near the Flavian Amphitheater in Rome there stands the magnificent Arch of Constantine. On its medallions tourists still can see the description in sculpture of that Emperor's victory in the battle of the Milvian Bridge on October 27, 312. The night before this decisive battle with Maxentius, Constantine dreamt he saw a flaming cross in the sky with the words around it, "In this sign shall you conquer." He ordered his soldiers to put that on their shields and banners. The next day he won a victory that overwhelmed his foe. According to the Church historian Bishop Eusebius, this "vision and victory", along with the example of the Emperor's Catholic mother, Saint Helen, were the elements that contributed most to his eventual conversion to Christianity.

In the coming week, which is the holiest and most sacred in the year, the words of Constantine's dream can well be made into our own motto and guiding slogan. The "Following of Christ" says, "In the cross is salvation; in the cross is life; in the cross is peace and protection from enemies; in the cross is heavenly sweetness; in the cross is wisdom and strength of mind; in the cross is height of virtue and joy of spirit." Saint Thérèse of Lisieux said that during Holy Week we should "look at His adorable face, His glazed and sunken eyes, His wounds, His cross, and see how much He loves us."

MARCH 29, 1996

5

EASTER

Resurrection

Jesus was "put to death for our trespasses and raised for our justification" (Rom 4:25). The central fact and pivot of Christianity is involved in Christ's death and Resurrection. As Michael Ramsey says, "Jesus Christ came not only to preach a Gospel, but to be a Gospel. He is the Gospel of God in all that He did for the deliverance of mankind." The Resurrection of our Savior is indeed one of the Christian "mysteries", that is, something that is a sign, something that both conceals and reveals a deeper reality.

CHRIST AS SIGN

Jesus is the sign of the saving act of divine love. Divine wisdom, power, and love in Christ assume visible, human form. Jesus is such a sign in the acts and expressions of His life. This sign reaches its dramatic and eternal completion in the risen Christ, reigning at the right hand of the Father. The Resurrection shows forth the divine acceptance of the sacrifice and victim offered by the High Priest on the altar of the Cross. The Resurrection is the core of Christ's redemptive activity. It marks the transition from this world to a new order of creation, from death to new life.

What our Lord claimed about Himself He proved to be true. God confirmed by extraordinary signs that Jesus is His legate and envoy and, ultimately, that Jesus is His divine Son. As Saint Peter preached in his Pentecost sermon: "Jesus of Nazareth, a man attested to you by God with mighty works and wonders and signs which God did through him in your midst, as you yourselves know. . . . This Jesus God raised up, and of that we are all witnesses. . . . Let all the house of Israel therefore know assuredly that God has made him both Lord and Christ, this Jesus whom you crucified" (Acts 2:22–36). Thus, the Resurrection of Christ is the greatest of all the confirmatory miracles by which God Himself validated and authenticated the testimony of the Carpenter from Nazareth. The glorious Resurrection of Jesus is a fact of history, a definite, datable, perceptible event.

Cajetan said that although Christ paid the price for our sins by His death, we should not have been justified unless He had risen, because we should not have believed. His Resurrection gave us an opportunity to believe and so to come to be justified, that is, to stand just before God.

The Resurrection of Jesus gives our faith a motive of credibility. It serves as a *kerygma*, or proclamation, that enables us to see that it is in accord with human reason *to believe* and not in accord with our rationality *to doubt or deny*. Faith, as supernatural, is not the mere result of our thinking, logical, intellectual processes. In the final analysis it is a gift from God. However, it must be seen as an act and habit that is far from irrational. Apologetically, the Resurrection assists in this.

The Resurrection confirms the testimony that Jesus gave about Himself. It is heaven's seal on His truthfulness. He was condemned to death for blasphemy, claiming to be the Messiah and the Son of God (Mt 26:63–66). His rising from the dead vindicated His claim to those titles and also vindicates His own proper prophecy about His future (Lk 11:29).

MYSTERY

The Resurrection is in the order of history and not, as a fact or event, so totally supernatural that it exceeds historic perceptibility. Nevertheless, it is also a supernatural happening and involves aspects beyond mere historicity. Christ's Resurrection is the transition from His state of bodily death to renewed and integral human life. Death is a part of the human experience that we all share since Adam. When Jesus died on the Cross, He shared this human experience, His body and soul "separating", His body being laid in the tomb owned by Joseph of Arimathea and His soul "descending into hell", that is, to the limbo of the just of the old Testament (1 Pet 3:19).

The adjective "glorious" is often used to modify "Resurrection" to indicate that, while His risen life is truly human and His humanity truly the same as He had before He died, they are of a special quality in many ways different from the ordinary human way of living. While the risen body of Christ is really material, it is obviously of a higher form than we are usually aware of (Lk 24:31–36; Mk 16:19). His risen body is the eminent exemplar of all future risen bodies of the saints. Saint Paul speaks of risen bodies as "spiritual" bodies as distinguished from "physical" bodies (1 Cor 15:44). The risen body of Jesus appears to be a "spiritual body" in that sense, but it did not receive its full external glory until after the Ascension (Acts 10:41; 2:33; Jn 20:17).

Whatever the *mysterious*, supernatural, and miraculous aspects of the

Resurrection, it must be remembered that there were also clear historical facts surrounding the event that point plainly to its truth: the empty tomb, the apparitions, the faith and preaching of the apostles, the angelic information, and the evident panic of Christ's enemies, who, in the words of Saint Augustine, tried to appeal to sleeping witnesses (Mt 28:11–15).

In the thought of F. X. Durwell, Christ, three days after His death, became, in His body, the new temple (Mt 26:61), the dwelling place of glory, the place of divine revelation, the point of contact between God and His people, the bond uniting the People of God together. He is, in His risen body, the house of prayer and praise where God's People would gather to worship in His sacrifice, sitting down at table with Him, in a temple not made by hands, where worship would be always in spirit and in truth (Jn 4:23).

Easter is the annual proclamation that eternal life is here and that victory has been won. It inspires us, the disciples of Christ, to toil more diligently upon the lake (Jn 21:3), knowing that He is on the shore waiting to greet us and love us and ask us to love Him in return. Easter reminds us that at every Mass He walks with us on the way to Emmaus (Lk 24:13–35), to tell us what little sense we have, to interpret for us every passage of Scripture, to make our hearts burn within us, so we can recognize Him in the "breaking of the Bread".

As theologians note, the fact that the Resurrection took place on the first day of the week is not without its meaning. Christian history began as a separate entity on a Sunday with the appearance of the risen Christ. The history of the new creation began on the first day of the week and will continue until it is enveloped in an endless sabbatical rest.

APRIL 9, 1993

Apostolic Proclamation

The New Testament decisively shows that the proclamation of the Resurrection of Jesus from the dead is at the very core of the preaching of the apostles. Everything leans on this historic fact, which they do not hesitate to announce even at the peril of their lives. From the beginning, the Resurrection is the keystone of the entire structure of Christianity that authorizes and validates everything before and after its occurrence. It is the sign that the historic figure of Jesus of Nazareth is identical to the Christ of history, enthroned at the right hand of God the Father.

PAULINE CREED

The paschal creed of Saint Paul is found in his First Epistle to the Corinthians (15:1–11), dating from about 56 or 57. This creed recalls to the minds of the Corinthian Christian community the catechesis that Saint Paul imparted to them about the year 50, approximately twenty years after Jesus rose from the dead. Paul had received his own catechism instruction shortly after his conversion, about 36 or 37. He was taught by the Apostles, including Peter and James, the "brother" of the Lord (Gal 1:19; Acts 11:26). He also consulted the apostles at the apostolic Council of Jerusalem (Acts 15; Gal 2:1–10), when he saw Cephas (Peter) again and also James and John.

In his creedal statement, Saint Paul uses the language of Jewish rabbinic schools, saying that he handed over what he had received. It is clear that the Twelve were the ones who handed it over to him, since he strives to vindicate his right to be called an "apostle", notwithstanding the fact that he was not among the first privileged witnesses of Christ's Resurrection. It is also quite clear that the death, burial, Resurrection, and post-Resurrection apparitions of Jesus are part and parcel of the earliest catechetical material of the Catholic Church, although the *private revelation* of Christ's appearance to Saint Paul at the time of his conversion did not form an essential part of the first Christian message.

When Saint Paul writes about the Resurrection of Jesus, it is plain that what he understands by "resurrection" is a dead person once more living in his earthly body. It is known that Paul agreed with the Pharisees against the Sadducees in the resurrection controversy (Acts 23:6) and that he announced the Resurrection in Athens and was met with disbelief precisely because of that (Acts 17:18–31). It seems from the context of the First Epistle to the Corinthians that Paul had to deal with a group of Greek Christians who denied the future resurrection of the dead. He uses the Resurrection of our Savior as an *a pari* argument to convince them of the future resurrection of all deceased persons.

Saint Paul also gives in the same chapter of that epistle (1 Cor 15:36–53) a theological explanation of the newness of the risen body. In writing about "flesh and blood", however, he was not denying the material reality of risen bodies but was referring to man in his present condition of infirmity and mortality.

NICENE–CONSTANTINOPLE CREED

Each Sunday is a "little Easter". The first day of the week was the one chosen by God for the greatest and most important event in human history to occur. This is why in the New Testament the Catholic Church, using the power of binding and loosing that her Founder gave her (Mt 16:19; 18:18), changed the Sabbath to Sunday.

As the present-day Christian community gathers to participate in the paschal mystery each Sunday, we proclaim our Catholic faith in the magnificent old words of the Nicene-Constantinople Creed. There we say that we believe that Jesus rose again on the third day according to the Scriptures, and, in union with our Christian ancestors in Corinth long ago as well as with Saint Paul and the Twelve, we say that we also believe in the "resurrection of the dead and life everlasting".

The question that should haunt and taunt us all week long after our creedal statement on Sunday is: How can we live this Creed rather than just recite it?

Easter should have a lasting resonance in our souls. For it is the feast that reminds us that God's life, sanctifying grace, is a share in the risen life of the Redeemer Himself. It is a solemnity that is intended to give or reinforce a spiritual elevation to union with God. In the words of the *Exsultet*, the Easter proclamation sung at the Easter Vigil, this solemnity "banishes enmities, drives out wickedness, washes away guilt, restores innocence, brings joy, establishes peace, and weds heaven to earth".

As Cardinal John Henry Newman puts it, the celebration of Easter is meant to help us know our place, our position, our situation as children of God, members of Christ, and inheritors of the kingdom of heaven. We are risen, and we know it not. It takes a long time for us to apprehend what we profess. We are like people waking from sleep who cannot collect their thoughts at once. But, little by little the truth should dawn on us. Let us pray, let us work, let us meditate and thus gradually comprehend what we are. As time goes on, we must struggle to give up the shadows and find the substance. "Each Easter, as it comes, will enable us more to rejoice with heart and understanding in that great salvation which Christ then accomplished". Saint Paul, each Easter season, calls out to us across the centuries "Our commonwealth is in heaven" (Phil 3:20). Let us answer that call all year long, by (in the words of Saint Gregory the Great) "perfumes of good acts and holy desires" until we see God's face and share Christ's victory forever.

APRIL 16, 1993

He Is Risen

Cardinal John Henry Newman wrote that now, since Christ has risen from the dead and ascended into heaven,

> let us approach Him, who walked upon the sea, rebuked the wind, multiplied the loaves, turned water into wine, made the clay give sight, and entered through closed doors, coming and vanishing at will. Ever more He is with us, a gracious Lord, whose garments smell of myrrh and aloes and cassia, of spikenard and saffron, calamus and cinnamon and all the trees of frankincense and all the chief spices. So may He be with us, moving our hearts within us, until the day breaks and the shadows flee away.

We "approach" Christ, of course, in His Church and, most particularly, in the Blessed Sacrament of that Church, the Holy Eucharist. It is the *risen* Christ Whose Body and Blood we receive in Holy Communion and Who gives us in this Easter sacrament the pledge and promise of our own resurrection. Jesus tells us after His Resurrection that He "is going before" us (Mk 16:6). Receiving this pledge allows our Easter Holy Communion to teach us, in the words of Cardinal Ratzinger, "that death is no longer a prison from which no one returns. Death is no longer a house with no exits, a place of no return."

The solid historical fact of the Resurrection of Christ demonstrates that Christianity is "neither legend nor fiction, nor mere exhortation nor mere consolation". Based on reality, our holy religion originated in a particular moment in the stream of history when all the centuries before and after found a pivotal event in the empty tomb, which forever consecrated the first day of every week until the end of time.

The Gospels record ten appearances of Jesus after His death and Resurrection: to Mary Magdalen (Jn 20:11–18; Mk 16:9) and to the holy women (Mt 28:1–10); to Peter (Lk 24:34; 1 Cor 15:5); to the disciples of Emmaus (Lk 24:13–35; Mk 16:12–13); to the apostles in the Cenacle (Jn 20:19–23; Lk 24:36–43); to the apostles eight days later (Jn 20:26–29); to the seven disciples on the lake shore (Jn 21:1–23); to the apostles in Galilee (Mt 28:16–17; Mk 16:14–15); to more than five hundred brethren at one time (1 Cor 15:6); to James (1 Cor 15:7); and to the apostles and disciples on Ascension Day (Acts 1:6–11).

The apologetic value of Christ's Resurrection is undoubted, for it vindicates His claims and fulfills His prophecies as nothing else could do. However, He did not rise from the dead to satisfy curiosity or even, in the first place, to prove the truth of what He said and did. For He Himself said: "If they do not hear Moses and the prophets, neither will they be convinced if some one should rise from the dead" (Lk 16:31).

Our risen Savior addresses Himself even to unbelievers such as Thomas and Paul. But He showed Himself mainly to chosen "witnesses" (Acts 2:32). His risen life goes beyond the realm of measurable data in physics and biology. Saint Peter affirms that the Resurrection is a perceptible fact (2 Pet 1:16), but revelation tells us it is much more. God raised Christ from the dead that His risen life, an entirely new kind of life, might be introduced into humanity. This is why He did not go to the Sanhedrin or Pilate or Herod and show them His scars and Himself. Rather, He approached only those who would respond in faith and love, in gratitude and joy, only those who had the capacity to say "My Lord and my God" (Jn 20:28).

The Solemnity of our Lord's Resurrection is a great "water feast", surpassing in importance the other "water feasts" of the liturgical year, Pentecost and Epiphany. It is the special time for new Baptisms and for the renewal and recalling of all Baptisms. All Christian Baptism is dying and being buried with Christ and then rising with Him to newness of life (Rom 6:4). Each Easter we are called upon to remember our own Baptism, renew the vows we made then either directly or through our sponsors, and be determined, insofar as it is in us, to die to sin and become alive once more in Jesus Christ our Lord (Rom 6:11).

At our Baptism our souls are infused with, along with sanctifying grace, the powers that enable us to direct our lives toward God, Who is our beatitude and eternal happiness. These powers, or theological virtues, of faith, hope, and love should also be recalled and renewed at every celebration of Easter. These virtues are supernatural and do not depend on logic or reason in themselves. Nevertheless, they have a rational component that is based on the reality of Christ's Resurrection. Saint Paul writes: "If Christ has not been raised, then our preaching is in vain and your faith is in vain" (1 Cor 15:14), and "If for this life only we have hoped in Christ, then we are of all men most to be pitied" (1 Cor 15:19). He goes on: "But in fact Christ has been raised from the dead" (1 Cor 15:20).

Saint Gregory the Great said that, like the holy and faithful women, "we, who believe in the Lord Who died for us, should seek Him at each Easter bearing the perfume of personal virtue, joined to our good works, coming to the sepulcher with sweet spices. The holy women saw angels, and this should teach us that citizens of heaven may be seen readily by such as go forth with good acts and holy desires to seek the Lord."

Fragrance of Easter

Speaking of the Easter season, Cardinal Joseph Ratzinger says, "These fifty days of joy are the answer to the forty days of tribulation and preparation by which the Church leads up to Easter. In Old Testament numerology forty signified the age of the world; it is an intensification of four, which recalls the four corners of the earth and hence, the brokenness, the finite, incomplete, and toilsome nature of all earthly existence. The forty prepare for the fifty, the fragmentary for the complete, and the Lord's Resurrection is at the axis of both."

Father Joseph Manton observes, "Nature itself at Easter has thrown away its winding sheet of snow, and coming forth from the grave of winter, walks abroad in its new, glorified body of radiant spring. Easter spells joy for all. Caesars, pharaohs, kings, emperors, czars had all in their time been laid in tombs and that was their end. But, only Christ came back!"

Cardinal John Henry Newman said, "O blessed day of the Resurrection, which of old time was called the Queen of Festivals, and raised among Christians an anxious, nay contentious diligence duly to honour it! Blessed day, once only passed in sorrow, when the Lord actually arose, and the disciples believed not; but ever since a day of joy to the faith and love of the Church!" Gilbert Keith Chesterton noted, "People are quite prepared to shed pious reverential tears over the sepulcher of the Son of Man. What they are not prepared for is the Son of Man walking once more upon the hills of morning."

CELEBRATION

It is difficult to imagine a truly devout Catholic who would not ardently want, if the possibility presented itself, to participate in the beautiful, unique, and uplifting liturgies of the Sacred Triduum (the title for the days of Holy Thursday, Good Friday, and Holy Saturday). Of all the liturgical actions throughout the year, the most important, special, and solemn is that of the Easter Vigil on Holy Saturday evening, when the newest members of Christ's Mystical Body are welcomed into our Catholic family and when all of us renew again our dying and rising with Jesus in Baptism and in the Holy Eucharist.

The Resurrection of our Savior is central to our religion. Jesus saved us not only by His death but also by His Resurrection (Jn 16:19–22). Father Karl Rahner calls the rising of Jesus "the consummation of God's saving activity for the world and for mankind". The *Catechism of the*

Catholic Church says, "The Resurrection of Jesus is the crowning truth of our faith in Christ, a faith believed and lived as the central truth by the first Christian community; handed on as fundamental by Tradition; established by the documents of the New Testament; and preached as an essential part of the Paschal mystery along with the Cross" (CCC 638). Pope Saint Leo the Great said that Easter is one day on which it is "forbidden" to be sad.

MEANING

There is little doubt that the Resurrection of Christ has a powerful "apologetic value", that is, it serves to prove the validity of His claims to be the Messiah and, indeed, to be divine, even if that is not the principal and major purpose of this greatest of all miracles. The empty tomb and the numerous appearances of Jesus after His death, as historically reliable documents and witnesses affirm, offer an overwhelming argument in favor of the truth of our religion and the rational support of our faith (see 1 Cor 15:5-8).

Nevertheless, the *Catechism* states that there is a yet deeper significance to the Resurrection. It has as "its object an event which is historically attested to by the disciples, who really encountered the Risen One. At the same time, this event is mysteriously transcendent insofar as it is the entry of Christ's humanity into the glory of God" (CCC 656). "Christ, 'the first-born from the dead' (Col 1:18), is the principle of our own resurrection, even now by the justification of our souls (cf. Rom 6:4), and one day by the new life he will impart to our bodies (cf. Rom 8:11)" (CCC 658). Christ's rising from the dead profoundly affects us who are His followers (Rom 6:3-4), and, thus, the celebration of Easter should have the highest priority in our lives, since Easter has the highest significance for our destiny.

POETRY

Ordinary prose seems to fail utterly when speaking of the mystery of Christ's Resurrection and how it affects us. The Resurrection is the supreme act of the Father's power, testifying that Jesus is "Lord" and that He is the new, cosmic "Adam". The *Exsultet*, or Easter Proclamation, sung at the Easter Vigil says, "O truly blessed night, which alone deserved to know the time and hour when Christ rose from the dead; night truly blessed when heaven is wedded to earth and man is reconciled with God!"

The Proclamation also exclaims, "Father, how wondrous your care for us! How boundless your merciful love! To ransom a slave you gave away your Son! This is the night when Jesus Christ broke the chains of death and rose triumphant from the tomb."

Although Christ now is at the right hand of the Father, He also continues to abide with us, as our risen Lord. He is present through time and space in the Catholic Church, His Bride and Body. He is also present in that Church in a substantial and real way in the Eucharistic Banquet.

As Cardinal Newman said:

> Let us, as far as is permitted us, approach Him, Who walked on the sea, rebuked the wind, multiplied the loaves, turned water into wine, gave sight to the blind, and entered and left through locked doors. Evermore may He be with us, a gracious Lord, whose garments smell of myrrh, aloes, cassia, spikenard, saffron, calamus, cinnamon, frankincense and all the chief spices. So may He be with us evermore, moving our hearts within us, until the day breaks and the shadows flee away.

At Holy Communion during the Easter Vigil, may we experience the fragrance of Easter.

APRIL 14, 1995

Greater Than All Others

Saint Gregory the Great said, "It is fitting that we should speak to you about the nobility of this feast, since it is greater than all others. In it we have the model of our resurrection, and the way of hope is open to us, which is the way to the kingdom of heaven to which we aspire." Saint Bernard of Clairvaux wrote, "The Lion of the tribe of Judah has conquered. Wisdom has prevailed over malice." Saint Augustine wrote, "All days are the work of the Lord, but this day (Easter) is the day which He has made especially, and in which shines forth the light of His Word in the hearts of the faithful." Cardinal Joseph Ratzinger writes that Easter faith is designed to give us "the ability to look across from evening to morning, from the part to the whole, and thus to journey toward the joy of the redeemed which springs from the morning of the third day which first heard the message: Christ is risen."

Cardinal John Henry Newman wrote, "The grave could not detain Him Who had 'life in Himself' (Jn 5:26). He rose as a man awakes in the morning, when sleep flies from him as a thing of course. Corruption had no power over that sacred Body, the fruit of a miraculous conception. The bonds of death were broken, witnessing by their feebleness that He was the Son of God." Saint John Chrysostom preached, "Let us celebrate this greatest and most shining feast, in which the Lord has risen from the dead. Let us celebrate it with joy and in equal measure with devotion. For the Lord has risen and with Him He has raised the whole world. He has risen because He has broken the bonds of death."

Sacred Scripture records ten apparitions of our Redeemer after His Resurrection. C. H. Dodd, writing about the appearances of Jesus, says, "The incidents are reported in stories of various types, some concise and almost bald, stating the bare minimum of fact; some told at length with deliberate artistry. But, the pattern is the same; the disciples are 'orphaned' (the phrase is John's) of their Master; suddenly He is there—it may be in a room, on the road, in a garden, on a hillside, beside a lake, wherever they happen to be."

There can be no doubt that the empty tomb and the appearance of the angelic visitors played a part in the belief of the disciples in the Resurrection of Christ. However, the Gospels indicate that the "clincher" was the repeated appearances of our Savior, sometimes to a few persons, but sometimes to as many as five hundred at once (1 Cor 15:6). Father Karl Rahner says of the post-Resurrection appearances of Jesus that they show "the Father's supreme act of power, the decisive testimony given of Himself by the Son, the inauguration of the last days . . . the full recognition of Jesus as the Messiah, the Servant of Yahweh, the Son of Man, the second Adam, the cosmic Man (Colossians and Ephesians), the Lord (*Kyrios*) present to His Church in His glorified state."

Saint Thomas Aquinas said that Jesus rose from the dead for five principal reasons. The first was to show divine justice to the universe, to vindicate His claims, and to validate His mission. The second was to strengthen our faith in His Godhead and in the power of God shining forth in this miracle of miracles (2 Cor 13:4). The third reason was to raise up our hope. Saint Paul writes, "If for this life only we have hoped in Christ, we are of all men most to be pitied" (1 Cor 15:19). Our risen Savior not only gives us, His people, hope, but He actually is our Hope.

The fourth reason for the Resurrection was to give us an example and reference point for our own moral resurrection. We are exhorted to walk in newness of life (Rom 6:4) because the sanctifying grace we possess is, in a certain sense, the very risen life of Christ. Because Christ has risen from the dead, we are to set our "minds on things that are above" (Col 3:1–2). The fifth reason that Jesus rose from the dead, according to Saint Thomas, was to complete the work of our salvation. "He was put to death for our trespasses and raised for our justification" (Rom 4:25). His death saved us from evil, and His rising from the dead enveloped us with the supreme good.

One of the best ways to capture in our hearts and lives the "spirit of Easter" is to pay attention to the various exhortations and homilies of our present Holy Father and of past popes. Pope John Paul II said:

> We have followed Christ's footsteps. We have travelled the roads of His words and of the signs that He worked. On Golgotha we have been filled with astonishment and when the final night fell, we have kept watch by the tomb, a watch kept by the Church that is in Rome, a watch kept by the Church throughout the world. And, behold, a day has dawned before us, "the day that the Lord has made" (Ps 117:24), a most special day in the history of the universe and in human history. This is the day that springs from the night of watching. It is the day on which God revealed that He is the God of the living and not of the dead (Mk 12:27). And, He has revealed it in that precise place where the death of the Man had been sealed as a definitive and irreversible fact. The liturgy puts into the mouth of Christ the words, I will become your death, O death.

Pope Pius XII wrote:

> Having once overcome the sting of death, our Lord Jesus Christ not merely opened to the faithful who believe in Him the gates of heaven, but also a new and happier era began for the whole human race. Truly, just as the sun, rising over the tops of the mountains, puts to flight the mist and the darkness, bringing once more light, warmth, and life, so Jesus Christ, on rising alive from the tomb, puts crime to flight, washes away sins, gives innocence to those who are fallen, joy to those who are sad. He removes hatred and prepares the way for happiness.

Pope John Paul II says:

> Take fresh hope. Sing Alleluia. Christ goes forward in our future. Easter is the miraculous day of victory, the passover of the Resurrection. May the proclamation of Easter joy be heard by all individuals and by all the peoples on the face of the earth. Christ first died but now He lives forever. He tells us: There is

nothing to fear. I am the First and the Last and the One Who lives. Once I was dead, but now I live forever, and I hold the keys of death and the nether world (Rev 1:17–18).

Happy Easter to all.

APRIL 5, 1996

Part Four

THE SACRAMENTS

1

SIGNS AND MYSTERIES

Mysteries

A sacrament is a sign. Saint Thomas Aquinas, perhaps the greatest of theologians, said it quite clearly: "It is in the genus of sign that one finds sacraments." The Latin word *sacramentum* is a translation of the Greek word *mysterion*. A mystery, we know, is something that we partly see and partly do not see. Every mystery has a hidden or invisible aspect. That which is visible both reveals and conceals the hidden part.

A sign leads to the knowledge of something else. For instance, words are signs of thoughts and lead one to the knowledge of someone else's thinking. An orange triangular highway sign with the word "danger" printed on it is a sign that leads a driver to the knowledge of some peril ahead on the roadway.

Signs also unite. Words, for example, unite people in common thought. A stop sign on a street unites the intention and action of the motorist with the desire and intention of the lawgiver.

We human beings need signs. We cannot exist without them. When God bends down to us in revelation, His self-disclosure comes to us under the form of signs.

CHRIST AND THE CHURCH

Jesus is the great Sign of God. His human nature, specifically His human body and Its words, gestures, and actions simultaneously conceal and reveal the Father to us (Jn 14:9). As the living Sign of God's love, pardon, and grace, our Lord leads us to the knowledge of the Father. His earthly life was a book of signs (Jn 21:25). As a Sign, Christ also unites. He joins humanity to divinity, and in His Mystical Body He unites human nature and human beings with His Divine Person. There is a certain legitimacy in calling Jesus a "kind of Sacrament of God".

In a certain sense, too, we can call the Church that Christ founded a "kind of sacrament", as does the Second Vatican Council. The Catholic Church meets perfectly the catechism definition of a sacrament: an outward sign instituted by Christ to give grace. The Church, which derives from and extends in time and space the Incarnation, is like her divine Spouse a "mystery", with a visible aspect that conceals and reveals a hidden part.

To distinguish this wider use of the word *sacrament* from the specific use of the term in referring to the seven great signs Christ instituted and gave to His Church in order to distribute the salvation won for us in the paschal mystery, it is customary to restrict the use of the word *sacrament* by calling our Lord and His Church a "kind of sacrament".

The sacraments that Christ instituted form a system like the solar system. They are like planets around the greatest or most blessed sacrament, deriving all their strength, beauty, and efficacy from the Holy Eucharist. They are external signs (things we can see, feel, hear, touch), involving the use of oil, water, gestures, words, wine, and bread. They must be understood as situated in the larger picture of what we have called a "kind of sacrament", that is, our incarnate Lord and the Catholic Church.

This is one of the reasons why, whenever possible, six of the sacraments are to be celebrated in and around Holy Mass, for they are all linked theologically with the Eucharist.

The sacraments are meant by Jesus to touch us in various stages of our earthly lives. They come from and lead to the Holy Eucharist. Their invisible aspects involve what is called "grace". They give us the life that Jesus won for us on the Cross, sanctifying grace (Jn 10:10), either initially or in a restored form or by way of increase. They also bestow particular supernatural helps and pledges of future actual or sacramental helps. Three of the sacraments give to those who receive them, in addition, a participation in the priesthood of Christ by way of an indelible character.

SACRAMENTAL MINISTERS

The usual minister of a sacrament is a deacon, priest, or bishop. However, there are exceptions. In Matrimony, for example, the ministers are the couple themselves who receive and bestow the sacrament on each other in their giving and taking of marriage consent. In emergency situations, Baptism can be administered by anyone who has the correct intention and who uses the correct matter and form.

Some sacraments require in the minister a certain kind of power that derives from Christ Himself and is given in certain of the sacraments. The power of Holy Orders, for instance, is needed to confect the Holy Eucharist. The fullness of Holy Orders is required to ordain priests and bishops.

The sacraments are acts of Christ. Saint Augustine said that when a priest baptizes, it is really Christ Who baptizes. This is why the efficacy of a sacrament does not depend on the holiness of a priest. Of course, a priest would commit a serious sin if he were to celebrate a sacrament in the state of mortal sin, but the sacrament itself would be unaffected by the priest's state of soul. If the sign is correctly placed and accompanied by the right intention, if there is no block or impediment, and if the minister possesses the appropriate power, it is Jesus Himself Who touches the recipient of the sacrament. It is the Lord Who bestows His grace, pardon, and love.

The sacraments are celebrations of liturgy. They are acts of worship given to God. This is why the basic or fundamental sacrament of Baptism is required for valid reception of the other six sacraments. Baptism gives to the recipient the indelible character that enables the person, as a sharer in the priesthood of Christ (the universal priesthood of all the faithful as distinguished from the ministerial priesthood that comes only from the sacrament of Holy Orders), to adore and give worship to the Father through Jesus Christ in union with the Holy Spirit.

In contemplating the sacraments, Saint Thomas Aquinas wrote: "Every believer is committed to receive that which belongs to the worship of God and to pass it on to others."

JUNE 4, 1993

Sacred Signs

The Second Vatican Council teaches: "The liturgy involves the presentation of man's sanctification under the guise of signs perceptible to the senses. . . . The liturgy is complete public worship performed by the Mystical Body of Jesus Christ, that is, by the Head and members." [1]

LITURGY AND MYSTERIES

Just as the liturgy is the worship given to God the Father by the "whole Christ", that is, Jesus our Head and us, joined to Him, so it is also worship given by our own entire being, not only our minds and souls, but also our bodies. Hence, our worship of God in the Church involves postures, gestures, words, music, listening, speaking, reading, and so on. Likewise incorporated into our official, public worship of God are the "things" that have "sign value", such as bread, oil, wine, water, light,

---

[1] *Sacrosanctum concilium*, no. 7.

color, clothing, art, architecture, fire, incense, cups, dishes, candles, and books.

The liturgy consists of the Mass, the sacraments, the sacramentals, the Divine Office (Liturgy of the Hours), and the sanctification of time (the liturgical year). The Second Vatican Council mentions the sublime character of liturgical worship: "Because it is an action of Christ, the Priest, and His Body, the Church, it is a sacred action surpassing all others. No other action of the Church can equal its efficacy. . . . The liturgy is the summit toward which all the activity of the Church is directed. It is also the font from which all her power flows." [2]

A sign is that which leads to the knowledge of something else. Saint Thomas Aquinas calls the signs of the liturgy "sacraments of the Church". The *Catechism of the Catholic Church* explains this: "The liturgy makes the Church present and manifests her as the visible sign of the communion in Christ between God and men" (CCC 1071). The ancient word that is often used for the liturgy, coming from the Greek language, is "mystery". The "sacred mysteries" are the signs that simultaneously conceal and reveal God to us.

In the Incarnation, the human nature of Jesus, His human body and human soul, veiled His divinity at the same time that it revealed God to us in Him. So, in the liturgy, external signs conceal at the same time they reveal hidden, supernatural reality.

Signs also join persons or things together. For instance, an advertisement joins our mind and attention to the product or service or intention of the signmaker. The stop sign joins our action and obedience to the command of the lawmaker. Words, which are signs of thoughts, join together the minds of the author and of the one who hears or reads his words.

Thus, the signs that make up the liturgy join us, when we are engaged in the official worship of the Church in a conscious, active, and fruitful way, to Jesus Christ. In Him we are joined to each other in a special way; and, of course, in Him, through the Holy Spirit, we are joined to God the Father.

LITURGY AND DIVINE LIFE

In the complex of signs that is the sacred liturgy, some signs have much more value and importance than others. The reason is that some signs were invented or instituted by Christ Himself. The *Catechism* teaches: "In this age of the Church, Christ now lives and acts in and with his

[2] Ibid., nos. 7, 9.

Church, in a new way appropriate to this new age. He acts through the sacraments in what the common Tradition of the East and the West calls 'the sacramental economy'; this is the communication (or 'dispensation') of the fruits of Christ's Paschal mystery in the celebration of the Church's sacramental liturgy" (CCC 1076).

The signs that Jesus instituted and gave over to the custody and care of His Catholic Church do more than signify. If they are properly placed and there is no obstacle to block their effect, they really do what it is they signify. They are efficacious. In each of the seven sacraments, Christ Himself is the principal celebrant. While Deacon Jones might be baptizing, or Father Smith might be anointing, it is really and actually Christ, as Saint Augustine says, who is baptizing and anointing. The *Catechism* states: "Christ indeed always associates the Church with himself in this great work in which God is perfectly glorified and men are sanctified. The Church is his beloved Bride who calls to her Lord and through him offers worship to the eternal Father".[3]

Jesus is not a "founder of a religion" in the sense of Buddha, or Mohammed, or John Wesley, or Martin Luther, that is, someone who created a religious organization that goes on functioning after his death according to the rules he gave at the beginning. Jesus not only founded the Catholic Church, but He continues to live in her here and now. He is risen from the dead and promised to be with us, His Church, until the end of time (Mt 28:20). As Father Roguet writes: "The Pope is not His successor, but His vicar. The priesthood of Christ did not cease with His death, but continues to function through the ministry of His Church, the ministry of His priests."

The Second Vatican Council says: "For it is in the liturgy, especially in the divine sacrifice of the Eucharist, that the work of redemption is accomplished, and it is through the liturgy particularly that the faithful are enabled to express in their lives and to manifest to others the mystery of Christ and the real nature of the true Church."[4]

SEPTEMBER 2, 1994

Mysteries of Faith

The word "mystery" comes to the English language through the Greek language, a mystery being something that is known or "seen" or revealed but which, in some sense, "conceals" something else. For many

---

[3] CCC 1089, quoting *Sacrosanctum concilium*, no. 7.

[4] *Sacrosanctum concilium*, no. 2.

centuries, churchmen have translated the Greek word *mystery* by the term that comes from the Latin language, "sacrament".

In its root meaning, then, a sacrament is a sign or symbol that both reveals and conceals. Among the ancient Romans, the word "sacrament" also meant a soldier's oath or pledge.

The seven sacraments of the Catholic Church are, of course, symbols that Jesus, the Founder of our Church, instituted. They are the principal means by which He Himself encounters His People and by which He bestows on them divine life, the grace that He won by His death and Resurrection. The Second Vatican Council teaches, citing Saint Augustine of Hippo, "By His power, Christ is present in the sacraments, so that when a man baptizes, it is Christ who baptizes." [5]

These signs of grace, which really do what they signify, are "outward" or external. They can consist of works alone (Penance), or words and gestures (laying on of hands in Holy Orders), or words, gestures, and material things (water, words, and pouring or dipping in Baptism).

Jesus is the Word of God made flesh (Jn 1:14). His human nature simultaneously reveals and conceals God to humanity in one Divine Person. He has both a divine and human nature in all their fullness. He is the unique Priest of the New Testament. Christ continues His work through time and space in His Mystical Body, His Catholic Church (1 Cor 12:12–31).

Pope John XXIII spoke about "the Church of Christ, that human and divine institution, which, from Jesus, takes its name, its grace, and its meaning". What our Lord won by His paschal mystery, He distributes and applies to humanity through this great sign He instituted to "give grace", the Church. This is why the Second Vatican Council calls the Catholic Church "a kind of sacrament". Like Christ, the Church has an aspect that is both visible and invisible. The Church participates in the "incarnational principle" by which God has decided to redeem and save the human race from eternal torment.

The seven sacraments, which contain and communicate the grace Christ gained by His dying and rising, are rooted and grounded in His Mystical Body. Therefore, it is the Church that, through her teaching authority (Magisterium), determines all questions about legitimacy as well as about validity in regard to the sacraments. This includes those matters determined by divine law and direct institution by our Redeemer as well as those of Church order and discipline.

Provided there is no obstacle present and the minister of a sacrament has the necessary authority and power, a sacrament will always impart the

---

[5] *Sacrosanctum concilium*, no. 7.

grace, holiness, justification, and sanctification that it signifies. If a priest or other minister of a sacrament were to administer a sacrament while in the state of serious sin, such a minister would certainly be committing another mortal sin of sacrilege. Nevertheless, the sinfulness of the minister would not affect the result of the sacrament, which does not depend on the holiness of the minister. This is because a valid sacrament is fundamentally an action of Jesus Christ, Who can do His work even by means of a seriously defective instrument, such as a sinful minister.

The *Catechism* says: "Since Pentecost, it is through the sacramental signs of his Church that the Holy Spirit carries on the work of sanctification. The sacraments of the Church do not abolish but purify and integrate all the richness of the signs and symbols of the cosmos and of social life. Further, they fulfill the types and figures of the Old Covenant, signify and make actively present the salvation wrought by Christ, and prefigure and anticipate the glory of heaven" (CCC 1152).

The more faith, fervor, love, devotion, preparation, thanksgiving, and contrition we bring to the reception of any of the sacraments, the more fruitful and grace-filled will be our encounter with Christ. Our intention, when we receive any of the sacraments, should be to have more in our hearts and souls than just the bare minimum necessary for their worthy reception.

It is important, however, to recall occasionally some of the minimum requirements for a worthy reception of the sacraments. We know, for instance, that two of the sacraments are nicknamed "sacraments of the dead" because they are the only two that we can licitly receive when we are supernaturally dead, that is, when we have on our soul an unforgiven mortal sin. These are Baptism and what is called "the second plank after spiritual shipwreck", Penance.

The other five sacraments, including the greatest of all the sacraments, the Holy Eucharist, are nicknamed "sacraments of the living", because we may not receive them if we are conscious that we are guilty of a mortal sin. We know, too, that the only ordinary way we can have mortal sins forgiven is to submit them to the forgiveness of God in the sacrament of Penance, sometimes called now Reconciliation.

If we knowingly receive a "sacrament of the living" with an unforgiven sin on our conscience, we not only do not receive any grace from such an act, but we commit a further heinous mortal sin of sacrilege. Of course, the objectivity and validity of the sacrament would not be affected in such a case. For example, were some Catholics to be married with mortal sins on their souls, they would truly and validly be married, but without any of the grace of God and with an additional grave sin burdening their consciences.

If a Catholic were to receive Holy Communion, conscious that he had an unforgiven grievous sin on his soul, such a person would truly receive the Body and Blood of Jesus, but not to any spiritual benefit, but rather to his spiritual detriment. This is what Saint Paul meant when he wrote about unworthy reception of Holy Communion, "Whoever, therefore, eats the bread or drinks the cup of the Lord in an unworthy manner will be guilty of the body and blood of the Lord. . . . For any one who eats and drinks without discerning the body eats and drinks judgment upon himself" (1 Cor 11:27–29).

AUGUST 25, 1995

Sacramental Mysteries

The seven sacraments, or mysteries, that Jesus bequeathed to His Catholic Church form a system. They are not simply haphazard symbols or signs, but they are ordered to each other and, in a most important way, to the Blessed Sacrament. The *Catechism* states, "In this organic whole, the Eucharist occupies a unique place as the 'Sacrament of sacraments'" (CCC 1211). Saint Thomas Aquinas asserts that "all the other sacraments are ordered to the Eucharist as to their end."

One of the benefits of the liturgical renewal deriving from the Second Vatican Council is the reemphasis on this insight, which is brought about by having the sacraments administered, when possible and feasible, in direct proximity to the Mass or even during the course of the celebration of the eucharistic sacrifice and banquet. Since Christ in the Holy Eucharist is contained, offered, and received, and since He is the Source and Author of all sanctifying grace and supernatural life, it is obvious that the Blessed Sacrament is, in the words of the *Catechism*, "the heart and summit of the Church's life" (CCC 1407).

PERSONAL AND ECCLESIAL

In one sense our encounter and union with our Lord in the sacraments are utterly and simply personal. In another sense, however, this encounter and union are achieved only insofar as we are members of a community or assembly, which is to say, of that Church willed by our Savior to be His Body and the instrument by which His paschal mystery is conveyed to us across the centuries. All the sacraments are public acts of worship and adoration of God the Father, brought about by our High Priest, Jesus Christ.

All seven sacraments are acts of praise, petition, and thanksgiving raised to God. They are actions of the "whole Christ", Head and members—that is, of the Mystical Body. Not only the so-called "social sacraments" (Matrimony and Holy Orders), but all the sacraments have a social or horizontal (Church-directed) dimension as well as a vertical (God-directed) aspect. Jesus saves us as individuals, but He saves us only "in community".

The two sacraments that are most constitutive of the Church are Baptism and the Holy Eucharist. This is why, in God's providence, it was water and blood that flowed from the pierced side of Jesus on the Cross. Thus the Second Vatican Council, following the teaching of the Fathers of the Church, proclaimed that the Catholic Church was born "from the side of Christ as He slept the sleep of death on the cross".[6] In the Mass for the Solemnity of the Sacred Heart, the liturgy says, "His wounded side, flowing with blood and water, is the fountain of grace renewing the Church with sacramental life." In the Bible, Saint John speaks about the "witnesses" to Christ, which are the Holy Spirit, the water, and the blood (1 Jn 5:8).

SALVATION AND FAITH

In the divine condescension, when the Almighty stoops down to touch our planet and intervene in our history, He comes in the form of the familiar. Thus in the liturgy we say that God willed that we be saved by "One like us". Christ, remaining the eternal and all-powerful God, became like us in all things but sin. He walked down our streets, spoke our languages, ate our food.

When He left behind His abiding presence in His Church in order to distribute what He won by His dying and rising to all generations until He returns, He also used the familiar. So the great signs He invented, which we name sacraments, are the familiar, charged and filled with invisible grace. He uses things we can see, feel, hear, touch, and experience. He uses grapes and wheat, oil and water, gestures and words.

Bishop Wuerl says:

> Sacraments are thus gifts of Christ by which He confers divine life and exercises divine power through expressive signs adapted to our human nature. In the sacraments Christ reaches out to all people of every place and in every area. In His earthly life, Christ shared our finite limitation to one place and time.

---

[6] *Sacrosanctum concilium*, no. 5.

Through the sacraments the glorified Christ puts aside these limitations and draws us by visible signs appropriate to our condition to the new world of eternal life, already present but hidden.

The sacraments are essentially signs or expressions of faith. This does not mean that their validity somehow depends on the faith of the minister or even of the recipient. If a sacrament is administered properly, it is true and not prejudiced by unbelief, although it could be without any effect in an unbelieving recipient.

The faith that makes a mere liturgical ritual into a sacrament is the faith of the Church. This is the faith that is called upon every time a sacrament is administered. The community of the Church is not simply those people who presently constitute the Catholic Church on earth but also those who "have gone before us with the sign of faith", the early Christian community, the Pentecost gathering, which was initially filled with the Holy Spirit and passed on to us the foundation on which the structure of our Church was built, "not solely by reason of the hierarchic powers handed down through apostolic succession, but also by reason of the faith which accepted the Word of God in the flesh of Jesus". It is this faith that enters into the intimate structure of the sacraments.

By means of the sacraments Christ reaches out to the human race, and the Church, "joined to Him as His Body, extends His healing and sanctifying action to all His members". Quoting Bishop Wuerl again: "The sacraments are signs of faith by which we cling in worship to Christ to share the fruits of His paschal gift. They are the instruments by which Christ, through the liturgical acts of His Church, in fact confers the graces symbolized by the sacraments."

SEPTEMBER I, 1995

The Water Mark

The seven sacraments are grouped in various ways. For instance, Baptism, Confirmation, and the Holy Eucharist are called the sacraments of initiation. The *Catechism* says, "Christian initiation is accomplished by three sacraments together: Baptism which is the beginning of new life; Confirmation which is its strengthening; and the Eucharist which nourishes the disciple with Christ's Body and Blood for his transformation in Christ" (CCC 1275).

The sacraments are also divided into those "of the living" and those "of the dead". This does not pertain to physical death but rather to Baptism and Penance, which can be licitly received even when one is "spiritually dead" in the state of grave sin, and the other five sacraments, which can be received legitimately only when one is in the state of sanctifying grace. Sometimes the sacraments are divided into those that are "social", that is, Matrimony and Holy Orders, and the others, which are called "individual".

One important grouping is the listing of the three sacraments that can be validly and licitly received only once. Baptism, Confirmation, and Holy Orders are unrepeatable, because they stamp upon our very person the mark of Christ, the High Priest. Those three sacraments imprint on the human soul of the one who receives them an indelible character and eternal conformity to Jesus, which adds to one's glory and happiness if one is saved but to one's torment and suffering if one is damned.

SHARING IN THE PRIESTHOOD OF JESUS

In the New Testament, Jesus Christ is the one and only Mediator between God and man (1 Tim 2:5). He is the only priest, but He incorporates others into His unique priesthood. The indelible character imprinted on a Christian soul in Baptism, Confirmation, and Holy Orders is a share in the very priesthood of Jesus. Of course the share that one receives in Baptism, we are told by the Second Vatican Council, is different not only in degree but in essence from that share which is received in Holy Orders.

Keeping that difference in mind, we should nevertheless remember that by Baptism we become part of the Catholic Church, which is a kingdom of priests for Christ's God and Father (1 Pet 2:5; Rev 1:6). The *Catechism* states, "The whole community of believers is, as such, priestly" (CCC 1546).

As part of a priestly people, once we are stained with the indelible share in Christ's priesthood by Baptism, we have the right and the duty to worship God by receiving the other sacraments. We also have the right and the duty to become active participants rather than mere onlookers at Holy Mass. After the Holy Eucharist is effected by the ordained priest—for only one who has received Holy Orders has the power and authority to do that—all the baptized who are present take part in actually "offering" the sacrifice of Jesus to God the Father. In the First Eucharistic Prayer the priest speaks of "we Your people and Your ministers". Even at the preparation of the gifts he speaks of "our sacrifice".

The *Catechism* says: "Incorporated into the Church by Baptism, the faithful have received the sacramental character that consecrates them for Christian religious worship. The baptismal seal enables and commits Christians to serve God by a vital participation in the holy liturgy of the Church and to exercise their baptismal priesthood by the witness of holy lives and practical charity" (CCC 1273).

A PRIESTLY PEOPLE

Among the religious errors propagated by Protestants is the blurring of the clear distinction between the priesthood of all the faithful and the ministerial priesthood possessed only by those men who receive Holy Orders. To remain faithful to the gospel of Christ, the Church has had to emphasize the reality of this distinction. However, this necessity should not prevent us from recalling the eternal priestly character that is one of the great effects of receiving the sacrament of Baptism. The *Catechism* teaches, "No sin can erase this mark, even if sin prevents Baptism from bearing the fruits of salvation. Given once for all, Baptism cannot be repeated" (CCC 1272).

The Second Vatican Council repeats what the Catholic Church has always taught, namely, that the faithful exercise their baptismal priesthood through their participation, each according to his vocation, in Christ's mission as priest, prophet, and king. Through the sacraments of Baptism and Confirmation, the faithful are consecrated to be a holy priesthood.[7] Saint Peter says we are "a chosen race, a royal priesthood, a holy nation, God's own people" (1 Pet 2:9).

A significant, although by no means essential, part of the rite of Baptism is the naming of the person. In the case of infants, parents usually have already chosen and imposed a name by the time of the Baptism. Adults who are baptized usually have carried their names for many years before receiving the sacrament. However, at the time of Baptism the name is indicated and called out "in the Christian assembly". It is, therefore, inscribed in heaven and attaches forever to the one named. It is part of the "identity of the person". (There are many reasons why Christians should always select the names of saints for their children, but that is another topic.)

Some scholars see an analogy between the naming at Baptism and the invisible, but real, "water mark" that Baptism places upon the soul of the Christian. Just as a certain name attaches to the person who is baptized, so the indelible mark that distinguishes that person as part of the "priestly people" of Jesus Christ is received at Baptism. This mark, says Saint Irenaeus, is "the seal of eternal life". If it is "kept" until the end, it

---

[7] See *Lumen gentium*, no. 11, and *Apostolicam actuositatem*, no. 2.

carries the expectation of the blessed vision of God and the hope of the resurrection. Let all who share by Baptism in the priesthood of Christ exercise that priesthood with fidelity and joy.

SEPTEMBER 22, 1995

2

Baptism

The Water Sign

Last Sunday an event of great historical importance occurred in our Diocese of Lincoln. For the first time in our one-hundred-and-eight-year history, our diocese held a Eucharistic Congress this past year, and this past Sunday saw its solemn closing. Several thousand of our diocesan family gathered around Jesus in the Blessed Sacrament to love, honor, and adore Him in a special way. Those who were there remember that the Mass began with the blessing of holy water and its sprinkling, to remind all present of their Baptism.

Last August 31, another event of historical significance took place in our Diocese of Lincoln, the solemn funeral liturgy and entombment of our seventh ordinary, Bishop Glennon Patrick Flavin. That funeral liturgy, as in the liturgy for every deceased Catholic, began with sprinkling holy water upon the coffin, to remind all present of the Baptism of the departed person.

Both of these events, solemn and important, began with a reminder of the sacrament of Baptism. Each time we enter one of our church buildings to participate in the sacred liturgy, we are encouraged "to take" holy water and make the sign of the cross with that sacramental. This serves, of course, to remove our venial sins, if it is done and used with devotion and contrition. However, the primary purpose of the holy-water stoops at the doors of our church buildings is to remind us of our Baptism and to recall that, as we touch water entering this building called a "church", so it is through the waters of Baptism that we enter the spiritual family of God on earth called the "Church". Each time we "go to church", then, we should remember our Baptism.

WATER AND LIFE

The overwhelming majority of the surface of our planet is covered with water. The greatest part of our body weight, as human beings, is composed of water. Even before we are born, we are surrounded by water in our mother's womb. We are indeed people of water.

Life as we know it depends on water. When the Viking satellites were sent to Mars and Venus, they had technical equipment aboard to detect any signs of H₂O. Lack of water would mean lack of life. When one flies over Africa, one can notice the Sahel, the fringe of the Sahara Desert, impinging into the green areas of the continent. Where there is more water, there is more life, and vice versa.

It is understandable, then, why Christ chose this common and vital substance, water, to be the initial and fundamental sign or symbol by which He could convey to His People the divine life He won by His dying and rising and the way by which He could mark out His own. The *Catechism of the Catholic Church* says, "Baptism is the first and chief sacrament of forgiveness of sins because it unites us with Christ, who died for our sins and rose for our justification, so that 'we too might walk in newness of life' (Rom 6:4)" (CCC 977).

Water played an essential role in the history of salvation. In the Old Testament it served as a foreshadowing of Baptism. In the poetic language of the Book of Genesis, water formed part of the primordial chaos that antedated the major part of creation. It was over the water that the breath or spirit of God moved (Gen 1:1–2). The Deluge too was a prefiguring of Baptism (1 Pet 3:20–21). But, as the *Catechism* puts it, "above all, the crossing of the Red Sea, literally the liberation of Israel from the slavery of Egypt, announces the liberation wrought by Baptism" (CCC 1221). The crossing of the Jordan River also was a prophecy *in deed* regarding Baptism (Jos 3:14–17).

Our Savior, Jesus Christ, summed up in His life and works all the Old Covenant prefigurations. Thus, He, the divine Author of New Testament Baptism, chose to be baptized by His cousin and precursor, Saint John the Baptist, in the Jordan River to fulfill "all righteousness" (Mt 3:15) and as another manifestation of His "kenosis" or self-emptying (Phil 2:7). The *Catechism* tells us, "The Spirit who has hovered over the waters of the first creation descended then on Christ as a prelude of the new creation, and the Father revealed Jesus as his 'beloved Son' (Mt 3:16–17)" (CCC 1224).

WATER AND FAITH

There can be no doubt that Baptism is linked strongly to faith (Mk 16:16). For someone who has the use of reason (for most people this begins about the age of seven), it is necessary to profess the Catholic faith before being baptized. Baptism itself effects the infusion of supernatural faith into the soul of the one receiving the sacrament. Nevertheless, a preliminary expression of belief is required before the sacrament is administered. In the case of infants, it is obvious that it is the faith of the Church, the believing community, that is present and made manifest generally in the profession of faith made on the child's behalf by parents and godparents.

The *Catechism* teaches that "the faith required for Baptism is not a perfect and mature faith, but a beginning that is called to develop. . . . For all the baptized, children or adults, faith must grow *after* Baptism. For this reason the Church celebrates each year at the Easter Vigil the renewal of baptismal promises. Preparation for Baptism leads only to the threshold of new life. Baptism is the source of that new life in Christ from which the entire Christian life springs forth" (CCC 1253–54).

Whenever we celebrate great historical events, such as the conclusion of a Eucharistic Congress or the burial of a bishop, and, indeed, whenever, we enter a church and "take" holy water, let us recall the symbol and the sacrament that ennobled and enriched us beyond exaggeration, our Baptism, the water sign.

SEPTEMBER 15, 1995

Primordial Calamity

Those who study the place of water in divine revelation notice that this substance seems to have two aspects that are emphasized. On the one hand, it is destructive. It wipes out most of the human race in the great Deluge. It drowns the Egyptian army at the Red Sea. On the other hand, it is salvific. It saves people. It saves, for instance, the eight people of Noah's family in the ark, and it saves the Chosen People of the Old Testament, the Hebrews, at the Red Sea crossing.

In choosing water as the material part of His sacrament of Baptism, our Savior also emphasizes these two aspects. Water in Baptism is destructive of sin, wiping out and destroying original sin and, in the case of adults who are baptized, all actual sin too. This negative aspect of water in Baptism is balanced by its positive aspect of bestowing life. For Baptism not only symbolizes the giving of new, supernatural life to the one baptized but actually is the efficacious sign that pours this life of God into the person's soul. Saint Clement of Alexandria wrote, "Being baptized, we are illuminated. Being illuminated, we become sons. Being made sons, we are made perfect. Being made perfect, we are immortal."

ORIGINAL SIN

Saint Thomas Aquinas said, "The whole human race is in Adam, as in one body of one man." The *Catechism* teaches, "By this 'unity of the human race' all men are implicated in Adam's sin, as all are implicated in Christ's justice. . . . By yielding to the tempter, Adam and Eve committed a *personal sin*, but this sin affected the *human nature* that they would then transmit *in a fallen state*. . . . [O]riginal sin is called 'sin' only in an analogical sense: It is a sin 'contracted' and not 'committed'—a state and not an act" (CCC 404). Original sin is not merely the "bad example" of our first parents but an actual condition of being deprived of God's grace and of a supernatural destiny. Pope Paul VI wrote, "We hold, with the Council of Trent, that original sin is transmitted with human nature *by propagation and not by imitation*." [1]

The sin of Adam and Eve introduced great disorder into the universe. There is now natural disorder. Hence, we have tornadoes, earthquakes, babies suffering from pain and death, hail, floods, and so on. There is also now great moral disorder, and so we have crime, war, human violence, and so on. This moral disorder extends into the very fiber of every human being. The Second Vatican Council says, "What revelation makes known to us is confirmed by our own experience. For when man looks into his own heart, he finds that he is drawn toward what is wrong and sunk in many evils which cannot come from his good Creator." [2]

The *Catechism* states, "Following St. Paul, the Church has always taught that the overwhelming misery which oppresses men and their inclination toward evil and death cannot be understood apart from their connection with Adam's sin and the fact that he has transmitted to us a sin with which we are all born afflicted, a sin which is the 'death of the soul' " (CCC 403).

THE REMEDY: BAPTISM

In the water and words of Baptism, the justice or righteousness of Jesus becomes our own (1 Cor 1:30). The redemption that Christ won on the Cross and by His Resurrection is applied to our souls (Gal 3:27). Original sin and our actual sins are not simply "covered over" or disguised by this justice or righteousness, but original sin is destroyed and wiped out entirely (Eph 4:22). The effects of original sin still remain, however. The moral and physical disorder, being subject to suffering and death, the

[1] Paul VI, *Credo of the People of God.*
[2] *Gaudium et spes*, no. 13.

earning of bread "in the sweat of our brow", and the concupiscence of our eyes and heart are not taken away. These will only be gone at the Second Coming of Christ. Nevertheless, Baptism makes us pure and free from all stain of sin and gives us a true share in the very nature of God Himself (2 Pet 1:4).

Sometimes the inclination to sin that remains in all human beings, even after original sin is removed by Baptism, goes by the name of "sin" (Rom 6:12). This concupiscence is not sin in the regenerated and re-born in the true and proper sense of that word but goes by that name, says the Council of Trent, "only because it is from sin and inclines to sin".

In the ceremonies surrounding the administration of Baptism, there are several dramatic moments. One of these is when the baptismal garment is given to the newly baptized. This symbolizes the garment of sanctifying grace, God's life, which clothes the soul of a baptized person, making that person immaculate and totally unsullied by his inherited share of the primeval disaster called original sin.

Another such moment occurs when the head of the newly baptized is anointed with sacred chrism in the form of a crown, showing that Baptism makes one a sharer in the very kingship and priesthood of Christ. Sacred chrism is the holy oil used in anointing kings and priests. The *Catechism* asks:

> *Why did God not prevent the first man from sinning?* St. Leo the Great responds, "Christ's inexpressible grace gave us blessings better than those the demon's envy had taken away." And St. Thomas Aquinas wrote, "There is nothing to prevent human nature's being raised up to something greater, even after sin; God permits evil in order to draw forth some greater good. Thus St. Paul says, 'Where sin increased, grace abounded all the more', and the Exultet sings, 'O happy fault, . . . which gained for us so great a Redeemer!' " (CCC 412).

The Second Vatican Council says, "The world has been established and kept in being by the Creator's love. It has fallen into the slavery to sin, but has been set free by Christ, crucified and risen to break the power of the evil one." This is part of the glory of Baptism.

SEPTEMBER 29, 1995

Baptism: Spiritual Adoption

Some years ago I happened to spend some time in a family court in Wisconsin, helping some of my parishioners with child-custody matters. While waiting for their case to come up, I observed the finalization of several adoption proceedings. What characterized each of these proceedings was the overwhelming joy of the new parents in being able to adopt a child. In one instance the child was an eleven-year-old boy. It was hard to distinguish in all the tears of happiness whether the adoptive parents or the boy was the more joyful.

Unfortunately, the wholesale killing of little babies in our country by the heinous activity of abortion makes adoptions quite rare nowadays. Still there are some mothers (and fathers), especially when young and unmarried, who recognize it is best for their child and for themselves to give a child up for adoption. Agencies, such as Catholic Social Services in our diocese, assist in such adoption procedures. Often adoptive parents can be more loving and caring than biological parents. Sometimes, too, neglected, handicapped, special-needs, or abandoned children are available for adoption by loving couples who want to have a child and provide a happy family environment for such a child to grow and learn in.

One of the great effects of the sacrament of Baptism is that we who are baptized are adopted. The joy of becoming an adopted child of God should be one of the principal reasons why we thank Him continually for the privilege of being numbered among the baptized.

When a child is adopted in civil law, the state declares through appropriate acts that these parents, legally and before the law, are the parents of this particular child. However, it is obviously beyond the power of any court to make people who are not the the child's biological parents into his natural parents.

When God adopts us in Baptism, it is quite different. It is not an adoption that is merely forensic or a legal fiction. It is a genuine change in us, making us sharers in the very nature of God Himself (2 Pet 1:4). This share in God's nature, which is called sanctifying grace, transforms us remarkably. God is immutable and cannot change, but we are changed into something very special, His children.

In Baptism we are touched by the dying and rising of Jesus. By means of this sacred sign we are recreated. From nothing, through dust and ashes, clay and dirt, we are made into God's creatures, His images. Then we are called to be His friends. Finally, in the sacrament of water and words, we are summoned to glory and are made over into His children.

It normally would be terribly blasphemous for creatures, such as we are, to be familiar with our Almighty Creator. It is only because we are baptized that we dare to call God "our Father" (Mt 6:9–13). We recite the Lord's Prayer so frequently that we often forget how outlandish it is for us, who are basically nothing, to address the Ground of All Being as "Father". Saint Peter Chrysologus said, "When would a mortal dare call God 'Father', if man's innermost being were not animated by power from on high?" The *Catechism* states, "In *Baptism* and *Confirmation*, the handing on (*traditio*) of the Lord's Prayer signifies new birth into the divine life. . . . Those who are 'born anew . . . through the living and abiding word of God' learn to invoke their Father by the one Word He always hears" (CCC 2769).

Saint Paul, writing to the Galatians, says, "And because you are sons, God has sent the Spirit of his Son into our hearts, crying, Abba! Father!" The words "Abba" and "Father" are equivalent. Saint Paul repeats the Hebrew word in Greek, because it is so central and so important for our Catholic faith (see Gal 4:4–6). Indeed, Saint Paul says that "God sent forth his Son, born of woman, born under the law, to redeem those who were under the law, so that we might receive adoption as sons." Saint Cyprian wrote, "The new man, reborn and restored to his God by grace, says first of all, 'Father!' because he has now begun to be a son."

BAPTISM AND HOLINESS

Baptism is the sacrament by which we are plunged into the death of Jesus so that we might rise with Him to newness of life (Rom 6:4–5). This life of God, sanctifying grace, simultaneously comes into the soul of a baptized person the instant original sin is washed away by this symbol. An immediate effect of this new life, the life of God, the life of our risen Savior, is to make us adopted children of God (Rom 8:15–16).

Saint John, the Beloved Disciple, wrote, "See what love the Father has given us, that we should be called children of God; and so we are. The reason why the world does not know us is that it did not know him. Beloved, we are God's children now; it does not yet appear what we shall be, but we know that when he appears we shall be like him, for we shall see him as he is. And every one who thus hopes in him purifies himself as he is pure" (1 Jn 3:1–3).

The eleven-year-old boy I saw adopted long ago in a Wisconsin court remarked at the time, "This is awesome." How much more awesome it is to be adopted by the eternal God. To be adopted by God means sharing His very nature, His life. What effort we should put into preserving and increasing sanctifying grace in our souls!

Saint Cyprian said, "We must remember and know that when we call God 'Our Father', we ought to behave as sons of God." Saint Augustine of Hippo remarks, "Our Father: at this name love is aroused in us . . . and the confidence of obtaining what we are about to ask. . . . What would He not give to His children who ask, since He has already granted them the gift of being His children?"

OCTOBER 6, 1995

Necessity of Baptism

Jesus gave a solemn duty to His apostles before He ascended into heaven. "Go therefore and make disciples of all nations, baptizing them in the name of the Father and of the Son and of the Holy Spirit" (Mt 28:19). The reason for this "duty", of course, is that Baptism is linked to eternal salvation itself (Mk 16:16), for Christ said he who believes and is baptized "will be saved".

The *Catechism* says, "The Lord himself affirms that Baptism is necessary for salvation" (CCC 1257). Jesus said unambiguously, "I solemnly tell you, unless a man is born again of water and the Spirit, he cannot enter the kingdom of God" (Jn 3:3). The *Catechism* goes on to say, "The Church does not know of any means other than Baptism that assures entry into eternal beatitude; this is why she takes care not to neglect the mission she has received from the Lord to see that all who can be baptized are 'reborn of water and the Spirit'" (CCC 1257).

Baptism is the sign or symbol by which Christ first touches the heart and soul of a person and bestows on such a human being in this sacrament the redemption He won for all men on the Cross. Jesus saved the human race by His dying and rising, but He initially applies this salvation to each individual through the sacrament of Baptism, which He instituted. To stand just and righteous before God is impossible for any human being because of Adam's sin. However, Jesus puts His righteousness and justification upon us at the moment of our Baptism.

FORMS OF BAPTISM

The first three hundred years of the existence of the Catholic Church were marked by hideous and almost continuous persecution. To be a Christian meant being subject to torture and death. Membership in the Catholic Church was a capital offense in the ancient Roman Empire.

In many instances catechumens, those studying to become Catholics, were arrested along with members of the faithful and then were put to death. It was the instant teaching of the Church that those who die for her or for Christ (there is an identity, of course, between the Catholic Church and Jesus Christ, for the Church is His Mystical Body and Bride) receive by their martyrdom the effects of Baptism, even if they have not received the sacrament itself.

The *Catechism* states, "The Church has always held the firm conviction that those who suffer death for the sake of the faith without having received Baptism are baptized by their death for and with Christ. This *Baptism of blood*, like the *desire for Baptism*, brings about the fruits of Baptism without being a sacrament" (CCC 1258).

There can be no doubt that the earliest teaching of the Church contains also the belief that those who desire to be baptized but who through no fault of their own are unable to be baptized can be saved by what is called the "Baptism of desire". Sacred Scripture tells us that God wishes all men to be saved and to come to a knowledge of the truth (1 Tim 2:4). The only thing that can obstruct God's universal salvific will is willful sin. Those people, therefore, who are not saved are damned because of their refusal of God's pardon, love, and grace.

The Baptism of desire can be either explicit or implicit. The *Catechism*, quoting the Second Vatican Council, teaches:

> "Since Christ died for all, and since all men are in fact called to one and the same destiny, which is divine, we must hold that the Holy Spirit offers to all the possibility of being made partakers, in a way known to God, of the Paschal mystery" [*Gaudium et spes*, no. 22 § 5]. Every man who is ignorant of the Gospel of Christ and of his Church, but seeks the truth and does the will of God in accordance with his understanding of it, can be saved. It may be supposed that such persons would have *desired Baptism explicitly* if they had known its necessity (CCC 1260).

The possibility of a Baptism of desire, however, should not diminish our missionary zeal and our work to carry out the great commission of Jesus. We have no idea which people ever achieve the mind-set or live in invincible ignorance that would enable them to have a Baptism of desire, and we have no assurance that they are many. Furthermore, it is clearly very difficult to be saved by a mere implicit baptism and implicit membership in the Catholic Church.

MINISTERS OF BAPTISM

Because Baptism is a sacrament of the Church and an ecclesial act of worship and adoration, the ordinary minister of the sacrament is a man in Holy Orders, that is, a deacon, priest, or bishop. However, because of the absolute necessity of Baptism for salvation, anyone can baptize when there is danger of someone dying without the sacrament. Such a Baptism would be perfectly valid, but, of course, anyone doing an emergency Baptism should inform a priest as soon as possible afterward.

Baptism is an act of Christ. Saint Augustine said, "When a man baptizes, it is really Christ Who baptizes." As long as the sign is correctly placed (water is poured or the person is dipped into water with the words: "I baptize you in the name of the Father and of the Son and of the Holy Spirit" said at the same time) and as long as the intention of the minister is correct (to do what Christ or what the Catholic Church intends by this act), the faith or sinful condition of the minister is of no account. Even an unbeliever can validly baptize in such circumstance.

When someone over the age of seven is baptized, the minister should first ascertain, if possible, that person wishes to be baptized and then, if possible, obtain from the person an act of faith (the Creed) and an act of contrition.

Baptism is a key that unlocks the first door that leads to salvation. Without possession of this key, one cannot enter.

OCTOBER 13, 1995

Other Baptismal Matters

One of the great joys and privileges of being a parent is the selection of a name for a newborn infant. Parents often spend some time and have much discussion about this important matter. With the use of ultrasound nowadays, parents sometimes choose to know the sex of their child before birth. Among other things, this enables them to focus even more on the name they will choose for their child.

Frequently, there are various factors that enter into the decision about a child's name. These can range from family or ethnic customs to giving an infant the name of a rich aunt or uncle for rather obvious reasons. However, for a conscientious Catholic couple, the most significant factor ought to be the saint after whom the child will be called. A "Christian name" means the name of some saint, who will be the child's lifelong patron in heaven and who will be a model on which the child can construct a spiritual life while on earth.

At Baptism a name is registered forever in heaven when it is called out by the parents at the beginning of the ceremony. Parents should be certain that it is a saint's name that will be given to their child. Parents should learn about the life of that saint and, when the child is old enough to understand, teach the child about his patron saint. Families should celebrate name days, that is, the feastdays of the members' patron saints. Surely parents should inform their children about the dates of their baptisms, which, in the eyes of heaven, are even more important dates than their birthdays. As the Easter proclamation puts it, "It profits us nothing to be born if we are not saved."

Christian parents should not unduly delay having their children baptized. Of course, if there is any danger of death, a child should be baptized immediately. In olden times, when there was more infant mortality, children were usually baptized the day after birth.

Unless there is a very serious reason for delay, Catholic couples should have their children baptized within a month of birth. Baptism is absolutely essential for salvation, and unnecessary postponement could be tragic. If in doubt about the timeline, parents should certainly consult their parish priest.

It would be wrong to baptize a child against the wishes or without the knowledge of the parents or if there were not a well-founded hope that the child would be raised as a Catholic. However, if a child is in danger of death, the right of the child to salvation takes precedence over the rights of parents and over other rights.

What happens to unbaptized infants who die? The most honest answer is that we do not know. God did not choose to tell us. Saint Augustine and other theologians who followed him postulated the existence of a place or state of natural (rather than supernatural) happiness, which he named "limbo" (from the Latin word *limbus*, meaning "fringe"). This is, of course, only a guess. There are other theologians who postulate a moment of enlightenment, when an infant before death receives the use of reason for a time to make a decision for or against Christ, much like a "Baptism of desire" for someone who has the use of reason. There is no shred of evidence for such a thing, but they base this conjecture on the universal salvific will of God (1 Tim 2:4: "God . . . desires all men to be saved and to come to the knowledge of the truth"), whereas Saint Augustine based his idea on the clear teaching of Jesus about the need to be baptized (Jn 3:5: "Truly, truly, I say to you, unless one is born of water and the Spirit, he cannot enter the kingdom of God").

The *Catechism* states:

> As regards *children who have died without Baptism*, the Church can only entrust them to the mercy of God, as she does in her funeral rites for them. Indeed, the great mercy of God who desires that all men should be saved, and Jesus' tenderness toward children which caused him to say: "Let the little children come

to me and do not hinder them," allow us to hope that there is a way of salvation for children who have died without Baptism. All the more urgent is the Church's call not to prevent little children coming to Christ through the gift of holy Baptism (CCC 1261).

Among the attributes of God are His absolute justice and His perfect and complete goodness.

Godparents have much more than a merely honorary role to play in the life of the person for whom they are sponsors. They take on a duty to pray for the person they sponsor and to give that person the good example of a devout and practiced Catholic life. The *Catechism* says that godparents "must be firm believers, able and ready to help the newly baptized—child or adult—on the road of Christian life. Their task is a truly ecclesial function" (CCC 1255).

The law of the Catholic Church is quite specific about the qualifications that are necessary before one can be a baptismal sponsor. Parents, of course, should be aware of these qualifications before they ask people to be godparents, or else there can be serious embarrassment and anger when a priest would be obliged to refuse to accept certain persons as baptismal sponsors. (Catholics living in an "invalid marriage" or in a state of fornication, for instance, would be disqualified from being baptismal sponsors.)

It is a very useful and beautiful custom for godparents to help a person recall the date of Baptism with a card or phone call or visit. Namedays, too, can be remembered often with the help of thoughtful godparents. To the extent possible, it is a practice in accord with Christian tradition for godparents to participate in the other sacraments of Christian initiation for the person they sponsored, that is, in first Holy Communion and Confirmation, and to help the person link those three sacraments together as a beginning of the Christian life and the gateway to heaven.

3

EUCHARIST

HOLY MASS

A saint once said that, if you prayed and did penance every moment of your life and added to that all the prayers and merits of the Blessed Virgin Mary and the angels and saints, all of this would not even begin to equal the value of one Mass. For each Mass makes present again the dying and rising of Jesus Himself and the perfect adoration and gratitude He gives to God the Father through His paschal mystery.

The Mass is the core of the sacred liturgy and, therefore, as the *Catechism of the Catholic Church* teaches, it is "the heart and summit of the Church's life, for in it Christ associates his Church and all her members with his sacrifice of praise and thanksgiving offered once and for all on the cross to his Father" (CCC 1407).

Holy Mass has an identity with the act of Jesus on Mount Calvary, when, as our High Priest, He offered Himself as a spotless victim in sacrifice to His heavenly Father to take away our sins. The only differences are that on Golgotha Christ won salvation for us and in the Mass He distributes and applies this salvation. Also, on the Cross His sacrifice was a horrible separation of His Body and Blood, whereas, in its being presented again on our altar, this same sacrifice is mystical and sacramental and unbloody.

A MARVELOUS EXCHANGE

A very old prayer calls the Mass an *admirabile commercium*, or a "marvelous exchange". This is basically what the Mass is. Each part of the Mass is an exchange with God.

In the first part of the Mass we exchange "words" with God. We speak to Him, through Christ, in the Holy Spirit, in the prayer that the priest says on our behalf. We beg His forgiveness and praise His glory. Then, God speaks to us in the words of Holy Scripture, especially in the very words of Jesus in the Gospel, and in the preaching of the Church.

In the second and more important part of the Mass, we exchange gifts with God. We give to God our bread and wine, which symbolize our work and recreation, our tears and smiles, our lives and ourselves. Our contribution in the collection basket also represents the gift of ourselves. Fundamentally, we realize that our gifts are intrinsically worthless in God's eyes. At the best, they are only things that God Himself has first given to us, and, at worst, they are flawed and sullied by our selfishness and sins. They become acceptable to God simply because they are accompanied by our sincerity and contrition.

Then, at the climax of the Mass, Christ takes our worthless gifts and changes them, through the invocation and blessing of the Holy Spirit and the words of institution, spoken by the ordained priest, into His gift of Himself to God. Thus, our gifts, joined to His, become of infinite worth and of unsurpassable value. This is what makes each Mass, even when imperfect with defective music, ceremonies, rubrics, or homily (although we must deplore and overcome such defects), infinitely meritorious before God.

Finally, the exchange of gifts concludes when we receive back our gifts, now transformed and "transubstantiated" into the Body and Blood of our Redeemer, in Holy Communion.

Saint Thomas Aquinas called the Mass "the holy banquet in which Christ is received, the memory of His Passion is recalled, the soul is filled with grace, and there is given to us a pledge of future glory". It is wrong to oppose the two aspects of the Mass, that is, as a supper and as a sacrifice, for the Mass is truly both. The *Catechism* states, "The Mass is at the same time, and inseparably, the sacrificial memorial in which the sacrifice of the cross is perpetuated and the sacred banquet of communion with the Lord's body and blood" (CCC 1382).

In another place the *Catechism* emphasizes this unicity of the Mass: "The Eucharistic celebration always includes: the proclamation of the Word of God; thanksgiving to God the Father for all his benefits, above all the gift of his Son; the consecration of bread and wine; and participation in the liturgical banquet by receiving the Lord's body and blood. These elements constitute one single act of worship" (CCC 1408).

THE EYES OF FAITH

An unbeliever who happened in upon the Mass would probably "see" only a largely incomprehensible ceremony. The view that faith provides allows us to "see" something far more profound. In sign and symbol, in word and sacrament, we see the reality of Christ's Last Supper and the reality of His Passion and death on the Cross. The sacrifice of Christ and the sacrifice of the Eucharist are one single sacrifice.

The Council of Trent says, "The victim is one and the same. The same Priest, Who offered Himself on the cross, now offers the same sacrifice through the ministry of His priests. Only the manner of offering is different. In this divine sacrifice which is celebrated in the Mass, the same Christ Who offered Himself once in a bloody manner on the altar of the cross is contained and is offered in an unbloody manner." When we participate in Mass as we ought, in a conscious, prayerful, and active way, let us strive to "see" with the eyes of faith what is really going on and bring the utmost devotion and love to what we do.

SEPTEMBER 9, 1994

It Is a Sacrifice

The Mass is many things, such as a solemn prayer and a sacred banquet. However, our understanding of the Mass would not be clear unless we meditated on the words of the Council of Trent, which declared, "The Mass is a genuine sacrifice and a propitiatory one, although it is nothing else than the sacrifice of the cross. There is one and the same victim in the Mass and on the cross and one and the same Priest, Who offers Himself through the ministry of priests."

In order really to know what is going on when we attend Mass, it is important to keep in our minds that word "sacrifice". Because the Mass is, above all, a sacrifice, the altar is the most important part of the furnishing of any Catholic church, and the ordained ministers in the Catholic Church are not merely ministers but priests.

Religious anthropologists tell us that sacrifice is the most ancient and widespread of all religious rites. Sacrifice is found in a great variety of forms and with varied significance over an enormous range of human religious practices. It seems indisputable that the urge to "make sacrifice" is as instinctive in human nature as is the urge to "practice religion", both being implanted in the human heart by the Author of all nature.

Sacrifice is the offering of a gift to God. Usually, this is the first of something (first lamb of springtime, first cutting of the harvest, and so on) and the best gift possible. This offering is done for the purpose of adoring God, of acknowledging His sovereignty over the universe, of praising Him, of thanking Him, of making reparation for sins against Him, and for petitioning Him for needs and favors. Invariably, sacrifice involves the changing and destruction or immolation of the gift given to God, to show that it no longer belongs to the giver but to God alone. Some theologians maintain that this destruction indicates a sinner telling God he is worthy of death. Other theologians hold that the "sacrifice instinct" has to do with man understanding himself as dining with God or, inversely, with God inviting man to His table to commune with Him. Both interpretations are disputed among experts.

When a collectivity or group offers sacrifices, it almost always happens that a person or class of persons is designated as the mediator or go-between, to do the offering in the name of the group. Such persons are called priests.

THE OLD TESTAMENT

What God planted in human hearts He specified and codified in His divine revelation in the Old Testament. In the earliest days of humanity, the father or patriarch of the clan acted as the priest and offered sacrifice to God. Examples would be Noah, Abraham, and the mysterious priest-king, Melchizedek. Later on, the Hebrew race's sacrifices were regulated by the Pentateuch, especially the part of the Book of Exodus called the "Code of Holiness" and the entire Book of Leviticus.

There are some who say that the original sacrifice of the Jews was the Passover memorial and that all subsequent codification of the rituals practiced in the tabernacle and temple derived in some way from the Passover experience. Prophetic influence, particularly in the later Old Testament period, tended to emphasize the spiritual and internal aspect of ritual sacrifice and the need for interiority in the offering of gifts to God. The psalms and prophets often mention that external sacrifice is worthless unless accompanied by proper internal dispositions.

THE NEW TESTAMENT

Of course, all of the Old Testament sacrifices with their accompanying priesthood and, indeed, all of the human tendency toward sacrifice were only shadows and hints of what was to take place in these "last days" (Heb 1:1–2). The sacrifice of Jesus on Mount Calvary was the definitive Passover, the completion and fulfillment of all the sacrifices of the Old Testament and of all men of all time. In this one act, Christ, acting as our High Priest and as the only Mediator between God and us (1 Tim 2:5), gave perfect adoration and worship to God, offered the Father perfect satisfaction for all sins of all people, gave to the Father infinite gratitude on behalf of the human race, and begged all necessary and useful favors from God for needy and sinful humanity.

Whenever we attend Holy Mass, it is this once-and-for-all sacrifice of Jesus that is made present again for us so that we may participate in it in an intimate way. There is now no need for further sacrifices on the part of the human race, but there is a continual need for the re-presentation of the death and Resurrection of Jesus under the appearances of bread and wine. Divine ingenuity has contrived a way in which our instinct to offer sacrifice to God and in which the shadows of the Old Testament can be fulfilled in our lives.

At the Last Supper, as Father Louis Bouyer puts it, Jesus "gives His death a sacrificial significance and makes the community meals of His People in the future the memorial of the New Covenant until the end of time".

We who live in these New Testament times should be conscious of how our involvement in the Mass requires from us a type of continuous behavior and conduct that serves to reduce our fundamental unworthiness to be sharers in the very dying and rising of the Messiah. This is why Saint Paul tells us, "Present your bodies as a living sacrifice, holy and acceptable to God . . . your spiritual worship" (Rom 12:1).

SEPTEMBER 16, 1994

Breaking of the Bread

The death on August 27, 1995, of the Bishop Emeritus of our Diocese of Lincoln, Bishop Glennon Flavin, threw our diocesan family into bereavement and grief. The grand and noble priestly and episcopal service that he gave to us all over more than a quarter of a century, however, served to console and comfort us in our loss and sorrow.

His funeral in the Cathedral of the Risen Christ was a physical and tangible expression of the unity of our diocese. His passing from this world served to continue his pastoral work among us by bringing us together to pray for his soul, to remember his work in our midst, and to remind us of our basic oneness in our common Catholic faith.

Another physical and tangible expression of our diocesan unity is scheduled for the Catholic Center at Waverly, just outside of Lincoln, when we gather as a sort of *statio orbis* for the conclusion of our year-long, diocesan Eucharistic Congress. United around Jesus present in the Blessed Sacrament, our diocesan family will beseech our Lord to bless our homes, our families, our state, and our nation. In a special way we shall ask Christ to bless our diocesan Synod in 1996 and to be with us as we prepare to celebrate the great Holy Year, the year 2000, which will mark the beginning of a new century and a new millennium. Everyone is invited to be present for the Mass and eucharistic procession.

The Holy Eucharist unites us to Christ and then, in that unity, to each other. Like spokes in a wheel, which draw closer to each other as they draw closer to the hub, so when we are united to Christ in Holy Communion, we are also drawn closer to our fellow Christians. The *Catechism* teaches, "Through [the Eucharist,] Christ unites [those who receive Him] to all the faithful in one body—the Church. Communion renews, strengthens, and deepens this incorporation into the Church, already achieved by Baptism. In Baptism we have been called to form but one body (cf. 1 Cor 12:13). The Eucharist fulfills this call" (CCC 1396).

Saint Augustine said, "If you are the body and members of Christ, then it is your sacrament that is placed on the table of the Lord; it is your sacrament that you receive. To that which you are you respond 'Amen'('yes, it is true!') and by responding to it you assent to it. For you hear the words, 'the Body of Christ' and respond 'Amen.' Be then a member of the Body of Christ that your 'Amen' may be true." This saint elsewhere says, "O sacrament of devotion, O sign of unity, O bond of charity!"

In addition to the sublime unity symbolized and effected by our receiving Holy Communion together to conclude our Eucharistic Congress, our gathering in common worship of Jesus will also reply to a theological and pastoral need. Pope John Paul II said, "The Church and the world have a great need for Eucharistic worship. Jesus awaits us in this sacrament of love. Let us not refuse the time to go to meet him in adoration, in contemplation full of faith, and open to making amends for the serious offenses and crimes of the world. Let our adoration never cease." [1]

The expression "breaking of the Bread" is used many times in the New Testament (Mt 14:19; 26:26; Mk 6:41; 14:22; Lk 9:16; 24:30; 22:19; Acts 2:42; 20:7–11; 1 Cor 10:16; 11:24). Some of these refer, it is clear, to the Holy Eucharist. Two of the references in the Acts of the Apostles are most specific in this regard.

The "breaking of the Bread", of course, refers to the entire eucharistic action and the amazing change that takes place in every Mass, when the dying and rising of Christ are made present that we may obtain what He won for us on Mount Calvary.

The Council of Trent teaches:

> The Church of God has always believed that, immediately after the consecration, the true body and blood of our Lord, together with His soul and divinity, exist under the species of bread and wine. His body exists under the species of bread and His blood under the species of wine, and His soul under both species in

---

[1] CCC 1380, quoting John Paul II, *Dominicae cenae*, no. 3.

virtue of the natural connection and concomitance which unite the parts of Christ our Lord, Who has risen from the dead and now dies no more (Rom 6:9). Moreover Christ's divinity is present because of its admirable hypostatic union with His body and soul. It is, therefore, perfectly true that just as much is present under either species as is present under both. For Christ, whole and entire, exists under the species of bread and under any part of that species, and similarly the whole Christ exists under the species of wine and its parts.

The Council goes on to say: "Through the consecration of bread and wine there is a transformation of the whole substance of bread into the substance of the body of Christ our Lord and of the whole substance of wine into the substance of His blood. This transformation, the Catholic Church rightly and in a true sense calls transubstantiation."

The *Catechism* calls the Holy Eucharist a memorial, a sacrifice, a thanksgiving, and a presence. The Holy Eucharist is the way God Himself has designated that He is to be adored and worshipped. We give true and authentic worship to our heavenly Father only when we do so through Christ, the Head of our Church, as He makes present His sacrifice on our altars in Holy Mass.

However, we also give authentic worship to God when we genuflect and bow to the Blessed Sacrament. As Pope Paul VI put it, "The Catholic Church has always offered and still offers to the sacrament of the Eucharist the cult of adoration, not only during Mass, but also outside of it, reserving the consecrated hosts with the utmost care, exposing them to the solemn veneration of the faithful, and carrying them in processions." [2] May the conclusion of our diocesan Eucharistic Congress bring to us all, all unity, peace, and grace, and may it effect the eternal repose of the souls of Bishop Flavin and all the faithful departed.

SEPTEMBER 8, 1995

Worthy Reception

Prefigured by the Old Testament manna, promised in the hills of Galilee, instituted in the Cenacle, and enacted on Mount Calvary, the Holy Eucharist is a supreme and divine Gift, Sacrifice, Presence, and Food. Without a doubt, the Blessed Sacrament is the most precious legacy Jesus left to the Catholic Church that He founded.

[2] CCC 1378, quoting Paul VI, *Mysterium fidei*, no. 56.

If this sacrament is neglected, it is to the eternal peril of the Church's members. We must constantly adore the Holy Eucharist, as we do at the elevation of the Mass, in the tabernacle of the altar, at the repository on Holy Thursday, during Benediction, during Forty or Thirteen Hours, in our Corpus Christi processions, during the exposition at Holy Hours, and in our visits to our churches.

Even if we are impeded from going to Holy Mass each day, every Catholic should strongly want to do so. Pope Saint Pius X said: "The desire of Jesus Christ and of the Church is that all Christians should daily approach the Holy Banquet." Saint Francis de Sales wrote: "Two classes of persons should receive Holy Communion often, the perfect, because, being well prepared, they would be wrong not to approach the Fount of all perfection, and the imperfect, that they might acquire perfection."

DISPOSITIONS

One of the great blessings of the liturgical renewal that has taken place in our century in the Catholic Church is the frequency with which God's faithful now receive Holy Communion. The last shreds of Jansenism seem to have been dissipated, and Holy Communion is seen, not as a "reward" for goodness, but as a healing remedy for sinners.

However, it must not be forgotten that certain minimal dispositions for receiving Holy Communion always remain in place. Two of the basics are faith and Baptism. Baptism is fundamental. It is the sacrament that makes it possible to receive validly the other six sacraments. The unbaptized who would attempt to receive Holy Communion perform an act that is both illicit and invalid.

Holy Communion not only brings about deeper and greater unity among Christ's followers but is, before that, a sign of an already existing unity among them. Therefore, even baptized non-Catholics cannot usually be admitted to Holy Communion. Those who do not profess the fullness of the Catholic faith, even if it is not their fault, cannot receive Holy Communion with us, for this would be inauthentic and a mere pretense that unity in faith exists, when in reality it does not. This kind of intercommunion would be a lie, unworthy of the disciples of Jesus.

REQUIREMENTS

To receive Holy Communion worthily three other demands are made on us: the state of grace, the proper intention, and the eucharistic fast. The Holy Eucharist is called one of the five "sacraments of the living", which means that one can receive Holy Communion only when one is spiritually "alive", that is, in possession of sanctifying grace, God's life. If a person is spiritually "dead" with an unforgiven lethal or mortal sin on his soul, receiving Holy Communion would be not only worthless but an additional mortal sin of sacrilege. To get a deadly sin forgiven, it is necessary to have recourse to the "power of the keys", which is to say, to go to Confession with appropriate sorrow and contrition (Jn 20:23).

When approaching our Lord in Holy Communion, one must do so with proper motivation, from a desire to be more closely united to Christ and, in Him, to be more closely united with His People. It would be base and wrong to go to Communion out of human respect or out of fear that others would think poorly of us if we did not go.

Because of reverence for the Blessed Sacrament, in addition to the demands of the divine law, Church law requires that we observe the eucharistic fast. At the present time, this means abstaining from eating or drinking anything (except water or medicine, which can be taken any time) for one hour before receiving Holy Communion, unless we are sick, in which case we are excused from this Church requirement. Also, the *Catechism* observes about Holy Communion: "Bodily demeanor (gestures, clothing) ought to convey the respect, solemnity, and joy of this moment when Christ becomes our guest" (CCC 1387).

Saint Paul, in the inspired words of the New Testament, is unequivocally clear about the damnation that awaits those who communicate unworthily. "Whoever, therefore, eats the bread or drinks the cup of the Lord in an unworthy manner will be guilty of profaning the body and blood of the Lord. . . . For anyone who eats and drinks without discerning the body eats and drinks judgment upon himself" (1 Cor 11:27–29).

Even those who do not approach Holy Communion in total unworthiness must still pray as the centurion, "Lord, I am not worthy . . . but only say the word" (Mt 8:8). The *Catechism* cites the prayer recited before receiving Holy Communion by those Catholics of the Eastern Rites, who use the Divine Liturgy of Saint John Chrysostom, "O Son of God, bring me into communion today with your mystical supper. I shall not tell your enemies the secret nor kiss you with Judas' kiss. But, like the good thief, I cry, Jesus, remember me when you come into your kingdom" (CCC 1386).

Yet, we dare not stay away from Holy Communion. Our Redeemer tells us, even today, with the utmost solemnity, "unless you eat the flesh of the Son of Man and drink his blood, you have no life in you" (Jn 6:53). The *Catechism* tells us, "To respond to this invitation, we must prepare ourselves for so great and so holy a moment" (CCC 1385). May our preparation to receive Holy Communion always demonstrate the seriousness of what we do.

OCTOBER 21, 1994

Holy Eucharist: Before and After

A well-known horticulturist was once asked the secret of his beautiful summer lawn. There was no doubt that his lush grass was the glory of his neighborhood. He replied that once you have excellent grass seed, the secret is good soil, soil that is rich, balanced, and well prepared. He also mentioned that once the grass seed was planted, it had to be properly cared for as well.

PREPARATION

It is our Catholic doctrine that the sacraments impart grace "automatically" (*ex opere operato*), that is to say, when the sign that constitutes the sacrament is properly placed by someone with the power to do so and there is no obstacle to the sign, Christ's action takes place, and Jesus touches the recipient of the sacrament directly with His love and favor.

However, the grace of the sacrament is proportionately greater and longer lasting when the one receiving a sacrament brings to that reception a greater degree of devotion, fervor, preparation, and thanksgiving. Just as grass seed thrown on almost any soil will germinate and grow, but will only flourish when the soil is well prepared and then cared for after the planting, so the soil of our souls will prove rich and fertile only if we bring to the celebration of the sacraments the highest measure of care, thought, and consideration both before and after we encounter Christ in these seven signs that, in His infinite mercy, He has instituted.

The general principle of a good preparation before and a devout thanksgiving after receiving a sacrament applies in a special way to the greatest and most important of the sacraments, the Blessed Sacrament, the Holy Eucharist. It is true that, if we attend Mass and receive Holy Communion with no "obstacle" in the way, grace will come to us, always assuming the presence of faith and Baptism. An obstacle would, of course, be an unforgiven mortal sin on one's soul, an improper intention, or lack of the eucharistic fast.

Nevertheless, the action of Jesus within us will be enormously enhanced when we receive Holy Communion with a fervent preparation and follow that reception with a devout thanksgiving. The *Catechism* tells us that the Lord addresses an invitation to us, urging us to receive Him in the sacrament of the Eucharist: "Truly, truly, I say to you, unless you eat the flesh of the Son of man and drink his blood, you have no life in you" (Jn 6:53) (CCC 1384). To respond to this invitation, we must prepare ourselves for so great and so holy a moment.

Preparing to receive Holy Communion is done in two ways, remotely and proximately. In a certain way, our whole Catholic life must be a remote preparation for receiving Holy Communion. Our participation in liturgical prayer as well as our private prayer life must be directed toward as well as derived from our sharing in the most holy sacrament of the altar. Especially when confronted with decisions and moral challenges in our business, work, family life, recreation, and leisure should we be conscious of our past and future "eating the flesh and drinking the blood" of our Savior.

For example, a certain man I know told me that he is able to control his urge to use profane language and to tell "off-color" stories by remembering that his lips and tongue are made purple and sacred by the very blood of our Redeemer when receiving Holy Communion.

Proximate preparation must involve a careful and attentive participation in the forepart of the Mass, the Liturgy of the Word. There the word of God in Sacred Scripture and in the preaching of the Church, a response on God's part to our official prayers offered by the priest in our name, plows and cultivates the soil of our soul so that our reception of Holy Communion can be more fruitful.

Official documents of the Church tell us: "The Church has always required from the faithful respect and reverence for the Eucharist at the moment of receiving it. . . . 'It is strongly recommended that, coming up in procession, they should make a sign of reverence before receiving the sacrament. This should be done at the right time and place, so that the order of people going to and from Communion is not disrupted.' " [3] Usually, a slight bow shows the required reverence suggested here.

Saint Augustine of Hippo is cited in the *Catechism* saying: "If you are the body and members of Christ, then it is your sacrament that is placed on the table of the Lord; it is your sacrament that you receive. To that which you are you respond 'Amen' ('Yes, it is true!') and by responding to it you assent to it. For you hear the words, 'The Body of Christ' and respond 'Amen.' Be then a member of the Body [the Church] of Christ that your *Amen* may be true."

---

[3] Sacred Congregation for the Sacraments and Divine Worship, Instructions on Certain Norms Concerning the Worship of the Eucharistic Mystery, *Inaestimabile donum* (April 3, 1980), no. 11.

The *Catechism* states that the Eucharist "is an action of thanksgiving to God", recalling His great works, namely, creation, redemption, and sanctification (CCC 1328). It is entirely possible that one of the reasons that the effects of our receiving Holy Communion are sometimes not very long lasting in our lives is that we neglect to thank God appropriately for being able to share in this "action of thanksgiving".

Official Church documents say: "The faithful are to be recommended not to omit to make a proper thanksgiving after Communion. They may do this during the celebration, with a period of silence, with a hymn, psalm or other song of praise, or also after the celebration, if possible by staying behind to pray for a suitable time." [4]

In Holy Communion we eat the "Bread of Life", the "Food of angels", which "preserves, increases, and renews the life of grace received at Baptism. . . . [It is] bread for our pilgrimage until the moment of death, when it will be given to us as viaticum" (CCC 1392), after which we shall no longer see Christ under signs but, sharing His Resurrection, shall gaze on His lovely face forever.

JANUARY 6, 1995

Body of Christ

English can be sometimes a rather ambiguous language. Our English tongue is a widespread and living language, and, as a result, the meanings of words can fluctuate and vary from time to time and place to place. This is one of the reasons why theologians will often resort to the use of ancient, archaic,and even dead languages to attach a very precise meaning to a particular word.

LATRIA

This is the case in the use of the word *latria*. *Latria* means worship or adoration, but it is restricted to that worship and adoration due exclusively to God. To give *latria* to any creature, including the most splendid and glorious creature that God made, the Blessed Virgin Mary, would be a mortal sin of idolatry.

The veneration and honor given to the saints in heaven and the prayers we address to them go by the technical term *dulia*. The very

[4] Ibid., no. 17.

special veneration and devotion given to the Mother of God is called *hyperdulia*. Both *hyperdulia* and *dulia* are far different from *latria*, just as all creatures are infinitely beneath the dignity and majestic transcendence of God.

Pope Paul VI wrote: "The Catholic Church has always offered and still offers the cult of Latria to the Sacrament of the Eucharist, not only during Mass, but also outside of it, reserving Consecrated Hosts with the utmost care, exposing them to solemn veneration and carrying them processionally to the joy of great crowds of the faithful."[5]

Origen, one of the earliest Fathers of the Church, said that faithful Catholics always understood themselves as guilty, and they were right in this, if even the smallest fragment of a sacred Host fell to the floor through inadvertence.

The faith of the Catholic Church in the real and substantial presence of our risen Savior in the consecrated Species has always remained one and the same. In the Holy Eucharist Jesus Christ is present in His Body and Blood, Soul and Divinity. Not only is He offered and received, but He is also there "contained". He remains with us in the Holy Eucharist after Mass is over for the benefit of our sick and for our own personal adoration and worship.

To quote Pope Paul VI once more: "From [the Feast of Corpus Christi, which was extended to the Universal Church by Pope Urban IV] have originated many practices of Eucharistic piety which under the guidance of divine grace have increased from day to day, and with which the Catholic Church is striving ever more to do homage to Christ, to thank Him for so great a gift and to implore His mercy."[6]

DEVOTION TO THE EUCHARIST

In the fourth century, Saint Cyril of Jerusalem said: "As a life-giving sacrament, we possess the sacred Flesh of Christ and His precious Blood under the appearances of Bread and Wine. What seems to be bread is not bread, but Christ, and what seems to be wine is not wine, but Christ's Blood."

Our own prayer life should be centered in the Holy Eucharist. The abiding presence of our Savior among us should give us a solid and continuous reason to make frequent visits to our Lord in the Blessed Sacrament. Attendance at daily Mass ought to be an ideal for which all Catholics strive. However, even when that proves impossible, a regular

---

[5] Paul VI, encyclical *Mysterium Fidei* (September 3, 1965), no. 56.
[6] Ibid., no. 63.

visit to Christ in the tabernacle could be part of a daily or, at least, weekly routine.

Thoughtful genuflections that are genuine acts of *latria* should mark our comportment in entering and leaving Catholic churches or when passing in front of the tabernacle. Silence in church when the Blessed Sacrament is present and bowing the head in reverence and, for men, tipping a hat or cap whenever passing a Catholic church where the Holy Eucharist is reserved should be the type of behavior taught to children and practiced by all.

Many parishes in our Diocese of Lincoln are able to have hours of eucharistic adoration set aside each week or even each day. Some of the larger parishes can have perpetual adoration of Jesus in the Blessed Sacrament. With what joy should parishioners "sign up" and participate in such eucharistic adoration when it is available! The sacrifice of the Mass is the greatest of all possible acts of *latria*. Our worship of Jesus in the Blessed Sacrament outside of Mass must be seen as the "overflow" from the adoration we give to God the Father in and through Christ at Mass. The ceremony of Benediction with the Blessed Sacrament should be seen as an extension of the elevation of the Mass.

Christ continues to abide within us in a sacramental way after we receive Him in Holy Communion, as long as the Species remain recognizable as "bread and wine". This is why we must not neglect to remain for some time in prayer after Mass, thanking and adoring Christ within us, if this is at all possible. In any event, we should try to be respectful and silent in church after Mass, in consideration of those who may be trying to make their thanksgiving prayers.

Above all, we should strive to remain in church until Mass is finished and the priest has left the altar, unless a real and true emergency makes this impossible. The old, sarcastic sign sometimes deserves revival: "Judas was the first one to leave Mass before it was finished."

Saint Thomas Aquinas asks: "What is more wondrous than this holy sacrament? Is it not beyond human power to express the ineffable delicacy of this sacrament in which all spiritual sweetness is tasted at its very Source?" Chesterton calls the tabernacle: "The hidden room in man's house, where God sits all the year, the secret window whence the world looks small and very dear."

JUNE 3, 1994

4

PENANCE

Sacrament of Mercy

When asked once why he became a Catholic, Gilbert Keith Chesterton said, "To get my sins forgiven." There are few more precious signs that Christ left to His Church than the sacrament of Reconciliation. This Easter gift (Jn 20:22) is one of the vital ways in which the pardon and peace and salvation that Jesus won on the Cross for all mankind were confided to the Church He founded, to be distributed and applied through the centuries until He comes again.

It is during this holy season of Lent that the stark and somber reality of our human condition should be the object of our careful reflection. As one writer puts it, "Life is short; death is certain; and the world to come is everlasting." It is in this perspective perhaps that we should prepare for our Easter Confession, taking advantage of the understanding and forgiveness of Christ (Lk 23:34) to be reconciled with God through the sacrament of Penance.

There are people who would not drive a car off the lot of the dealership where it was purchased without being certain that the automobile is insured. Yet these same people will risk eternal damnation by living for long periods of time in a state of estrangement from God, placing their eternal happiness in jeopardy by living in a condition of mortal sin.

FREQUENT CONFESSION

To spurn a precious gift gratuitously given at great cost is the height of ingratitude. The gift of God's forgiveness in Confession was purchased for us at the immeasurable price of Christ's suffering and death. To go to Confession with frequency is simply accepting the embrace and love of Jesus, Who awaits us in the person of His priest, to tell us, as He did so often in earthly life: "Your sins are forgiven" (Mt 9:2).

Even when there are no serious sins to confess, we ought to approach Christ in the sacrament of Penance and willingly pay the small price of the natural embarrassment that comes to everyone in confessing and owning up to one's shortcomings and in making the effort of true contrition in order to receive the increase in sanctifying grace that comes from reception of the sacrament and to receive the added sacramental graces that will help us avoid sin in the future.

In exhorting us to frequent Confession, Pope Pius XII wrote: "By it genuine self-knowledge is increased, Christian humility grows, bad habits are corrected, spiritual neglect and tepidity are countered, the conscience is purified, the will is strengthened, salutary self-control is attained, and grace is increased in virtue of the sacrament itself."

THE TEACHING OF THE CHURCH

Like her Founder and Spouse, the Catholic Church is hard and hateful to sin but loving and tender to sinners. So long as there is a determination not to sin again and genuine sorrow for the sins committed, a sinner will always find forgiveness in the motherly embrace of the sacrament in the Church.

Pope John Paul II says, "There has always remained firm and unchanged in the consciousness of the Church the certainty that, by the will of Christ, forgiveness is offered to each individual by means of sacramental absolution given by the ministers of Penance." The Second Vatican Council states: "Those who approach the sacrament of penance obtain pardon from God's mercy for the offences committed against Him and are, at the same time, reconciled with the Church which they have wounded by their sins, the Church which, by charity, by example, and by prayer, works for their conversion." [1]

Again our present Holy Father teaches, "For a Christian the sacrament of Penance is the ordinary way of obtaining forgiveness and the remission of serious sins committed after Baptism." Indeed, we must remember that perfect contrition, which can remit serious sins before the sacrament is received, is not perfect if it does not include the intention of going to confession as soon as possible.

The Council of Trent instructs us: "Since God is rich in mercy (Eph 2:4) and knows our frail structure (Ps 102:14), He has prepared a remedy of life for those who, after Baptism, have given themselves over to the slavery of sin and to the power of the devil. This remedy is the sacrament of Penance and through it the benefit of Christ's death is applied to those who have fallen after Baptism."

On the first Sundays of Lent we hear about the temptations of Jesus in the desert, after His forty-day fast, and about His Transfiguration on Mount Tabor. Our own situation can be recalled in these two events.

---

[1] *Lumen gentium*, no. 11.

For we too are subject to the tribulation of temptation (and, unlike our Savior, we actually and often fall into sin as a result) but are called to be "transfigured" once more by God's grace into His image in which we were originally created.

Lent is preeminently the season for preparing for Baptism and reception into the Church and for preparing for a "rebirth" into baptismal innocence by a good Easter confession. If we are not catechumens, may this Lent find us being, as we should be, penitents.

FEBRUARY 18, 1994

The Call of Penance

Our Holy Father, Pope John Paul II, has stated that the very term and concept of penance is complex. Despite this complexity, Lent is a most appropriate time of the year to examine this concept and term. Penance is undoubtedly linked to the Greek word *metanoia*, which is found in Holy Scripture. This word, in its root meaning, indicates a total and inmost change of heart, based on the word of God and done in the perspective of the kingdom of God (Mt 4:1; Mk 1:15). Just as the Chosen People of the Old Testament were taught by God the necessity of deliverance, not merely from external enemies like the ancient Egyptians, but also from internal enemies such as egoism and idolatry, so we, the Chosen People of the New Testament, must be taught by penance that our radical "deliverance" is the fruit of an interior struggle, in which suffering and distress accepted in faith are conditions for a truly new Christian life.

Penance, however, is much more than a change of heart. It is also a change of life in harmony with a change of heart. From across the centuries, Saint John the Baptist tells us each Lent: "Bear fruits that befit repentance" (Lk 3:8). In a certain sense, doing penance means directing one's existence to a continuous striving for what is better. The Holy Father reminds us, moreover, that "doing penance" is authentic and effective only if it is translated into "acts and deeds of penance". Penance is a conversion that passes from our hearts to our deeds and then to our entire lives.

In Sacred Tradition and Sacred Scripture, as divine revelation comes to us through the teaching of the Catholic Church, God addresses us each year anew with a fresh call to take up our cross and follow Jesus (Mt 16:24-26). Annually, we are exhorted to put the element of Christian asceticism into our lives once more, to "put off your old nature and put on the new" (Eph 4:22-24), to overcome what is of flesh so that which is spiritual will prevail (1 Cor 3:1–20), and to "seek the things that are above, where Christ is" (Col 3:1).

Lent, from the oldest days of the Church, is the season when catechumens are prepared for Baptism. But it has always been the season when the faithful, through penance, prepared for a "second baptism". The work of interior purification must be for us Christians a constant and ongoing task. Yet during Lent it must be intensified, so that, under God's grace, baptismal innocence might once again be ours, regained by sharing on Easter in the Resurrection victory of Jesus.

Penance is not a value in itself. Christianity is not just a species of the stoic philosophy. Rather, penance is closely connected with reconciliation, with a radical break with sin and the regaining of lost friendships and relationships, or at least with the strengthening of those friendships and relationships, which, as time goes on, can become strained and feeble. The primary friendship and relationship, of course, the one on which all others must be based, is our friendship and relationship with God. This is why penance must be joined to conversion and then to reconciliation.

Reconciliation is basically a gift and grace from God. It is God Who takes the initiative through Jesus of Nazareth, Christ, the divine Son made man. Saint Paul tells us: "If while we were enemies we were reconciled to God by the death of his Son, much more, now that we are reconciled, shall we be saved by his life" (Rom 5:10). He says too: "God was in Christ reconciling the world to himself" (2 Cor 5:19), so, by His grace, the Apostle of the Gentiles says: "Be reconciled to God" (2 Cor 5:21).

By her prayer, by her preaching, and by her pastoral action, the Catholic Church is the agent of and indeed herself the "great sacrament of Reconciliation". In her Lenten work of exhorting her children to penance, she undertakes to lead them to the pardon, understanding, and forgiveness of Christ, found in the Easter sacrament (Jn 20:23) of Confession and peace.

Sometimes it is useful to review the teaching of the Church about the sacrament of Reconciliation and Penance. The Council of Trent teaches:

> As regards venial sins, which do not exclude us from God's grace and into which we fall rather frequently, it is proper and advantageous to mention them in confession. Nevertheless, they can be left unsaid without committing a sin of sacrilege and can be atoned for in other ways. But, since all mortal sins, even mortal sins of thought, make men children of wrath (Eph

2:3), it is necessary to beg God's pardon of all of them in a candid and humble confession.

Those who knowingly hide some mortal sins present nothing in confession to be remitted by divine Goodness through the priest. For if a sick man is ashamed to show the physician his wound, the physician cannot treat what he is ignorant of.

As we prepare during Lent for our Easter Confession, we should not forget that "contrition, which ranks first among the acts enjoined on a penitent, is a deep sorrow and detestation for sins committed with a resolution of sinning no more. Contrition is always necessary to obtain forgiveness."

May this Lent and every Lent of our lives find us people of penance, eager to experience conversion and reconciliation.

MARCH 4, 1994

A Biblical Parable

Every third year of the cycle of readings in the liturgy, the Fourth Sunday of Lent presents us with one of the most beautiful parables spoken by our Lord (Lk 15:11–32). Not found in the other evangelists, the parable of the prodigal son is unique to Saint Luke, whom many biblical scholars have called the "writer of the loving kindness of God". There is probably no passage of Sacred Scripture that should give us greater joy to hear during the season of Lent than this parable. Father Lagrange said that the parable is too narrowly named. It should be called the parable of the father who is as prodigal in loving and forgiving as the son is in spending.

FORGIVENESS

Pope John Paul II writes, "The most striking element of the parable is the father's festive and loving welcome of the returning son. It is a sign of the mercy of God, who is always willing to forgive. Let us say at once that reconciliation is principally a gift of the heavenly Father."[2] Our Holy Father goes on to say, "The parable of the Prodigal Son is above all the story of the inexpressible love of a Father—God—who offers to his child when he comes back to him the gift of full reconciliation."[3]

---

[2] *Reconciliatio et paenitentia*, no. 5.
[3] Ibid., no. 6.

In the same chapter in which he relates to us the parable of the prodigal son, Saint Luke cites the words of Jesus that are illustrated by the parable: "I tell you, there will be more joy in heaven over one sinner who repents than over ninety-nine righteous persons who need no repentance" (Lk 15:7) and "There is joy before the angels of God over one sinner who repents" (Lk 15:10).

Lent, Saint Ambrose tells us, is the season to prepare ourselves to be touched by water, either the water of Baptism, for those preparing for that sacrament, or the water of tears, for those already baptized who are preparing for a new conversion and repentance. Change of heart or repentance (*metanoia* in the Greek New Testament) is truly a gift from God, but a gift that must be sought by us in our prayer and Lenten self-denial and, once received, must be taken into our lives by our mortification and our use of the sacrament of Confession.

Our Holy Father says, "The Prodigal Son is man—every human being: bewitched by the temptation to separate himself from his Father in order to lead his own independent existence; disappointed by the emptiness of the mirage which had fascinated him; alone, dishonoured, exploited when he tries to build a world all for himself; sorely tried, even in the depths of his own misery, by the desire to return to communion with his Father."[4]

It is only when the wayward son "comes to his senses" that the return to the Father can begin. So it is only when we recognize our sinful situation, admitting our folly and intending to present ourselves in humility before God, that our heavenly Father will see us "while we are still far off" and rush out to meet us and forgive us.

The *Catechism* recalls the words of the Apostle Saint John, "If we say we have no sin, we deceive ourselves, and the truth is not in us" (1 Jn 1:8). Our Lord Himself, says the *Catechism*, taught us to pray daily "forgive us our trespasses" (Mt 6:12) (CCC 1425). The prayer, penance, and almsgiving of Lent are a valuable means for us to come to a better knowledge of our personal situation before God and, in humility, to recognize our need for His pardon. It is the season for each of us to "come to his senses".

THE ELDER SON

Our Pope tell us that "every human being is also this elder brother. Selfishness makes him jealous, hardens his heart, blinds him and shuts him off from other people and from God. The loving kindness and

---

[4] Ibid., no. 5.

mercy of the father irritate and enrage him; for him the happiness of the brother who has been found again has a bitter taste. From this point of view, he too needs to be converted in order to be reconciled."[5] The older brother, too, needs to "come to his senses". Notice in the parable that the elder son speaks to his father disdainfully about "this son of yours", while in answering him the father speaks of "your brother".

When we first hear this parable, we tend to share the point of view of the devoted and loyal older son. After reflection, however, we realize that, while his steadfast dedication to his father is commendable, his anger and envy are not. The happiness and generosity of the father take nothing away from "what he has coming". Our point of view in this parable changes too when we remember that we are more to be identified with the young prodigal who returns than with the brother "who has no need of repentance".

CONFESSION

Pope John Paul II said, "The Lord Jesus Himself instituted and entrusted to His Church, as a gift of His goodness and loving kindness, a special sacrament for the forgiveness of sins committed after Baptism. The confession of sins, included in this sign, takes on such importance that for centuries the usual name of the sacrament has been and still is that of Confession."

Archbishop Fulton Sheen said, "In confession it is the penitent himself who is his own prosecuting attorney and even his own judge. One indispensable condition of receiving pardon is the open avowal of guilt, such as the prodigal son made when he returned again to his father's house." It is through Confession, Cardinal John Henry Newman tells us, that "we who are children of wrath are made into children of grace, and our pains, which are a foretaste of hell, become, by the sprinkling of Christ's blood, a preparation for heaven."

Each Confession is an anticipation of that time when we shall close our eyes in death and then open them to see God our Father, Who will run to greet us and put a cloak on our shoulders, sandals on our feet, and a ring on our finger. He will invite us into our true home then, where there will be music and feasting and dancing forever.

MARCH 24, 1995

---

[5] Ibid., no. 6.

5

HOLY ORDERS

The Priesthood

One of the happiest days in the life of any diocese is the day the bishop ordains priests. The Second Vatican Council says: "By sacred ordination and by the mission they receive from their bishops, priests are promoted to the service of Christ, the Teacher, the Priest, and the King. They share in His ministry of unceasingly building up the Church on earth into the People of God, the Body of Christ, and the Temple of the Holy Spirit." [1] Saint Alphonsus Liguori writes: "The entire Church cannot give to God as much honor nor obtain so many graces as one priest by saying one Mass." Cardinal Cicognani said: "In view of the lofty and infinite value of the divine gifts of which he is the dispenser, a good priest is the most precious endowment of a parish or an institution, of a village or a city."

The *Catechism of the Catholic Church* says of the priesthood: "Through the sacrament of Holy Orders, priests share in the universal dimensions of the mission that Christ entrusted to the apostles. The spiritual gift they have received in ordination prepares them not for a limited and restricted mission, 'but for the fullest, in fact the universal mission of salvation "to the end of the earth"' [*Presbyterorum ordinis*, no. 10], 'prepared in spirit to preach the Gospel everywhere' [*Optatum totius*, no. 20]" (CCC 1565). Saint John Chrysostom wrote, "A priest is the common father of the whole world", and Saint Justin Martyr wrote, "The apex of all dignities is the priesthood." Saint Thomas Aquinas wrote, "In this age, the whole worship of the Christian religion is derived from Christ's priesthood."

INSTITUTION OF THE SACRAMENT

Jesus Himself instituted the sacrament of Holy Orders at the Last Supper (Lk 22:19). Christ founded a priesthood that is eternal (Heb 7:24; 5:4–6), making His priests "fishers of men" (Mt 4:19), sending them to

---

[1] *Presbyterorum ordinis*, no. 1.

preach the "good news" (Mk 16:15), with His own authority (Jn 20:21), endowing them with the power to dispense the forgiveness of sins, a power that He won on the Cross (Jn 20:23). According to the Second Vatican Council, paraphrasing the Epistle to the Hebrews (Heb 5:1), "Priests are taken from among men and appointed for men in the things that pertain to God, in order to offer gifts and sacrifices for sins."[2]

Pope Benedict XV said: "It was the desire of Jesus Christ, once He had wrought the redemption of the human race by His death on the altar of the cross, to lead men to obey His commands and thus win eternal life. To attain this end He uses no other men than His priests, who are His heralds, whose work it is to announce to mankind what they have to believe and do in order to be saved."

Jesus intends His triumphant sacrifice, His death and Resurrection, along with His memory, to be perpetuated to the end of time (1 Cor 11:24–34). This is why the "primary duty of priests" (as the Second Vatican Council puts it) of proclaiming the word of God reaches its zenith when a priest, standing in the very Person of Christ Himself, makes present in our midst the dying and rising of our Savior.

The *Catechism* teaches:

> "It is the Eucharistic cult or in the *Eucharistic assembly* of the faithful (*synaxis*) that they exercise in a supreme degree their sacred office; there, acting in the person of Christ and proclaiming his mystery, they unite the votive offerings of the faithful to the sacrifice of Christ their head, and in the sacrifice of the Mass they make present again and apply, until the coming of the Lord, the unique sacrifice of the New Testament, that namely of Christ offering himself once for all a spotless victim to the Father" [*Lumen gentium*, no. 29]. From this unique sacrifice their whole priestly ministry draws its strength (CCC 1566).

RESPECT FOR PRIESTS

No one knows better than priests themselves their unworthiness of the honor of their priesthood. Conscious of their personal sinfulness and weakness, priests must rely on grace and strength from God in their lives and ministries. Divine revelation says: "And one does not take the honor upon himself, but he is called by God, just as Aaron was" (Heb 5:4). Father Daniel Lord once noted, "There is no life in this world like that of a priest. No one deserves it. A lucky few are

---

[2] Ibid., no. 3.

prayed into it, inspired into it, or drawn into it by some miracle of God's condescension."

Yet the office of the priest always deserves the greatest respect from God's People. When you know about a priest's sins, tell them to God and, if necessary, to his bishop, but never allow gossip about priests to feed the frenzy of anticlericalism, so widespread today among contemporary bishop-bashers, feminists, priest-eaters, and the usual chorus of anti-Catholics. Saint John Chrysostom said, "He who honors a priest, honors Christ, while he who insults a priest, insults Christ." Saint John Vianney said, "After God, a priest is everything in a parish. Leave a parish twenty years without priests, and the people will worship beasts." Cardinal Suhard observed, "A priestless parish is not a sick parish. It is a dead parish."

Certainly all members of the Catholic Church should take most seriously the solemn charge of the Second Vatican Council: "The task of fostering vocations devolves upon the whole Christian community, which should do so in the first place by living in a fully Christian way." [3] All members of a diocese should join in celebration whenever priests are made by the sacrament of Holy Orders in their midst and should fervently pray for the newly ordained and for all priests. "Keep them we pray Thee, dearest Lord, keep them for they are Thine, Thy priests, whose lives burn out before Thy consecrated shrine."

MAY 13, 1994

Mediators

The Bible is very clear: "There is one mediator between God and men, Jesus Christ the man" (1 Tim 2:5). Because He is true God and true Man, Christ is the perfect and only go-between, bringing God to humanity and humanity to the Almighty.

The remarkable aspect of this reality, however, is that Jesus chooses to exercise His unique mediatorship by using human agents and instruments. This is why the ancients often referred to Catholic priests as "other Christs". The *Catechism* teaches: "In the ecclesial service of the ordained minister, it is Christ himself who is present to his Church as Head of his Body, Shepherd of his flock, high priest of the redemptive sacrifice, Teacher of Truth. This is what the Church means by saying that the priest, by virtue of the sacrament of Holy Orders, acts *in persona Christi Capitis*" (CCC 1548).

[3] *Optatam totius*, no. 2.

Pope Pius XII wrote, "Now the minister, by reason of the sacerdotal consecration which he has received, is truly made like to the high priest and possesses the authority to act in the power and place of the person of Christ himself."[4] The *Catechism* goes on to say, "Through the ordained ministry, especially that of bishops and priests, the presence of Christ as head of the Church is made visible in the midst of the community of believers" (CCC 1549). Cardinal Vaughn wrote, "It sounds more like fable than fact that God should come down to earth and associate men with Himself in the exercise of the most astonishing and unheard of spiritual powers."

Cardinal Manning once remarked that a priest saying "This is My Body" is using a sentence that has no equal except "Let there be light." Saint John Vianney said, "A priest himself will not understand the greatness of his office until he is in heaven. If he understood it on earth, he would die, if not out of fear, then out of love."

The *Catechism* states, "The redemptive sacrifice of Christ is unique, accomplished once for all; yet it is made present in the Eucharistic sacrifice of the Church. The same is true of the one priesthood of Christ; it is made present through the ministerial priesthood without diminishing the uniqueness of Christ's priesthood" (CCC 1545). Saint Thomas Aquinas said, "Only Christ is the true priest, the others being simply His ministers."

The Council of Trent (whose 450th anniversary we are celebrating in 1995) teaches: "Sacred Scripture makes it clear and the Tradition of the Catholic Church has always taught that the priesthood was instituted by our Lord and Savior, and that the power of consecrating, offering, and administering His Body and Blood, and likewise the power of remitting and of retaining sins, was given to the Apostles and to their successors in the priesthood."

SANCTIFICATION OF THE CLERGY

Our Holy Father, Pope John Paul II, has asked that annually there be in every diocese of the world a "Day for the Sanctification of the Clergy". He has suggested that the Solemnity of the Sacred Heart of Jesus would be a suitable day. The Pope has asked for this day so that all the priests and laity of the Church might implore from God the graces and gifts needed for holiness for our priests. I have asked that in each parish of our Diocese of Lincoln special prayers be offered to God for our priests on that day. In addition, there will be an annual "Day" cele-

---

[4] CCC 1548, quoting Pius XII, *Mediator Dei*: AAS, 39 (1947): 548.

brated with all the priests of our diocese on Monday of every Holy Week.

Certainly there is a universal call to holiness, given by God to every Catholic. However, there is a particular need in our time to ask God to be especially generous in bestowing this holiness upon our priests, who have been called and consecrated in a special way to serve Him and all of us.

The *Catechism* gives us the reason quite plainly:

> This presence of Christ in the minister is not to be understood as if the latter were preserved from all human weakness, the spirit of domination, error, or even sin. The power of the Holy Spirit does not guarantee all acts of the ministers in the same way. While this guarantee extends to the sacraments, so that even the minister's sin cannot impede the fruit of grace, in many other acts the minister leaves human traces that are not always signs of fidelity to the Gospel and consequently can harm the apostolic fruitfulness of the Church (CCC 1550).

As one lady told me recently, "Let's face it; our priests really need our prayers."

Since the priesthood is linked so essentially to the Holy Eucharist, it is my hope and desire as well that on the Solemnity of the Body and Blood of Jesus (Corpus Christi) special prayers for our priests and our seminarians will also be offered throughout our Diocese of Lincoln.

The Second Vatican Council says, "By their vocation and ordination, priests of the New Testament are indeed set apart in a certain sense within the midst of God's People. But this is not so they may be separated from this People or from any man, but that they may be totally dedicated to the work for which the Lord has raised them up. They cannot be ministers of Christ, unless they are witnesses and dispensers of a life other than this earthly one."[5]

The Baroness de Hueck wrote, "Have you ever stopped to consider the blessing of the mere presence of a priest? If your soul is sensitive to God and the things of God, that blessing is almost palpable. The priest does not necessarily have to speak, just to be in some place. His being there will impart a blessing, bring God's grace closer to you, and, oh, do so many strange and almost miraculous things." Saint Ephraem said, "The priesthood is an astounding miracle, great, immense, and infinite." Saint Alphonsus preached, "The entire Church cannot give to God as much honor nor obtain from Him so many graces, as one priest saying one Mass."

Priests bring us to God and God to us. They are truly our go-betweens.

MAY 26, 1995

5 *Presbyterorum ordinis*, no. 3.

6

MARRIAGE AND FAMILY

Marriage: Basis of the Family

The United Nations declared 1994 to be the year of the family, an occasion to reflect on the basis of every true family, which is marriage, an institution of God, raised by Christ for His followers to be a sacrament of the New Testament.

At the creation of the human race (Gen 1:27–28), the Creator instituted marriage (Gen 2:18–24). Before the coming of Christ, marriage was simply a natural contract, but after His coming, it became for Christians a sacrament of the New Law. Thus marriage continues to be for non-Christians a natural contract, enjoying liceity and validity. However, for Catholics, marriage is a sublime sign of the union of Christ and His Church (Eph 5:32), an efficacious sign that imparts grace (see Mt 19:4–9). For Catholics it is certainly a sacred and legitimate contract instituted by God, but it is much more. It is a grace-filled covenant binding in an unbreakable lifelong union one man and one woman in mutual love and respect, with children as its crown and glory.

All real family life must be based on and traced to marriage. Families are the fundamental building blocks of human society, both Church and state. Consequently, marriage must be of the highest interest to all of human society. The Second Vatican Council teaches: "The well-being of individual persons and of natural and Christian society is intimately linked with the healthy condition of that community which is produced by marriage." [1]

It is surely fitting, then, to use an international celebration such as the year of the family to see our Catholic families as both the objects and the agents of a renewed "family evangelization", bringing to bear on family life prayerful thought and the teaching of our faith about this "basic building block".

Although the Second Vatican Council concluded in 1965, the insights of that important gathering of the successors the apostles have lost none of their impact. With careful understatement, the Fathers of the Council

---

[1] *Gaudium et spes*, no. 47.

said that the excellence of family life "is not everywhere reflected with equal brilliance". They then spoke about the "plague of divorce" and how married love is "too often profaned by sexual promiscuity, excessive self-love, the worship of pleasure, and immoral practices against human generation".[2] The years have not shown any clear improvement in family life, at least in Western civilization. Cruelty, spousal and child abuse, alcohol and drug addiction, decline in religious practices, unwillingness to sacrifice, desertion of solemn commitments, interfering in-laws, materialism, unconcern about justice, and lack of reflection about the shortness of time and the length of eternity are elements quite familiar to every observer of the contemporary scene. Too often the media are not simply an amoral mirror reflecting such decadence and degradation but are active promoters of "modern values" that could make a pagan or heathen blush.

The Second Vatican Council puts forward the evangelizing duty of Catholic spouses:

> Authentic conjugal love will be more highly prized and wholesome public opinion created regarding it if Christian couples give outstanding witness to faithfulness and harmony in that same love, and to their concern for educating their children; also if they do their part in bringing about needed cultural, psychological, and social renewal on behalf of marriage and family. Especially in the heart of their own families, youth should be aptly and seasonably instructed about the dignity, duty, and expression of married love. Trained thus in the cultivation of chastity, they will be able at a suitable age to enter a marriage of their own after an honorable courtship.[3]

The initial effort in family evangelization must be directed to recapturing the holiness of all marriage. That which comes from the hand of God is holy. All of creation has been marred and smeared by the effects of original sin and of our actual sins. Nonetheless, marriage remains, as the ritual states, as one blessing not forfeited by original sin or washed away in the flood.

The sanctity of married love and life is, as the Second Vatican Council states, "qualified by the laws of the Creator. It is rooted in the wedded covenant of irrevocable personal consent. Hence, by that human act by which spouses mutually bestow and accept one another, a relationship arises which by divine will and in the eyes of society is a lasting one. For the good of the spouses and their offspring, as well as for the good of

[2] Ibid.   [3] Ibid., no. 49.

society, the existence of this sacred bond no longer depends on human decisions alone."[4]

There must be in our Catholic community a solemn realization that marriage and family life "have a very decisive bearing on the continuation of the human race, on the personal development and eternal destiny of the individual members of a family, and on the dignity, stability, peace, and prosperity of the family itself and of human society as whole".[5]

May all married couples and all couples preparing for marriage, may every member of every family reinforce our Catholic convictions about marriage and family life and bring to bear on all around us the weight of those convictions. There are so few institutions today that do anything to protect and foster genuine married love and family life. It falls to families themselves, especially to Catholic families, to perform such a service for the family of man.

JANUARY 7, 1994

The Sacrament of Matrimony

The sacrament of Matrimony is one of the seven signs that Jesus instituted, by which the salvation He won on the Cross is distributed to His redeemed people. Jesus took the institution of marriage that He, as God, created when the Father created humanity and purified it and elevated it to be a means and vehicle of grace (Gen 2:24; Mt 19:5). The Council of Trent teaches: "Since Matrimony under the law of the Gospel is, due to the grace given through Christ, superior to the marriage unions of earlier times, our holy Fathers, the ecumenical councils, and the tradition of the Catholic Church have always taught that Matrimony should be included among the sacraments of the New Law."

When two Catholics marry, their wedding is a special moment of consecration. Matrimony is unique among the seven sacraments in that the usual minister is not a deacon, priest, or bishop, but rather the couple themselves, who, in the giving and taking of matrimonial consent, not only receive a sacrament but also administer a sacrament. Of course, to be licit and valid, this must be done properly and ordinarily before a priest and two witnesses.

Therefore, the first and best wedding present a Catholic couple receive is God's grace. Because the sacraments are usually and correctly

---

[4] Ibid., no. 48.   [5] Ibid.

administered in connection with Mass, since all are oriented to the "great" or "blessed" sacrament, the couple's first meal together as husband and wife is the Body and Blood of the Lord in Holy Communion. It is difficult to imagine that any Catholic couple would not want to make the best spiritual preparation for their marriage, with a careful confession of sins and a prayerful attitude of respect and reflection.

A CONTRACT

Archbishop Fulton Sheen loved to say that it takes three to get married: a man, a woman, and God. Marriage vows are made by a couple not just to each other, but to God. This accounts, in one sense, for the indissoluble character of marriage. God is the third party to the contract, and thus, even if the couple mutually were to desire to break their marriage covenant, they could not, for they are joined together not just by each other's agreement but by God (Mk 10:9).

An early Father of the Church wrote: "How can I ever express the happiness of a marriage that is joined together by the Church, strengthened by an offering, sealed by a blessing, announced by angels, and ratified by the Father? . . . How wonderful the bond between two believers, united in a single hope, a single desire, a single observance, a single service! The couple are brother and sister in the true faith and fellow servants of Christ. There is no separation between them in the spirit and in flesh."

Pope John Paul II said: "By virtue of the sacramentality of their marriage, [Catholic] spouses are bound to one another in the most profoundly indissoluble manner. Their belonging to each other is a real representation, by means of the sacramental sign, of the very relationship of Christ with the Church."[6]

In the Old Testament, God, in divine revelation, used the image of marriage to describe His love for His Chosen People. When the prophets condemned prostitution and adultery, they were inveighing not only against violations of the sixth commandment, but also of the first. Disobedience to God and idolatry, into which Israel often fell, were violations of that People's conjugal fidelity pledged, promised, and vowed to God.

The Old Testament, of course, was a shadow and preparation for the New Testament. The spousal image of the relationship of God with His Chosen People took on a new and deeper meaning since marriage was instituted by Christ as sacrament to be a sign of His unbreakable bond

---

[6] John Paul II, *Familiaris consortio* (November 22, 1981), no. 13.

with His Bride, the Catholic Church (Eph 5:32). Jesus called Himself the Bridegroom (Mt 9:15).

As a sign manifesting to the world the union of Christ and His Church, Christian marriage should have the qualities of irrevocable commitment (Mt 28:20) and unselfish love (1 Jn 4:7–11).

THE GRACE OF MARRIAGE

As a so-called "sacrament of the living" (that is, one that can be licitly received only by those in the state of grace), Matrimony bestows an increase in God's life, sanctifying grace, when the sign of the sacrament (the exchange of consent) is properly placed. Sanctifying grace cannot be understood only in quantitative terms, but it is a capacity for eternal happiness, and the greater the capacity at the moment of death, the greater the happiness.

Matrimony, moreover, bestows actual grace, the sacramental grace that enables a married couple to live their vocation as spouses and parents with perseverance and fidelity, even if the time comes that the vows mention: "for worse . . . in sickness . . . for poorer". It is this special help from God that permits couples to face sometimes enormous trials: mental illness, hopeless incompatibility, betrayal, desertion, or separation by death.

"The future of humanity passes by way of the family", says Pope John Paul II.[7] The foundation of a Catholic family is Christian marriage. May this truth be better understood by every Catholic who is called to the state of Matrimony.

JANUARY 14, 1994

Fidelity in Marriage

In an "International Year of the Family" [1994] it seems important to focus initially on the basis of every Catholic family, which is Christian marriage. Begun in the sacrament of Matrimony, their wedding day should be for a Catholic couple the beginning of a long, exciting, and interesting adventure. Marriage was made by God in such a way that a couple should be more in love and closer to each other on their thirtieth wedding anniversary than they were on their honeymoon, in a different sort of way, of course. A Catholic marriage should grow and deepen as the years go on.

[7] Ibid., no. 86.

A schoolboy once responded in a test to the question: "What is another name for Christian marriage?" His reply: "Holy acrimony!" Quarreling and arguments are not usually fatal to marriages, although they can have a corrosive effect upon family harmony and on the sensitive minds of children. However, adultery is a horrible reality that can be deadly in time and in eternity. It is a sin against justice as well as against purity.

God designed marriage to be one man and one woman. This exclusiveness was made lifelong by Jesus when He raised marriage to the dignity of a sacrament (Mt 10:3–9). The famous "I do" on a wedding day means "I don't" to everyone else in the world. The sacrament of marriage is a sign of the union of Christ and His Bride, the Catholic Church. Just as Christ and His Church are faithful to each other "until the close of the age" (Mt 28:20), so Christian spouses must not only say but intend and mean till death do us part (Mk 10:2–12).

Fidelity is of two kinds, internal and external. God made us with bodies and souls, a material and a spiritual component. External observance of marital fidelity is simply the exteriorization of what is already in one's mind and heart. Marriage, just like the single life, requires a Christian to keep careful control of the internal senses and the mind. Unfaithfulness in marriage begins in the memory or imagination and then goes into the intellect. From there it is only a short step to a violation of marriage vows. Imagination and desire can exert a tremendous pressure on the human will. Our divine Lord clearly teaches us that there is such a thing as illicit lust and "adultery in [one's] heart" (Mt 5:27–28).

The variant of the Chinese saying "If you want to avoid the journey, do not take the first step" is quite valid in regard to faithfulness in marriage. To avoid the slippery slope of serious sin, we must avoid unnecessary occasions of sin. This is simply the wise principle that says: "If you do not want to fall off a cliff, do not sit on the edge of it."

In marriage, as in every human institution, there is "gain and loss". When one makes a purchase in a store, one obtains the desired product but loses the money in the exchange. Similarly in marriage, one gives up a certain "freedom" and certain kinds of comportment, which may be legitimate for a single person, in exchange for the greater and more desirable state of Matrimony. It is easy for a married person to rationalize and say to himself that what he is doing is not a sin. In the heart and voice of conscience, however, one can see in certain circumstances that this may be a step in a direction that ultimately can lead to separation from God and the sin of adultery.

All of us human beings, with the exception of the Blessed Virgin Mary, were conceived and born with original sin on our souls. And, although the sin itself is washed away in the waters of Baptism, the effects of that sin remain within us. Concupiscence accompanies every human journey. It is not possible to be human in our present condition without experiencing external and internal temptations to sin. Family life and marital happiness depend on the ability of marriage partners to resist temptations to sin.

Conscientious Catholic couples who want to remain faithful and loyal in marriage will always understand their personal human weakness and capacity for error. Regular prayer, especially family prayer; meticulous avoidance of occasions of sin; frequent recourse to the sacrament of Penance, with truthful and integral confession; and stern self-control, particularly of one's interior life, will assist those who are called to the state of marriage to make proper use of the sacramental graces that God pledges to them in the sacrament of Matrimony.

Faithfulness in marriage is treated very lightly in our day. The media report about marital infidelity practiced even by high and important figures in politics, sports, and society. The entertainment industry laughs at faithful spouses and fosters adultery. Many married people fall prey to the pagan climate in which they are immersed.

Some people are perpetual adolescents who have never learned the need for self-discipline, the value of commitment, or the meaning of sacrificial love. Slaves to their hormones and glands, they follow their impulses, no matter how depraved. Other adulterers wallow in self-pity, allow alcoholic drinks to loosen their inhibitions, or look for "excitement" after years of raising children and "enduring domesticity".

Because Christian marriage is so beautiful, its perversion and misuse are correspondingly evil. May those called to marriage live their commitments in joy and love and lifelong fidelity.

JANUARY 21, 1994

Love and Prayer in Christian Marriage

Love is central to Christian marriage. Pope John Paul II wrote: "Without love a family cannot live, grow, and perfect itself as a community of persons."[8] Family love begins with the love of the spouses in marriage. The love between a husband and wife grows into the love between parents and children, among brothers and sisters, and among relatives and members of a household.

[8] John Paul II, *Familiaris consortio* (November 22, 1981), no. 18.

In our cultural setting, love is dreamed about, sung about, talked about, but rarely understood and examined intellectually. Because we have bodies as well as souls, both are involved in love, especially married love. It can be good that love involves sentiment, passion, ardor, desire, and the like. However, these emotions can come and go and sometimes can depend upon things other than our free will.

To lift love from the level of *eros* to that of *agapé*, it is necessary to purge love of selfishness and egoism. A married couple must strive, day in and day out, to root and ground their love in sacrifice and giving. To build a structure of love on a foundation of emotion is to build on sand.

Human love (in marriage, as in all human love) is elevated to the level of the divine by sacrifice and giving. Jesus said that "God so loved the world that he gave his only Son" (Jn 3:16), and He also said, "Greater love has no man than this, that a man lay down his life for his friends" (Jn 15:13). Love in marriage is simultaneously a gift of God that must be sought and prayed for as well as an action of the free will of the couple.

To be successful in marriage, each party must be willing to forget personal comfort, pleasure, and desire in order to please the other partner, in order to make the other spouse happy. If both are willing to do this and do it always (without one being a giver and the other a taker or, worse, without both being takers) and if this kind of unselfishness dominates their entire relationship, that marriage is going toward success.

Before, during, but especially after the wedding ceremony, a Catholic couple will want to introduce into their life together the essential element of prayer. Since God is the third party in every marriage contract, it is logical and sensible, from the very beginning of a marriage, to keep a dialogue and close relationship with Him. Later on, if God gives a couple the privilege of parenthood, they will be able to welcome their children into a household where prayer is already a usual and daily occurrence.

A military chaplain once hung a sign outside his office door. It said, "If you have troubles, come and visit us or pray in the chapel. If you do not have any trouble, come in and tell us how you do it!" Every marriage, even the proverbial one "made in heaven", has trouble sometime or another. The part of marriage vows that speaks of "worse . . . poorer . . . and sickness" is a reality that can be confronted successfully only by a couple who know how to pray and who do pray. Certainly, a couple who can kneel down each evening and say to God "forgive us as we forgive", and really mean those words, will be able to face, with a truly Christian disposition, whatever tensions and problems their lives may encounter.

The slogan of Father Patrick Peyton—"The family that prays together, stays together"—might seem trite to our cynical age. However, it contains more than a little truth. Pastors, who get to see marriages in every state of growth, development, and decay, can attest to the fact that marriages without a strong prayer component are almost certainly doomed to fail.

Pope John Paul II has written: "The Christian family's actual participation in the Church's life and mission is in direct proportion to the fidelity and intensity of prayer with which it is united with the fruitful Vine Who is Christ the Lord."[9]

The proverb that says "absence makes the heart grow fonder" is simply untrue. Marriage needs the "presence" of the partners. Togetherness is vital to married success and married happiness. Common interests and common activities are necessary in every marriage relationship.

Nevertheless, it is a flawed marriage that smothers every vestige of the "inner person" or that is hyper-possessive because of a lack of trust or because of a false love that disguises possession, ownership, or manipulation. Varied and divergent interests and activities are useful and valid in married couples so long as they are not excessive and provided the couple give total priority to the "together aspect" of married life.

Sharing not only a house but thoughts and feelings can make marriage a state in life in which the couple really assist each other in striving for sanctity and holiness. Respecting one another's conscience, giving good example to each other (and most of all to the children), leaving room for some privacy while being willing to give and sacrifice out of love for each other are "keys" in marriage that unlock the doors of temporal and eternal happiness.

JANUARY 28, 1994

Parenting

Christian marriage is very important for the cause of vocations of special consecration to God, that is, vocations to the priesthood and religious life. Although there are exceptions, it is usually only from solid Catholic families that an abundance of priestly and religious vocations can come. If there is a lack of such vocations in our time, it may be due to the impoverishment and decadence of family life.

If the Church has in great numbers Catholic mothers and wives and fathers and husbands who understand their role, who understand the

[9] Ibid., no. 62.

dignity and splendor of Christian marriage, and who are dedicated to conjugal fidelity and conjugal chastity, and has families where the priesthood and Church are esteemed and respected, God will bestow on the Church more than sufficient vocations of special consecration.

In marriages that are truly lifelong and faithful to the end, priests and religious themselves receive a good example of faithful commitment. In families where purity and obedience are taught by parents to children from a tender age, there will be deep respect and reverence for a vocation to consecrated celibacy and holy virginity. Indeed, the future flourishing of the Church herself depends on such Catholic family life.

Each child is an unrepeatable act of God, Who creates a human soul each time parents cooperate with Him in bringing a baby into existence. God has chosen to make no two human beings exactly alike. Even identical twins have separate and different personalities. Humans beings are as diverse as snowflakes from each other. Parents, of course, must understand and respect this diversity in their children. This does not mean, however, that there are no standards of socially desirable behavior and general human comportment that all children are required to abide by.

It can be a mistake to force all children into a common mold in their looks or their actions. On the other hand, common sense and good order demand that there be times "when the ducks must walk in a row". Thoughtful parents will strive to understand and encourage the special talents and characteristics of each child, while, at the same time, teaching children that for good family operation and family policy, some measure of conformity will be their duty.

It is a very serious matter to cooperate with God in bringing new human life into the world. Parents know that it is a heinous crime to bring children into the world and then not feed them, clothe them, educate and train them. However, while physical abuse of children ranks among the most terrible of human actions, spiritual abuse is even worse. Physical abuse can result in harm and even death, but spiritual abuse can result in eternal death.

Catholic parents must see to it that their children are baptized as soon as possible after birth. Since they must answer to God for the care not only of their children's bodies but also of their immortal souls, they must always give their children good example. Saint Pius X used to tell parents that "what you tell your children is too quiet; they will never hear it because of the loud noise of what you do". Needless to say, Catholic parents have a duty to pray for their children. Just as children themselves must love and respect their parents and pray for them, even after they are emancipated from the obligation of obedience, so parents must pray for their offspring always, even after they leave home and "are on their own".

From a child's first waking moments, he should be conscious of a home where Christ lives and abides, a home that is basically happy because every family member knows about the eternal destiny that God in His love has planned for the family. A Catholic home should be adorned with daily family prayers. Sunday Mass should be "not just part of the week, but the heart of the week". The natural virtues in a Catholic home (such as honesty, courtesy, unselfishness, and truthfulness) should be penetrated with supernatural strength and meaning (in hope, charity, meekness, obedience, justice, and so forth).

A Catholic home is supposed to be the first and best wedding preparation course for future spouses, as well as the first seminary and the first convent. In that kind of home, discipline is administered by parents in love and not in anger, and such parents know that being too indulgent and permissive is being as cruel to their children as being too severe and demanding.

A mosaic is composed of many tiny stones and bits of glass. No one piece is essential, but cumulatively they make a picture. So a Catholic home atmosphere is composed of many little things. Celebrations of saints' days and name days and celebration of the seasons and feasts of the Church year are important. So too is the use, without abuse or superstition, of sacramentals, such as a crucifix, statues and pictures of saints, holy water, rosaries and scapulars, blessed candles, palms, and ashes. In the heathen and godless modern culture in which we live, it is the Catholic family that will have to assume the undertaking of passing on to children our Catholic heritage. May God give our Catholic families His protection and His grace.

FEBRUARY 4, 1994

'Til Death Do Us Part

Speaking about Christian marriage, the Second Vatican Council says, "As a mutual gift of two persons, this intimate union, as well as the good of the children, imposes total fidelity on the spouses and argues for an unbreakable oneness between them." [10] The reason, of course, that the Catholic Church teaches the irrevocable character of the marriage vows is because Jesus Christ, her Founder, insists upon this. He said, "Whoever divorces his wife and marries another, commits adultery against her; and if she divorces her husband and marries another, she commits

---

[10] *Gaudium et spes*, no. 48 § 1.

adultery" (Mk 10:11–12). Therefore, a valid, sacramental, and consummated marriage cannot be ended by any power on earth, either by the Church or by the state. It can be terminated only by the death of a spouse. Governments and divorce courts cannot change what is reality in God's eyes.

It really takes three to be married, a man, a woman, and God. The vows that a couple make on their wedding day are not simply made to each other but are also made to God. Because God is the "third party" in a marriage contract and covenant, it cannot be broken, even by the mutual agreement of the spouses.

For Catholics, marriage is something even more than a three-way pact between a man, a woman, and God. It is a sacrament, one of the mysteries of faith. A sacrament is basically a sign. Christian marriage is fundamentally a sign or symbol of the union between Christ and His Bride, the Catholic Church (see Eph 5:21–33). Just as Christ has irrevocably committed Himself to the Catholic Church, promising to be with her until the end of time (Mt 28:20), so Christian spouses must show forth this indissoluble union of Jesus and His Church by their own lifelong and unbreakable union with each other.

Sacraments, of course, are far more than mere signs. They are signs that Christ instituted. Furthermore, they do more than symbolize. They actually do what they symbolize. They are efficacious signs of grace.

Of all the seven sacraments, Matrimony is unique. In the other six sacraments the ordinary minister is someone in Holy Orders. In Matrimony, however, the couple not only receive the sacrament, but, in their mutual exchange of consent, they also bestow the sacrament on each other. The couple themselves are really the ministers as well as the recipients of the sacrament. Naturally, a priest normally must be present as the official witness of the Church for the liceity and validity of the sacrament.

In marriage, then, the first and best wedding present that a Catholic couple receive is the gift of grace that they give to each other. When the sacrament is given and received during Mass, as it is supposed to be, the first meal that the couple has together as husband and wife is the Body and Blood of Jesus in the Holy Eucharist. For Catholics, Matrimony is a serious and beautiful event. A Catholic's wedding day should be a day of special prayer and consecration. It should always be preceded by a good and sincere sacramental Confession.

Besides an increase in God's life, sanctifying grace, the sacrament of Matrimony, like all sacraments, gives to those who receive it special help from God, called sacramental grace. Sacramental grace is a type of actual grace, which generally enlightens our minds and strengthens our wills to carry out whatever it is that the sacrament commissions us to do. The *Catechism of the Catholic Church* says:

> This grace proper to the sacrament of Matrimony is intended to perfect the couple's love and to strengthen their indissoluble unity. By this grace they "help one another to attain holiness in their married life and in welcoming and educating their children" [*Lumen gentium*, no. 11 § 2]. *Christ is the source of this grace.* Christ dwells with them and gives them the strength to take up their crosses and so follow him, to rise again after they have fallen, to forgive one another, to bear one another's burdens (CCC 1641–42).

One aspect of this sacramental grace of Matrimony is that it contains a pledge from God for future graces. It is something like a spiritual credit card, which entitles a Catholic married couple to call upon their Lord for the special help they need in both prosperity and adversity, in joy and in unhappiness, in tension and in relaxation. This "right" to special help from God, which in reality is a gratuitous gift from God, is not only for their wedding day but for all their married life together, as they carry out their vocation to be husband, father, wife, and mother.

There can be no doubt that we live in a "divorce culture". The United States is the world's acknowledged leader in divorces. Our Holy Father has called divorce "a plague". A wise and perceptive observer has noted that there are no such things as "failed marriages", only "failed spouses". The damage that derives from divorce is almost incalculable. It is the leading cause for people abandoning the Catholic faith and thereby forfeiting their eternal salvation.

The social fall-out is terrible. Joan Beck, a fanatic feminist by the way, has observed, "No-fault divorce laws, adopted in almost all states since 1970, have turned out to be enormously unfair to women and children. They have pushed millions of mothers and young children into poverty." During the divorce referendum campaign in Ireland, a billboard read, "A woman voting for divorce is like a turkey voting for Christmas." Sometimes divorce can seem to solve some problems, but it inevitably causes more and worse problems than it seemingly solves.

May all those called by God to the high and noble vocation of marriage never fail to call upon Him for help to keep their commitments and vows. May all Catholics respect the holy state and sacrament of Matrimony.

JUNE 16, 1995

Married Love

For Christians, Matrimony is one of the seven sacraments, which are symbols instituted by Jesus Christ to give grace. A Catholic wedding is the beginning of a lifelong pact, covenant, agreement, and contract in which a man and a woman give their free consent "to have and to hold" each other until one of them dies. It is a moment of solemn consecration. As the old ritual used to say, it is a union that is most sacred and most serious.

The wise words of that ritual also say that no greater blessing can come to married life "than pure, conjugal love, loyal and true to the end". The Bible clearly tells us what God says: "I hate divorce, says the Lord the God of Israel" (Malachi 2:16). It is genuine married love that protects the indissoluble character of Christian marriage. Love, in the full sense of that word, should be the guardian of every Catholic marriage and, consequently, of every Catholic home.

The Second Vatican Council teaches, "Authentic married love is caught up into divine love and is governed and enriched by Christ's redeeming power and the saving activity of the Church. Thus this love can lead the spouses to God with powerful effect and can aid and strengthen them in the sublime office of being a father or a mother." [11]

Feelings are something like fire. Fire can cook our food and heat our home, but, when not controlled, it has the capability to destroy. Human beings, with bodies as well as souls, experience feelings, and sometimes strong feelings. In themselves these are not "bad or wicked" and sometimes can be important and helpful. However, these must be seen for what they are.

Feelings such as passion, ardor, desire, sentiment, and emotion often precede and accompany married love. But these are merely the escorts of married love and not the "real thing". Sometimes, indeed, these feelings can be a mere mask or camouflage for selfishness and egoism. Generally, it is good for married love to involve profound feelings, so long as the spouses realize that authentic love is not measured by the intensity of their emotion but rather by their mutual desire for sacrifice for each other and for their children.

Whether one spouse really loves another is better measured by a willingness to give. If each spouse says to himself, I am not primarily interested in my own desires, wishes, comforts, pleasures, but what I want to do is make my marriage partner happy, even at great cost to myself, such

---

[11] *Gaudium et spes*, no. 48.

a marriage is marked by genuine love. Of course, this giving and sacrifice should come from both spouses. Saint Paul teaches, "The wife does not rule over her own body, but the husband does; likewise the husband does not rule over his own body, but the wife does" (1 Cor 7:4–5).

For all of us, and this obviously includes married couples, it is a difficult and continuing labor, which lasts as long as life, to purge selfishness and egoism from our love. This ongoing task needs the assistance of God's grace. To use the technical Greek terms, we must strive to pass from the love called *eros* through that called *philaea* to arrive at the love called *agapé*. In Latin this kind of love is called *caritas*, or charity. Our labor here is made more difficult because of the tendency to backslide in this area of our lives, due to the weakness we all experience from the effects of original sin.

When human love of any kind (for instance, the love of parents for children and children for parents, the love of celibate virgins for Christ, the love of Christian spouses for each other) is marked by giving and sacrifice, it is spiritualized, elevated, and it enters, by grace, into the realm of the supernatural.

In such instances our human love becomes like God's. Jesus said, "God so loved the world that He gave His only Son" (Jn 3:16). Notice the word "gave". Our Lord also taught, "Greater love has no man than this, that a man lay down his life for his friends" (Jn 15:13). Notice that the greatest love is marked by sacrifice. Successful marriages require each spouse to give to the other and to sacrifice for the other daily.

Such love seems possible only for people who have the life of God, called sanctifying grace, in their souls. This is because God not only is absolute and total in His love for us but is truly identified with love itself. Saint John tells us in Sacred Scripture that "love" is another name for God (1 Jn 4:8).

When we see things in our world that are truly beautiful, such as a breathtaking sunset over our Nebraska plains, an act of heroism, the mountains of our continent, or splendid works of art, we can safely say that we are viewing a "hint of God". Of all such things, however, that which is most like God is true and genuine love, "His other name".

Authentic married love, then, for Christians, must rest upon the great principle of self-sacrifice. As the ritual says, marriage must begin with the voluntary and complete surrender of two individual lives in the interest of the deeper and wider life that is to be had in common. The Second Vatican Council says, "For this reason Christian spouses have a special sacrament by which they are fortified. . . . By virtue of this sacrament they are penetrated with the spirit of Christ. This spirit suffuses their whole lives with faith, hope, and charity." [12]

The same Second Vatican Council goes on, "Authentic conjugal love will be more highly prized in our world, and wholesome public opinion created regarding it, if Christian couples give outstanding witness to faithfulness and harmony in that same love." [13] Our world desperately needs the help of such "witness" from all our Catholic spouses. This gives, in a certain sense, a new twist to the proverb: charity begins at home!

JUNE 30, 1995

[12] Ibid.   [13] Ibid., no. 49.

Part Five

LIVING THE CHRISTIAN MYSTERY

1

VIRTUE AND MORALITY

Basic Morality

Nature itself seems to proclaim to us that we must "do good and avoid evil". Granting this call from nature, how would we know what is good and what is evil? What are the criteria for morality?

There are really two criteria of morality: law and conscience. The objective norm of morality comes from law, while the subjective norm of morality comes from conscience.

The supreme objective norm of morality is the eternal law, which is the divine plan of God from all eternity, directing all created things to one end, which is God Himself. By means of the natural moral law and the positive divine law, God has made His will known to His rational creatures, after their creation and in the context of time. He also makes His will known by means of ecclesiastical law and, in some instances, by the civil laws of the state.

A law can be defined as a permanent, rational norm for free activity, enacted and properly promulgated by the superior of a public community for the sake of the common welfare.

The divine positive law is found in divine revelation, that is, in Sacred Scripture and Sacred Tradition as these are interpreted by the teaching authority of the Catholic Church. Church, or ecclesiastical, law is found in the Code of Canon Law, while civil laws are found in the official documents of governing bodies. But let us leave these aside for now and consider today only the natural law.

NATURAL LAW

God is the highest and supreme Lawgiver. We speak often about "laws of nature", meaning such things as laws of gravity, mathematics, chemistry, and physics. Over and above such "laws" there is also the natural moral law, which, Saint Paul says, is "written on [our] hearts" (Rom 2:15). This law is called natural because it accords with the very nature of a human being, while it is distinguished from supernatural law, which comes from divine revelation.

All law and all relationships have to be built upon the notion of natural law. This, of course, presupposes a Lawgiver, Who is God. When the Author of the natural law is set aside, as Pope Pius XII said, there is no room for the natural law itself, which reposes, "as upon its foundation, on the idea of God, the Almighty Creator and Father of us all, the Supreme and Perfect Legislator, and the wise and just Rewarder of human conduct".

Subrational creatures and inanimate objects *must* obey the "laws of nature", but human beings, endowed as we are with the priceless gift of freedom (since we are made in God's image), are free to disobey the natural law. Under the grace of Christ (needed since the fall of our primordial ancestors from God's favor), humans are true to their nature when they obey the dictates of the natural moral law and fall lower than the brute animals when they disobey this law. As Pope Pius XII wrote:

> The Church does not admit that in the sight of God mankind is totally corrupt and absolutely sinful. In the eyes of the Church, original sin did not inherently corrupt human attitudes and strength, but has left essentially intact the natural light of human intelligence and freedom. Undoubtedly, human nature is seriously weakened and injured by the heavy inheritance of the fall, deprived as we are at conception and birth of supernatural and preternatural gifts. However, with the powerful assistance of the grace of Christ, every human being is obliged to observe the natural law, so he can live as the honor of God and dignity of humanity requires.

WHO MUST OBEY THE NATURAL LAW?

Natural law is in some ways independent of the divine positive law contained in divine revelation. Its first principles are common to all human beings (except those who lack the use of reason). Nevertheless, knowledge of natural law is greatly helped by knowledge of God's revelation, especially when dealing with the secondary and derived principles of natural law, which are not as immediately self-evident as its primary conclusions and requirements. For most of humanity, words like "intuition", "practical reason", and "synderesis" tell us that this law is ingrained by God in the very nature of a human being.

Saint Thomas Aquinas taught that all the moral precepts of the Old Testament or the Old Law pertain to the natural law. The first three commandments of the Decalogue also, according to the Angelic Doctor, pertain to the divine positive law, inasmuch as they demand help from God to see just how they are consonant with human reason. The last seven pertain simply to the natural law, since we do not need special help from God to see how they are consonant with human reason, all being derived from the general natural-law principle that "good is to be done always and evil is to be avoided."

If Jesus did not come to abolish but to fulfill the law of the Old Testament (Mt 5:17), much less did He come to abolish the natural law. Since God is perfectly just, no good act or deed will go unrewarded or any deliberate and unrepented disobedience go unpunished. The Christian law of mercy did not repeal divine justice but rather makes it more clear, calling Christians to repentance in Christ Jesus.

Sometimes civil and ecclesiastical laws adopt and enforce parts of the natural law with appropriate sanctions. Sometimes, too, virtue brings its own rewards and satisfactions, vice and sin their own misery. One reaps what one sows (see Mt 7:16–17).

It is very difficult to imagine a case where any human being could be free from guilt and divine sanctions if he were to violate a primary principle of the natural law. There is a greater possibility of ignorance or lack of reflection mitigating the guilt of violators of the secondary or derived principles of natural law. Occasionally we all should reflect on the words of the poet: "The mills of God grind slowly, but they grind exceedingly small. Though in patience He stands waiting, with exactness He grinds all."

APRIL 23, 1993

Divine Law

It is a constant teaching of the Catholic Church that there are two measures of criteria by which we tell right from wrong, good from bad. These are law and conscience. These interact with each other and determine, one objectively and the other subjectively, what is moral or immoral. Lawlessness is the same as sin (see Mt 24:12).

Law can be natural, binding all human beings who have the use of reason, because it is written on the human heart (Rom 2:15). Law is also divine and positive, coming to us through divine revelation, Sacred Scripture, and Sacred Tradition, mediated to us and interpreted for us by the teaching authority of the Catholic Church. There is also Church law and civil law.

Not content to leave us in our fallen state, seriously wounded by original sin and by our own sins, God in His infinite mercy deigned to legislate for humanity, not merely leaving it to us to discern the law "written on our hearts". Those who are the recipients of revelation have a grave duty to learn what God legislates and to obey Him totally and completely.

Revelation itself came to mankind in stages, in the stream of history from the time of Abraham to the death of the last apostle. As the Second Vatican Council teaches, public revelation is now over until the Second Coming of Jesus.

OLD TESTAMENT LAW

In the earlier part of revelation, the Old Testament, which prepared for the coming of our Savior, God gave a great deal of law. In fact, the first five books of the Bible are called "Torah", or law. This law of the Old Testament is threefold: liturgical, civilly juridical, and moral.

The Old Testament is merely a preparation for the New Testament. Consequently, the ceremonial and cultic practices of the Old Testament were abrogated when the New Covenant was announced and enacted. Christ fulfilled the law (Mt 5:17). The liturgy of the Old Testament was meant to keep alive a yearning for the Messiah and a sense of sin and the need for salvation.

Similarly, the civilly juridic law of the Old Testament was replaced in its spiritual and temporal norms by the coming of Christ and the founding of the Catholic Church. This law was meant to segregate the Chosen People from the Gentiles, keep alive their identity, and make it easier for them to be the "bearers of the covenant of election".

Unlike the liturgical and civilly juridical, however, the moral law of the Old Testament still abides and still binds. It is basically a restatement in explicit terms of the natural moral law. It is found in the Ten Commandments and the two Great Commandments of love of God and love of neighbor. It should be noted that the "binding force, interpretation, and sanctions for this moral law derive not from the Old Testament but from the New". God revealed parts of the natural law and made it positive, so that it could be known, as the First Vatican Council says, by all people, easily and without fear of error. Keeping the Commandments is still a condition in the New Testament for entering eternal life (Mk 10:17–19).

NEW TESTAMENT LAW

Jesus perfected the Old Law (Mt 5:43) with His divine sovereignty: "You have heard it said . . . but I say to you." He made it internal as well as external (Mt 5:22). The law of love was now to be measured by His own love rather than by human standards (Jn 13:34). He purged the Old Law of merely human traditions (Mk 7:7) and of a sterile letter that lacked the correct spirit (Mt 23:23). He restored the perfection of the Old Law (Mt 19:5).

Jesus not only was the new Moses, giving a New Law and enacting a "new and eternal covenant" with the blood of His Cross, but He, in His very Person, replaced the Mosaic law as an institution.

Because the earliest Christians were Jewish converts, the apostles observed some of the civilly juridical norms of the Old Testament, including kosher and purification laws, even though they were not required to do so and, as a matter of fact, abandoned these later in their missionary work among the Gentiles (Gal 2:11). However, out of respect for Jewish Christians, under the advice of Saint James, a few of the civilly juridical laws were imposed on the Gentile converts to the Catholic faith (Acts 15:19–20) on a temporary basis.

What moral theologians call the "imperatives of the law" were reinforced by Christ so that the New Testament is more demanding and more severe than the Old. But our Redeemer also gave us, along with His New Testament, justification by faith apart from the works of the law (Gal 2:16) as well as the tender and merciful possibility of pardon and forgiveness from God (Mt 9:2), so long as there is repentance and conformity to His injunction "Sin no more" (Jn 5:14).

Divine positive law in the New Testament is a law of liberty (James 2:12) because nobody is truly free unless obedient to God. The alternative is ignorance, disorder, and strife. Until our Lord comes again on the clouds of glory, we are required to obey the "Law of Christ" (Gal 6:2), which is the law of love, and to bear bravely the burden and yoke of the gospel, which are light and easy (Mt 11:30).

APRIL 30, 1993

Civil Law

We know what is right and wrong, moral or immoral by means of law and conscience. There are various kinds of laws: natural law, the divine positive law, canon or Church law, and also civil laws, that is to say, laws made by governments and rulers.

There are frequently serious questions about exactly how civil law fits into the determination of morality. Can disobedience to civil laws be a sin? Do they bind us in conscience?

Some civil laws are merely specifications and concretizations of other laws that bind us, such as the natural law or divine positive law or even

Church law. Such civil laws obviously bind us in conscience, and we commit a sin if we disobey them. Examples of such laws would be those civil laws that forbid and punish stealing, perjury, and the like. Civil outlawing of rape, sodomy, murder, fraud, drunken driving, and so on, would be specifications on the civil level of other laws that bind us in conscience.

In some countries, there are laws against blasphemy and speaking and writing against the Church and the saints. Some countries have civil laws forbidding desecration of the Blessed Sacrament. These are examples of civil laws that overlap and bring civil sanctions to bear on Church or canon law.

Sometimes civil laws are unjust and even wicked. Such laws must never be obeyed. Laws in communist countries that impede or forbid the practice of the Catholic faith, laws that permit divorce and remarriage of Christians who have had previous valid marriages, laws that foster or even command heinous crimes such as abortion, homosexuality, and confiscation of legitimate private property would be examples of such laws.

There is a certain benefit in doubtful situations that must be given to legitimate governments. Nevertheless, we must avoid the pitfall of legal positivism, the idea that civil laws can make things moral or immoral, simply by the action of the legislator. Everything that is civilly "legal" is not by that very fact morally good. Indeed, some civilly "legal" things can be extremely deadly sins. While, on the one hand, we Christians are obliged to obey legitimate authority, which can bind us in conscience to obedience to civil law (1 Pet 2:12–17), and we know that antinomianism is foreign to Christianity, on the other hand, we are heirs of the apostles, who proclaimed: "We must obey God rather than men" (Acts 5:29). When Saint Thomas More was about to be executed for his refusal to swear an oath that King Henry VIII was the "supreme head of the Church of God on earth", he said: "I am the king's good servant, but God's first."

What about just civil laws? Merely because we may disagree with the wisdom of a law does not make it unjust. Do we commit a sin every time we disobey such a law? Everyone would agree that such disobedience is often sinful. Usually, it involves some "overlap" that may be rather obscure or hidden at first glance. To tell a lie is always a sin, and such things as cheating on taxes frequently involve lying. Breaking some traffic laws may involve a violation of the fifth commandment. We are bound not only to practice legal and distributive justice but also social justice, and sometimes the demands of this latter, which come from the gospel, are not immediately perceptible. Such duties as patriotism and fostering the common good may make small acts of civil disobedience cumulatively evil.

There are some moral theologians who say that every time we deliberately violate a just civil law we commit a sin. They cannot conceive of any case where civil disobedience is morally allowed. If there are certain instances where it appears less than sinful to defy civil legislation, they might opt for what is called *epikaia*. We are free to hold this opinion, which has many convincing arguments and many great teachers and writers on its side.

There are other moral theologians who hold that there is such a thing as "purely civil penal law". They maintain that civil legislators are concerned with external conduct and do not intend to bind in conscience. Some civil laws, they say, even those that stand apart from those that overlap other laws (such as those that require us to pay just taxes), do bind to obedience under pain of sin. But, they say, there are other laws whose violation (such as going a mile or two over a posted speed limit, gambling in a locality where this is forbidden) obliges us to pay the penalty only if we are apprehended in our disobedience. According to these thinkers, we commit no sin in not complying with such legislation. The arguments for "purely civil penal law" are not as strong as the opposite arguments, but we are free to follow this opinion if we wish.

In all observance of all law, when there is a conflict in obligation, that is, two laws simultaneously obliging but only one of which can be observed, the higher law must prevail. Thus, the natural law takes precedence over all positive law. The divine positive law takes precedence over Church law and civil law. Canon law takes precedence in our conscience over civil law. For instance, a Catholic on the way to Sunday Mass, to obey the Church law requiring us, under pain of serious sin, to keep holy the Lord's Day by assisting at Mass, could be obliged, by the higher divine positive law of charity, to stop and assist at the scene of an accident, even if this meant necessarily missing Mass that Sunday.

We are excused from obeying laws by invincible ignorance about the law. Vincible ignorance, on the other hand, does not excuse us from obedience or from sin. Physical impossibility excuses from all law. Moral impossibility excuses from laws that are not negative or do not involve intrinsically evil acts. We are never excused, even to save our life, from the laws forbidding idolatry, contraceptive intercourse, blasphemy, and so on. "Blessed is the man . . . [whose] delight is in the law of the Lord, and on his law he meditates day and night" (Ps 1:2).

MAY 21, 1993

Conscience

George Washington wrote: "Labor to keep alive in your breast that little spark of celestial fire called conscience." The term "conscience" has been used and misused down through the centuries. Sometimes it is imagined as "a small voice within our mind" telling us right from wrong. Sometimes, used in simplistic slogans, it is an excuse for immoral conduct. Jesus told us that some people, claiming to be following their consciences, will be killers and persecutors of the Church (Jn 16:2).

Conscience is the mind making a judgment on the rightness or wrongness of an act. An "act" can be a thought, word, deed, or omission done with human deliberation and free will.

Just as law is the supreme objective or external norm of morality, so conscience is the supreme subjective or interior norm of morality. It is the proximate way in which a human being who possesses the use of reason decides about the application of the law to a particular case.

Must we always "follow our conscience"? The answer is really both Yes and No.

The reason why the answer is both Yes and No is because there is more than one kind of conscience. A certain kind of conscience we must always obey, while other kinds of conscience we are required to defy. One of the highest duties of Christian life is to strive always to have conscience anchored in objective morality or law. When the verdict of our reason conforms to objective moral truth, we have what is called a "correct" or "right" conscience. On the other hand, if the verdict of our reason is not in conformity to objective moral truth, we operate out of an erroneous conscience.

The next question that must be pursued is: How did our conscience "get that way" in those cases where it is erroneous? Because conscience is fundamentally our reason, we are dealing with knowledge and ignorance. We must ask ourselves whether our ignorance is "our fault" or not. If we are culpable in our ignorance, then we are not allowed to follow such a conscience. If we are able to overcome this ignorance, we are obliged to do so, but if that is impossible, we are said to be in a state of invincible or unconquerable ignorance. If we follow an erroneous conscience, knowing or suspecting that it is truly out of compliance with law, we are guilty of sin.

Consciences can be certain (even when erroneous) or doubtful. We must always follow a certain conscience. If, for instance, our conscience tells us (as it should) that it is a mortal sin to miss Mass on a Sunday or holy day of obligation, we must follow such a conscience. If, on the other hand, our conscience were to tell us (as it should not) that it is all right to tell a lie to keep someone from "being hurt", we must follow such a certain conscience, providing it is not our fault that we do not know that lying is always intrinsically evil.

Conscientious doubts can be of two types. We can be uncertain about a law or about a fact. When faced with a doubt of fact, we are forbidden to act. Such a doubtful conscience makes our act evil. The classic example is that of the hunter uncertain whether the movement in the bush is that of a deer or a human. Were the hunter to shoot in this state of doubt, he would be guilty of murder, even if the movement did turn out to be of a deer.

Doubt of law is quite another matter. Naturally, one must do all one can to ascertain the law and to follow it. If access to the lawgiver is available, it must be used to resolve the doubt. There is a great system of moral principle involved in deciding how to act in other circumstances when there is a doubt of law. The general rule is that we may follow a well-founded moral opinion in such cases.

Writers usually divide inclinations of conscience into three categories: the tender, the lax, and the scrupulous. We must strive under God's grace to acquire, maintain, and use a tender conscience. A lax conscience is one that does not see sin where sin is present or that sees venial sins where mortal sins exist. A scrupulous conscience is one that sees sins where none exist or that sees mortal sins where there are venial sins or faults or imperfections.

Ironically as it may seem, it is quite possible for a person to have a lax conscience in one area of morality and a scrupulous conscience in another. A person, for instance, may be tender or scrupulous about matters of chastity and purity at the same time that he is lax about matters of justice or charity. To follow a lax conscience is always a sin, and in matters that oblige gravely it would be a mortal sin.

A person with a perplexed problem is one who sees any act to be done as a sin. We are never bound to what is impossible. In such a case, therefore, a perplexed person must simply choose that which is the lesser of the evils seen.

Forming a correct and certain conscience is a lifelong labor for every Christian. We must, if we are followers of Christ and members of His Catholic Church, struggle to "know what is right". However, sin is not in the intellect but in the will. Not only must we strive to own a tender conscience, but we are obliged to "follow" and "obey" such a conscience. This requires not only the engagement of our free will but also the redeeming grace of Jesus Christ. Let us beseech our Savior for His grace that we may ever enjoy a "good conscience" and never be reproached by it or by Him.

MAY 28, 1993

What Is Sin?

Almost everyone remembers this famous incident from the life of President Calvin Coolidge. Asked by a newspaperman after a Sunday service what the minister preached about, "Silent Cal" is supposed to have answered in his laconic fashion, "sin". The newspaperman followed up by asking what the minister said about sin and was told, "He was against it."

Everyone is against sin, so it is said, but there is always disagreement on what constitutes sin. Jesus Christ told us, "Apart from me, you can do nothing" (Jn 15:5). In its essence, that is what sin is—nothing. It is a negation, a hole, an emptiness. This is the mystery of sin, the "mystery of lawlessness" (2 Th 2:7) Saint Paul writes about. From its introduction into the world by our primordial parents, who were tempted to it by the devil, there is an obscure and intangible element in sin. Clearly, sin is, in the words of Pope John Paul II, a product of human freedom. God created everything. All things are the product of divine, creative freedom. It is "nothing", emptiness, that man has introduced into creation (preceded by the similar "product" of the fallen angels). Still, there is also something beyond the merely human in sin. It is, as the Holy Father states, in that area where human will, sensitivity, and conscience are in contact with the dark forces of the universe (see Rom 7:7–25; Eph 2:2, 6:12).

Sin is, we know, a deliberate human act, knowingly done in contradiction to God's will. This "act" can be an action, a thought, an omission. Actual sin is an act of disobedience to God, an exclusion of God, a rupture with God. By analogy, we call the state in which human beings are conceived and born, as a consequence of their carnal descent from Adam and Eve, original sin. This "nothing", or emptiness, is somewhat similar to, yet altogether different from, that calamity which is sin done by our own free will.

Our human soul enjoys two faculties, intellect and will. These are rooted in the spiritual part of our human nature and are profoundly interrelated. Usually our will operates out of information provided by our reason. However, error, ignorance, and mistakes, unless they are deliberately and freely imposed upon our intellect by our will, are not sins. On the other hand, it is possible to know a great deal and still, by misusing free will, to do evil. A lawyer, for instance, might be very knowledgeable about criminal law and yet commit crimes. A medical doctor might know all about correct healthy behavior and yet engage in unhealthy practices. A person might be filled with "sex education" and still commit sins of impurity and unchastity. However, simple and unwilled error can never be a sin. It is said that a very plain woman told Saint Francis de Sales that she was constantly looking into a mirror, admiring her own beauty, and she was suffused with thoughts of vanity. The good Saint is said to have replied, "A mistake is never a sin!"

Saint John, in the Bible, writes about two kinds of sin. One kind leads to death, and the other kind does not (1 Jn 5:16). Following the texts both of the New and Old Testament, and in accordance with the most ancient traditions, the Church has always preached about sins called grave, serious, or mortal and those of lesser intensity called venial. Mortal sin, of course, is a radical rupture with God, a fundamental turning away from Him toward some created things. It is deadly in the spiritual sense and interrupts the pathway to God. It is the greatest of all evils. Saint Dominic Savio's motto, "Death rather than mortal sin", is a statement of realism and not fanaticism.

Sins are also divided by reason of the punishment they merit. Mortal sins, if unforgiven at the moment of death, lead to eternal punishment, the loss of God forever, and pain unending; while venial sins, evil as they are, nonetheless deserve only partial or temporal punishment, which can be expiated either in this life or in purgatory.

The Beloved Disciple writes, "If we say we have no sin, we deceive ourselves, and the truth is not in us. If we confess our sins, he is faithful and just, and will forgive our sins" (1 Jn 1:8). Our Lord taught us to pray by asking our Father in heaven for forgiveness (Mt 6:12). He made no exceptions. The greatest saints began their journey to God by recognizing their sinfulness and their need for salvation and redemption. Pope Pius XII once said that the greatest sin of our age is the denial of sin. Today we use euphemisms to attempt to disguise reality. Fornication is called "living together". Sodomy is called "adopting an alternate lifestyle". Killing innocent babies is called "women's rights" or "therapeutic abortion". Murdering the sick and elderly is called "euthanasia". Cheating and lying are called "sharp business tactics".

The woman at the well was promised "living water" by Jesus (Jn 4). May this water, the presence of the Holy Spirit, the forgiveness and pardon of God, sanctifying grace that gives us a share in the divine nature (2 Pet 1:4), come to us in abundance in this Lenten season. May we approach our understanding and pardoning Redeemer in the sacrament of Penance and experience His cleansing love. At all times, but especially during Lent, we should be consoled by knowing that Christ, Who hates and detests sin, still loves sinners, which means He loves us. The treasure that Jesus gave us as His Easter present the very night after He rose from the dead (Jn 20:22) was the sacrament of Reconciliation. We should use this treasure often and prepare for every Easter by the best of all possible confessions.

MARCH 12, 1993

Characteristics of Sin

In one of the ironical narrations that characterize the Gospel according to Saint John, a man born blind is shown to be better able to see spiritually than those born with normal eyesight (see Jn 9). The story of that man is in some sense a parable about people today.

At the beginning of a Lenten season, Pope John Paul II asked this question: "Throughout the course of history and today, too, have [people] not perhaps frenetically sought to wipe out the category of sin from their thought and life? In various ways they try no longer to call evil and good by their rightful names."[1]

Sins are known in their malice by three qualities: their object, their end, and their circumstances. Sometimes even good acts can be made bad by circumstances, as, for instance, were someone to give an alms only for the purpose of being admired by others. However, some sins are intrinsically evil by reason of their object and can never be made good, no matter what the circumstances; for instance, lying (deliberately telling an untruth for the purpose of deception) is always wicked.

For a sin to be mortal and end our relationship with God, it must be something serious or perceived to be serious, and it must be done with full knowledge and deliberate, free consent. Lacking one of these elements, such a human act is either a venial sin or no sin. But we must never fall into the habit of speaking of "only a venial sin". Although this kind of sin does not remove God's life from our soul, it is a terrible evil, nevertheless. Pope John Paul II said, "This must never be underestimated as though it were something that automatically can be ignored and treated as a sin of little importance."

In the most proper sense of the term, sin is always personal. It is a purposeful misuse of freedom by an individual. A human being has free will. We cannot disregard this truth in order to blame a person's sins on structures, systems, or other people. Merit for virtue and responsibility for sin are not transferable.

[1] "Repent! Now Is the Acceptable Time", *L'Osservatore Romano* 9 (March 3, 1993): 1.

There are, however, situations of sin called "social sins", systemic violations of God's laws (such as institutional discrimination on the basis of race, exploitation of the poor, and indifference to human misery). This can involve the collective behavior of social groups, even of whole nations and blocs of nations.

Yet, even here sin is individual. Social sins are an accumulation of many personal sins. They are the sins of individuals who cause evil or who support evil; of those who fail to avoid, eliminate, or mitigate social evils because of sloth, fear, secret complicity, or indifference; of those who sidestep the effort or sacrifice required. Real responsibility always lies with individual persons.

Situations, institutions, structures, and society are not the subjects of moral acts. At the heart of every sinful situation or structure are sinful people. We must be careful never to blame the victims of social sins for the sins themselves. As in the story of Lazarus and the rich man (Lk 16:19–31), the real sinners may be dining on the best cuisine in fine houses where people are dressed in purple linen. Indeed, we may be the "social sinners".

Is society to blame? A person *can* be conditioned, incited, tempted, and influenced by powerful external factors. It is, for instance, easier to become addicted to narcotics in a society where drugs are widely and easily available.

From within a person can come tendencies, defects, and habits. It is also part of the mystery of evil that the devil tempts us (see Rom 7; Eph 2).

Sometimes such external and internal factors can attenuate to a greater or lesser degree a person's liberty and responsibility. Nevertheless, we must not allow ourselves to fall into the false attitude of blaming others for our own free acts. Like a martini-drinking alcoholic who blames his problems on the olives, we can look foolish in the eyes of God.

Children confronted with an empty cookie jar have been known to say: "It's not you; it's not me; it's the fellow behind the tree." In the spiritual life we can adopt a similar attitude and be like the people in the gospel pericope who can see but who, ironically and in reality, are spiritually blind.

MARCH 19, 1993

Occasions of Sin

One of the first lessons taught to little children is that they are not to play with dangerous things. Fire, knives, guns, sharp tools, electrical cords and plugs, and some cleaning compounds can be fatal in certain circumstances. Some places and locations, too, are usually off-limits to children. Railroad tracks, highways, and the edges of cliffs are not safe places to recreate. Even adults learn to use some items and places with care and caution because of their inherent danger.

Concern about safety in our physical surroundings should be matched by a corresponding concern about spiritual dangers. It is part of the virtue of prudence to exercise appropriate caution in the use of some things and in some locations. Occasions of sin are persons, places, or things that can, when looked at with prudent foresight, lead a person into sin. As one of the cardinal virtues, prudence helps a Christian to recognize and avoid the peril of "playing with eternal fire".

Occasions of sin can sometimes be sins themselves, the sins of others or our own, that lead us to other or further sins. However, most often they are persons, places, or things that are "morally neutral", that is, that are not sinful in themselves but "bad" only insofar as they touch us.

Bad companions are a good example of a usual kind of occasion of sin—persons in whose company we may commit sins that, if alone, we would not do. Encouragement, praise, ridicule, humor, and language are some of the means by which bad companions can induce us to sin. A pornography store is another example of an occasion of sin. Someone who would enter, browse, patronize, or work in such a place would obviously be in an occasion of sin.

A bar or tavern could be an occasion of sin for a person afflicted with the disease of alcoholism, while for other persons it could be a perfectly legitimate place to relax and entertain. A game of chance could be harmless for some people, while for others it might be an occasion for sinfully spending the family's needed money.

There is a moral duty to avoid unnecessary occasions of sin. To place oneself in an unnecessary occasion of sin is in itself a sin against prudence, even if no other sin is committed. An example would be dating a divorced person whose previous marriage is still considered valid in the eyes of God and of the Catholic Church. Sometimes, however, being in an occasion of sin is a necessity, as, for instance, if one needed to retain a job to support a family, even though the workplace were filled with temptations to blasphemy, profane speech, and obscene language.

When an occasion of sin is considered necessary (this decision should be made only with the help of a confessor or priest–spiritual director), every effort must be made to make the occasion extremely remote and to extricate oneself as soon as possible from the situation. A businessman, for example, who finds it very easy to "fix weights" and to cheat his customers, must put in some controls so that this kind of sin will be impossible to commit without detection.

The greatest treasure that God has given us, even more precious than our human life, is our Catholic faith. Consequently, it is particularly and gravely sinful for us to place ourselves in an occasion of sin against our faith. Books, magazines, films, and friends that place our faith in jeopardy should be avoided with the utmost speed. Attending non-Catholic church services, viewing them on television, and participating in so-called nondenominational activities could very well be for many Catholics an unnecessary occasion of serious sin.

Among the foolhardy things we occasionally may do is to test our willpower by "sitting on the edge of the cliff" in regard to occasions of sin. This is utter folly. Even the wisest and strongest of the saints have taught that, wherever and whenever possible, we should flee from occasions of sin. Humble recognition of our own weaknesses and a continuous acknowledgment of our dependence on God's grace to avoid sin always help a sincere Christian to stay as far away as possible from those persons, places, and things that can lead him into evil.

Jesus was very clear about how to confront occasions of sin (see Mk 9:42–48). He told us to pluck out an eye or cut off a hand or foot if these proved to be occasions of sin for us. Surely, this obliges us, even at the cost of some discomfort, to separate ourselves from persons, places, and things that have led or could lead us into sin.

Especially in the season of Lent should we make a prayerful and faith-filled effort to examine our lives in the light of Christ's gospel and discard whatever has the potential to lead us away from Him. Sometimes this is not easy. However, as Cardinal John Henry Newman said: "Let us not deceive ourselves. There are not two ways of salvation, a broad and narrow way. The world chooses the broad way and, in consequence, hates and spurns the narrow way. Our blessed Lord has chosen for us the narrow way and teaches us to denounce and scorn the broad way."

Saint John Climacus advised, "Run from places of sin as from the plague." Saint Augustine said, "Familiarity with sinners is a hook which draws us into their vices." Saint Thomas Aquinas wrote, "To know whom and what to avoid is a great means of saving our souls." Saint Alphonsus said, "If one does not avoid the voluntary occasions of sin, it is morally impossible to persevere in the grace of God." The Bible tells us (Sir 3:26), "Whoever loves danger will perish by it."

MARCH 10, 1995

Temptations

The Ecumenical Council of Chalcedon teaches us that Jesus, the eternal Son of God, shared our human nature to the extent that "He is like us in all things but sin." This means, of course, that our Lord Himself submitted to something that all of us human beings endure: temptation. The temptations experienced by Christ, which we hear about each year on the first Sunday of Lent, were from the devil and external, touching that which is most attractive to human nature: pleasure, power, and possessions (Lk 4:1–13).

The proverb that states that God can write straight with crooked lines seems to apply to the matter of temptation. Deriving from His *permissive will* rather than from His *positive will*, temptations appear to be permitted by our Creator that greater good may result from the resistance that they excite. Saint Leo the Great said: "Virtue is nothing without the trial of temptation, for there is no conflict without an enemy, no victory without strife." Saint John Vianney said, "The devil only tempts those souls that wish to abandon sin and those in the state of grace. The others belong to him already and he has no need to tempt them."

SOURCES OF TEMPTATIONS

Temptations, no matter how severe, how protracted, how vivid, or how frequent, are never sins. To sin one must engage one's free will with sufficient reflection and adequate liberty. Temptations become sins only when one assents to them, accepts them, or follows them.

Tradition tells us that there are three sources of our temptations: the world, the flesh, and the devil. The world as it came from the hand of God was good. It became tainted and soiled by the primordial disaster we call "original sin". To this calamity we all add regularly by our own sins. Thus, this world of ours has the ability to lure us away from our final end, which is to be happy forever with God. Things and persons around us, from bad companions to the media that often glorify, exalt, and encourage base and evil conduct, can pull us toward acts or omissions, thoughts or words that violate God's law and our own human nature and dignity.

Even after original sin is removed from our souls by Baptism, the effects of that sin (and later of our own sins) remain within us. Human nature was not intrinsically corrupted by Adam's Fall, but it was deeply and seriously wounded. This is why we can speak of the flesh as a source of temptation. Naturally good inclinations, which God has put into us, have the capacity to be perverted and become a gateway to sin. For instance, God gives us an inclination to proper self-esteem, but this is easily distorted into pride. He gives us a strong instinct to self-preservation, which can be perverted into gluttony or sloth. He gives us an inclination to preserve the human race, which can be perverted into lust. The seven so-called "capital sins" (pride, anger, envy, sloth, lust, greed, gluttony) are really these perverted instincts that result from temptations of the flesh and cause these temptations.

The primary source of our temptations, however, comes from the prince of darkness, Lucifer, the fallen angel, whose principal name is Satan or Tempter. Envious of the everlasting joy that God intends us to have and filled with hatred for us and for his Maker, the devil and his fellow fallen angels are permitted by God to roam the earth. To regard the devil as a mere myth or a metaphor for wickedness is to deny a revealed truth of our Catholic faith (see Rev 12:7–9; Lk 10:18; Mt 25:41) and to play directly into the hands of the greatest enemy of our salvation.

The *Catechism of the Catholic Church* states: "Scripture witnesses to the disastrous influence of the one Jesus calls 'a murderer from the beginning' (Jn 8:44). . . . 'The reason the Son of God appeared was to destroy the works of the devil' (1 Jn 3:8). In its consequences the gravest of these works was the mendacious seduction that led man to disobey God" (CCC 394). "Behind the disobedient choice of our first parents lurks a seductive voice, opposed to God, which makes them fall into death out of envy" (CCC 391).

RESPONSE TO TEMPTATION

The wisdom of the saints enables us to frame a proper reply to temptation. They followed Christ in His victory over temptation after His desert fast that began His public life. Saint Dominic, for example, said: "A man who governs his passions is master of the world. We must either command them or be enslaved by them. It is better to be a hammer than an anvil." Blessed Angela of Foligno said, "The more you are tempted, the more you must persevere in prayer."

Saint John Climacus said: "The devil flatters us that he may deceive us, charms us that he may injure us, and allures us that he may slay us." Saint Bernard stated: "Nothing restrains anger, curbs pride, heals malice, quenches the passions, checks avarice, and puts unclean thoughts to flight, as does the name of Jesus."

Each year the season of Lent provides us, through the Church, with the opportunity to equip ourselves anew for the victorious struggle against temptation. With the threefold work of Lent: prayer, fasting, and almsgiving, we have, under the grace of Christ, the weapons that permit us to be confident in our ultimate success.

There are many reasons to take Lent seriously every year, not the least of which is the need to provide ourselves with the means to oppose temptations, which are our lot as long as we dwell in this "valley of tears". Daily Mass, daily Bible reading, daily rosary, extra prayer, both in quality and quantity, spiritual reading, frequent confession, and mortification and self-denial even in legitimate things are some of the ways to implore and invoke God to aid us with His all-powerful grace.

Each time we resist temptation we say "yes" once again to God and to His inestimable gifts to us. Each temptation to sin that is resisted is future merit for us and another defeat for all that draws us from our destiny, and we grow stronger with the strength of our Savior.

MARCH 3, 1995

The Good Fight

Saint Paul in the New Testament writes about having "fought the good fight" (2 Tim 4:7). The enemies of our salvation who were the foes of Saint Paul continue to be our enemies and will continue to be so until the end of time. These are the Archfiend, our Adversary, the devil, Lucifer and his fallen angels; also the temptations that come from the world and the flesh as well as from Satan; and the frequent effects of those temptations, namely, the sins we commit.

Perhaps, however, our greatest enemy is our inability to recognize our own sinfulness. Our present Holy Father cites his predecessor, Pope Pius XII, who wrote: "The sin of our century is the loss of a sense of sin." It is true that in some areas a greater sensitivity to some particular sin may be detected, as, for instance, regarding racism, but most of the human race seems more than ever to have lost a true sense of sin.

During the holy season of Lent, when we are expected to carry out our annual duty of returning to repentance, is an appropriate time to reflect on temptation, sin, and our understanding of how these affect us.

Pope John Paul II claims that the loss of a sense of sin in our time can be traced to secularism, erroneous evaluation of some of the human sciences, historical relativism, and a misunderstanding of sin itself.

Secularism causes a loss of the sense of sin since it is practical atheism, that is, living as if God did not exist. Secularists are totally absorbed in action, production, pleasure-seeking, and consumerism—people totally unconcerned about losing their souls. At the most, they see sin as something that offends human beings but not God.

The human sciences, such as psychology, strive sometimes to avoid "feelings of guilt" or "restrictions on freedom". These notions can be exaggerated and reduce or eliminate personal responsibility for human acts. Sociology can sometimes lead people to claim that all sins can be blamed on society, or anthropology can so emphasize historical and environmental conditioning as to deny the possibility of individual responsibility. Certain sectors of society would reduce all sin to "sickness".

Historical relativism means that people suppose all moral norms are relative and there are no fixed and absolute moral laws that declare certain human acts intrinsically evil. Sin itself can be misunderstood (sometimes deliberately), and the media can communicate, especially to young people, that sin is nothing but a morbid sense of guilt or a mere transgression of some arbitrarily imposed legal precepts.

The Second Sunday of Lent traditionally uses in the liturgy the Gospel passages about the Transfiguration of Jesus, when the apostles received a glimpse of His divinity shining through His humanity. Saint Gregory the Great wrote: "Were we to consider how great is that heaven promised us, our souls would despise everything that we find in this world, for compared to the eternal, they are not joys, but rather a burden." Our first weapon in the "good fight" should be a sense of proportion and perspective, seeing time and our earthly lives from the point of view of eternity. Lent is the ideal season for this.

Extra prayer, mortification, and compassion for others (1 Jn 4:20), which are practices particularly enjoined on us during Lent, are also invaluable in the struggle against sin and temptation. A rekindling of our faith through a more frequent encounter with Christ in the sacraments of Penance and Holy Eucharist is basic to moral equilibrium and to acquiring and maintaining "a sense of sin". The teaching of our Lord through the mouth of His Church will assist us in attaining the intellectual consistency that will permit us to live, not only in accord with the teachings of Christ, but in accord with our own rational nature at the same time. In these days, adult Catholics should know and study *The Splendor of Truth*, an encyclical of Pope John Paul II; the *Catechism of the Catholic Church*; and the apostolic exhortation *On Reconciliation and Penance*, of our Holy Father. Coupled with a regular reading of the Holy Bible, this kind of Lenten study must be pursued by anyone who takes his Catholic faith seriously, anyone determined to be well-equipped for "the good fight".

As Father Francis Canavan puts it: "Christianity means nothing if it does not mean salvation from sin and from the disordered passions that lead to it. In the Christian view, all is not well, and we need the constant help of divine grace . . . to save our souls." Saint Paul's simile of a "fight" to describe our Christian existence is most apt in any age, but especially in our own. Wordsworth asked: "Who is the happy warrior; who is he, that every man in arms should wish to be?" In the "good fight" of Lent and of life, may that be our title.

FEBRUARY 25, 1994

Moral Pollution

In our times many people are concerned, and rightfully so, about the abuse of our natural resources. Without being extremist in environmental matters, one can have legitimate worries about unnecessary and wanton pollution of our water and air, basic requirements for human survival on our planet.

For a long time, however, there has been in various places on earth, including our own country, another kind of pollution taking place, which is poisoning souls and bringing ruin to our civilization. Far more disastrous than ecological pollution is the poison of pornography. Once confined to dismal areas of big cities visited only by people suffering from depraved perversions, pornography has gradually seeped into films, videos, and large sections of the communications media, giving it not only a disguise of respectability but also access to the living rooms of families and the consciousness of children.

One of the lies perpetrated by the multibillion-dollar porn business (much of which is controlled and operated by organized criminal syndicates) is that pornography is "victimless". Often it uses drugged and otherwise exploited models. Pornography is destructive of family life and marital relationships. It degrades to the level of filth and obscenity the sacred and beautiful aspects of sexual embrace in marriage. It horribly exploits women and children and treats human beings as objects rather than persons made in the image of God. It foments violence and crime, encourages rape and parental irresponsibility, panders to the lowest and most shameless aspects of fallen human nature, and fosters the solitary vice of self-abuse.

Pornography dulls a soul's perception of supernatural reality and kills all taste for the things of God and the things of the spirit. It is the enemy of prayer and good works and the death of true art and beauty. It has the capacity to engender addiction to itself even to the point of fomenting self-destruction in its users.

By gradually introducing more and more "daring" things into television programming and into manipulative advertising, in both images and words, our culture is making an attempt to have smut become a regular visitor in our consciousness and perception.

Among the guardians of Christian chastity and purity is the virtue of modesty. The *Catechism* says, "Modesty protects the mystery of persons and their love. . . . Modesty is decency. It inspires one's choice of clothing. It keeps silence or reserve where there is evident risk of unhealthy curiosity. . . . It protests, for example, against the voyeuristic explorations of the human body in certain advertisements, or against the solicitations of certain media that go too far in the exhibition of intimate things" (CCC 2522–23).

The *Catechism* goes on to say, "Christian purity requires a *purification of the social climate*. It requires of the communications media that their presentations show concern for respect and restraint. Purity of heart brings freedom from widespread eroticism and avoids entertainment inclined to voyeurism and illusion" (CCC 2525).

Saint Augustine of Hippo once said, "Do not tell me your heart is chaste if your eye is unchaste, for an unchaste eye is the sign of an unchaste heart." He echoes what Jesus teaches us, "Every one who looks at a woman lustfully has already committed adultery with her in his heart" (Mt 5:28). The ninth commandment of the Decalogue commands us, under penalty of eternal damnation, to be chaste and pure in our thoughts. This is not possible in an atmosphere where pornography is allowed to run rampant and where carnal lust is presented as attractive entertainment and legitimate diversion.

It is true, as a wise old priest once told me, that God, Who gives us eyes, also gives us eyelids. Television sets have off buttons as well as on switches. However, it is also true that even the healthiest fish cannot long survive in totally polluted water. Pornography, because it is a type of serious social and moral pollution, cannot be counteracted simply by personal taste and the exercise of personal liberty. The *Catechism* teaches that moral permissiveness in this area rests on an erroneous conception of human freedom.

Purveyors and supporters of pornography often argue that violence, injustice, exploitation, and the like are the "real obscenities". This is, of course, a specious attempt to divert attention from their evil minds and wicked activities. Surely one type of sin and evil does not justify another. These shameless people also will sometimes attempt to acquire agreement with their positions by calling "censorship" any effort to counteract their foul and soul-destroying behavior.

Catholics involved in the area of entertainment and social communications surely have a duty to oppose pornographic presentations and discussions. Parents and teachers have many obligations in this area in regard to the children and youth committed to their care. Vigilance over young people's activities and work to fill young minds with real beauty, art, and truth are a never-ending task. Catholic politicians are duty-bound to oppose vice and immorality.

Writing letters of protest to advertisers who support pornographic publications and programs can frequently have a good effect if the letters are sincere, clear, forceful, and polite. Catholic organizations can have an impact on local businesses that may be indifferent to or even supportive of porn and smut. Prayer, certainly, is very important in every antipornography campaign. We should ever keep in mind the sixth beatitude. Our divine Lord said, "Blessed are the pure in heart, for they shall see God" (Mt 5:8).

JANUARY 26, 1995

Against Hope

Probably more than we suspect, we meet people who live outside of the virtue of hope. Hope is the supernatural virtue by which we trust totally and completely in God and in the merits of Jesus Christ as our Lord and Savior. In those merits we hope to obtain pardon for our sins and life everlasting.

The virtue of hope must be actualized, that is, expressed in acts. Like a muscle that grows flabby with disuse, so the virtues, implanted into us at Baptism, need to be used to be preserved. Once we achieve the use of reason, we must implicitly and explicitly begin to *hope*.

Along with supernatural love, hope completes and crowns our faith. Saint Paul says that Abraham became "the father of many nations", because hoping against hope, he believed (Rom 4:18).

Just as faith will pass into vision when we enter heaven, so hope will disappear when the object of our desire and hope is achieved, that is, when we possess God in eternity. That is why Saint Paul informs us that of the theological virtues, faith, hope, and love, "the greatest of these is love." When there is no need any longer for faith and hope, they will be gone, but love will abide (1 Cor 13:13).

However, while we walk on the journey of life in this world, hope is not only important but vitally necessary. This need is best understood when we look at the sins opposed to hope: despair and presumption.

Sinful despair does not mean emotional despondency, mental depression, or the like. Rather, despair that is sinful means a refusal to accept God's forgiveness, often involving a refusal to approach God with our sins and our repentance, motivated by the thought that "God will never forgive the horror of my crimes and sins" or by the misunderstanding of the justice of God in relationship to His mercy. Ironically, sometimes people suffering from mental depression and emotional despondency are, in a spiritual way, filled with supernatural hope.

Presumption is quite a prevalent sin in our world today. There are really two kinds of presumption: one that claims we can get to heaven on our own and one that claims God will save us without any effort on our part.

The first kind of presumption is akin to the attitude of the people who tried to build the Tower of Babel (Gen 11). There are people who *presume* to be able to reach heaven and to be saved without a Savior. They think they will be saved by "being good". As a matter of fact, we cannot even observe the moral law without the help of divine grace, but, even if we could, we are unable to save ourselves. Salvation, which is the result of justification or righteousness, is a gratuitous gift, basically undeserved. Jesus said, "When you have done all that is commanded you, say, 'We are unworthy servants; we have only done what was our duty'" (Lk 17:10).

Such presumptuous people often try to compare themselves favorably with others who are "religious". Thinking that they can get to heaven on their own terms, sometimes without Christ, without the Church, without the sacraments, they say: "That one is a drunk; that one is a wife-beater. I, at least, am better than they." Judas walked with Jesus and betrayed Him. Saint Dismas hung on the cross with Him only for three hours and, notwithstanding a lifetime of crime, was saved. There seems to be a temptation in all humanity to play the Pharisee, at least occasionally: "Thank You, God, that I am not like the rest of men."

The second kind of presumption is also widespread. It is the kind that imagines God will save a person even without his cooperation and consent. Saint Augustine wrote: "God, Who created us without our consent, will not save us without our consent." God owes nothing to anyone. He certainly does not owe us salvation. Having created us free so that we could participate in His happiness for eternity by love (which is possible only for those who are free), God chooses to wait upon the cooperation of our free will with His sovereign grace. Our justification does not initially come as *merit* from either faith or works (Rom 11:6).

We are justified through faith (Rom 3:22; Heb 11:6). But the Catholic Church teaches and has always taught that there is reward and merit on our part involved in salvation (James 2:24; Mt 25:31ff.).

It is presumptuous to think that it is sufficient to "believe on the Lord Jesus" or to suppose that merely having confidence (fiduciary faith) in the merits of Christ's Passion and death or in my personal forgiveness of sins or in Jesus as my "personal Savior" or in my antecedent predestination, with no further effort on my part, will be efficacious and sufficient for salvation. It is possible to speak of "gaining grace" or "persevering in grace" or "meriting grace", so long as we always remember, as the Council of Trent puts it, "God chooses to allow His gifts to be our merits."

People who habitually live in the state of mortal sin in the "confidence" that God will give them an opportunity to repent before they die are not simply playing Russian roulette with salvation but are also taunting God with the sin of presumption. Those who fling away the "pearl of great price" have no guarantee that a loving God will continue to give them a chance to recover it. Christ's repeated warnings about always being prepared incline a prudent person never to presume that God's invitation, once spurned, will be offered again (Mt 22:1–14).

With trust and confidence, then, in the infinite merits of Jesus and His suffering, dying, and rising, we must walk through this world in hope, "fearing all things from our weakness, while hoping for all things from His goodness".

OCTOBER 2, 1992

Holy Virginity

In the post-Christian, neopagan atmosphere of our culture, chastity and purity are not only disdained, but speaking and writing about that virginity which is embraced for the love of God often bring smirks and cynical ridicule from listeners and onlookers. The idols and false gods of the ancient heathen world were not adored with any greater fervor than are the modern idols of materialism, hedonism, and sensuality, nor are those who refuse to worship these false gods persecuted with any less zeal than were the early Christians.

Yet, despite the difficulties inherent in the task, the Catholic Church would not be true to the doctrine of her Master and Founder if she did not proclaim, even amid the sexual promiscuity and perversion of today, the exceptional value of a life of consecrated celibacy and virginity, undertaken for the love of God. Like every life of love, virginity and celibacy require some sacrifice, but all love worthy of the name involves some pain and discomfort.

When Jesus spoke about the indissolubility of marriage (Mt 19:3–12), His disciples remarked that, given the hardships and difficulties that marriage can involve, it might be better not to be married. Our Lord agreed but said that this applied only to those who would renounce their right to be married "for the love of the kingdom of heaven" and to those whose "hearts would be large enough for this". Christ made it clear that a free spiritual decision to embrace lifelong chastity and continence would be a gift bestowed by God, Who would invite some people to accept it.

From her earliest years, the Catholic Church has always especially esteemed those who receive and accept the gift of celibacy and virginity for the sake of the kingdom. Saint Paul himself wrote about this in the New Testament (1 Cor 7:32–34). Saint Cyprian said, "Those who have pledged themselves to Christ give up the desires of the flesh and devote themselves body and soul to God, seeking to gratify no one except their Lord and Master."

Saint Augustine said that genuine Christian celibacy and virginity cannot mean remaining single as an act of selfishness or as a flight from matrimonial responsibility or as some proud pharisaical show of bodily integrity. The Book of Revelation talks about those who "follow the Lamb wherever He goes" (Rev 14:4), and the New Testament gives us the example of Jesus Himself as well as Saint Paul.

Marriage and family life are profoundly respected and fostered by the Catholic Church. Married people are called to holiness and sanctity as are all of mankind. Indeed, there are many saintly married people, including canonized saints. It is entirely possible and often happens that a married person is more pleasing to God in fidelity to the married vocation than some virgin or celibate who is unfaithful or at least careless in his vocation.

However, it must be said, in the objective order, that (quoting Pope Pius XII) "in accordance with the clear teaching of the Church, holy virginity is better and higher than Matrimony. As some of our contemporaries are going astray on this subject and are exalting the married state to the point of placing it above virginity, thereby disparaging consecrated chastity and ecclesiastical celibacy, my sense of duty compels me to proclaim and defend the excellence of virginity."

The Council of Trent condemned anyone who says that the married state is to be preferred to the state of virginity or of celibacy and that it is not better and holier to remain in virginity or celibacy than to be joined in marriage.

Again, Pope Pius XII wrote, "Holy virginity and absolute chastity pledged to the service of God unquestionably take rank among the priceless values which the Church's Founder bequeathed to the society which He established. There is no counting the number of those who, from the foundations of the Church to our own day, have offered their chastity to God. Some there are who have always kept their virginity intact. Others have dedicated their remaining years to God after losing a husband or wife. Others again have embraced a life of absolute chastity on being converted from a life of sin."

The *Catechism* says, "Virginity for the sake of the kingdom of heaven is an unfolding of baptismal grace, a powerful sign of the supremacy of the bond with Christ and of the ardent expectation of his return, a sign which also recalls that marriage is a reality of this present age which is passing away" (CCC 1619). The *Catechism* goes on to say, "Esteem of virginity for the sake of the kingdom and the Christian understanding of marriage are inseparable, and they reinforce each other" (CCC 1620). Saint John Chrysostom wrote, "Whoever denigrates marriage also diminishes the glory of virginity. Whoever praises it makes virginity more admirable."

To be meritorious, virginity and celibacy for the sake of the kingdom must be as free as possible from ambition, lust for power, prudery, and resentment against life. This must be love reaching out in hope, a cheerful and joyful sublimation of a basic and common human component.

Holy virginity gives to the entire Church, the Family of God, a foretaste of heaven and of the resurrection (Lk 20:34–36). Those who are given this gift and accept it are "equal to angels", according to the words of our Redeemer Himself. They are the living images of that perfect integrity which forms the bond of union between the Catholic Church and her divine Bridegroom. Saint Cyprian says they are "the splendor of the grace of the Holy Spirit, flawless masterpieces of praise and worship, choicest firstlings of the flock of Christ, reflections of the holiness of the Lord, the generous flowering of the Church's glorious luxuriance".

AUGUST 11, 1995

Dare to Be Different

One of the words in the English language that is undergoing significant change is "unique". This word means "one and only". That which is unique is singular, with nothing else like it. Consequently, it is incorrect to say that something is "very unique". This kind of tautology is like saying "mostest". However, the word "unique" sometimes is now used in the sense of "unusual". It is in the old, original meaning of the word, however, that it is proper to say that being a Christian demands that one sometimes must be unique.

Within every human being there seems to be a tension between his uniqueness and that which is shared in common with other humans. This kind of tension extends as well to our Christianity. In a certain sense we are to be one with the world in which we live. We are to be its salt and light (Mt 5:13–16), according to Jesus. Indeed, we are to love the world as God does (Jn 3:16). On the other hand, Saint John warns us "Do not love the world or the things in the world. If anyone loves the world, love for the Father is not in him" (1 Jn 2:15).

One of the constant duties of a follower of Christ is to discern when conformity to the world is according to God's will and when it is contrary to His will. Our divine Lord tells us there are few things more worthless than salt that has lost its taste (Mt 5:13).

The millions of dollars that are spent to advertise various products and services in our civilization, particularly through the communications media, should alert us to the fact that we may be more amenable to persuasion, and perhaps even to manipulation and control, by outside factors than we suspect. In sometimes subtle ways this kind of persuasion, manipulation, and control can extend to false beliefs and evil morals. The young especially can be victims of an agenda far different from the beliefs and moral convictions of their parents. Unthinking adoption of some contemporary customs and activities can even lead to the loss of our immortal souls.

Our world, even in North America and Europe, has large pieces of geography that are not only inimical to the Catholic faith but are aggressively anti-Christian. Adoration and worship are given to the false gods of divorce, contraception, abortion, euthanasia, adultery, and fornication by great numbers (perhaps even the majority) of our fellow citizens. Public schools must be by law non-Christian and sometimes even totally godless and anti-Christian. Christmas is turned into a "winter festival", and, while Jesus Christ cannot be mentioned even in Christmas carols, snow or a bunny or some such thing is celebrated instead at Christmas and Easter.

The entertainment industry, frequently uninhibited by even a semblance of ethical or moral principles, often puts wickedness and evil before our eyes and ears in an appealing and attractive way, sometimes luring the unwary to their eternal damnation. Laudable civic and political tolerance is used as an excuse to promote religious indifference (which says such untrue things as "it does not matter what religion one belongs to" or "one church is as good as another"). Accusations of bigotry and prejudice often attend efforts to label sexual and other perversions as the sinful and reprehensible conduct it is. Sometimes this is done nowadays out of deference to a new, false god that has recently appeared on the scene, cloaking itself in the disguise of multiculturalism or pluralism.

Can a Catholic be an oxymoron? An oxymoron is a contradiction in terms, like a square circle, or God creating a stone so heavy He cannot lift it, or God telling a lie. A Catholic who embraces the false beliefs and evil morals that seem to penetrate a large sector of our contemporary culture is, in a real sense, an oxymoron.

It is not easy to be countercultural, as the gospel frequently requires us Catholics to be. The uniqueness that is conferred on us by our following of Christ is, in our present situation, often pressured by a pull to conform with a world that is not congruous with Christianity. Prayer and a ceaseless petition to God for His grace must be necessary accompaniments to our work of discerning when we should embrace the world with love and when we should fear and abhor the world. More often than not we must dare to be different, cost what it may cost.

Among oxymoronic Catholics would have to be included those who claim membership in intrinsically evil organizations, such as the freemasons and their associated groups, planned parenthood, and so on. These people would also have to include those who associate with schismatic groups, such as the so-called Society of Saint Pius X. Other oxymorons would be cowardly politicians who might claim to be Catholics but yet vote for and foster baby-killing, under the euphemism of "pro-choice", and perhaps even those Catholic citizens who vote for pro-abortion politicians.

To live and act always in conformity with the teachings of Jesus as they are given to us in their fullness in the Catholic Church definitely involves carrying a daily cross (Lk 9:23). This cross in turn involves being courageously countercultural when our Catholic faith demands it. In those moments we must rely heavily on the gift of fortitude we received when we were confirmed and on the pledge of sacramental grace we received on that occasion in our lives.

There are times and places when we must share in our common humanity the concerns and values of the world around us. There are other times when we must flee from them, oppose them with all our strength, and dare to be different. Even in this opposition, however, we must remember our duty to be salt and light and yeast (Lk 13:21) to our world and to our fellow travelers on the road to eternity.

JANUARY 5, 1996

2

GRACE AND JUSTIFICATION

Sanctifying Grace

One of the most remarkable passages in the New Testament is found in the second letter of our first pope, Saint Peter. Cephas tells us (2 Pet 1:4) that, by God's life, we have become sharers in the "divine nature". In other words, while remaining human beings, we actually share, when we are in the state of grace, in the very life of God Himself.

Were we to notice our pet dog playing chess or our cat operating our computer or our trees dancing or our rocks flying, we would laugh at the absurdity of it. It is beyond the nature of dogs to play chess, or cats to compute, or trees to dance, or rocks to fly. Even if we were fond of our dog, our cat, our trees, or our rocks, we could never elevate them above their nature. However, what is beyond our capacity to do for creatures beneath us, God can and does do for us, who are infinitely beneath Him. Keeping us fully human, He lifts us up to share His very life.

The *Catechism of the Catholic Church* tells us, "It is the *sanctifying* or *deifying grace* received in Baptism" which is "in us the source of the work of sanctification. . . . Sanctifying grace is an habitual gift, a stable and supernatural disposition that perfects the soul itself to enable it to live with God, to act by his love" (CCC 1999–2000).

Grace (sometimes translated as "God's favor" in newer scriptural versions) is, by its definition, completely gratuitous. It is a gift, pure and simple, utterly and absolutely beyond our ability to obtain on our own. Saint Paul says "all this is from God" (2 Cor 5:18). The *Catechism* says, "The grace of Christ is the gratuitous gift that God makes to us of his own life, infused by the Holy Spirit into our soul to heal it of sin and to sanctify it" (CCC 1999).

However, what about "earning grace" or "gaining grace" or "meriting grace"? These concepts and expressions are valid, so long as it is clear that in the ultimate and absolute sense one cannot earn, gain, or merit something totally beyond one's nature, any more than a clever dog could acquire the ability to play chess or a wise cat could learn to use a computer.

If a generous stranger were to put a million dollars in a bank in your name, this gift would be, like grace, unmerited and unearned. However, to use it, it would be necessary to go to the bank to withdraw it. Thus, your trip to the bank may enable you to say that you "gained or merited or earned" the money. This is one of the reasons why the Council of Trent says of God, "He allows His gifts to be called our merits."

By a system of infinite wisdom, God's primordial arrangements were for the human race not only to be created but at the same time to be "elevated". God made mankind from the beginning for the purpose of having not merely a natural end but a supernatural end, which is to be joined to God in perfect happiness and beatitude. However, because of a primeval catastrophe at the beginning of the human race, the gift or favor or grace of God was discarded by our earliest ancestors, and, consequently, we are conceived and born as "children of wrath", part of a *massa damnata*.

Rather than leave us to perish in misery and agony, God, in His unlimited mercy, came to save us personally. The second Person of the Blessed Trinity shared our human nature so that we could once again share His divine nature. That is why Jesus told us He came to give us "life" (Jn 10:10). He taught us that if we want to go to heaven, we must be "born again" (Jn 3:1–17). The life of God in us was the theme of our Lord's preaching (Jn 15:5–6; 6:48–51; 4:10–15). As God's creatures, human beings were only metaphorically God's children, until Christ's death and Resurrection made it possible for human beings to be truly God's children in a real and actual way (1 Jn 3:1–3).

Saint Paul says that "if anyone is in Christ, he is a new creation; the old has passed away, behold, the new has come" (2 Cor 5:17). Sanctifying grace in one's soul excludes mortal sin. When anyone is "born again" in the waters of Baptism, original sin and any actual sins committed are truly remitted and not merely covered over.

Are people who are in the state of grace, then, not sinners any longer? The answer is "yes and no". The effects of original sin and of our own sins always remain with us while we walk on earth, although the sins themselves are taken away in Baptism and Confession. The need for penance always remains. Venial sins, too, make us "sinners" even though they are compatible with the state of grace.

There is a sense, then, in which a Christian is "simultaneously just and a sinner". However, there is also an erroneous Protestant idea in this regard, dating from the time of Martin Luther, which holds that sins are not taken away by sanctifying grace but merely "covered over" as "snow covers over a disgusting pile of excrement" (to use Luther's vivid phrase). This "nominalist" view of Luther's, sometimes still held by modern non-Catholics, is, of course, incompatible with the data of divine revelation.

The *Catechism* sums up the doctrine of grace by saying, "Grace is *favor*, the *free and undeserved help* that God gives us to respond to his call to become children of God, adoptive sons, partakers of the divine nature and of eternal life. Grace is a *participation in the life of God*. It introduces us into the intimacy of Trinitarian life" (CCC 1996–97). The very last words in the Bible are: "The grace of our Lord Jesus Christ be with all. Amen." Let us add our own "Amen" to that!

FEBRUARY 10, 1995

Merit and Grace

Not even the smartest dog could be taught to play chess. The most brilliant goldfish could never learn to read. If by some power we were able to elevate dogs or goldfish to have such capacities, this remarkable happening would not even begin to illustrate what God does for us by His grace. Dogs who could play chess or goldfish who could read would be, in some way, "sharing" our human nature, which is far above theirs. When God bestows on us sanctifying grace, a created share in His life, we actually participate in His very nature (2 Pet 1:4). The difference between us humans and goldfish and dogs is great indeed. However, this difference is minimal compared to the distance between God and us.

Just as it is beyond the ability of dogs or goldfish to raise themselves to our level, so it is even more beyond our ability to raise ourselves to God's level. This is possible only by God's free action. The very nature of grace is that it is gratuitous. The supernatural order, entry into which is necessary for salvation, is totally and absolutely gratuitous on God's part.

In the late fifth century there was an English monk named Pelagius. He and his followers held that we could get to heaven by our own work and that Jesus had merely given us a good example to follow. The teaching of Pelagius was condemned repeatedly by the Catholic Church.

If we cannot offer to God, in the absolute sense, any achievement of our own, independent of Him, that He is required to reward, we must believe that our capacity for supernatural and meritorious acts and the acts themselves are gifts of God. In ultimate terms, God crowns and rewards His own gifts. The interaction between the utterly sovereign and almighty will of God and the created and dependent, yet really free, will of man remains always part of the mystery of our faith. We must maintain the truth that God owes us nothing while we owe Him everything. If we are saved, it is His doing, but if we are damned, it is totally our own doing.

Yet there is such a thing as merit. God Himself revealed that, once we are gratuitously justified before Him, we can bring forth fruit (Mt 13:8). The works of the justified, done in the atmosphere of both freedom and grace, are truly rewarded by God (Rom 2:6; 1 Pet 1:9; Mt 25:31–46). The *Catechism* states:

> With regard to God, there is no strict right to any merit on the part of man. Between God and us there is an immeasurable inequality, for we have received everything from him, our Creator. The merit of man before God in the Christian life arises from the fact that *God has freely chosen to associate man with the work of his grace.* The fatherly action of God is first on his own initiative, and then follows man's free acting through his collaboration, so that the merit of good works is to be attributed in the first place to the grace of God, then to the faithful (CCC 2007–8).

Sanctifying grace goes by various names. It can be called "God's life" or sometimes "the risen life of Christ". It can be called "God's self-communication and self-giving" or "everlasting and supernatural life". It can also be viewed as a capacity for eternal happiness.

In this latter sense it is obvious that sanctifying grace can be increased, once possessed, and, in the case of a lethal or mortal sin, it can be lost. To think in quantitative terms (which is not entirely accurate), the more sanctifying grace one has at the time of death, the greater will be one's eternal joy in heaven. Lack of sanctifying grace at the moment of death, of course, means everlasting damnation in the torments of hell. Everyone in heaven is perfectly happy, but some of the saints have a greater capacity for happiness, just as glasses and jugs of varying sizes can all be perfectly filled with liquid, but the larger have a greater capacity and can hold more. The Blessed Virgin Mary, who is "full of grace" (Lk 1:28), is the greatest of all the angels and saints, with the greatest capacity for happiness.

God chooses to link His freely giving more of His life to us to our works, such as our participating in and receiving the sacraments, especially the Holy Eucharist, our praying, our acts of charity and justice, our resisting temptations, and our obedience to His commandments. Thus, when merit is correctly understood, we can truthfully say that we can *merit* an increase in sanctifying grace. Christ promised that even in the smallest matters, we "shall not lose [our] reward" (Mt 10:42). However, this is because, in the beautiful words of the Council of Trent, God's goodness to men is so great that He wishes His gifts to be our merits.

The *Catechism* tells us, "The saints have always had a lively awareness that their merits were pure grace" (CCC 2011). It then cites the prayer of Saint Thérèse of Lisieux, "In the evening of this life, I shall appear before you with empty hands, for I do not ask you, Lord, to count my works. All our justice is blemished in your eyes. I wish, then, to be clothed in your own *justice* and to receive from your *love* the eternal possession of *yourself*." The *Catechism* tells us that "Grace, by uniting us to Christ in active love, ensures the supernatural quality of our acts and consequently their merit before God and before men" (CCC 2011).

Saint Peter wrote, "Brethren, labor the more that by good works you may make sure your calling and your election" (2 Pet 1:10), and Saint Paul wrote, "Work out your own salvation with fear and trembling" (Phil 2:12).

The Catholic Church, completely faithful to the New Testament, teaches us that, although they seem to be contradictory terms, spiritual reality contains both grace and merit.

OCTOBER 10, 1995

All from God

In the middle of the sixteenth century, Cardinal Reginald Pole wrote: "There is no point or article more expedient for a Christian man to seek, more necessary to find and to know, more comfortable rightly to understand, more profitable to remember and practice than is the true and right knowledge of his justification." The *Catechism* cites Saint Augustine: "The justification of the wicked is a greater work than the creation of heaven and earth", because "heaven and earth will pass away but the salvation and justification of the elect . . . will not pass away" (CCC 1994).

Justification, sometimes called "righteousness", means the act or operation by which God, out of His gratuitous love for us, makes us "just" or "righteous" in His sight. As the *Catechism* puts it: "Since the initiative belongs to God in the order of grace, *no one can merit the initial grace* of forgiveness and justification, at the beginning of conversion" (CCC 2010).

Justification makes us share in the very nature of God Himself (2 Pet 1:4). It is not simply an external or juridical imputation of holiness, but God's holiness itself given to us through faith and Baptism linked totally to the death and Resurrection of Jesus.

It is absolutely necessary for salvation that human beings who have reached the age of reason cooperate freely with God's grace of justification. In this sense we must *merit* our salvation. However, as the Council of Trent teaches, our merits are God's gifts, for grace must always go before us.

It is a constant temptation for autonomous, individualistic mankind, at the end of the twentieth century, to suppose that it is possible for us to go to heaven on our own. (This is the perennial temptation of the people of Babel [Gen 11:1–9].) It is thought that by simply observing some laws external to us, we will come to a debit and credit kind of ledger at our judgment, and, if the credits outweigh the debits, we will be saved. This is a type of "legalism" that leaves no room for grace, the death of Jesus, the Church, the sacraments, and so on, except simply as "moral aids", reducing Christ merely to someone who "gave us a good example". A heretical monk named Pelagius taught something similar in the early fifth century.

It must never be forgotten that salvation, even when we, by our free will, cooperate with God, is always a *gift*. Without God's actual grace we cannot fully or correctly observe His laws, given our fallen human nature. But, even if we could do so, we could not justify ourselves in God's sight. Heaven is supernatural, beyond our natural powers to attain. This is why Jesus taught us to say: "We are unworthy servants; we have only done what was our duty" (Lk 17:10).

The *Catechism* states: "With regard to God, there is no strict right to any merit on the part of man. Between God and us there is an immeasurable inequality, for we have received everything from him, our Creator" (CCC 2007).

Yet, as Saint Augustine observes: "God, Who created us without our consent, will not save us without our consent." Every human being is called by God to be joined to Him in the endless happiness of heaven. Jesus Christ died for the salvation of all. Those who are ultimately damned are those who have failed to cooperate with divine help and have failed to reach up, through faith and repentance, to take the free salvation offered or, worse, have thrown away by serious sin the most precious gift of justification once possessed.

We often hear people in their presumption remark that they "have no need of Christ, the Catholic Church, the holy liturgy and sacraments, and so on". Such people sometimes boast that they observe the societal conventions and the Commandments better than "churchgoers", whom they regard as hypocrites. The self-righteous are the most severely condemned people in the New Testament. There is an old story about a self-righteous man who told a woman, "I never go to church, because there are only hypocrites there." To which she replied, "Oh, come on, there is always room for one more!"

Saint Paul, who wrote so eloquently about justification by faith and not by the works of the law (Rom 3:28; Gal 2:16), also told us that we must "work out our salvation in fear and trembling" (Phil 2:12). He devoted vast sections of his epistles to the Romans and Galatians to moral instruction and exhortation. Saint James tells us in the Bible that man is "justified by works and not by faith alone" (James 2:24). Christ Himself tells us that when the Son of Man will come in His glory, "He will repay every man for what he has done" (Mt 16:27).

"Justification", says the *Catechism*, "establishes *cooperation between God's grace and man's freedom*" (CCC 1993). As the Council of Trent teaches: "When God touches man's heart through the illumination of the Holy Spirit, man himself is not inactive while receiving that inspiration, since he could reject it; and yet, without God's grace, he cannot by his own free will move himself toward justice in God's sight."

Justification detaches us from sin, is merited for us by the Passion of Jesus Christ, effects not only the remission of sins but also the sanctification and renewal of the interior human being, and is the excellent work of God's love. Every human being must ask himself not "How do I appear to others?" or "How do I esteem myself to be?" but, rather, "Am I really just and righteous in the sight of almighty God?" How God "sees" us at the moment of our death will determine whether we will be in pain and misery or in joy and gladness forever.

JULY 15, 1994

Indulgences

On November 2, All Souls Day, the faithful may obtain a plenary indulgence, applicable to the souls in purgatory, if they piously visit a Catholic cemetery or church and there recite the Apostles' Creed and the Lord's Prayer for the deceased.

To obtain a plenary indulgence, it is necessary to be in the state of grace, perform the "work", or act, required, receive Holy Communion and go to Confession within eight days before or after doing the work, pray for the intentions of our Holy Father (usually an Our Father and a Hail Mary), and be free from all affection toward sin, including venial sin.

To obtain a partial indulgence, it is necessary to be in the state of grace and to perform the work as indicated. Because of abuses that once crept into the practice and because of serious misperceptions, the use of money in any connection with the obtaining of indulgences is strictly forbidden. No indulgence can be obtained by any donation of money for any cause!

An indulgence is the remission in whole or in part of the temporal punishment due to sin. If all the temporal punishment is remitted, the indulgence is called "plenary"; if part, it is called "partial".

Every sin causes damage. Sometimes this "damage" is obvious, as in sins of stealing, slander, and homicide. Oftentimes the damage is spiritual and unseen. However, even the most secret sins, known only to God and the sinner, damage the Church, the soul of the sinner, and other souls as well.

Even after our sin is forgiven, the responsibility to "repair the damage" remains. This is one of the reasons why all Christians are required to practice penance, asceticism, mortification, and reparation. We are reminded of this responsibility when in the sacrament of Reconciliation, after our confession, the priest enjoins a symbolic or salutary penance upon us.

An indulgence is the help that the Church gives us in this duty of "damage repair". It is help given by the Church from her spiritual treasury, which consists of the infinite merits of Jesus Christ and the superabundant merits of the Blessed Virgin Mary and the saints. In the sacrament of Penance the guilt of sin and the eternal punishment due to sin are remitted, but the temporal punishment remains to be satisfied either in this world by extrasacramental remission or in purgatory.

Before the reform of indulgences enacted by Pope Paul VI in 1967, partial indulgences were given in terms of time (years, days, quarantines), but now they are simply called "partial indulgences". What the time element meant was *not* so much time less in purgatory (that state or place cannot be calculated in temporal terms) but, rather, the same amount of temporal punishment is remitted as one would obtain were he to spend that much time in long, hard, public penance.

Among erroneous views spread about indulgences, sometimes out of ignorance and sometimes out of malice, is the false assertion that an indulgence means permission to commit sin, or is the pardon of future sin, or is an exemption from a law or duty, or releases one from an obligation such as restitution, or forgives past sin, or buys salvation, or purchases release from purgatory.

Usually, indulgences can be obtained only for oneself, but, because of the wonderful and loving relationship of the Church Militant, the Church Suffering, and the Church Triumphant in the communion of saints, some indulgences can be obtained for the souls in purgatory.

Normally one may obtain a plenary indulgence only once a day. A partial indulgence can be obtained as often as one desires. Which prayers or good works will have an indulgence attached to them is a matter that is decided only by the authority of the Catholic Church. Among the acts or works to which a plenary indulgence is attached are reading the

Bible for at least fifteen minutes a day for a week, saying the rosary each day for a week, making the Stations of the Cross, making a retreat, and making a pilgrimage. Among the ways one can obtain a partial indulgence are the pious use of sacramentals (medals, holy water, cross, crucifix, rosary, scapular, and so on, which are blessed in the proper way), certain short prayers, and doing those works that obtain a plenary indulgence but not fulfilling all the conditions of plenary indulgence.

Pope Paul VI in writing about indulgences said:

> Today the Church invites all her sons and daughters to give careful consideration to the effectiveness of indulgences in enriching the lives of individuals and of the whole Christian community. Let us mention their principal advantages. In the first place they teach Christians how ill it goes with the man who forsakes the Lord his God (Jer 2:19). Believers in Christ who seek indulgences realize that their own powers are inadequate to atone for the harm they have brought on themselves and on the whole community. They benefit from this humble realization. Indulgences teach us how close is the union in Christ that exists between us all. They teach us how much each person's share of supernatural life can contribute to others so they too can be brought swiftly to enjoy a close union with God the Father. Indulgences arouse real love and make it really effective, since, by means of them, our brothers and sisters asleep in Christ receive our help.[1]

The First Vatican Council teaches: "The souls of those who die in the charity of God before they have done sufficient penance for their sins of omission or commission are purified after death by the punishment of purgatory."[2] The Council of Trent teaches "that there is a purgatory and that the souls detained there can be helped by prayers of the faithful, especially by the acceptable Sacrifice of the altar" (DS 983).

The ancient tradition of the Church Fathers and a number of ecumenical councils along with the pious practice of Christians throughout the centuries of praying for the dead confirm those truths, which also can be found in Sacred Scripture (see 2 Macc 12:39–45; Sir 7:33; Zech 13:9; Mt 12:32; 1 Cor 3:10–15; 2 Tim 1:18; and so on).

On this All Souls Day and more often than that, let us pray: May the souls of all the faithful departed through the mercy of God rest in peace. *Requiescant in pace.*

OCTOBER 30, 1992

---

[1] Paul VI, *Indulgentiarum doctrina*, no. 9.
[2] Schema of the Dogmatic Constitution on the Principal Mysteries of the Faith.

3

The Christian in Society

The Social Teaching of the Church

In 1991 the Church celebrated a significant anniversary—the one hundredth anniversary of the great social encyclical of Pope Leo XIII, *Rerum novarum*. Our present Holy Father wrote a new social encyclical, *Centesimus annus*, to commemorate the occasion, A knowledge of authentic Catholic teaching on social matters, which involves politics, economics, and social justice, all issues that are inextricably tied to morality, should be a desire of every Catholic layman for whom the goal of sanctifying the temporal order is taken seriously as a commission that is part of the lay vocation given by God Himself.

In recent times, unfortunately, authentic Catholic teaching in the field of social justice and social morality is sometimes obscured by self-appointed "teachers" who are known to insert their own views into this field rather than present that teaching which comes from the authentic teaching authority (Magisterium) of the Catholic Church. Potential and actual lay apostles can find authentic Catholic teaching in this field by paying the closest attention to the words of the popes, the successors of Saint Peter, particularly the writing of the recent Holy Fathers and especially the present Bishop in the See of Rome.

In this month when our country celebrates Labor Day, we might well revisit, in our thoughts and studies, the dedication of the Church to social justice on the local, national, and international levels.

It is difficult to excerpt any single part of the large body of Catholic teaching in this area. However, one principle that is among the most basic in Catholic social teaching is the principle of subsidiarity. This was expressed best in recent times by Pope Pius XI in the encyclical *Quadragesimo anno* in 1931:

> Just as it is wrong to withdraw from the individual and commit to the community at large what private enterprise and industry can accomplish, so too, it is an injustice, a grave evil, and a disturbance of right order for a larger and higher organization to arrogate to itself functions which can be performed efficiently

by smaller and lower bodies. This is a fundamental principle of social philosophy, unshaken and unchangeable, and it retains its full truth today. The true aim of all social activity should be to help individual members of the social body, but never to destroy or absorb them.

Nonetheless, the popes teach that it is part of moral, social teaching that there is such a thing as the "common good" and that this is more than simply the sum total of an accumulated series of individual goods.

They teach, too, that human beings have a right to private property. This right derives from the virtue of prudence that all are bound to practice as well as from the nature of humanity and the social relationships that govern the human race. Pope Leo XIII wrote, "Before all else this principle is to be considered basic, namely, that private ownership must be preserved inviolate." Pope John XXIII wrote, "The right of private property, including that pertaining to goods devoted to productive enterprises, is permanently valid and rooted in the very nature of things."

Yet, the popes teach that a true social order cannot come merely from a collection of selfishness. The Church has always taught more than that the rich are to be exhorted to generosity and the poor to resignation. Proper social order cannot be just the automatic product of market forces any more than it can come from Marxian laws of history or other "iron laws" of economics or politics.

Proper social order requires that morality and moral principles accompany human beings in this sector of their lives as in all aspects of human existence. The Catholic Church in her social teaching does "not propose economic or political systems or programs, nor does she show a preference for one of these over another". The social teachings of the Church are not some kind of intermediate or third state between liberal capitalism and Marxist collectivism. She simply states and applies the perennial, moral principles that derive from the gospel of our Savior.

The right to private property, the Church tells us, is not an absolute right that has no limits and carries no corresponding social obligations. On the contrary, everything comes from God, including our talents, our possessions, our abilities, our accomplishments, and all our property. We are the stewards of these things and must give an answer to God for how we use what He has confided to our care. Profit is not the only or the key motive for economic progress. Brutal competition is not the supreme law of economics.

The Church teaches that human beings are more important than things and that human labor is a participation in the creative activity of

God and that work itself has been sanctified by Jesus, the God-Man, Who chose to be known on earth as a carpenter and the son of a carpenter. Pope John Paul II writes: "The Book of Genesis is also in a sense the first Gospel of work, for it shows what the dignity of work consists of: it teaches that man ought to imitate God, his Creator, in working because man alone has the unique characteristic of likeness to God. Man ought to imitate God both in working and also in resting, since God Himself wished to present His creative activity under the form of both work and rest."

Let us listen to the voice of Christ as He continues to instruct us through the Church He founded. Let us not leave our morality and our faith outside our participation in agriculture, business, industry, commerce, art, culture, education, the professions, and the field of work and labor. But let us bring Christ and His teaching to every aspect of life and work. Studying and applying the social teaching of the Church take us in that direction.

SEPTEMBER 11, 1992

Darwin as Bible

The First Vatican Council taught:

> Everyone knows that, after having rejected the divine teaching office of the Church and abandoned religious questions to the private judgment of each individual, the heresies proscribed by the fathers at Trent gradually broke down into an infinite number of sects, which divided and fought among each other and that finally a considerable number of their members lost all faith in Jesus Christ. The Holy Books themselves, which Protestantism first claimed as the only source and sole rule of Christian doctrine, ceased to be regarded as divine. They even came to be ranked among the fictions of mythology. . . . This gave birth to rationalism and naturalism . . . in open opposition to the Christian religion.

One can imagine how in such an atmosphere, which describes a large part of nineteenth-century Europe, an atmosphere that already saw many thinking people posit a contradiction between faith and reason, between religion and science, the publication on November 24, 1859, of *The Origin of Species* by Charles Darwin was like a flame in the midst of a sea of gasoline.

Of course, there is no contradiction between faith and reason, religion and science. God is the God of truth, and truth does not contradict itself. The question of biological evolution, provided it does not exclude God's creation and direction and the divine creation of the human soul, is a matter for science, not religion, to solve. It might be noted, however, that modern scientists, even the most ardent proponents of evolution, no longer accept the particular teachings of Darwin on this matter, although they pay tribute to him as a scientific pioneer. Fossil hunters still hunt for "missing links".

In all of recorded history there is no century that has been as horrible as our own. This twentieth century, now rapidly drawing to an end, has seen the most exceptional and remarkable developments in human science and technology but at the same time the greatest slaughter of human beings by each other ever known. Among the many wars and their devastation that our century has witnessed and continues to witness, it may be difficult to pinpoint the principal causes of human misery. However, most historians and observers will agree that the twin ideologies of Nazism and communism are unsurpassed as the origin of the mass murders and havoc that have marred these years.

Interestingly, the fathers of both these monstrous movements, Hitler and Marx, were diligent students of Darwin. Marx even corresponded with him. Both were convinced that Darwin provided a key to the interpretation of history. Both of them established political parties and schools of economic theory. Both of them founded systems based on absolute atheism. Both claimed they represented "advanced and progressive humanity", and both insisted they represented "the cutting edge of scientific victory". Both managed to convince millions of devoted and even fanatic disciples that following their interpretation of Charles Darwin would bring utopian dreams to reality, despite intermediate agony and terror for some people.

The fundamental ideology of Hitler was that of racial superiority. He ardently held to the slogans derived from Darwin: survival of the fittest; favorable variations are to be preserved, and unfavorable ones to be destroyed; and so on. The National Socialist movement believed that tall, blue-eyed, blond people were superior to others and, following evolutionary theory, were to be "bred up", while other races were to be enslaved or exterminated.

The Nazis embraced eugenics, that is, the killing of the handicapped, the mentally ill, and the aged, who were called by them "useless eaters". They also supported and promoted abortion and contraception to decrease the population of what they called "inferior races". (Incidentally, Margaret Sanger, the foundress of the Planned Parenthood religion, was a great admirer and supporter of the Nazi programs.) Hitler believed that he could accelerate the process of evolution by applying his theories not only to Germany, where he had come to power, but to Europe and perhaps the world. All who joined the Nazi party were expected to be atheists, although many still clung to some vestiges of other religions.

Pope Pius XI condemned Nazism in the encyclical *Mit Brennender Sorge* as totally incompatible with Christianity.

Karl Marx was convinced that evolutionary theory demonstrated that blind matter, with no direction or spiritual dimension, was evolving toward a classless society. The end or goal of all evolution, as he saw it, was a synthesis in which the thesis of a wealthy middle class was exterminated by the antithesis of the proletariat (the downtrodden, or lower class) to form the synthesis, a utopia where all would work according to their ability and receive according to their need. Denial of original sin and its effects, denial of the right to private property, hatred between economic and social classes, and hatred of religion are inherent in communist doctrine. In communist societies all individual rights and even individual existence are to be sacrificed to the good of the collectivity.

Marx conceived the Communist Party as the agent for accelerating the pace of evolution by means of violent revolution throughout the world. Communism was also condemned by Pope Pius XI as intrinsically opposed to the Catholic faith.

There is a true saying: Those who do not possess the true religion will most likely invent one of their own to follow. May God spare us from such inventions, particularly the ones using Darwin as their bible!

NOVEMBER 18, 1994

Gratitude

Harvest festivals are probably as old as harvests. It is understandable, then, that harvest festivals should have marked the beginnings of our country's history, when the richness of our soil and characteristics of our climate as well as the industry of the settlers began to yield an abundance of good things to eat and wear.

The earliest Thanksgiving on record in what is now the United States undoubtedly took place in Florida, when Holy Mass was offered there. It is very possible that Mass was offered in Florida already in 1513, but certainly from 1565 on, the "Great Act of Thanksgiving" (Eucharist) was offered at Saint Augustine, Florida, with regularity.

Among the settlers from the English-speaking world, a Thanksgiving service was held in 1619 in Jamestown, Virginia, according to the Anglican (Episcopalian) rite. However, the best known of these harvest festivals was the three-day affair celebrated in 1621 at Plymouth Plantation in present-day Massachusetts by order of Governor William Bradford.

American legend tells of the hardships of the voyage of the *Mayflower* and the *Speedwell* (the latter returned to port) and how the Pilgrims were fleeing religious persecution (They lived for a while with their fellow Calvinists in Leyden, Holland, but did not much like the company.)

The Pilgrims, a sect of the Puritan religion, Calvinists with overtones of Presbyterianism, celebrated their survival (only fifty-five out of the original 102 were still alive) after the starvation winter of 1620–1621. The seeds they brought from England, except for their barley, did not take in the New World. They survived thanks to the Indians, who taught them to hunt, fish, and plant corn. According to the account that has now entered American folklore, Edward Winslow explained how the Governor sent the men hunting; how, with the harvest in, they "rejoiced together after they gathered the fruit of their labor"; and how Chief Massasoit with ninety Indians showed up to join in the fun, supplying in the course of the three days five deer they had killed.

We live in an age of "political correctness", of demythologizing, of revisionist history, and of the debunking of legends. So it is inevitable that some of the Pilgrim myths be punctured. For instance, while they fled religious persecution from the Anglican Church in England, they had no intentions of giving religious toleration to any but their coreligionists. They quickly passed laws against "Papists and Quakers" and had a great abhorrence for Christmas. (Christmas was outlawed in Massachusetts for many decades, and it was a crime not to report for work on December 25. Indeed, for much of New England, Thanksgiving was a Christmas substitute.)

Their relationships with the Indians quickly soured. Several Indian wars and disease wiped out the tribes that came into contact with the Pilgrims. Evarts described the Pilgrims as "the pious ones of Plymouth, who, reaching the rock, first fell upon their own knees, then upon the aborigines". Samoset and Squanto, who spoke English (they had escaped from English slave traders—the English Puritans were among the greatest slave traders in history), were quickly forgotten.

New England poets (such as Emerson and Whittier) made the New England celebration of Thanksgiving part of our American heritage. There is no evidence that Massasoit and the Pilgrims had turkey, cranberries, or pumpkin pie for their feast, but later New England customs demanded these foods as part of the holiday.

George Washington issued the first presidential Thanksgiving Proclamation in 1789, saying: "I do recommend and assign Thursday the twenty-sixth day of November next to be devoted by the people of these States to the service of that great and glorious Being . . . for His signal and manifold mercies and the favorable interpositions of His providence."

Other presidents occasionally followed suit, but it was Abraham Lincoln (under the prodding of Sarah Josepha Hale) who made Thanksgiving on the fourth Thursday of November an annual custom, with its religious, harvest, civil, and patriotic aspects. With one variation (in 1939), it has continued so ever since.

Although Thanksgiving Day is not specifically a Catholic holy day, it is a wonderful national observance. The feasting, the family gatherings, the football, and the like should be subordinate to an annual recollection of our constant need to thank God.

The word "Eucharist" means "to give thanks". At every Mass we say: "Let us make a Eucharist", that is, "Let us give thanks." Our worship of God consists, in large measure, of giving thanks. When Jesus instituted the Holy Eucharist, He gave thanks, the Evangelists tell us (Mt 26:27; Mark 14:23; Luke 22:19). Repeatedly, our Lord gave thanks to His Father in the course of His earthly life (Mt 15:36) and even after His Resurrection (Lk 24:30).

We ought to thank God for the natural gifts He has bestowed on us, including such things as our talents, our health, our very breath, our family, our freedoms, and our occupations. How much more, however, ought we to thank Him for those supernatural gifts that go beyond our capacity even to imagine! These gifts given gratis (the root meaning of the word "grace") lift us to another level, making it possible for us, while remaining fully human, to participate in the divine nature, to have the ability in eternity to know and love as only God can know and love. In Christ, God has given us the Gift of Himself so one day we may enjoy happiness that defies exaggeration. "What no eye has seen, nor ear heard, nor the heart of man conceived . . . God has prepared for those who love Him" (1 Cor 2:9).

We should not neglect to thank God even for our hardships and sorrows and pains. Francis Thompson suggested that these are only the shadow of His arm stretched out lovingly. Joyce Kilmer said we ought to thank God for the roar of the world, the tide of fears against us hurled, the sting of His chastening rod . . . and "oh, thank God for God." Old Aesop said: "Gratitude is the sign of noble souls", and Cicero wrote: "Thanks is not only a great virtue, but the parent of all other virtues."

Saint Paul exhorts us: "Whatever you do, in word or in deed, do

everything in the name of the Lord Jesus, giving thanks to God the
Father through him" (Col 3:17). Let us make this our resolution, not just
on the fourth Thursday of every November, but every day of our lives.

NOVEMBER 26, 1992

Let Us Give Thanks

Harriet Beecher Stowe wrote, about the Thanksgiving season: "The
apples were all gathered and the cider was made and the yellow pump-
kins were rolled in from many a hill in billows of gold, and the corn was
husked and the labors of the season were done and the warm late days of
Indian Summer came in, dreamy, calm, and still, with just enough frost
to crisp the ground of a morning, but with warm traces of benignant,
sunny hours at noon." Like Mrs. Stowe, few Americans, especially those
whose lives touch agriculture, either directly or indirectly, would be unfamiliar with the completion of harvest time and with the great American harvest festival of Thanksgiving.

Unfortunately, this typically American holiday, which was begun in a
highly religious atmosphere and which possesses a name ("Thanksgiving") that cries out for the recognition of God as the Giver of all good
gifts (James 1:17), is starting to be soiled by the secularization that appears to be taking over large portions of our national culture. Forgetting
its origin and purpose, many Americans make this holiday simply the
time to start Christmas shopping, to begin putting up Christmas decorations, and to indulge in purposeless overeating.

Harvest festivals throughout the world are doubtlessly as old as harvests. These celebrations were brought from Europe to our shores by
many immigrants, including the English settlers in Virginia, the Pilgrims
in Massachusetts, and the French in Maine. What commonly seems to
have characterized all these festivals was their religious component.
While not always specifically Catholic in their American settings, these
celebrations certainly were Christian and invariably found a place for
the words of Psalm 100: "Know that the LORD is God. . . . Enter his
gates with thanksgiving. . . . Give thanks to him, bless his name."

Special American days of thanksgiving were proclaimed by Presidents
George Washington, John Adams, and James Madison. However, the
present kind of celebration derives basically from the proclamation issued by Abraham Lincoln in 1863. All the U.S. presidents since Lincoln
have issued similar proclamations. While their sincerity in some instances may be questioned, all these presidents never failed to include, as

the primary thrust of what they proclaimed, the need and usefulness of thanking Almighty God on the part of the nation's citizens.

Of course, as Catholics, we have an obligation to thank God at all times, not just at harvest time (Col 3:17). From Him alone comes all that we have and are. He is the One Who bestows on us our breath, life, talents, friends, indeed everything in the natural order. He gives us even more in the supernatural order, including a share in His very life, and then, when it seems impossible to imagine anything more we could receive from God, He gives Himself in Jesus Christ. This Supreme Gift is given to us again and again in a particular way in the Holy Eucharist.

Ironically, it is this Gift of the substantial presence of Jesus in the Holy Eucharist that is the means by which we are capable of rendering suitable and appropriate thanks to God. Jesus instituted the Blessed Sacrament by giving thanks (Lk 22:19). Gratitude is a basic part of every eucharistic act, including those of worship, contrition, and petition. The very word "Eucharist" is from the Greek, meaning "to give thanks".

At each Mass the priest invites us: "Let us give thanks to the Lord our God", and we affirm that it is "right to give Him thanks and praise". Were this exchange to use the Greek word, it would say: "Let us make a *Eucharist* to the Lord our God." Shakespeare said: "Beggar that I am, I am even poor in thanks." However, in the Holy Eucharist we are actually enabled to show adequate gratitude to God, because we render thanks perfectly through Jesus Christ.

The most difficult things to appreciate and to be grateful to God for are adversity and agony. Pain, sorrow, and suffering, which God sometimes permits, come, not directly from Him, but from the effects of original sin in ourselves and our world. They are nonetheless used by God for our ultimate benefit. They are, in the words of Francis Thompson, the "shade of His hand, outstretched caressingly".

Only in eternity will the mystery of why God permits evil be solved for us. As the poet wrote: "Full oft He weaveth sorrow and I in foolish pride, forget He sees the upper, and I the under side". Joyce Kilmer told us that we should thank God for toil and sorrow and "the sting of His chastening rod . . . and, oh, thank God for God". It helps to remember too that the Eucharist is the re-presentation of the sacrifice of the Cross, and without the Cross there can be no crown. Implicit in presently sharing the Cross is our gratitude for our glory to come.

The Book of Psalms asks a question for us: "What shall I render to the Lord for all He has given to me?" Fortunately, an answer follows immediately: "I will lift up the cup of salvation and call on the name of the LORD" (Ps 116:12–13). The psalmist goes on to urge: "Give thanks to the Lord, for He is good" (Ps 118:1). Let us not allow our national holiday to become merely "turkey day", but may it always be "Thanksgiving Day".

NOVEMBER 25, 1994

An American Holiday

In a moving passage in his Epistle to the Philippians, Saint Paul says that he gives unceasing thanks to God (Phil 1:3). This text is a symbol of how the notion of "giving thanks" penetrates the pages of Sacred Scripture. In the Old Testament, the Chosen People were required to be a people who praise and thank God continually for His gifts (Lev 7:12–13; 1 Chron 16:8–18).

The Apostle of the Gentiles not only was himself a person who lived in a perpetual attitude of gratitude to God, but he constantly exhorted his converts to the Catholic faith to be people of thanks. "Have no anxiety about anything, but in everything by prayer and supplication with thanksgiving let your requests be made known to God" (Phil 4:6). "Whatever you do, in word or deed, do everything in the name of the Lord Jesus, giving thanks to God the Father through him" (Col 3:17).

Before Christ worked His great miracle of multiplying the loaves and fishes, the evangelists noted that He gave thanks (Mk 15:36). Jesus praised the cured leper, who alone out of ten returned to give thanks and glory to God (Lk 17:15–19). Our Lord thanked His Father for hiding religious truth from the learned and clever and, instead, revealing Himself to the little ones (Mt 11:25; Lk 10:21).

The Gospels show clearly that Christ, in instituting the Holy Eucharist at the Last Supper, surrounded this sacred act with thanks (Mt 26:27). So much was "giving thanks" part of what Jesus did that the entire sacrament and sacrifice took on the name of "thanksgiving", or Eucharist (which, in the Greek language, means "to give thanks").

At the beginning of the Great Prayer of the Mass, in the course of which the dying and rising of our Savior are made present again on our altars and His substantial presence is made real among us under the species of bread and wine, the priest invites us not only to lift up our hearts but also to "give thanks" (to "make a Eucharist") to the Lord our God. We reply that it is right and just "to give Him thanks", that is, to make a Eucharist.

It is surely part of following Christ, then, to be grateful to God and to have this attitude as a sort of perpetual and regular outlook on life. The most casual meditation will demonstrate the obligation that all rational creatures have to manifest their continual thanks to their Creator. All that we are and have comes from God (Acts 17:28)—except for our sins and the evil and pain that are the result of those sins. To God we owe everything that is good, beautiful, holy, and true. Even more than for natural gifts ought Christians to be grateful to their heavenly Father for His supernatural gifts, especially the supreme gift of Himself in Christ Jesus.

We Catholics are, by our holy religion, called to be people who are always thankful to God. Every Mass, every Catholic celebration is an occasion for special gratitude. Our principal act of worship is named "Eucharist". Nevertheless, it is fitting that we join our fellow Americans in this land on the fourth Thursday of every November for our national holiday and harvest festival, which, although not specifically Catholic, is nonetheless an appropriate and fitting custom and tradition.

As a matter of fact, in the increasingly godless and secular atmosphere in our country, it would be wise to work to maintain the religious overtones of this holiday. In this regard the term "Thanksgiving" is so much more proper than something so crass as "turkey day". In our own families it may be better to emphasize thanking God on this day even more than the feasting and merrymaking. Certainly, attending Mass on Thanksgiving Day, if possible, would be the best way to indicate our gratitude to God and to seek His blessings for our health and happiness and for our material and spiritual prosperity. It would also seem important for us to be mindful of those who are hungry and less fortunate than we are with suitable gifts and to help in that direction.

Even adversity and sorrow, when seen in the light of eternity, can be an occasion for giving thanks to God. As the poet Francis Thompson remarked, these sometimes are simply the "shadow of His arm" outstretched lovingly. A surgeon serving in the U.S. Continental Army remarked at Valley Forge, "Mankind is never truly thankful for the benefits of life until they have experienced the want of them."

The Pilgrims in Massachusetts and almost all the early American settlers who celebrated Thanksgiving put great emphasis on the Book of Psalms in the Bible. There is no reason why we cannot follow this example. Psalm 100, for instance, says, "Enter his gates with thanksgiving, and his courts with praise. Give thanks to him." Psalm 111 says, "I will give thanks to the LORD with my whole heart." George Washington said we should celebrate Thanksgiving to thank God for His "signal and manifold mercies". Abraham Lincoln said this holiday should be "a day of thanksgiving and praise to our beneficent Father Who dwelleth in the heavens". Franklin Roosevelt said it should be a day when we learn "the ancient truth that greed and selfishness and striving for undue riches can never bring lasting happiness or good".

Thanksgiving is a wonderful day of parades, football, delicious food, and happy family gatherings. Its full meaning, however, involves gratitude to God. We would be unfaithful to our national heritage if we allowed that aspect of this quintessential American holiday to slip away.

NOVEMBER 24, 1995

Catholic Patriotism

The geography of our country is replete with Catholic names: San Antonio, Santa Fe, Saint Louis, San Diego, San Francisco, Los Angeles, Corpus Christi, Saint Paul, and so on. In a similar way, the history of our land and nation is marked by Catholic names. Those who opened our continent to European exploration and colonization were men who also shared our Catholic faith, Christopher Columbus and Leif Eriksson.

De Soto, Coronado, and Jolliet were among those whose heroic exploring of the wilderness contributed greatly to continental development. Catholic explorers, if not missionaries themselves, as they sometimes were, were almost always accompanied by missionary priests. One thinks immediately of the proto-martyr of America, Father Juan Padilla, who suffered death in 1544, in what is now Kansas (reputable historians sometimes argue that it was actually here in Nebraska) while trying to convert the Guas Indians. In our nation's capitol building, statues honoring Blessed Junipero Serra and Jacques Marquette testify to the "Catholic imprint".

Anti-Catholic bigotry and hatred were all too characteristic of many of the English colonies, especially those settled by the Puritans in New England. The Quebec Act of 1774, allowing tolerance for the Catholic religion in Canada, recently conquered by England in the French and Indian War, particularly enraged the New Englanders as much or more than the Stamp Act and similar British legislation. It is not surprising then that, when the Americans invaded Canada during the Revolutionary War, Catholic Canadians refused to join their army to fight against the British.

Too late the Continental Congress realized its mistake in leaning too much toward New England's Catholic bashing. It tried to make up for the error by sending a delegation to persuade the Canadians to join the revolution. The delegation consisted of the Catholic patriot (and richest man in Maryland and probably in America) Charles Carroll, his cousin Father John Carroll, Benjamin Franklin, and Samuel Chase. Bishop

Briand of Quebec strongly opposed the Americans, due to his memory of New England's anti-Catholicism, and so the delegation was a failure.

In the colonies themselves, however, the tiny minority of Catholics were very prominent. Charles Carroll signed the Declaration of Independence from Maryland and ardently supported the "glorious cause". His family were staunch Catholics as well as devoted patriots. His cousin Daniel Carroll (along with the Catholic Thomas Fitzsimmons) helped draw up and later signed the Constitution.

Stephen Moylan, a major general in the Continental army, whose brother was a Catholic bishop in Ireland, was the principal secretary and aide to George Washington during the war. John Barry, from Philadelphia, was the "Father of the United States Navy". Anthony Wayne was a prominent United States general officer.

Almost immediately upon assuming command of the Continental army, Washington forbade the celebration of the vile, anti-catholic "Guy Fawkes Day". Most of the help from abroad that enabled the colonies to triumph over the British was "Catholic". The names tell the story: Lafayette, Pulaski, d'Estaing, Rochambeau, Kosciuszko, John Fitzgerald, and so on.

Once France and Spain entered the war on our side, the Continental Congress itself attended Catholic services on occasion, such as a solemn *Te Deum* in Saint Mary Church, Philadelphia, on July 4, 1779, to commemorate the third anniversary of the Declaration of Independence; the Requiem Mass for the Spanish Ambassador at Saint Joseph Church in Philadelphia in 1781; and the Mass of thanksgiving for the victory at Yorktown on November 4, 1781, again at Saint Mary's.

After the Revolutionary War, George Washington wrote to the Catholics of the United States: "I presume that your fellow citizens will not forget the patriotic part you took in the accomplishment of their revolution and the establishment of our government or the important assistance they received from a nation (France) where the Roman Catholic religion is professed."

Father John Carroll (who later became the first bishop and archbishop in the United States) wrote: "The blood of Catholics flowed as freely in proportion to their numbers to cement the fabric of independence as that of any of their fellow citizens. They concurred with perhaps greater unanimity than any other body of men in mending and promoting that government from whose influence America anticipates all the blessings of justice, peace, plenty, good order, and civil religious liberty."

As our country approaches its annual celebration of national independence, it is well occasionally to recall that we Catholics "belong".

There is today, as there has been in the past, an almost visceral anti-Catholicism in certain sectors of our national culture, which colors the media and which tries to depict the Catholic Church and her members as "bigots", "intolerant", and worse. The liberal establishment becomes especially angry (after all, "anti-Catholicism is the anti-Semitism of the liberal") when its "orthodoxies" are challenged, particularly in the areas of sexual ethics, abortion, suicide, and the like.

As Catholic laymen take seriously their duty of sanctifying the temporal order, as the Second Vatican Council requires them to do, let them remember they are walking in the paths already trod by their fellow Catholics whose lives gained additional luster from their patriotic endeavors.

JULY 1, 1994

Television

Very few parents would be so irresponsible as to seat their children alone in their living room, open the door to invite in strangers they might notice passing by, and tell these strangers to talk to and instruct their youngsters, while they went about their business in another part of the house. Yet, many parents who would be appalled at the thought of such behavior do something quite like that. They allow their children to be formed, educated, and instructed by strangers who are invited into their living rooms by means of the remarkable machine called the television set.

Television is indeed a twentieth-century marvel. Brilliant colored pictures transport reality and fiction thousands of miles in an instant, from places as distant as Tokyo, Berlin, and Rome. Millions of people all over the planet can be united in viewing the same pictures. (Actually, several programs have claimed over a billion viewers.)

Television has a great potential for good. It can be extraordinarily educational, it can increase awareness, cause vocabulary growth, provide distraction and entertainment, and it can be a blessing in hospitals, waiting rooms, nursing facilities, and other places where it can allay boredom and anxiety.

For all its positive potential, however, television can be (like fire) a good servant but a bad master. For this reason, some families (very few) do not have TV sets in their homes. However, most American families do make use of television rather extensively. For instance, it is said that by the time an average American child reaches the age of seven, he watches TV six hours a day!

Living the Christian Mystery

There is some empirical evidence that excessive TV viewing, especially in younger children, can actually cause mental retardation. The
passivity that TV generates can be a source of physical as well as mental
damage to children whose viewing is not restricted, monitored, and limited by parental control.

Enslavement of our minds and emotions is never pleasant to admit,
but sometimes the media, and most especially the queen of the media
(TV), can oftentimes control and manipulate us far more than simply by
consuming our time, better used in other directions. It can slowly in-
sinuate into our attitudes, our lives, and our culture sets of values and
outlooks that are alien to our Christian convictions, and it can form our
opinions and, even worse, those of our children, in directions that, if
followed, lead to a loss of salvation.

As one U.S. Senator puts it:

> Through the power of television, millions upon millions of
> people are persuaded to buy this or that automobile or this or
> that deodorant or this or that political candidate. Are we so na-
> ive, then, as to assume that millions of viewers are not being
> swayed by a constant diet of foul language, debased behavior,
> outrageous violence, and sexual promiscuity?
>
> With each dose of vulgarity, profanity, pornography, assault,
> murder, and other violence, we become and less uncomfortable
> with those crimes and vices, until at last our consciences lose
> the ability to object to them.

One family told me that the most difficult Lenten penance they ever
undertook was to unplug and closet the TV set for the duration of that
season. Like any addiction, television viewing can be subtle in its gradual
control of our lives. We can deceive ourselves into thinking that the
remote control device is still under the direction of our free will, when
oftentimes it is no longer. Entertainment of a certain sort can harm the
formation of children even by lessening or hurting the desire and need
to read or by destroying the art of enjoyable conversation.

Some perceptive priests have observed that the artificial excitement
created by some television programs has had a deleterious effect upon
participation in the liturgy by children and upon their desire to grow in
the grace of God. Not only can television exterminate innocence, but it
also has the potential to cripple imagination.

Parents who take seriously their God-given duties and rights to be
the primary and inalienable teachers and educators of their children will
certainly want to control their children's television viewing. It would be
foolish to be totally negative about the media, including television view-

ing. Wise parents will positively affirm the values and the good that can come from some television viewing. At the same time they would be derelict in their vocation as parents if they did not only exercise control over this aspect of their children's formation (and this includes children of high-school age) but also develop in their children a sense of criticism and a valid set of Christian beliefs and Catholic principles that can be used as the criteria for such criticism.

It is shocking to learn that parents who would scruple about the kind of food their children ingest, who study carefully the labels on food packages to be sure that their youngsters are not eating harmful or questionable things, are hopelessly indifferent about the poison that can come from the media, especially television, to pollute, damage, and cripple the minds of their children, to say nothing of causing their souls' eternal happiness to be placed in serious jeopardy.

True parental love, as all parents eventually learn, means occasionally having to say no and teaching children the importance of deferred gratification. Parents who are too lenient with children are as cruel as those who are too severe. This supposes, of course, that the parents themselves have mastered the art of self-discipline in the use of the media. As Saint Pius X said, "What parents say to their children cannot be heard because of the loud noise of what they do."

Many wonderful and conscientious people, including fine Catholics, work in the media, including television. These people often struggle to insert gospel values and decency and morality into their professional labors. This is why, when the occasion calls for it, we should not hesitate to send letters and cards of praise to channels, stations, sponsors, and so on to accentuate the positive as well as to express strongly our displeasure with the negative.

OCTOBER 9, 1992

4

PRAYER AND SPIRITUAL LIFE

The Three Ways

Very few people are familiar with the name of Evagrius Ponticus, but he accomplished an interesting and somewhat important task many centuries ago. After carefully studying the Sacred Scriptures and the writings of the Fathers of the Church, he drew up a division of stages or steps or "ways" through which one ordinarily must pass in the development of the spiritual life. These are traditionally called the purgative, the illuminative, and the unitive ways.

These ways, or steps, in spiritual development are not mutually exclusive. They interpenetrate each other. In a special way, the annual celebration of Lent bids all Catholics to revisit these steps, either in memory or in actual fact.

THE PURGATIVE WAY

The first phase, the purgative way, is sometimes called the way of beginners. It is that stage in our spiritual life when, under God's grace, we struggle against all sin. It is the effort that our free will makes to remain not only free from mortal sins but also from all habitual sins and all vices that encumber us. It is the time and place to rid ourselves of all attachment to sin. Saint Paul tells us that it is God Who works in us both the will and the performance, and yet it we who must "work out [our] salvation in fear and trembling" (Phil 2:12–13). What God does in us is truly His, and yet it is also ours.

The purgative way is not entirely negative. For virtues can grow at the same time that vices are restrained. The three customary practices of Lent are especially suited to those in the purgative way. Fasting, prayer, and almsgiving are eminently fine means to control the urges inside of every human being that, when out of control, are the source of all sins. We call these urges the seven capital sins. Interior drives that were inserted into us at our creation, these urges become the sources of evil when they are unrestrained. Disorder in their regard was introduced into our human condition when our first parents were beguiled into disobedience in the Garden of Eden. Their names are well known to us: pride and anger, lust and sloth, gluttony, envy, and greed.

THE ILLUMINATIVE WAY

When in our lives virtues take on more significance than sin and begin to outweigh the evil in our motives, we acquire a certain conformity between what we profess in our faith and how we live and act daily and hourly. In this stage of our development, we become able to be lifted from the realm of the sensual and the merely sensible impressions that have hitherto dominated us and, again under God's grace, to be "illuminated".

When one is well advanced in the illuminative way, there is not only the avoidance of all deliberate venial sins but also, in periods like Lent, a genuine effort at interior mortification along with that which is exterior, mortification of imagination and memory, for instance. Christ becomes the center of one's thoughts and affections in this phase. Works of charity done in His name and for His sake are done in joy. Peace and interior serenity, affective and frequent prayer mark one's growth from a tepid and moderately devout soul into a person of profound fervor. In the illuminative way, the theological and moral virtues are embraced, and their practice is a basic part of a Christian's life.

It is in this time of spiritual development that liturgical prayer becomes so much more than a Christian duty and a Catholic obligation. Involvement in the Mass and the sacraments becomes the highest of privileges, and participating in these "actions of Christ", even on a daily basis, becomes a longing and a spiritual craving. It is also in this stage of spiritual development that a deep sensitivity to orthodox truth, to the fullness and completeness of God's revelation, is manifested in a Catholic's attitude and concern.

THE UNITIVE WAY

Once one has walked up the steps of purgation and illumination, the highest stage or way of the spiritual life is called unitive. Meditation and prayer take on, in this phase, a superior quality brought about by infused contemplation. In a certain sense the Second Sunday of Lent with its annual account of the Transfiguration of Jesus (Mt 17:1–9) gives one a glimpse of what this third way is about. There is in the unitive way a more direct experience of God in Christ, and His love is poured into one's heart, enabling God the Holy Spirit to crown with His gifts the labors of struggle against vice and the acquisition of virtue.

The list of the Holy Spirit's gifts (which, incidentally, each Catholic receives in embryo in Baptism and in fullness in Confirmation) basically represents the internal growth of this third way (see Is 11). One begins with fear or awe of God and then progresses to piety and fortitude, advances to counsel, supernatural knowledge, and spiritual understanding. The supreme achievement is the actualization of the gift of wisdom, which makes one see all things as God sees them and which gives one a perpetual and unfailing "taste" for the things of heaven.

Evagrius Ponticus is not a name worth remembering. However, what he systematized long ago was very much in the tradition expressed in the writings of Saint John and Saint Paul, of Saint Augustine and Saint Gregory of Nyssa, of Saint Maximus and Saint John of the Cross, of Saint Teresa of Avila and Saint Catherine of Siena, of the whole tradition of the Fathers and Doctors of the Church. It is the reality of that tradition that is worth remembering, especially in this holy season of Lent.

Saint Peter tells us that we are "partakers of the divine nature" (2 Pet 1:4). As we journey in this period from ashes to glory, may we also go from purgation through illumination to union with Him whose nature we share by sanctifying grace.

MARCH 5, 1993

Prayer

The great prayer of the Catholic Church is the sacred liturgy, when the "whole Christ, Head and members", worships God the Father in the Holy Spirit. However, this essential, public prayer of the Church must spill over into the private life of each Christian. Each of us must have a secret life of prayer that is ours personally (Mt 6:5–13).

Some people have found it surprising that the *Catechism of the Catholic Church* has devoted such a large part of its content to a treatment of prayer. Once the vital importance of prayer for our Catholic life and faith is understood, however, it is logical and consistent for prayer to occupy a significant portion of a Catholic's time and attention. Tennyson wrote: "More things are wrought by prayer than this world dreams of." Saint John Chrysostom said, "It is simply impossible to lead, without the aid of prayer, a virtuous life." And Saint Alphonsus Liguori wrote, "Prayer is necessary for salvation, and, therefore, God, Who desires that we should be saved, has enjoined it as a precept."

For many centuries, the Church has used the definition of prayer formulated by Saint John Damascene: "Prayer is the raising of one's mind and heart to God or the requesting of good things from God." Prayer, of course, can be either mental or vocal. But all prayer, including vocal prayer, in order to be authentic and valid, must have an interior component. Saint Francis de Sales said, "A single Our Father said devoutly is better than many prayed in haste and without thought."

Prayer can be either spontaneous, that is, words composed by the one praying, or formal, words given to us by someone else. The most glorious of all formal, vocal prayers is the Lord's Prayer, the Our Father, given to us by the lips of our Savior Himself. Because they are derived from God, the primary Author of the Bible, the Psalms and the Hail Mary have a very special aspect to them as prayers even when used privately.

In its most profound reality, prayer is a gift from God. In humility, we human beings must first acknowledge that "we do not know how to pray as we ought" (Rom 8:26). The *Catechism* tells us that "God thirsts that we may thirst for Him" (CCC 2560) and that prayer "is the action of God and of man, springing forth from both the Holy Spirit and ourselves, wholly directed to the Father" (CCC 2564).

The purpose or goal of prayer is fourfold. First, prayer is worship. We most often pray directly to God, but even when praying to the Blessed Virgin Mary and the saints, our prayers are ultimately directed to the adoration of the one, true God. Second, both implicitly and explicitly, all prayer must be filled with gratitude. Thanksgiving (in Greek, *Eucharist*) should be a perpetual attitude of every Christian. In Holy Writ, Saint Paul instructs us: "Whatever you do, in word or deed, do everything in the name of the Lord Jesus, giving thanks to God the Father through him" (Col 3:17).

Third, prayer must have an aspect of contrition or sorrow for sin. Some prayers are directly acts of repentance for sin, but all prayer must implicitly acknowledge our continual need for God's pardon and forgiveness and our profound unworthiness to approach Him.

Fourth, prayer should also be petition and request. The Lord knows what we want and need before we ask (Mt 6:8), but still Christ has taught us to seek and beg (Mt 7:7) and to be humble and persevering in our prayers (see Lk 18:9–14; 11:5–13; 18:1–8; Mt 15:21–28). God answers every prayer (Jn 16:23). Sometimes He answers "yes", sometimes "no", and sometimes "wait".

Every loving parent knows that sometimes it is necessary, for a child's own good, to answer childish requests with those responses (yes, no, or wait). God is our Father and knows far better than we do what is for our own good. Saint Bernard said: "God either gives us what we ask for, or He gives us something better for us." The great Bishop of Hippo remarks: "God is more anxious to bestow His blessings on us than we are to receive them. He would not urge us to ask, unless He were willing to give."

Both by His instruction and by His example, our Redeemer taught us how to pray and how necessary prayer is for His followers and disciples (Mk 11:24). Prayer, according to Christ, cannot be merely saying "Lord, Lord", but must derive from faith, conversion of heart, and resignation to the will of God (Mt 7:21; 9:38).

Jesus taught us that our prayers should be done in His name (Jn 14:13). He also taught us to pray sometimes directly to Him (Mt 9:27), and He assured us that prayer will be a source of genuine happiness in our lives (Jn 16:24). "Spiritual joy arises from purity of heart and perseverance in prayer", said Saint Francis of Assisi. Saint Augustine said of the prayer of Jesus: "He prays for us as our Priest, prays in us as our Head, and is prayed to by us as our God. Therefore, let us acknowledge our voice in Him and His in us."

At every Mass we hear the priest say: "Let us pray." May this be a slogan and motto for our entire life.

AUGUST 12, 1994

Saints and Prayer

There can be no doubt that one of the functions God intends His saints to perform is that of good example for us who follow after them. The Solemnity of All Saints, which ushers in the month of November, provides an occasion to look again at the heroes of heaven, the saints, especially those the Church has canonized, and to learn from them the place and importance of prayer. The *Catechism* states that the Christian discovers the "[example of holiness] in the spiritual tradition and long history of the saints who have gone before him and whom the liturgy celebrates in the rhythms of the sanctoral cycle" (CCC 2030).

Every saint was a man or woman of prayer. This is evident from their biographies and from their very words. Saint Alphonsus Liguori said, "Prayer is necessary for salvation, and, therefore, God, Who desires that we should be saved, has enjoined it as a precept." Saint Augustine of Hippo stated, "As our body cannot live without nourishment, so our soul cannot be kept alive spiritually without prayer." Since the call from God to holiness is universal, we too must respond to this call by being men and women of prayer.

INTERCESSION OF THE SAINTS

The *Catechism* is quite eloquent in regard to the intercessory power of the saints: "The witnesses who have preceded us into the kingdom, especially those whom the Church recognizes as saints, share in the living tradition of prayer by the example of their lives, the transmission of their writings, and their prayer today. They contemplate God, praise him and constantly care for those whom they have left on earth. . . . Their intercession is their most exalted service to God's plan. We can and should ask them to intercede for us and for the whole world" (CCC 2683).

Pope Leo XIII wrote: "We are taught by our Catholic Faith that we may pray not only to God Himself, but also to the Blessed in heaven, although in an entirely different manner. From God we ask as from the Source of all good, but from the saints as from intercessors. We pray to the holy angels and saints, not that God may learn our petitions through them, but that by their merits and prayers, our own prayers may be efficacious." When she was dying, Saint Thérèse of the Child Jesus said, "I will spend my heaven doing good upon earth." On his deathbed, Saint Dominic remarked, "Do not weep, for I shall be more useful to you after my death and I shall help you then more effectively than during my life."

We can and ought to pray for each other. We can ask family and friends to pray for us. Death does not interfere with this kind of mutual help. The marvelous "communion of saints", in which we believe, enables us to be assisted by the prayers of those who are now in heaven but, while on earth, shared our membership in the family of the Catholic Church.

TEACHING OF THE SAINTS

Besides giving us good examples in regard to prayer and continuing to pray for us while enjoying the beatific vision, the saints have left for us a great deal of wisdom in what they have written and spoken about prayer.

Saint Teresa of Avila said, "It is essential to begin the practice of prayer with a firm resolution of persevering in it. Never address words to God while you are thinking of something else." Saint Bonaventure said, "When we pray, the voice of the heart must be heard more than that proceeding from the mouth." Saint Catherine of Siena stated, "By humble and faithful prayer, the soul acquires, with time and perseverance, every virtue." Saint John Chrysostom taught, "It is simply impossible, without the aid of prayer, to lead a virtuous life."

Saint Thomas Aquinas wrote, "For prayer to be effective, our petitions should be for benefits worthily to be expected from God." Saint Benedict taught his monks, "Prayer ought to be short and pure, unless prolonged by special inspiration of divine grace." Saint Alphonsus preached, "The prayer of a humble soul penetrates the heavens and presents itself before the throne of God and does not leave without God's looking on it and hearing it."

Saint John Baptist de la Salle, who lived in the early eighteenth century, told his brothers, "We should have frequent recourse to prayer and persevere a long time in it. God wishes to be solicited. He is not weary of hearing us. The treasure of His graces is infinite. We can do nothing more pleasing to Him than to beg incessantly that He bestow them on us." Saint John Vianney, the pastor of the French village of Ars, preached, "Prayer is to our soul what rain is to the soil. Fertilize the soil ever so richly, it will remain barren unless fed by frequent rains." Saint Aloysius Gonzaga said, "Diligence in prayer is the perfection of the Gospel." Saint Thérèse of Lisieux wrote, "For me prayer is a surge of the heart. It is a simple look turned toward heaven. It is a cry of recognition and of love, embracing both trial and joy."

When we learn from the saints, we learn from Christ. They followed the example and teaching of Jesus, and, in following them, we follow our Divine Master. In reply to the plea of a disciple (Lk 11:1), Christ taught His disciples how to pray. In this lesson He taught all the saints of all the centuries, and in teaching them, He teaches us as well. As our companions and helpers in prayer, the saints take nothing away from the unique mediatorship of Jesus, Who is the only Mediator between God and man (1 Tim 2:5–6). Rather, they lead us to Him and keep us close to Him in our affections and thoughts, until, with them, we shall enjoy a share in His victory and triumph forever.

The Epistle to the Hebrews tells us that Jesus Himself "offered up prayers and supplications" (Heb 5:7–9). The saints reflect our Lord in prayer. It is our duty to do this also.

NOVEMBER 11, 1994

The Psalms: Prayer Book of the Church

Whenever an inquiry is made as to what constituted the principal prayers of the early Christians, it is clear that only one answer could be given: the Psalms. Our Catholic ancestors in the primitive Church knew the Psalms by heart and used them daily in their prayer life. The Psalms were used in both the public and private prayer of the ancient Jews, and, consequently, it can be assumed that our Lord and His apostles knew and used them from childhood.

It is understandable that the Psalms passed immediately into the prayer life of the Catholic Church. They constitute the core and major portion of the Liturgy of the Hours (or Divine Office, the fixed and official daily prayer of the Church) and are widely used in all the celebrations of the sacred liturgy. Saint Ambrose said, "The Psalms are loved by pious souls of every age. We find in them instruction as well as beautiful poetry. We sing them to enjoy the latter and we study them to profit by the former."

Saint Paula, a Roman matron of the fourth century, wrote of the early Christians singing the Psalms: "The farmer at his plow used to sing them; the sweating harvester lightened his labor with them; the vintager chanted snatches of David's poetry."

The word *psalm* is Greek for a chant or song. The one hundred and fifty Psalms, gathered into five books, constitute an entire section in the Old Testament of the Bible, called the Psalter. Since they are the inspired word of God, when they are used as prayer, we address God in His own words. Thus, the Psalms have a heavenly or mystic quality from their very origin.

In their human origin the Psalms are attributed by legend, at least in general inspiration, to King David, the ancestor of our Lord. They are hymns and prayers, lamentations and thanksgivings, royal chants and songs of wisdom, individual and communal, and songs of pilgrimage. The *Catechism* notes that there are certain constant characteristics of all the Psalms: simplicity and spontaneity, desire for God and for the good of His creation, and presentation of the distraught condition of the believer who is beset by a host of enemies but who is loyal and submissive to God in the certitude of His love. All psalms contain the element of praise (CCC 2589).

Jesus is the center of the entire Bible. All of Sacred Scripture, including the Psalms, must be read in the light of the Christ-event in human history. Although composed at an earlier stage of revelation than the New Testament and, consequently, more "primitive" and undeveloped than later poems and prayers, the Psalms nevertheless are an important part of the continuous and basic plan of God and, indeed, contain many prophetic aspects that bear directly on our divine Lord (for example, Heb 1:5–13).

In the "Christ-perspective" of the Psalms, we should, when reading or singing them, see Jerusalem as a type of the Church, the king as that of the Messiah, the temple sacrifices as that of the Cross, and so on. We should see in the struggle with the forces of evil a symbol of that final battle which shall culminate in the glory of the resurrection on the last day. The Psalms provide us with some early and temporary images of our own eternal salvation. The *Catechism* calls the Psalms "the master-work of prayer" and says, "They extend to all dimensions of history, recalling God's promises already fulfilled and looking for the coming of the Messiah" (CCC 2596).

Father Roland Murphy explains that the Psalms can be, from some points of view, not an easy "prayer book" to use. This is because they "represent a wide range of Israel's beliefs and history over some seven hundred years". To get to know them well requires some effort to learn about the Old Testament and about how God gradually revealed Himself to Israel and then, in Jesus, to the whole of mankind.

Nonetheless, the Psalms express the basic reactions of human beings before God: faith, fear, joy, trust, and praise. They have a universal quality that makes them accessible to every person who is acquainted with them. The study of ancient Hebrew poetry and prayer can be long and difficult and definitely is not an area that many people are called to. However, it is not necessary to master the complications of scientific study in order truly to use and enjoy using the Psalms as prayer. The experience of the Catholic Church in almost two thousand years teaches us that the Psalms are a useful and even necessary form of prayer for all people of all classes and all times.

In his *Confessions*, Saint Augustine recounts how the singing of the Psalms played a role in his conversion: "As the music flowed into my ears and Your truth trickled into my heart, the tide of devotion swelled high within me and the tears ran down, and there was joy in those tears."

Saint Ambrose wrote: "A psalm is a blessing on the lips of people, the praise of God, the assembly's homage, a general acclamation, a word that speaks for all, the voice of the Church, a confession of faith in song." The *Catechism* says, "Prayed and fulfilled in Christ, the Psalms are an essential and permanent element of the prayer of the Church. They are suitable for men of every condition and time" (CCC 2597).

SEPTEMBER 30, 1994

The Christian Mantra

Some years ago observers were startled when Pope John Paul II, asked about the rosary, remarked: "The rosary, why that's my favorite prayer." It may seem strange that a very sophisticated scholar with two doctorates, a mastery of more than a dozen languages, and work and concern for a billion Catholics throughout the world would find in the rosary his "favorite prayer". The Holy Father personally leads the rosary over Vatican Radio once a month and is shown in many photographs fingering his rosary in the course of his travels and his daily recreational walks in the Vatican gardens. In my last visit to Rome, he gave me a beautiful rosary as a souvenir of my audience with him. Perhaps his example may help us, in this month of the rosary (October), to reexamine our own attitude toward this prayer form, which has been used for so many centuries in the Church.

The origins of the rosary go back into the mists of history. Historians generally agree that the 150 Hail Marys are somehow linked to an attempt by lay people to do something similar to the recitation of the 150 Psalms, from the Old Testament Psalter, which was done on a daily or weekly basis, from a very early time in Church history, by hermits and monks, and which, by the Middle Ages, was done weekly by all clerics in major Orders. The best guess is that lay people, who because of their secular occupations and sometimes their illiteracy were unable to recite the Psalms, kept track of their 150 Hail Marys by means of beads or pebbles. These, for convenience' sake, were strung on a wire or cord. To make such an apparatus less cumbersome, it was reduced in size, and thus we have the generally used five-decade (or one-third) rosary of the present day.

The use of the rosary was widespread in Western Christendom by the thirteenth century, with variances in its devotional emphasis deriving from various religious Orders (Franciscans, Dominicans, and so on). A pious legend grew up at the end of the thirteenth century that Saint Dominic, who was given the task of trying to convert the Albigensian heretics with his newly formed band of mendicant friars, received a vision of the Blessed Virgin Mary and was told by her to promote the rosary among Catholics to insure his success. It is difficult to verify the facts involved in this legend, but, without any doubt, by the end of the thirteenth century, the Dominicans and especially Alan de la Roche in southern France were ardent exponents of rosary devotion.

The impetus toward use of the rosary was enhanced when the great Dominican pope Saint Pius V ordered all Christians to say the rosary for the success of the Christian fleet in 1571, trying to turn back the Turks, who were determined to make all of Europe Muslim. The victory of Lepanto on October 7 not only gave a new feast to the Church year and a new title to Mary in her litany (Help of Christians) but caused Catholics everywhere to make even greater use of the mysteries of the rosary, which a Protestant minister once called: "One for Sorrow and Two for Joy!"

The worry beads of Muslims and prayer chains of Buddhists are the result of cross-cultural influence and, except for physical resemblance, have no other relationship to the rosary.

The rosary, of course, is primarily a mental prayer. This is what makes it so suitable for such a broad spectrum of people and useful for family prayer. It can be used by the wisest philosopher or by the simplest rustic. While we recite the Hail Marys we are to concentrate on the mysteries in the life of our divine Lord that are presented for our consideration. These mysteries also include the life of the Church, of which the Virgin Mary is the type, model, and exemplar. The Hail Marys and the Our Fathers and doxologies are to be a sort of chant in the background, while our minds rest in the application of the mysteries of divine revelation to our circumstances and our lives.

Far from violating Christ's injunction against needless repetition in our prayers (Mt 6:7–8), the rosary supplies us with an excellent means to fulfill our obligation to have a private or secret prayer life that is a spillover from our liturgical worship of God.

The rosary is a fine way to introduce children to the practice of individual and family prayer. It is quite suitable for use by travelers on their journeys and is a more grace-filled way to fall asleep than counting sheep.

From the most ancient times, the custom arose of crowning victors in sporting events and wars and political contests with some type of vegetation. Often this was laurel or myrtle or rare flowers. Since roses were frequently the rarest and most costly of flowers, Christians in the Middle Ages, thinking about the shape that rosaries had assumed, imagined them to be "garlands" of spiritual roses for the Blessed Virgin Mary. Hence, the name of "corona" or "crown" or "rosary" arose for this type of devotion.

The Church has richly blessed the practice of reciting the rosary and has encouraged its use by bestowing many indulgences and blessings upon people who engage in the practice. It is true that some people find the rosary to be a type of prayer that is not congenial to their temperament or personality. There is nothing obligatory about its use. Nonetheless, most Catholics, when the rosary is properly explained to them and correctly used, find themselves deeply enamored of it and want the "beads" not only to accompany them through life but to be entwined around their fingers in death.

Speaking of the rosary, Pope Paul VI said: "As the history of the Church so frequently testifies, this duty of prayer, so abundant in its fruits, is efficacious in averting evils and calamities and greatly fosters Christian living."[1] Pope Pius XI wrote: "Above all, the rosary nourishes

[1] "Rosaries to the Mother of Christ".

the Catholic faith, which, by timely meditation on its sacred mysteries, gains new strength, and it lifts the mind to the contemplation of divinely revealed truths."

Again, Pope Paul VI wrote: "It is a solemn custom of the faithful, during the month of October, to weave with the prayers of the rosary, a spiritual garland to the Mother of Christ. This we heartily approve, following the example of our predecessors." [2]

His successor in the See of Peter continues this line of thought and exhortation. It is, after all, his "favorite prayer". Perhaps we could make it our favorite as well.

OCTOBER 16, 1992

Mary's Crown

We Americans are often accused of a lack of historical sense and perspective. This may be true in part because of the relative youth of our continent and our nation. Yet, America was open to European exploration and settlement more than five hundred years ago, and our own country is more than two hundred years old, with one of the longest continuous forms of government on earth. Perhaps we should take not only our own history but all history more seriously.

There are many anniversary dates that mark the milestones of Western civilization that go unnoticed. There is one that occurs each October, however, that deserves annual consideration. It is October 7, the liturgical feast of Our Lady of the Rosary, which marks the anniversary of the great battle and Christian victory at Lepanto. It was there that the Christian fleet, under the command of Don Juan of Austria, put to destruction and flight the Turkish fleet, bent on conquering Europe for Islam and forcing the Muslim religion on all of mankind.

The Catholic Church at that time, October 7, 1571, was guided by an aged and brilliant saint, Pope Pius V. That good Pope had all of Christendom praying the rosary while the Christian fleet was trying to protect Christian Europe. When news of the victory arrived in Rome, he instituted the feast we still celebrate every seventh of October and added the title "Help of Christians" to the litany of Loreto. As Chesterton put it: "The Pope spread his arms about for agony and loss and asked the kings of Christendom for swords around the cross. . . . The

[2] Ibid.

vain Queen of England was looking in her glass and the shadow of the Valois was yawning at the Mass."

The vanity and the yawns have not vanished from our world. The threat continues even now to inundate the earth. It is not a Turkish fleet, however, but rather a fleet of false ideologies that today demands from the Church, not a military crusade, but missionary and evangelical energy, accompanied, as in the sixteenth century, by all of Christendom praying the rosary.

These ideologies can range from moral consequentialism to radical feminism. Resurgent Marxism, racism, consumerism, materialism, hedonism, liberalism, and false notions of freedom and autonomy would have to be included on any list of such a contemporary "fleet". Nor could one neglect to include the collective attempts to systematize and legitimize the killing of innocent human persons, whether unborn babies or the aged and infirm.

Modern popes, not less than Saint Pius V, have continued to exhort us to recite the rosary. Our liturgical prayer in Holy Mass, the sacraments, the sacramentals, and the Liturgy of the Hours should spill over into our private and secret lives. One of the very effective ways to accomplish this is to put the rosary into the prayer habits of our household and our hearts.

In this month dedicated to the most holy rosary, the remarkable victory at Lepanto reminds us that what threatens Christendom today can be destroyed and put to flight if confronted by united and determined prayer and resolute Catholic action.

Pope Saint Pius V wrote: "Once this method of praying becomes known, the faithful begin to be enlightened as a result of their meditation and enkindled by these prayers. . . . the darkness of heresy is dispelled and the light of the Catholic faith shines brightly."

The components of the rosary date back to the beginning of Christianity. The sublime words of the Lord's Prayer were given to us by Jesus Himself. They are unsurpassed in their perfection and beauty. The *Ave* came from heaven too, being delivered initially by an archangel. The Holy Spirit, God Himself, inspired a part of the Hail Mary, as it came from the lips of Saint Elizabeth, the mother of John the Baptist.

The rosary combines vocal and mental prayer in a remarkable way. In contemplating the fifteen mysteries that go to make up the "Dominican rosary", we are presented, "graphically and comprehensively", with the truth of our Catholic faith.

Pope Leo XIII wrote: "Saint Dominic composed the rosary in such a way that the mysteries of our salvation are recalled to mind in succession. This method of meditation is interspersed and, as it were, interlaced with the Hail Mary and with the prayer to God, the Father of our Lord Jesus Christ. We who are seeking a remedy for evils similar to those in the time of Saint Dominic have a right to believe that, by using the same prayer . . . we too will see the calamities of our times disappear."[3]

Pope Paul VI wrote: "The rosary of the Blessed Virgin Mary . . . consists of various elements disposed in an organic fashion: contemplation, in communion with Mary, of a series of mysteries of salvation, wisely distributed into three cycles, which express the joy of messianic times, the salvific suffering of Christ and the glory of the risen Lord which fills the Church. This contemplation by its very nature encourages practical reflection and provides stimulating norms for living."[4]

Each month our present Holy Father recites the rosary over Vatican Radio, his voice beamed to millions of listeners the world over. He is rarely without a rosary in his hands, especially when hiking or walking for recreation. Many times I have personally received a rosary as a gift from him after a visit or an audience. My mother treasures and uses daily the beautiful white rosary he personally gave her.

In a spiritual, not material, way, the call to the crusades comes even to us in our times. The enemy "fleet" is at hand to kill and plunder spiritually. Let us see to our duties. Let us take up our beads.

OCTOBER 15, 1993

The Family and the Rosary

October and the year of the family are slipping off rapidly into the realm of memory. Before they disappear, however, it may be good to pause for a moment and reflect on how the month of the rosary and the year of the family may touch each other. Pope Paul VI wrote, "It is a solemn custom of the faithful during the month of October to weave with the prayers of the rosary a spiritual garland to the Mother of Christ."[5]

That same Pope also expressed his desire "to recommend strongly the recitation of the family rosary".[6] It is obvious that our present Holy Father is equally strong in promoting and fostering the praying of the rosary, which he calls his "favorite prayer". Pope John Paul II prays the rosary publicly, even over Vatican Radio, and privately many times in the course of each day.

---

[3] Leo XIII, *Supremi apostolatus officio* (On Devotion of the Rosary) (September 1, 1883), no. 8.
[4] Paul VI, *Marialis cultus* (February 2, 1974), no. 49a.
[5] Paul VI, "Rosaries to the Mother of Christ".
[6] Paul VI, *Marialis cultus*, no. 52.

The Second Vatican Council calls a Catholic family "the domestic Church".[7] That Council also mentions that a Catholic family is seen to be a "domestic Church" when its members, each according to his proper place and tasks, all together promote justice, practice the works of mercy, devote themselves to helping their brothers and sisters, take part in the apostolate of the parish community, and play their part in their parish's liturgical worship.[8] In addition, each family must have, according to the popes and the Council, a place and time for communal family prayer. Otherwise, says Pope Paul VI, "it would lack its very character as the domestic Church."[9] The Holy Father went on to say, "The rosary should be considered as one of the best and most efficacious prayers in common that a Christian family is invited to recite. When a family gathering becomes a time of prayer, the rosary should be a frequent and favored manner of praying."[10]

Family life in our time often can be filled with stress. Various duties and employment, as well as diverse interests and entertainment, can sometimes pull modern families apart to such an extent that their time spent together as a family is reduced to a bare minimum. Regular family prayer together invokes God's grace upon a household, helps family members grow in natural and supernatural love for each other, assists family members in their obligation of forgiveness for each other's faults, and gives a correct perspective to family goals and projects. Father Patrick Peyton's slogan might seem trite, but it remains true: The family that prays together stays together.

In my more than thirty-four years of priestly ministry, I have never known a family that recites the rosary together each day to become (to use the modern term) dysfunctional. It is true that not all the families I have known to have this practice have always enjoyed complete health. Some have had to face enormous and painful problems, including great financial strain, alcoholism, serious chronic illness, physical and mental handicaps, accidents, and death. Still, the family rosary seems to sustain all families who practice it, in tears as well as in smiles, as a source of strength and consolation.

Because the rosary is basically a type of contemplative or mental prayer, it is very suited to family use. It can be used by the most sophisticated and learned person at the same time that it is used by simple and unlettered children. Pope Paul VI points out, "This contemplation by its very nature encourages practical reflection and provides stimulating

[7] *Lumen gentium*, no. 11.
[8] *Apostolicam actuositatem*, no. 11.
[9] Paul VI, *Marialis cultus*, no. 52.
[10] Ibid., no. 54.

norms for living."[11] The *Catechism* says, "Christian prayer tries above all to meditate on the mysteries of Christ, as in the *lectio divina* or the rosary".

When reciting the rosary, of course, our attention should be focused on the mystery of salvation that accompanies each decade. The litany-like succession of Hail Marys in the background, which numbers one hundred and fifty in the complete rosary, presents, according to Pope Paul VI, "a certain analogy with the Psalter and is an element that goes back to the very origin of the exercise of piety".[12]

What an extraordinary introduction to life it is when a young child, from his most tender years, can recall his parents on their knees each day saying "I believe in God"! What a marvelous opening this provides, in such an environment, for parents to begin to exercise their rights and duties as the primary, inalienable, and indispensable teachers of their children in the ways of the faith! Needless to say, the Apostles' Creed, which begins the rosary, should be the basis of parental introduction to the truths of our Catholic religion.

The most sublime of all prayers is, in the rosary, the anchor between each of the decades. The Lord's Prayer, by its origin from the lips of Jesus Himself, is unsurpassed in magnificence. Each time a family recites the Our Father in the rosary, there is a new occasion to think again about each of the petitions.

Even the most ideal families experience occasional tension and disagreement. There is no family on earth that does not need to say and truly mean each day, "Forgive us . . . as we forgive." The *Catechism* says, "It is called the Lord's Prayer because it comes to us from the Lord Jesus, the master and model of our prayer. [It] is the quintessential prayer of the Church" (CCC 2775–76). The Our Father is called by the *Catechism* what the popes have called the rosary: "a summary of the whole gospel" (CCC 2761).

Finally, the doxology, or Glory Be, reminds us always that the triune God is the ultimate object of all our prayers. The doxology in the family rosary provides an occasion when a Catholic family and all its members can exercise their serious obligation to have a private and personal prayer life, alongside the liturgical worship that all Catholics are required to render to the Almighty. Let us not allow the month of the rosary and the year of the family to slip away without some of these thoughts.

NOVEMBER 4, 1994

---

[11] Ibid., no. 49a.   [12] Ibid., no. 49c.

The Stations of the Cross

There is probably no extraliturgical devotion for Lent and Holy Week that comes more readily to mind than that called the Stations or Way of the Cross. No Catholic who is truly devout would want to allow Holy Week, especially Good Friday, to pass by without "making" the Stations, either privately or with a parish community.

For the last several decades it has been the custom in Rome for the pope, after the Solemn Good Friday Liturgy of the Passion and Death of Jesus, to go to the ancient Colosseum and the ruins of the Imperial Roman Forum and there to follow the Stations of the Cross. In recent times this has been televised worldwide and is usually carried in the United States by the EWTN network of Mother Angelica.

This exercise in Christian piety consists in walking, either personally or through a leader, along a pathway, usually in a church but sometimes outdoors, and stopping at some halting places ("stations") to think about the Passion and death of our Savior. The Church lavishes her gift of indulgences on those who piously make the Stations of the Cross, granting even a plenary indulgence when this is done properly, with appropriate sorrow for sin and with the observance of the usual conditions for such a favor.

It is quite clear that the devotion of the Stations of the Cross originated in the visits of Catholic pilgrims to the Holy Land. Saint Jerome and other early Christian writers described their visits to the various holy places, remembered as the places where this or that event in the journey of Christ to Golgotha happened. Indeed, in a private revelation, a sort of vision, Saint Brigid said that she learned that the Blessed Virgin Mary, after the Ascension of Jesus, went back to visit those holy places.

However, it was in the twelfth and thirteenth centuries that great devotion to the suffering of Jesus arose in Europe, and this was given strong emphasis by the return from the Holy Land of veteran knights of the crusades. In this context the devotion of the Stations of the Cross became gradually better known among Catholics. There is evidence of this devotion in Europe as early as the fifth century, but it was when the Franciscan Friars took over the custody of the shrines and holy places in the year 1342 that they considered it their duty to promote this devotion throughout the Christian world.

Certain saints' names are closely associated with this devotion, the most famous being Saint Leonard of Port Maurice, who enthusiastically fostered this devotion in the eighteenth century. It was in that century that the practice and customs we know became stabilized, largely through the work of Pope Clement XII. Saint Francis of Assisi and Saint Alphonsus Liguori composed sets of prayers for the Stations of the Cross that are still in widespread use today.

It is sometimes surprising to learn that the number of stations currently in most frequent use (fourteen) is not prescribed and that the names of the stations as well as their number admit of certain variance. In some places there were as few as five stations, and in others as many as twenty, thirty, and more. The number of the "falls of Jesus" extend from one to seven.

Some of the stations still in use in some places include the agony in the garden of Gethsemane, the kiss of Judas, and the *Ecce Homo* (Behold the Man) from Pilate's praetorium. The current sixth station (Veronica) is a rather recent addition, associated with one of the precious relics in St. Peter's Basilica in Rome, an ancient veil, said to be that of a pious woman, with the image of Christ's face on it. The name of the woman, a contemporary of our Lord, is linked with her veil, that is, in Latin, *vera ikona* or "true image".

Originally the stations were set up backward to our present Way of the Cross. They began with Christ's death and worked back to the agony in the garden. The thirteenth and fourteenth stations were not used often in the centuries before the eighteenth.

There are people today who insist that there should be a fifteenth station, depicting the Resurrection of Christ, since recalling His Passion and death is "psychologically and theologically incomplete" without a commemoration of the Resurrection as well. However, traditionally, pilgrims to the Holy Land, praying at the empty tomb of Jesus at the fourteenth station, remembered both His being placed in the sepulcher and His rising from the dead.

Strictly speaking, the devotion of the Stations of the Cross is to be associated only with a set of wooden crosses that are blessed by a bishop or an authorized priest. The statues or paintings that line the walls of our churches are meant to assist us in contemplating Christ's redeeming pains and death, but they are not essential to "do the devotion" in the correct way. The stations should now be set up in a "progressive way", that is, from the beginning of Christ's Passion to His death and burial. It is probably best, from a devotional point of view, to keep to the traditional fourteen stations with which we are most familiar. On certain occasions, however, it may be useful to focus the devotion of Stations of the Cross in certain directions. For instance, there are prayer compositions for the Stations of the Cross for an end to abortion, for captive communist lands, and for social justice, all with quotations from Sacred Scripture.

While making the Stations of the Cross, especially during Holy Week, it is often useful to think of some phrase that rests like a leitmotiv in the back of our mind as we meditate on the awesome reality of the Son of God carrying a cross. Saint Francis said, "Love is not loved!" and the liturgy of the East says: "Holy God, Holy Strong One, Holy Immortal One, have mercy on us!" Make the Stations of the Cross. Follow Jesus in this as He told us to do (Lk 14:27).

APRIL 7, 1995

Spiritual Reading

It is said that we become what we eat. In a certain crude sense this is a truism. If this is true to a certain extent when we speak of material food, how much more correct it is to apply this slogan to spiritual food. Professor William May loves to point out that, in a sense, we become what we do, that is to say, if we do evil, we become evil, and if we do good, we become good. Similarly, then, we can say that reading forms and transforms us, perhaps more than we realize.

Although television and some of the other nonprint media have made reading a fading activity for large portions of the population and although illiteracy plagues many parts of the world, including our own country, reading maintains a special place in the arena of information, entertainment, instruction, and cultural tradition. Images, no matter how effectively transmitted, stored, and conveyed, cannot replace the written and printed word. Indeed, there are families and individuals who have discovered the joy and even the importance of self-discipline in subordinating the nonprint media to the written and printed media.

Saint Augustine of Hippo recounts how a large part of his conversion to Christ came about when he heard the little child chanting the children's call "*Tolle, lege*", which is Latin for "Take and read." His experience and that of many others affirms that reading can be spiritual nourishment. It can form as well as inform us, as we journey through life toward the eschaton.

For a Christian, of course, the first thought of reading should be turned to Sacred Scripture. Bibles are often prized family possessions but sometimes are rarely used. It is true that Holy Scripture read in the course of the sacred liturgy provides us with ample amounts of God's written words. Nevertheless, Bible reading should be part of our family life and household devotion. Many devout Catholic families make it a point to read the *entire* Bible. Needless to say, a good, solid, Catholic commentary on the Bible is a fine accompaniment to our careful encounter with Holy Writ. Children especially can memorize large portions of Sacred Scripture when exposed to the word of God in a prayerful and fervent atmosphere.

Our Catholic heritage provides us with a library of possible books to read. There are currently many excellent translations of the writings of the Fathers of the Church. The *Confessions* of Saint Augustine and his *City of God* would have to be on any list of Catholic "Great Books". The *Imitation of Christ*, by Thomas à Kempis, is a classic that every adult Catholic should be acquainted with. Spiritual giants through the years have left an impressive literary legacy for us. We need only think of the *Introduction to the Devout Life* of Saint Francis de Sales, the *Spiritual Exercises* of Saint Ignatius Loyola, and the *Summa Theologiae* of Saint Thomas Aquinas.

Anyone interested in advancing in the spiritual life would want to know the writings of Saint John of the Cross, Saint Teresa of Avila, and Saint Catherine of Siena.

Closer to our own era, the writings of Gilbert Keith Chesterton, Hilaire Belloc, Ronald Knox, Étienne Gilson, Jacques Maritain, Caryll Houselander, Frank Sheed, and Fulton Sheen would add luster to anyone's bookshelves and to anyone's mind.

Novels such as *Quo Vadis?* by Henryk Sienkiewicz and *Fabiola* by Cardinal Nicholas Wiseman are certain to strengthen the faith of any Catholics who read them. The literary work of Cardinal John Henry Newman is a must for any Catholic who wants to be considered knowledgeable. His elegant prose and renowned poetry polish any intellect they touch. His *Apologia, Dream of Gerontius, Essay on the Development of Christian Doctrine, Grammar of Assent*, and his *Idea of a University* are landmarks in English literature, widely appreciated even by many non-Catholics.

Since the time of Pope Leo XIII, the custom has grown up of the popes writing encyclical letters. These documents, covering a wide spectrum of subjects, are often available at reasonable cost and can provide hours of pleasant thought and learning. Our present Holy Father, Pope John Paul II, has written many major encyclicals as well as apostolic exhortations and other documents of significance and great interest.

Although it is somewhat "pricey", *L'Osservatore Romano*, the semi-official newspaper of the Holy See, is available in a weekly English edition. Those fortunate enough to have a subscription find in that edition a vast compendium of news about the activity of the Holy See and a documentary collection of the many speeches, homilies, letters, sermons, and work of Pope John Paul II and the departments of the Holy See that assist him in shepherding the Church.

Our interior life will be a reflection of what we spiritually "eat". The secular world around us, which is indifferent and often hostile to the Catholic faith, provides mountains of sweet-tasting poison for us to consume. Let us reject such "bait" and consume with our eyes and hearts genuine Christian and Catholic reading.

OCTOBER 22, 1993

5

MARY: OUR MOTHER AND MODEL

Mary and the Church

The month of May is traditionally the time when thoughts turn to motherhood, since for several decades the second Sunday in this month (probably to the great delight of restaurant owners, florists, and candy manufacturers) has been designated as Mother's Day. Although this can be a time of exaggerated sentiment and overblown emotions, it can also be an appropriate moment for reflection on the high vocation of mothers and a time of explicit gratitude for her whose knee, in the words of Miner, became our altar, where we learned the faith that opened hidden doors for us, leading to peace and eternity.

This month of motherhood, when the refreshing warmth of springtime elicits flowers in our Northern Hemisphere, is properly dedicated to the Blessed Virgin Mary. The Second Vatican Council says of her: "In an utterly singular way she cooperated by her obedience, faith, hope, and burning charity in the Savior's work of restoring supernatural life to souls. For this reason she is a mother to us in the order of grace. . . . By her maternal love, Mary cares for the brethren of her Son who still journey on this earth, surrounded by dangers and difficulties, until they are led to their happy fatherland."[1]

In giving us Mary, as one of His last and most precious gifts from His Cross (Jn 19:26), Jesus gave us the archetype and model of His Church. The Second Vatican Council says again:

> The Church, contemplating Mary's mysterious sanctity, imitating her charity, and faithfully fulfilling the Father's will, becomes herself a mother by accepting God's word in faith. By her preaching and by baptism, the Church brings forth to new and immortal life children who are conceived of the Holy Spirit and born of God. The Church herself is a virgin, who keeps whole and pure the fidelity she has pledged to her Spouse. Imitating the Mother of her Lord, and by the power of the

[1] *Lumen gentium*, nos. 61–62.

Holy Spirit, she preserves with virginal purity an integral faith, a firm hope, and a sincere love.[2]

Saint Ambrose said that, like Christ's Mother, the Catholic Church is married but a virgin who conceives us spiritually by the Holy Spirit and bears us without travail. The name of the first woman, "Eve", means "mother of all the living". So, Mary is the new Eve, the mother of all the spiritually alive, and, potentially, the Church is the mother of all the living as well. Saint Augustine said that just as our Lady became the mother of many through the birth of One, so the Catholic Church, by bringing many to spiritual birth, becomes the mother of human and Christian unity.

Commentators often remark about Christ's use of the word "woman" in speaking to His Mother (see Jn 2:4; 19:26). In English this word sounds harsh, but in Aramaic, which Jesus spoke, the word is not harsh but exceptionally formal, something like *madonna* in Italian. It seems apparent that the word "woman" has a special theological meaning for Saint Paul (Gal 4:4) and that it has great significance for the seer of the Apocalypse (Rev 12). It is the study of these aspects of divine revelation that led many of the Fathers of the Church to concur in the saying of Serlo: "Mary is prefigured in the Church, and the Church is figured in Mary."

The theologian Carl Feckes wrote: "As Mary bore the earthly Christ, so the Church bears the Eucharistic Christ. As the whole life of Mary is centered upon the bringing up and protecting of Christ, so again the deep life and solicitude of the Church is centered on the Eucharist."

Mary belongs to the Church. She is her first, principal, and highest member. She is a daughter of the Church, the first disciple. But, in another sense, she is the Mother of the Church. She is a daughter of the Jerusalem that is our Mother from on high, but she is also the Mother of the new Jerusalem that we constitute.

The glory of Mary is a foretaste of the glory of the Church that Christ founded. The last two glorious mysteries of the rosary (the Assumption of Mary into heaven and her coronation as Queen of heaven and earth) are mysteries not merely about her destiny but about ours. For the Church, too, is destined to be assumed into heaven, body and soul, and she too is to be crowned when she comes as a Bride adorned for her husband to the eternal nuptials with her Savior (Rev 21:2).

The litanies of our Lady are also litanies of the Church. Her beautiful titles are also titles of the Mother that she foreshadows. The ancient

[2] Ibid., no. 64.

writers say of Mary and the Catholic Church that they both are a "sacrament of Jesus Christ carrying in their hearts a living Gospel"; both are faithful virgins, immaculate as Woman and as City, surrounded by angels; both are the "House of gold, the Scepter of orthodoxy, the Dawn heralding salvation, the Fleece of Gideon, the Tabernacle of the Highest, the Gate of heaven, the valiant Woman of the Book of Proverbs, the Sign in the sky clothed with the sun in the Book of Revelation, and the Ark of the new and everlasting covenant."

The Second Vatican Council teaches: "In the bodily and spiritual glory which she possesses in heaven, the Mother of Jesus continues in this present world as the image and first flowering of the Church as she (the Church) is to be perfected in the world to come."[3]

As we celebrate Mother's Day this year, let us remember that long ago God kissed Mary in Galilee and now, in the Church, He kisses us and gives us in our earthly mothers a reminder of the loving maternity that is meant to lead us to gaze on His face forever.

MAY 7, 1993

'Tis the Month

Some people expressed surprise that the concluding section of our Holy Father's encyclical *The Gospel of Life* (*Evangelium vitae*) should be dedicated to the Blessed Virgin Mary. However, when it is understood how Mary's life and very existence were a loving reply to God, Who visited her with His gifts and grace, and how she is the exemplar and archetype of the Catholic Church responding to God's gifts and grace, the logic of the Pope's thought becomes clear and apparent.

Pope John Paul II wrote:

Mary, "like the Church of which she is the type, is a mother of all who are reborn to life. She is in fact the mother of Life by which everyone lives, and when she brought it forth from herself she in some way brought to rebirth all those who were to live by that Life." As the Church contemplates Mary's motherhood, she discovers the meaning of her own motherhood and the way in which she is called to express it. At the same time, the Church's experience of motherhood leads to a most profound

---

[3] Ibid., no. 68.

understanding of Mary's experience as the incomparable model of how life should be welcomed and cared for.[4]

The Fathers of the Church often said that Mary conceived in her heart before she conceived in her womb. The meaning of that expression, of course, is that after God took the initiative in lavishing His love upon her, she responded with her consent and her own love. Especially in this her month of May ought we to look to her example to learn how we are to reply to the unlimited and overwhelming love of God given constantly to us.

The Fathers of the Second Vatican Council were very desirous to link the Blessed Virgin Mary and her place in the redemptive economy of God to the supernatural mystery of the Catholic Church. This is why they placed that Council's extensive treatment of Mary in their dogmatic constitution on the Church. The *Catechism of the Catholic Church*, quoting *Lumen gentium*, teaches, "By her complete adherence to the Father's will, to his Son's redemptive work, and to every prompting of the Holy Spirit, the Virgin Mary is the Church's model of faith and charity. Thus she is a 'preeminent and . . . wholly unique member of the Church' (53); indeed, she is the 'exemplary realization' (63) . . . of the Church" (CCC 967). The *Catechism* also calls Mary the "eschatological icon of the Church" (CCC 972), saying that "she shines forth on earth, until the day the Lord shall come, as a sign of certain hope and comfort to the pilgrim People of God."[5]

Our Holy Father writes that, in Mary,

> the Church recognizes an image of her own mystery: present in history, she knows that she transcends history, inasmuch as she constitutes on earth the "seed and beginning" of the kingdom of God [*Lumen gentium*, no. 5]. The Church sees this mystery fulfilled in complete and exemplary fashion in Mary. She is the woman of glory in whom God's plan could be carried out with supreme perfection. . . . Mary becomes the model of the Church, called to be the "new Eve", the mother of believers, the mother of all the "living" (Gen 3:20).[6]

All throughout the year, but with special intensity in the month of May, do the children of the Church, showing that they are also by that fact children of Mary, turn to her, asking that she join her prayers to theirs in a special way, for she is, in the words of the Council Fathers,

[4] *Evangelium vitae*, no. 102.
[5] CCC 972, quoting *Lumen gentium*, no. 68.
[6] *Evangelium vitae*, no. 103.

"for us a sure sign of hope and solace".[7] In the ninth century, Saint Theophilus wrote, "The prayers of His mother are a pleasure to the Son because He desires to grant all that is granted on her account and thus recompense her for the favor she did Him by giving Him His Body."

Saint Francis de Sales said, "Let us run to Mary like little children and cast ourselves into her arms with perfect confidence." Saint Bonaventure wrote, "The gates of heaven will open to all who confide in the protection of Mary", and Saint Thomas Aquinas wrote, "As sailors are guided by a star to their port, so are Christians guided to heaven by Mary."

While we stand in awe of Mary's intrepid faith (Lk 1:45), her virginal purity, her valor and courage (Jn 19:26), it is probably her prayers on our behalf that excite us most and that make her the "Cause of our joy". Saint Alphonsus preached, "She is truly our mother, not indeed in the flesh, but spiritually, the mother of our souls and of our salvation. By giving us Jesus, she gave us true life and afterward, by offering the life of her Son on Calvary for our salvation, she brought us forth to the life of grace." Saint Bernard said, "Let us cast ourselves at the feet of this good mother and, embracing them, let us not depart until she blesses us and accepts us as her children."

These words of the Second Vatican Council have a perennial value, but they have a worth that is more focused and emphatic in each month of May:

> Let the entire body of the faithful pour forth persevering prayer to the Mother of God and the mother of men. Let them implore that she, who aided the beginnings of the Church (Acts 1:14) by her prayers, may now, exalted as she is in heaven above all angels and saints, intercede with her Son in the fellowship of the saints. May she do so until all the people of the human family, whether they are honored with the name of Christian or whether they still do not know their Savior, are happily gathered together in peace and harmony into the one People of God, for the glory of the Most Holy and Undivided Trinity.[8]

Pope Paul VI said:

> We must not lessen our devotion to the Virgin Mary, we modern people who more than ever demand evangelical authenticity and who seek out the mysterious ways of divine transcendence. We must remain faithful and fervent in this devotion,

---

[7] *Lumen gentium*, no. 68.
[8] Ibid., no. 69.

in the love, in the imitation, in the invocation of Blessed Mary. Due devotion to our Lady is a sign of the correct interpretation of the Christian Religion and of our Catholic Faith in particular. The Church sees Mary maternally present and sharing in the many complicated problems which today beset the lives of individuals, families, and nations. She sees Mary helping the Christian People in the constant struggle between good and evil.

Our present Holy Father says, "As we make our way in confidence toward the new heavens and the new earth (Rev 21:1) we look to her."[9] Let us follow the teaching of the saints, the popes, and the councils and turn to Mary "now and at the hour of our death".

MAY 12, 1995

The Immaculate Conception

An annual parenthesis in our celebration of Advent each year is the Solemnity of the Immaculate Conception. Observed on December 8, exactly nine months before the feast of Mary's birth on September 8, the celebration of this solemnity enables us to remember how God, by a singular act of His providence, kept Mary from every stain of sin from the first moment of her existence in the womb of her mother, Saint Ann. Although Mary was conceived in the normal way by which all children come into our world, God nevertheless effected her redemption through Jesus Christ in an anticipated and unique manner. As Pope Pius IX wrote: "She is redeemed in a more exalted fashion by reason of the merits of her Son."[10]

The truth of Mary's Immaculate Conception was always held by the Catholic Church and is contained implicitly in the deposit of faith. However, the Church's awareness of the meaning of "full of grace" enabled Pope Pius IX to declare as a dogma of our faith in 1854: "The most Blessed Virgin Mary was, from the first moment of her conception, by a singular grace and privilege of almighty God and by virtue of the merits of Jesus Christ, Savior of the human race, preserved immune from all stain of original sin."[11]

---

[9] *Evangelium vitae*, no. 105.
[10] *Ineffabilis Deus*.
[11] Ibid.

OUR PATRONESS

Not long after Pope Pius IX proclaimed the dogma of the Immaculate Conception, the bishops of the United States, gathered in a meeting in Baltimore, arranged that Mary, under that title of her Immaculate Conception, should be the principal patroness of our country. Just as providence arranged that the flagship of the little fleet of Christopher Columbus should be named *Santa Maria*, so God also arranged that Mary, the most favored of all His creatures, should be the one pleading on behalf of our land before His throne in heaven.

Our Diocese of Lincoln, too, enjoys a special benefit joined to the Solemnity of the Immaculate Conception. Because our first cathedral was named "Saint Mary", she is our principal patroness before God, and December 8 is the main feastday of our diocese. Her prayers have assisted us through the years of our diocesan existence and have helped us to do the work of her divine Son.

Since December 8 is our diocesan patronal feast, it is most fitting that we begin our diocesan Eucharistic Congress on that date and conclude it on the Sunday nearest the feast of her nativity, September 10, 1995. It is fitting also that our prayers for the success of the Eucharistic Congress and for the diocesan Synod that will follow in 1996 should be linked to our diocesan pilgrimage, next February, to the National Shrine, the Basilica of the Immaculate Conception in Washington, D.C. I hope that many people from our Diocese of Lincoln will find themselves able to make the pilgrimage and that those who are unable to go will spend some special time at prayer back here.

The Eucharistic Congress will be a unique time of prayer for our entire diocese, permitting us to concentrate in a particular way on Christ, present in the Blessed Sacrament among us, as the Center of our lives and work here in the Diocese of Lincoln. This holy season of Advent offers a wonderful opportunity for all of us to rededicate ourselves to Jesus in the most Blessed Sacrament of the altar and to prepare our hearts and souls for Christmas by frequent attendance at daily Mass and by adoration of our Lord in the tabernacle.

MARY AND THE EUCHARIST

There are many ways in which Mary is linked to the Holy Eucharist. It was, after all, she who gave to God the body and blood that He joined to the soul of Jesus, which He created and then united to His divinity in her womb. This is the Body, Blood, Soul, and Divinity of Christ that we receive in Holy Communion.

Many commentators see a strong eucharistic strain in the great prayer of Mary, her Magnificat (Lk 1:46–55). She speaks of the hungry who are "filled with good things" and the rich and haughty who are sent away empty. She speaks of being called "blessed" as a result of God's goodness to her. So also in the Holy Eucharist, we, all undeserving, become holy with the holiness of God Himself.

The wedding feast at Cana (Jn 2:1–11) was undoubtedly a prefiguring of the eucharistic "miracle". Jesus changed water into wine as He would later change wine into Blood. The "good wine" (the New Covenant) was saved until last. Of course, at Cana it was at Mary's behest that Jesus worked His first "sign" even though His "hour [had] not yet come".

Our diocesan pilgrimage, Eucharistic Congress, and Synod are all connected to each other. The Synod will have no success without prayer preceding it. ("Unless the Lord build the house, they labor in vain who build it" [Ps 127].) Thus we see the need for the pilgrimage and Eucharistic Congress. The entire ensemble (pilgrimage, Congress, and Synod) is a preparation for the end of this century and the beginning of the great holy year and millennium of the year 2000. Our Holy Father has declared that 1997 will be a year dedicated to Christ our Lord, 1998 to God the Holy Spirit, and 1999 to God the Father. Our 1995 Congress and pilgrimage and 1996 Synod will lead up to these significant events.

May the prayers, intercession, and example of the Blessed Virgin Mary continue to accompany us as we journey into the future and prepare to welcome Christ and rendezvous with our Creator.

DECEMBER 9, 1994

Love of Mary

Traditionally, the month of May has been dedicated by Catholics the world over to honor the Blessed Virgin Mary. More than twenty years ago, the Catholic bishops of the United States expressed concern about the decline in Marian devotions. They wrote:

> No survey is needed to show that all over the country many forms of Marian devotion have fallen into disuse, and others are taking an uncertain course. In an age avid for symbols . . . , the use of Catholic Marian symbols, such as the scapular and the Miraculous Medal, has noticeably diminished. Only a few years ago the use of the rosary was a common mark of a Catholic, and it was customarily taught to children, both at home and in courses of religious instruction. Adults in every walk of life

found strength in this familiar prayer which is biblically based
and is filled with thought of Jesus and his mother in the "mysteries". . . .

We view with great sympathy the distress our people feel
over the loss of devotion to our Lady, and we share their concern that the young be taught a deep and true love for the
Mother of God.[12]

There is no better time for parents and all Catholic households to
reinvigorate devotion to Mary than annually during the month of May.
Spiritual riches of a significant kind will come to families that inaugu-
rate or revive the practice of the family rosary. It is deeply impressive to
see little children construct a "May altar" every year and to witness families gathered in common faith and prayer.

The *Catechism* says of Mary:

[The Mother of Jesus] gave herself entirely to the person and to
the work of her Son; she did so in order to serve the mystery of
redemption with him and dependent on him, by God's grace:
As Saint Irenaeus says: "Through her obedience she became the
cause of salvation both for herself and for the whole human
race [*Adv. haeres*, 3, 22, 4: PG 7/1, 959A]". Hence not a few of
the early Fathers gladly assert . . . : "The knot of Eve's disobedience was untied by Mary's obedience: what the virgin Eve
bound through her unbelief, Mary loosened by her faith
[ibid.]". Comparing her with Eve, they call Mary "the Mother
of the living" and frequently claim: "Death through Eve, life
through Mary [*Lumen gentium*, no. 56]" (CCC 494)."

Pope Paul VI, in his famous *Credo of the People of God*, says: "We believe that the most holy Mother of God, the new Eve, Mother of the
Church, continues in heaven her maternal role towards the members of
Christ, in that she cooperates with the birth and growth of divine life in
the souls of the redeemed."

The Second Vatican Council declares:

Let the entire body of the faithful pour forth persevering prayer
to the Mother of God and the Mother of men. Let them implore that she who aided the beginnings of the Church by her
prayers may now, exalted as she is in heaven above all the saints
and angels, intercede with her Son in the fellowship of all the

---

[12] National Conference of Catholic Bishops, "Behold Your Mother: Woman of
Faith", (Nov. 21, 1973), nos. 92–93.

saints. May she do so until all the peoples of the human family, whether they are honored with the name of Christian or whether they still do not know their Savior, are happily gathered together in peace and harmony into the one People of God, for the glory of the most holy and undivided Trinity.[13]

Again, the Catholic bishops of our land wrote: "The Gospels summon us all to recognize the special place the Mother of Jesus has in God's plan for the salvation of mankind. The teachings of the Popes and Councils lead us to an ever clearer understanding of Mary's privileged position in the Church. Singular honor has been given her in piety, art, music and literature. Surely this Catholic tradition is the fulfillment of her prophecy: All ages to come shall call me blessed (Lk 1:48)."[14]

According to the *Catechism*, "Jesus is Mary's only son, but her spiritual motherhood extends to all men whom indeed he came to save: 'The Son whom she brought forth is he whom God placed as the first-born among many brethren, that is, the faithful in whose generation and formulation she cooperates with a mother's love' [*Lumen gentium*, no. 63]" (CCC 501).

Archbishop Sheen once said: "As one searches for the reasons for the universal love of Mary among peoples who do not even know her Son, it is to be found in four instincts deeply embedded in the human heart: affection for the beautiful, admiration for purity, reverence for a queen, and love of a mother. All of these come to a focus in Mary."

Quoting the American bishops once more:

> Sometimes anxiety is expressed that devotion to Mary may detract from the position of Jesus, our one Lord and Mediator. Such fear is unfounded. The more we know and love Mary, the more surely will we know and love Jesus and understand His mission in the world. It is also true that the more we know Jesus and love Him, the better we will appreciate His Mother's place in God's plan for man's redemption. This is the teaching of the Second Vatican Council. Her motherly intercession . . . in no way diminishes the unique mediation of Christ, but rather shows its power.[15]

Pope Paul VI wrote: "Devotion to the Virgin Mother of God does not stop with her, but has to be regarded as a help which of its very nature leads to Christ."[16]

---

[13] *Lumen gentium*, no. 69.
[14] "Behold Your Mother", no. 1.
[15] Ibid., no. 6.
[16] *The Pope Speaks*, 10 (1965): 140.

Our present Holy Father, Pope John Paul II, said that devotion to Mary in our country has "ancient roots". He noted: "It is not without significance that the ship on which Christopher Columbus crossed the Atlantic was named *Santa Maria*. And many of the immigrants who moved to this vast country brought with them a strong attachment to their faith and to a special love for the ever Virgin Mary, whom they addressed under many titles." The month of May should help us recollect these things each year.

APRIL 29, 1994

Marian Devotion

In the Middle Ages, it was customary to recite the axiom "about Mary one can never say enough" (*de Maria numquam satis*) as a slogan. Those who breathe Catholic air and live in the Catholic tradition know almost instinctively that genuine devotion to Mary leads to Christ. If such devotion is authentic and balanced, it enhances a person's spiritual life immeasurably.

In a talk in April 1993, our Holy Father reiterated the truth that the mystery of the Incarnation is at the center of the entire Bible. There is no access to this central truth of our faith apart from considering the virginal maternity of Mary. This is why it is more than useful to set aside a certain period each year when attention can be focused on the "lowly handmaid of Nazareth" whom God created as the most grace-filled of His creatures. The custom has arisen of concentrating this focus in the month of October, dedicated to the holy rosary, and in the month of May, dedicated to motherhood and beauty.

When he visited our country last year, Pope John Paul II called Mary the "model of Christian love" who "contemplates her Son in glory and intercedes for the members of His Body on earth".[17] He asked her, as the patroness of the United States, "to look upon the people of this great nation, so richly blessed with material and spiritual resources".[18]

Great saints and learned writers have found over the centuries many symbols and types of Mary in the Old Testament. For example, there is the earthly paradise (Gen 2:8–14), which symbolizes Mary, who is full of grace and thus the earthly paradise of the new Adam, Jesus Christ. There is the dove with the olive branch in its mouth (Gen 8:8), which symbol-

---

[17] John Paul II, "May Christians Be the Leaven of God's Kingdom in American Society", *L'Osservatore Romano* 4 (October 11, 1995): 16.
[18] Ibid.

izes Mary, who brings to the world Jesus, the Prince of Peace (Is 9:6). The rainbow, too (Gen 9:11–17), is a symbol of Mary, whose life signaled the end of sin and a new beginning of goodness.

Pope Pius IX noted that the Fathers of the Church saw many of the Old Testament symbols as foretelling "the sublime dignity of the Mother of God, her unsullied innocence, and her holiness of life".[19] Among these symbols are the golden candlestick (Ex 25:31–40), the fleece of Gideon (Jg 6:36–40), the tower of David, and the throne of Solomon (1 Kings 10:18–20). One cannot overlook the rod of Aaron (Nb 17:1–11), for Mary is truly the lily of the valley (Song 2:1), nor neglect to see her shadow in the cloud bringing life-giving water to the world (1 Kings 18:42–45), and in the burning bush that nonetheless was not consumed (Ex 3:2–6). This latter symbol is often seen as prophesying Mary's virginity, which remained even after the birth of her Son.

Of all the Old Testament symbols, the ark of the covenant seems to have a special place as a model or type of the Blessed Virgin Mary (Nb 10:35). The infancy narrative in the Gospel according to Saint Luke (1:39–44) seems to apply to Mary what the Old Testament says about the ark (2 Sam 6:2–11).

The highest dignity and honor that Mary possesses is that of being the Mother of God. It was the Council of Ephesus (which took place in A.D. 431) that declared that Mary was "Theotokos", that is, the Mother of God. The reason for this is that mothers are mothers of persons and not merely of natures. Jesus is the eternal Son of God, the second Person of the Blessed Trinity, Who unites to His divine nature a human nature, like us in all things but sin. He remains, however, a divine Person. Mary is truly the Mother of Christ, the Mother of Jesus. She gave Him, through the power of the Holy Spirit, His flesh by which He redeemed the world. As God, He created her and keeps her in existence. Yet He took His flesh in her womb. As God, He exists from all eternity. As Man, He began to exist in time and human history when He was conceived in Mary.

The Second Vatican Council teaches, "For, believing and obeying, Mary brought forth on earth the Father's Son. This she did, knowing not man but overshadowed by the Holy Spirit. She was the new Eve, who put her absolute trust not in the ancient serpent, but in God's messenger. The Son she brought forth is he whom God placed as the firstborn among many brethren (Rom 8:29), namely, the faithful. In their birth and development she cooperates with a maternal love."[20]

[19] Pius IX, *Ineffabilis Deus* (December 8, 1854).
[20] *Lumen gentium*, no. 63.

Jesus is the one and only Mediator between God and man (1 Tim 2:5–6). As the Second Vatican Council puts it so well, "The maternal duty of Mary toward men in no way obscures or diminishes this unique mediation of Christ, but rather shows its power." [21] Her prayers for us, her mediation, depend entirely on His and draw all their power from Him. They do not impede the immediate union of the faithful with Christ but rather foster such union.

The Council goes on to teach, "Just as the one priesthood of Christ is shared in various ways both by the sacred ministers and by the faithful, and as the one goodness of God is in reality communicated diversely to His creatures, so also the unique mediation of the Redeemer does not exclude but rather gives rise to a manifold cooperation which is a sharing in this one and only source." [22]

The *Catechism* says, "Jesus is Mary's only son, but her spiritual motherhood extends to all men whom indeed he came to save" (CCC 501). Jesus gave her to us to be our mother (Jn 19:25–27). The *Catechism* says, " 'This motherhood of Mary in the order of grace continues uninterruptedly from the consent which she loyally gave at the Annunciation and which she sustained without wavering beneath the cross, until the eternal fulfilment of all the elect. Taken up into heaven, she did not lay aside this saving office.' " [23]

May is the month of Mary. Let us invoke her intercession. Let us honor her and so fulfill what she herself predicted: "All generations will call me blessed" (Lk 1:48).

MAY 3, 1996

---

[21] Ibid., no. 60.
[22] Ibid., no. 62.
[23] CCC 969, quoting *Lumen gentium*, no. 62.